Marie Doug

1787 Col. Rd.

HUGO'S

FRENCH
SIMPLIFIED

COMPLETE—CONSISTING OF

I.—A SIMPLE BUT COMPLETE GRAMMAR

Containing all the Rules necessary for
Speaking and Writing French correctly

The Pronunciation of Every Word Exactly Imitated

II.—FRENCH PRONUNCIATION SIMPLIFIED

Easy Anecdotes, with the Translation and Pronunciation of every
word; including Complete Rules of Pronunciation

III.—FRENCH IDIOMS

A Collection of Practical Conversational Sentences, introducing
all the Important Idioms, and Peculiarities of French Construction

IV.—A KEY to the EXERCISES in the GRAMMAR

PHILADELPHIA

DAVID McKAY, Publisher

604-8 S. Washington Square

HUGO'S

FRENCH

SIMPLIFIED

COMPLETE—CONSISTING OF

I.—A SIMPLE, YET COMPLETE GRAMMAR

*Containing all the Rules necessary for
Writing and Making French Correctly*

The Pronunciation of Every Word Exactly Indicated

II.—FRENCH PRONUNCIATION SIMPLIFIED

*Easy Anecdotes with the Translation and Pronunciation of every
word, including Complete Rules of Pronunciation*

III.—FRENCH IDIOMS

*A Collection of Practical, Conversational Sentences Introducing
all the Important Idioms and Peculiarities of French Conversation*

IV.—A KEY to the EXERCISES in the GRAMMAR

PHILADELPHIA

DAVID McKAY, Publisher

CONTENTS.

INSTRUCTIONS TO STUDENTS.

After acquiring a general idea of the Pronunciation, learn five or six lessons in the Grammar. This can best be done by reading carefully several times through each rule, pronouncing the examples and new words aloud, and writing out the translation to the Exercise which follows that rule. Then compare your work carefully with the Key, sentence by sentence, marking all errors, and afterwards reading again through the examples to the rule forgotten or misunderstood. Repeat this process until you can translate every sentence correctly and unhesitatingly.

After having mastered five or six lessons in this way, a page or two of the anecdotes may advantageously be worked through with each lesson. This will relieve the monotony of learning so many rules, and greatly enlarge the number of words at the student's command, if each page is gone through two or three times. No attempt need be made to learn the words in the reading pages by heart ; they will be acquired gradually, and without effort.

The Conversational Sentences will well repay the trouble of careful study ; but at least twelve or fourteen lessons should be learned before this section is attempted.

Advanced Students can derive great benefit from writing out the LITERAL TRANSLATION of the Anecdotes, and of the Conversational Sentences, afterwards re-translating this literal English into French, without reference to the original.

FRENCH
GRAMMAR
SIMPLIFIED

AN EASY AND RAPID
SELF-INSTRUCTOR

EXERCISES AND VOCABULARY
With the
PRONUNCIATION OF EVERY WORD
EXACTLY IMITATED

Revised and entirely Rewritten

PHILADELPHIA
DAVID McKAY, Publisher
604-8 S. Washington Square

PREFACE.

THE numerous reprints of HUGO's "FRENCH SIMPLIFIED" having completely worn out the Stereo-plates, it has been necessary to reset the book in fresh type. The present "STANDARD" EDITION has been entirely rewritten, and is practically a new work, in which the special advantages which made former editions so popular have been carefully preserved; while the new features make the work of the same value to schools that it has hitherto been to travellers and business men.

We have given in an Appendix the irregular Feminine and Plural forms, as these—although most of them useless for practical purposes —are unfortunately required in nearly all examinations.

These exceptions are given in full, to absolve us from the charge of incompleteness; but we hold strongly that irregular Feminines and Plurals (except of very common words), and seldom used Defective Verbs, should only be learned by advanced students. It takes as long to learn the plural of *ciel* (bed-tester), a word which not one Englishman in 10,000 ever requires to say in French, as to learn that S is generally added to form the Plural. Yet the former applies to one word only, the latter to many thousands. This mixing up of unimportant exceptions with fundamental rules is a great defect in most Grammars; but Hugo's principle is—a clear explanation of important Rules in their natural order.

The Appendix also includes—for reference—the full conjugation of the Regular and Auxiliary Verbs; but it is never advisable to attempt to learn a Verb straight through. By working on Hugo's rules for forming one Tense from another, nine-tenths of the labour can be saved. But we have not wasted space by following the ridiculous practice of giving in full the Interrogative and Negative Forms, and the Compound Tenses. Students generally think that these formidable tables have to be learnt, and are naturally confused and disheartened; whereas every Interrogative Form in the language follows one simple rule, as does also every Negation. As regards the Compound Tenses, how can three or four pages of tables be necessary to teach a student that *il a été* is "he has been," when he already knows that *il a* is "he has," and that *été* is "been"?

HUGO'S SYSTEM is now so widely known that there is little need to enlarge on its merits; but we may point out that ours are the only grammars written throughout from the *learner's point of view*. Others are compiled more or less for teachers, and contain technical explanations quite unintelligible to ordinary students, who sometimes hardly know one part of speech from another. For this reason we consider a grammatically arranged "Contents," convenient though it undoubtedly is for teachers, of little help to the average learner, for whose use we give in the Vocabulary a reference to every Paragraph relating to words which undergo a grammatical change. Students can by this means readily look up any word without even knowing what part of speech it is.

Simple and concise as they are, Hugo's Grammars are complete, inasmuch as they contain every rule a foreigner need know. The contents do not correspond with the early lessons only in the larger books sold at six or eight times the price. Hugo's books contain the *gist of the whole*, the careful manner in which the matter is condensed and simplified being their chief beauty.

ADDITIONAL EXERCISES.

The Exercises on each right-hand page are simply intended as *extra practice* for junior pupils, who as a rule are not anxious to learn, and can therefore only be taught by constant repetition. **No fresh words or rules are introduced in these exercises,** so that adult students, who usually want to learn for their own sakes, are recommended to confine themselves to the left-hand pages, which constitute in themselves a complete grammar.

CONTENTS.

Students should begin with the FIRST LESSON (*see page 4*) after having read over the following Rules, which are for reference only, and NEED NOT BE LEARNT AT ONCE.

THE FRENCH ALPHABET ;

with the names of the 26 letters. (W and K do not occur in real French words, and are sometimes omitted from the Alphabet.)

A	B	C	D	E	F	G	H	I	J	K
ah	beh	seh	deh	eh	eff	sheh*	ahsh	ee	shee*	kah

L	M	N	O	P	Q	R	S	T	U	V
ell	emm	enn	o	peh	kü†	airr	ess	teh	üt	veh

W	X	Y	Z
doohbl-veh	iks	ee-greck	zaid

* **sh** to be sounded like the *s* in *measure*. † ü like *ee* with rounded lips.

GENERAL RULES ON PRONUNCIATION.

CONSONANTS (i.e. all letters except *a, e, i, o, u, y*) are pronounced as in English, except the following :—

c before *e, i, y*, sounds like *s* ; otherwise like *k*.

ç (ç cedilla) always sounds like *s*.

g before *e, i, y* sounds like the *s* in *measure* ; otherwise like *g* in *go*.

h is generally silent.

j always sounds like the *s* in *measure*.

s between two vowels sounds like **z**.

r is stronger than in English.

ch=*sh*, **qu**=*k*, **th**=*t*.

Important Rule.—*Consonants* are not pronounced when the last letter of a word, except **c, f, l, r**, which are pronounced.

FRENCH WORDS are divided into SYLLABLES by the following general rule :—Finish with a *Vowel*, and commence with a *Consonant*. Two Consonants are divided, but if the second is *l* or *r*, both belong to the next syllable.

PRONUNCIATION OF VOWELS.

(The Stress in French is very slight, and is placed on the last syllable.)

a like *ah*, but very short ; as,

1. a par cas fatal chacal
   has by case fatal jackal
   (*for Pronunciation see below*)

e in the middle of a syllable like *ai* ; as,

2. mer fer sel merci
   sea iron salt mercy

e at the end of a syllable like *u* in *fur* ; as,

3. je cela cheval matelas
   I that horse mattress

e is mute at the end of a word of more than one syllable ; as,

4. tasse place malade salle
   cup place ill hall

IMITATED PRONUNCIATION.

(*r* in italics not to be pronounced ; **sh** in thick type like *s* in *measure* ; Vowels before double Consonants to be pronounced short ; *ah* very short.)

PRON.—1. ah, pahr, kah, fah-tahll, shah-kahll ; 2. mair, fair, sell, mair-se ; 3. **sh**er, ser-lah, **sh**er-vahll, mah-ter-lah ; 4. tahss, plahss, mah-lahdd, sahll.

é (acute accent) like the interjection *eh !* as,

5. été répété café thé blé
been repeated coffee tea corn

è (grave accent) and **ê (circumflex accent*)** like *ay* ; as,

6. père frère élève rêve
father brother pupil dream

i (or y) like *ee* if long, and like *i* in *ill* if short ; as,

7. il ami vide syllabe lit
he friend empty syllable bed

o somewhat like *o* in not ; as,

8. botte dormir chose rose
boot (to) sleep thing rose

u like *ee* pronounced with rounded lips ; as,

9. reçu sur rue dur futur
received on street hard future

ai, ei like *ay* ; as,

10. mais paire reine haleine
but pair queen breath

au, eau like *oh* ; as,

11. chaud mauvais cadeau
warm bad present

eu, œu like *u* in *fur* ; as,

12. neuf heure œuf sœur
nine hour egg sister

oi like *wah* or *o'ah* short ; as,

13. loi roi mois boire
law king month (to) drink

ou like *oo* ; as,

14. ou roue couteau mouche
or wheel knife fly

* The *Circumflex Accent* lengthens the pronunciation : Vowels are otherwise generally short. The *Grave Accent* is used to distinguish between words spelt alike (la, *the* ; là, *there*), and only alters the pronunciation of e.

---

5. eh-teh,† reh-peh-teh, kah-feh, teh, bleh ; 6. pair, frair, eh-laiv, raiv ; 7. ill, ah-me, veedd, sill-ahb, lee ; 8. bot, dor-meer, shohz, rohz ; 9. rer-sü, sür, rü, dür, fü-tür ; 10. may, pair, rain, ah-lain ; 11. shoh, moh-vay, kah-doh ; 12. nerff, er, erf, ser ; 13. lo'ah, ro'ah, mo'ah, bo'ahr ; 14. oo, roo, koo-toh, moosh.

---

† In the Imitated Pronunciation, the sound of *é* is indicated by *eh*, and that of *è* by *ai* or *ay*, though in English *eh* and *ay* have practically the same sound.

NASAL SOUNDS.

Any vowel before *m* or *n* is pronounced nasally, thus :—

o before *m* or *n*=*ong* in s*ong* (therefore om, on sound alike); as,

1. long plomb non nom
long lead no name

u before *m* or *n*=*ung* in l*ung* (therefore um, un sound alike); as,

2. parfum un humble brun
perfume one humble brown

a or e before *m* or *n*=*ahng*, similar to *aun* in *aunt* (am, an, em, en sound alike) ; as,

3. dans enfant temps champ
in child time field

i before *m* or *n*=*ang* in s*ang* (im, in sound alike) ; as,

4. impôt fin vin simple
tax end wine simple

The nasal sound of *i* is always used if there is an *i* or a *y* in the syllable ; therefore *im, in, ym, yn, aim, ain, eim, ein* are all pronounced alike.

The nasal sound *en* at the end of a syllable, preceded by *i* or *y*=*in* ; as,

5. faim main teint nymphe bien chien
hunger hand complexion nymph well dog

PRONUNCIATION : (nasal sounds are indicated by *italics*, *ng* not being pronounced distinctly). 1. lo*ng*, plo*ng*, no*ng*, no*ng* ; 2. pahr-fu*ng*, u*ng*, u*ng*-bl, bru*ng* ; 3. dah*ng*, ah*ng*-fah*ng*, tah*ng*, shah*ng* ; 4. a*ng*-poh, fa*ng*, va*ng*, sa*ng*-pl ; 5. fa*ng*, ma*ng*, ta*ng*, na*ng*f, be-*ang*, she-*ang*.

NOTE.—There is no nasal sound if *m* or *n* is followed by a vowel, or if there are two *m*'s or two *n*'s ; as,

inutile (PRON. ee-nü-teel) ; une (ün) ; bonne (bonn) ; homme (omm).

LIQUID SOUNDS.

ill and il, if liquid=*ee-e*.

il is only liquid if at the end of words, and following a vowel ; as,

1. travail   fauteuil   soleil
   work   armchair   sun

ill is always liquid except in words commencing with *ill*, *mill*, or *vill* ; as,

2. billet   brouillard   famille
   ticket   fog   family

gn=*ni* in *companion* ; gne if final sounds similar to *ing* ; as }

3. signal   agneau   campagne
   signal   lamb   country

The above is the general pronunciation, but some pronounce *il* or *ill* like ill-yer, and final *gne* like n'yer.

PRONUNCIATION.—1. trah-vah'e, foh-ter'e, so-lay'e ; 2. bee-yay, broo'e-yahr; fah-mee-ye, 3. seen-yahll, ahnn-yoh, k*ahng*-pah'ing or k*ahng*-pahn-yer.

IMPORTANT REMARKS.

er at the end of words of more than one syllable=*é* (eh) ; as,

1. parler   donner   fumer
   (to) speak (to) give (to) smoke

ez final sounds like *é* (eh) ; as,

2. nez   fermez   commencez
   nose   shut   commence

y between two vowels is equal to *i-i* or *i-y* ; as,

3. royal=roi-ial payer=pai-ier
   royal   (to) pay

ti unless beginning a word is usually pronounced *si*, especially if between two vowels ; as,

4. diplomatie   révolution
   diplomacy   revolution

But in the terminations *stion*, *xtion*, *tié*, *tier*, *tière*, *tième*, the *t* is pronounced as in English; as,

5. question   amitié   litière
   question friendship litter

PRONUNCIATION.—1. pahr-leh, donn-eh, fü-meh ; 2. neh, fair-meh, komm-*ahng*-seh ; 3. ro'ah-yahll, pay-yeh ; 4. de-plo-mah-se, reh-vo-lü-se-*ong* ; 5. kess-te-*ong*, ah-mee-te-eh, lee-te-air.

If a word beginning with a vowel or an *h* mute follows a final Consonant, this consonant (even if otherwise mute) is joined to the second word, *whenever no pause could be made between the two words.* When thus linked to the following word, s and x sound like z, d like t, and f like v ; as,

1. vous êtes   ont-ils?   deux hommes   vend-il?   pas encore
   you are   have they?   two men   does he sell?   not yet

PRON.—1. voo z'ayt, *ong*-t'ill, der z'omm, v*ahng*-t'ill, pah z'*ahng*-kor.

4

FIRST LESSON.

1. **a (or an) is translated** { UN before a *Masculine Noun*; UNE „ „ *Feminine Noun*;

IMITATED PRONUNCIATION.—*ung*, ün.

1. a soldier, un soldat.
2. a lady, une dame.
3. a friend, un ami.
4. an aunt, une tante.
5. an hotel,* un hôtel.*
6. a church,* une église.*

PRONUNCIATION (see foot-note).—1. *ung* soll-dah, 2. ün dahmm (*ah* very short), 3. *ung* n'ah-me, 4. ün ta*h*ngt, 5. *ung* n'oh-tell, 6. ün eh-gleez.

EXERCISE I.

The small numbers after a word refer to the translation and pronunciation at the foot of the Exercise.

1. a brother[1]; 2. a sister[2]; 3. a soldier[3]; 4. an aunt[3]; 5. a day[4]; 6. a door[5]; 7. an hotel[3]; 8. a church[3]; 9. a friend.[3]

1. frère, 2. sœur, 3. see Examples, 4. jour (*masculine*), 5. porte (*feminine*).
PRON.—1. frair, 2. ser, 4. shoohr (sh=s in *measure*), 5. port.

*Names of things are MASCULINE in French, except those ending in e, which are FEMININE (those in té, eur, ion, son are also Fem.)

2. **the is translated** { LE before a *Masculine Singular Noun*; LA „ „ *Feminine Singular Noun*;

PRON.—ler, lah (*ah* always very short).

1. the soldier, le soldat.
2. the lady, la dame.
3. the day, le jour.
4. the door, la porte.

3. **L'** is used instead of *le* or *la* before a vowel or *h* mute (all *h*'s are mute unless we indicate the contrary); as,

1. the friend, l'ami.
2. the church, l'église.
3. the man, l'homme.
4. the hour, l'heure.

PRON.—1. lah-me, 2. leh-gleez, 3. lomm, 4. ler.

EXERCISE II.

1. the paper[1]; 2. the door; 3. the uncle[2]; 4. the church; 5. the table[3]; 6. the bag[4]; 7. the address[5]; 8. the day; 9. the hour[6]; 10. the hotel; 11. the soldier; 12. the friend.

1. papier (*masc.*), 2. oncle, 3. table (*fem.*), 4. sac, *m.*, 5. adresse, *f.*, 6. heure, *f.*
PRON.—1. pah-pe-eh, 2. *ong*-kl, 3. tah-bl, 4. sahkk, 5. ah-dress, 6. er.

In French words the last vowel pronounced is stressed very slightly, so that beginners should pronounce all syllables with equal emphasis; but they must on no account stress any syllable except the last one pronounced.—For explanation of *italics*, etc., in Imitated Pronunciation, see pages 1 to 3.

CONVERSATIONAL SENTENCES.

Où[1] est[2] l'église ?	Where[1] is[2] the church ?
L'é lise est là.[3]	The church is there.[3]
Qui[4] est à[5] la porte ?	Who[4] is at[5] the door ?
Un homme est à[5] la porte.	A man is at the door.
Qui a[6] le papier ?	Who has[6] the paper ?
Le frère a le papier.	The brother has the paper.
Où est la porte ?	Where is the door ?
La porte est ici.[7]	The door is here.[7]
Qui est la dame ?	Who is the lady ?
L'oncle a un ami.	The uncle has a friend.
Où est le soldat ?	Where is the soldier ?
La tante a un sac.	The aunt has a bag.

IMITATED PRONUNCIATION.

1. oo, 2. ay, 3. lah, 4. kee, 5. ah, 6. ah (*ah* always very short), 7. e-se.

———o———

ADDITIONAL EXERCISES.

These Additional Exercises are specially intended for School use, the Key being supplied to Teachers only.

Students desirous of quickly acquiring a general knowledge of French may omit them altogether, as they contain no new Rules.

1.

1. L'oncle a (*has*) un ami. 2. L'église a (*has*) une porte. 3. La dame a une sœur. 4. La tante a le sac. 5. Le soldat a l'adresse. 6. La tante a un frère. 7. L'homme a un oncle.

2.

1. an uncle ; 2. a lady ; 3. a day ; 4. a church ; 5. the brother ; 6. the sister ; 7. the bag ; 8. the door ; 9. the friend ; 10. the hotel ; 11. the church ; 12. the hour.

3.

1. the soldier ; 2. an aunt ; 3. the address ; 4. a man ; 5. the table ; 6. a church ; 7. the hotel ; 8. a bag ; 9. the day ; 10. the door ; 11. the paper ; 12. the friend.

4.

1. The hotel has (*a*) a door. 2. The brother has the bag. 3. The sister has the paper. 4. The man has a table. 5. The lady has the address. 6. The soldier has an uncle.

4. the must always be translated *LES* if followed by a *Plural.*
(The *s* which is added to form the Plural of Nouns is not sounded).

1. the sisters, les sœurs.
2. the friends, les amis.
3. the men, les hommes.

4. the days, les jours.
5. the churches, les églises.
6. the hours, les heures.

PRON.—1. lay ser, 2. lay z'ah-me, 3. lay z'omm, 4. lay shoohr (sh==s in *measure*), 5. lay z'eh-gleez, 6. lay z'er.

EXERCISE III.

1. the papers ; 2. the uncles ; 3. the tables ; 4. the bags ;
5. the hotels ; 6. the addresses ; 7. the soldiers ; 8. the hours.

5. PRESENT TENSE *of* (to) have, *avoir.*

1st person	I have	*j'ai*	we have	*nous avons*
2nd „	thou hast	*tu as*	you have	*vous avez*
3rd „	he has	*il a*	they (*m.*) have	*ils ont*
3rd „	she has	*elle a*	they (*f.*) have	*elles ont*

PRON.—sheh (sh==s in *measure*), tü ah, ill ah, ell ah ; noo z'ah-vong, voo z'ah-veh, ill z'ong, ell z'ong.

The Third Person (*has*, a, or *have*, ont) must be used after a Noun ; as, the man has, *l'homme a* ; the men have, *les hommes ont.*

EXERCISE IV.

1. He has bought[1] a house.[2] 2. We have found[3] two[4] bags.
3. They (*f.*) have received[5] a letter.[6] 4. The brother and[7] the sister have bought[1] an hotel. 5. I have received[5] two[4] parcels.[8]
6. You have found[3] the addresses. 7. She has a chair.[9]

1. acheté, 2. maison,*f.*, 3. trouvé, 4. deux, 5. reçu, 6. lettre,*f.*, 7. et, 8. paquet, *m.*, 9. chaise, *f.* PRON.—1. ahsh-teh, 2. may-zong, 3. troo-veh, 4. der, 5. rer-sü, 6. lettr, 7. eh, 8. pah-kay, 9. shayz.

6. our, NOTRE, Plural, NOS ; **your**, VOTRE, Plural, VOS ; **their**, LEUR, Plural, LEURS.

The Plural form must be used if the following Noun is in the Plural. PRON.—notr, noh ; votr, voh ; ler, ler.

our brother, notre frère.
your sister, votre sœur.
their uncle, leur oncle.

our brothers, nos frères.
your sisters, vos sœurs.
their uncles, leurs oncles.

EXERCISE V.

1. from[1] our door ; 2. to[2] your hotels ; 3. the doors of[1] the church ; 4. at[2] their table ; 5. from your house[3] to our garden[4];
6. at their church ; 7. of our chairs ; 8. of their friends.

1. *of* or *from*, de, 2. *to* or *at*, à, 3. maison, *f.*, 4. jardin, *m.*
PRON.—1. der, 2. ah (very short), 3. may-zong, 4. shahr-dang.

CONVERSATIONAL SENTENCES.

Où est votre maison ?	Where is your house ?
Notre maison est là (ici).	Our house is there (here).
Qui a trouvé les papiers ?	Who has found the papers ?
J'ai trouvé les papiers.	I have found the papers.
Qui a reçu les lettres ?	Who has received the letters ?
Ils ont reçu les paquets et[1] les lettres.	They have received the parcels and[1] the letters.
Notre oncle a acheté une maison et[1] un jardin.	Our uncle has bought a house and[1] a garden.
Elle a trouvé les lettres.	She has found the letters.

PRON.—1. eh. The *t* of *et* is never pronounced, even if a Vowel follows.

:0:0:

ADDITIONAL EXERCISES (Optional, see notes on page 5).

5.

1. Il a reçu votre lettre. 2. Nous avons trouvé les adresses. 3. Ils ont acheté les papiers. 4. L'église a deux portes. 5. La dame a trois frères. 6. Leurs frères ont acheté un hôtel. 7. Votre sœur a reçu le paquet. 8. Notre oncle a trouvé les hommes.

6.

1. the soldiers and the friends ; 2. the ladies and the men ; 3. the churches and the doors ; 4. the hours and the days ; 5. the hotels.

1. our uncles ; 2. your aunt ; 3. their brothers and their sisters ; 4. our house ; 5. your parcels ; 6. their garden ; 7. our friends.

7.

1. from the church to our hotel ; 2. the garden of your house ; 3. at their church ; 4. to your papers ; 5. from our friends.

8.

1. nous avons ; 2. elle a ; 3. ils ont ; 4. j'ai ; 5. tu as ; 6. elles ont ; 7. il a ; 8. vous avez.

1. he has ; 2. they (*f.*) have ; 3. we have ; 4. thou hast ; 5. they have ; 6. she has ; 7. you have ; 8. I have.

9.

1. He has two houses. 2. You have an hotel. 3. They (*fem.*) have the paper. 4. I have one brother and two sisters. 5. We have the address. 6. The church has two doors.

10.

1. I have bought an hotel. 2. We have received your parcels. 3. She has found the bag. 4. You have received two letters. 5. They have bought our house. 6. He has found their addresses.

SECOND LESSON.

7. The *Plural* in French is *nearly always* formed by adding s to the *Singular*, as in English (see Rule 4).

The following additional Rules apply to comparatively few words.

(a) Words ending in *s, x, z*, do not change in the Plural : as,

1. a month, *un mois*.	two months, *deux mois*.
2. a price, *un prix*.	two prices, *deux prix*.
3. the nose, *le nez*.	the noses, *les nez*.

(b) Words ending in *au* or *eu* add x ; as,

4. a hat, *un chapeau*.	two hats, *deux chapeaux*.
5. a nephew, *un neveu*.	two nephews, *deux neveux*.

(c) Words ending in *al* change *al* into aux ; as,

6. a horse, *un cheval*.	two horses, *deux chevaux*.

PRON.—1. *ung* mo'ah, der mo'ah, 2. *ung* pree, der pree, 3. ler neh, lay neh, 4. *ung* shah-poh, der shah-poh, 5. *ung* ner-ver, der ner-ver, 6. *ung* sher-vahll, der sher-voh.

EXERCISE I.

1. a knife,[1] the knives ; 2. one[2] arm, two arms ; 3. the journal,[4] the journals ; 4. the voice,[5] the voices ; 5. the fire,[6] the fires ; 6. one[2] son,[7] three[8] sons.

1. couteau, *m.*, 2. =a or an, 3. bras, *m.*, 4. journal, *m.*, 5. voix, *f.* (exception to rule), 6. feu, *m.*, 7. fils (pron. *fiss*), 8. trois.
PRON. 1. koo-toh, 3. brah, 4. shoohr-nahll, 5. vo'ah, 6. fer, 7. fiss, 8. tro'ah.

8. The *Interrogative* (Question) of *j'ai*, etc., is formed as in English ; but a hyphen (-) is placed between the verb and pronoun, and in the third person singular a t between two hyphens (-t-) ; thus,

have I, *ai-je ?* hast thou, *as-tu ?* has he, *a-t-il ?* has she, *a-t-elle ?*
have we, *avons-nous ?* have you, *avez-vous ?* have they, *ont-ils ? ont-elles ?*

PRON.—aysh, ah tü, ah-til, ah-tel, ah-*vong* noo, ah-veh voo, *ong-t'*il, *ong-t'*el.

EXERCISE II.

1. Have I seen[1] your nephews ? 2. Have they sent[2] a letter ? 3. Have you written[3] the address ? 4. Have we received the journals ? 5. Has he seen the horses ? 6. Have they (*f.*) written to their friends ? 7. They have two sons. 8. Have you seen your friends ? 9. Have they bought your house ? 10. Has she received the parcel ?

1. vu, 2. envoyé, 3. écrit.—PRON. 1. vü, 2. *ahng*-vo'ah-yeh, 3. eh-kree.

CONVERSATIONAL SENTENCES

Avez-vous vu notre ami ?	Have you seen our friend ?
Oui,[1] j'ai vu votre ami.	Yes[1], I have seen your friend.
A-t-il acheté la maison ?	Has he bought the houes ?
Non,[2] il a acheté le jardin.	No,[2] he has bought the garden.
Ont-ils reçu nos lettres ?	Have they received our letters ?
Oui, ils ont reçu deux lettres.	Yes, they have received two ,,
Qui a trouvé l'adresse ?	Who has found the address ?
Notre sœur a trouvé l'adresse.	Our sister has found the address.
Où avez-vous vu nos chevaux ?	Where have you seen our horses ?
J'ai vu vos chevaux là.	I have seen your horses there.
Leurs neveux sont ici.	Their nephews are here.

PRON,—1. we or oo'e, 2. nong.

:o:o:

ADDITIONAL EXERCISES (Optional, see note on page 5).

11.

1. Avons-nous les couteaux ? **2.** A-t-elle votre adresse ? **3.** Avez-vous un frère et deux sœurs ? **4.** Ont-ils les chevaux ? **5.** Ai-je votre chapeau ?

6. J'ai envoyé le paquet à votre tante. **7.** A-t-il reçu une lettre ? **8.** Avez-vous vu leurs neveux ? **9.** Ils ont écrit à notre oncle. **10.** Nous avons acheté les journaux.

12.

1. the arm, the arms ; **2.** a newspaper,* three newspapers ; **3.** our nephew, our nephews ; **4.** your price, your prices ; **5.** their son, their sons ; **6.** one horse, three horses ; **7.** the nose, the noses.

13.

1. a-t-il ? **2.** avons-nous ? **3.** ont-elles ? **4.** ai-je ? **5.** avez-vous ? **6.** a-t-elle ? **7.** ont-ils ? **8.** as-tu ?

9. have I ? **10.** have we? **11.** has she ? **12** have they (*m.*) ? **13.** hast thou ? **14.** has he ? **15.** have you? **16.** nave they (*f.*) ?

14.

1. Have I your knife ? **2.** Has he the newspaper* ? **3.** Have they three sons ? **4.** Have you our papers ? **5.** Has she their letter ?

15.

1. We have lost your letters. **2.** Have you received our parcels ? **3.** She has seen their nephews. **4.** They have found our newspapers.* **5.** Has he sent the horses ? **6.** The lady has written to your uncle.

*newspaper. journal, *journal* (*m.*).

9. my, MON, MA, MES ; **his, her, its,** SON, SA, SES ; **thy,** TON, TA, TES. PRON. *mong, mah, may, song, sah, say, tong, tah, tay.*

mon, ton, son are used if the following Noun is MASCULINE SINGULAR.
ma, ta, sa,   „   „   „   „   FEMININE SINGULAR.
mes, tes, ses   „   „   „   „   PLURAL.

my brother, **mon frère.**	my sister, **ma sœur.**
his (or her) sister, **sa sœur.**	her (or his) brother, **son frère.**
my brothers, **mes frères.**	his (or her) sisters, **ses sœurs.**

NOTE carefully that *son frère* means her *brother* as well as *his brother*, and that *sa sœur* means his *sister* as well as *her sister*, because these words always take the Gender of the following Noun.

EXERCISE III.

1. my niece[1] ; 2. his father[2] ; 3. my hat ; 4. her mother[3] ; 5. my nephews ; 6. his nieces[1] ; 7. my room[4] ; 8. his pen[5] ; 9. her pen ; 10. her pencil[6] ; 11. his pencil ; 12. her hats.

1. nièce, 2. père, 3. mère, 4. chambre, *f.*, 5. plume, *f.*, 6. crayon, *m.*
PRON.—1. ne-ess, 2. pair, 3. mair, 4. shahng-br, 5. plüm, 6. kray-yong.

10. *mon, ton, son* are used before words beginning with a vowel or *h* mute, even if the Noun is FEMININE ; as,

my friend *(fem.)*, mon amie. | her address, son adresse.

Ex. IV.—1. her handwriting[1] ; 2. his school[2] ; 3. his room ; 4. her uncle ; 5. his street[3] ; 6. his church ; 7. her church.

1. écriture, *f.*, 2. école, *f.*, 3. rue, *f.* PRON.—1. eh-kre-tür, 2. eh-kol, 3. rü.

11. **not** is translated by the two words NE ... PAS.

PAS always occupies the same place in the sentence as the English word *not*, and *ne* (n' before a vowel) always *precedes the Verb* ; thus,

I have not, je n'*ai pas*	have I not ? n'*ai-je pas ?*
thou hast not, tu n'*as pas*	hast thou not ? n'*as-tu pas ?*
he has not, il n'*a pas*	has he not ? n'*a-t-il pas ?*
we have not, nous n'*avons pas*	have we not ? n'*avons-nous pas ?*
you have not, vous n'*avez pas*	have you not ? n'*avez-vous pas ?*
they have not, ils n'*ont pas*	have they not ? n'*ont-ils pas ?*

PRON.—sher neh pah, tü nah pah, ill nah pah ; naysh pah, nah tü pah, etc.

EXERCISE V.

1. Have you not my book[1] ? 2. He has not seen her handwriting. 3. We have not found the gloves.[2] 4. Have they not written to your friends ? 5. I have not read[3] his letter.

1. livre, *m.*, 2. gant, *m.*, 3. lu. PRON.—1. leevr, 2. gahng, 3. lü.

CONVERSATIONAL SENTENCES.

Avez-vous reçu un paquet par la poste[1] ?	Have you received a parcel by (the) post[1] ?
Non, mais[2] j'ai reçu deux lettres de Paris.[3]	No, but[2] I have received two letters from Paris.[3]
N a-t-il pas rencontré[4] sa nièce dans[5] la rue ? [chevaux ?	Has he not met[4] his niece in the street ? [horses ?
N'avez-vous pas acheté les deux	Have you not bought the two
N'ont-ils pas trouvé mon parapluie[6] ?	Have they not found my umbrella[6] ? [gloves ?
De qui a-t-elle reçu les gants ?	From whom has she received the
Elle n'a pas écrit à son père.	She has not written to her father.
N'avez-vous pas vu mes livres sur[7] la table ?	Have you not seen my books on[7] the table ?

PRON.—1. post, 2. may, 3. pah-ree, 4. *rahng-kong*-treh, 5. d*ahng*, 6. pah-rah-plwe (masculine,—exception to rule), 7. sür.

ADDITIONAL EXERCISES.
16.
1. Qui a acheté leurs gants ? 2. N'avez-vous pas vu son école ? 3. Nous avons vu son crayon et sa plume.

4. N'a-t-il pas trouvé nos livres sur la table ? 5. Nous n'avons pas écrit les lettres. 6. N'ont-ils pas envoyé les livres, les crayons et les plumes dans mon paquet ?

17.
1. my father ; 2. my mother ; 3. his book ; 4. her room ; 5. his gloves ; 6. her pens ; 7. her father ; 8. his mother ; 9. her pencil ; 10. his pen ; 11. my books ; 12. her glove ; 13. his pens.

18.
1. il n'a pas ; 2. n'ai-je pas ? 3. nous n'avons pas ; 4. n'ont-ils pas ? 5. tu n'as pas ; 6. n'avez-vous pas ? 7. elles n'ont pas.

8. has he not ? 9. I have not ; 10. have we not ? 11. they have not ; 12. hast thou not ? 13. she has not ; 14. have you not ?

19.
1. from his house ; 2. to her address ; 3. of our street ; 4. at her school ; 5. from her father ; 6. to his mother.

20.
1. Has he not found my gloves ? 2. We have not received his letter. 3. Have you not seen my niece ? 4. My nephew has not bought the horses. 5. They (*f.*) have not seen my handwriting.

THIRD LESSON.

12. **which? what? what a!** are translated:—
Sing. Masc. QUEL, Fem. QUELLE; Plu. Masc. QUELS, Fem. QUELLES.
PRON. *of all four forms*—kell.

which niece? **quelle nièce?** | which hats? **quels chapeaux?**

EXERCISE I.

1. which school? 2. what month? 3. which rooms? 4. what
a man! 5. what hats? 6. which hour? 7. which parcels?

---

13. this } Masc. CE, Fem. CETTE; Plural { these } CES.
that } { those }
PRON.—*ser*, sett, say.

this (*or* that) book, **ce livre.** | **these** (*or* those) books, **ces livres.**
that (*or* this) street, **cette rue.** | **those** (*or* these) streets, **ces rues.**

EXCEPTION.—**cet** is used instead of **ce** if the next word begins with a
vowel or *h* mute; as,

this (*or* that) friend, **cet ami.** | that (*or* this) man, **cet homme.**

PRON. set ah-me, set omm. NOTE.—*cet* is never used instead of *cette* or *ces.*

EXERCISE II.

1. this carriage[1]; 2. that gun[2]; 3. these knives; 4. those
forks[3]; 5. this inkstand[4]; 6. that handwriting; 7. this hour;
8. those days; 9. this hotel; 10. these gardens; 11. this ink.[5]

---

1. voiture, *f.*, 2. fusil, *m.* (L silent), 3. fourchette, *f.*, 4. encrier, *m.*, 5. encre, *f.*
PRON.—1. vo'ah-tür, 2. fü-zee, 3. foohr-shet, 4. *ahng*-kre-eh, 5. *ahng*kr.

14. *Possessive Cases* like the following must be changed thus:

my father's hat *into* the hat of my father; your sister's husband *into* the
husband of your sister; the girls' friends *into* the friends of the girls.

Begin with the word coming after the apostrophe ('), *placing* 'the' *before it.*

EXERCISE III.

1. my niece's husband[1]; 2. the officer's[2] horse; 3. these
soldiers' guns; 4. my sister's umbrella[3]; 5. which lady's
carriage? 6. those officers' horses; 7. your friend's address.

8. Have you found this lady's umbrella? 9. Her husband
has written to his nephew's friend. 10. Their nieces have
not read this lady's letter. 11. Our neighbour's[4] windows.[5]

---

1. mari, 2. officier, 3. parapluie, *masc.*, 4. voisin, 5 fenêtre, *fem.*
PRON. 1. mah-re, 2. off-iss-e-eh, 3. pah-rah-plü'ee, 4. vo'ah-*zang*, 5. fer-nay-tr

CONVERSATIONAL SENTENCES.

Où est la voiture de votre père ?	Where is your father's carriage ?
Elle est là (ici).	It (=she) is there (here) [stand ?
Quel est le prix[1] de cet encrier ?	What is the price[1] of this ink-
Qui est cet homme ?	Who is that man ?
N'avez-vous pas lu[2] ce livre ?	Have you not read[2] this book ?
Quel est votre chapeau ? [dame.	Which is your hat ? [writing.
Je n'ai pas vu l'écriture de cette	I have not seen that lady's hand-
Elle a envoyé son fils[3] à l'hotel.	She has sent her son to the hotel.
Avez-vous trouvé l'adresse de cet homme ?	Have you found that man's address ?

PRON. 1. pree, 2. lü, 3. fiss.

:o:o:

ADDITIONAL EXERCISES.

21.

1. Avez vous vu la voiture de son mari ? 2. J'ai acheté ce couteau et cette fourchette. 3. Quel livre a-t-il écrit ? 4. Qui a vu les gants de ces dames ?

5. Le cheval de l'officier est à la porte. 6. Quel est le fusil de ce soldat ? 7. Ils n'ont pas trouvé le parapluie de votre nièce. 8. N'avez-vous pas reçu les lettres de votre frère ?

22.

1. which school ? 2. what hat ? 3. what a carriage ! 4. which knives ? 5. what forks ? 6. what a fire ! 7. what street ? 8. which houses ? 9. what a handwriting !

23.

1. the officer's gloves ; 2. the man's bag ; 3. your brother's niece ; 4. these soldiers' guns ; 5. our uncle's carriage ; 6. your friend's knife ; 7. those men's papers ; 8. his sister's address ; 9. our nieces' house ; 10. my nephew's voice.

24.

1. this soldier ; 2. that lady ; 3. this man ; 4. these horses ; 5. those rooms ; 6. this handwriting ; 7. that officer ; 8. these newspapers ; 9. those streets ; 10. that voice ; 11. these letters.

25.

1. Which day ? 2. Your nephew's friend. 3. Have you sent the man's books ? 4. He has bought his uncle's garden. 5. They have bought these hats. 6. Has she written this letter ? 7. We have received that parcel. 8. Have you seen those houses ? 9. We have written to that man 10. Have you sent those addresses ?

HPS?

15. PRESENT TENSE of *(to) be*, **être**.

I am,	*je suis*	we are,	*nous sommes*
thou art,	*tu es*	you are,	*vous êtes*
he is,	*il est*	they *(m.)* are,	*ils sont*
she is,	*elle est*	they *(f.)* are,	*elles sont*

PRON. (sh=s in *measure*) sher swe, tü ay, ill ay, ell ay; noo somm, voo z'ayt, ill song, ell song.

The Third Person *(are,* sont) must be used after a Noun; as,
The soldiers are in the street. *Les soldats* sont *dans la rue.*

EXERCISE IV.

1. Who[1] is there[2]? 2. Where[3] are our knives? 3. I am very[4] tired.[5] 4. He is very rich.[6] 5. She is at (the) church. 6. We are at his hotel. 7. You are late.[7] 8. The inkstand is on the table. 9. Who are these men? 10. Where are our newspapers (=journals)? 11. Your friends are at the station.[8]

1. qui, 2. là, 3. où, 4. très, 5. fatigué, 6. riche, 7. en retard, 8. gare. PRON.—
1. kee, 2. lah, 3. oo, 4. tray, 5. fah-te-gay, 6. rish, 7. *ahng* rer-tahr, 8. gahr.

16. Adjectives form the Feminine by adding **e** (those ending in **e** do not change). **s** is generally added in the Plural (see Rule 7).

	MASCULINE.		FEMININE.	
	Singular.	Plural.	Singular.	Plural.
right,	droit,	droits	droite,	droites
left,	gauche,	gauches	gauche,	gauches
large,	grand,	grands	grande,	grandes
small,	petit,	petits	petite,	petites

PRON.—*Masc.* dro'ah, gohsh, grahng, per-te,
Fem. dro'ahtt, gohsh, grahngd, per-tit.

17. Adjectives take the Gender of the word to which they refer; as,

The man is tall.	L'homme est grand.
The lady is tall.	La dame est grande.
The men are tall.	Les hommes sont grands.
The ladies are tall.	Les dames sont grandes.

EXERCISE V.

1. Our friends are absent.[1] 2. These men are rich. 3. His house is too[2] small.[3] 4. We are tired. 5. This water[4] is warm.[5] 6. That ink is bad.[6] 7. You are very polite.[7] 8. I am ill.[8] 9. Her hat is too small. 10. My gloves are too large.

1. absent, 2. trop, 3. petit, 4. eau, *f.*, 5. chaud, 6. mauvais, 7. poli, 8. malade.
PRON.—1. ahb-*sahng*, 2. tro, 3. per-te, 4. oh, 5. shoh, 6. moh-vay, 7. po-le, 8. mah-lahdd.

CONVERSATIONAL SENTENCES.

N'êtes-vous pas malade ?	Are you not ill ?
Non, mais je suis très fatigué.	No, but I am very tired.
Cette eau est très mauvaise.	This water is very bad.
Est-elle grande ou petite ?	Is she tall or short ?
Elle est assez[1] grande.	She is rather[1] tall.
Ne sont-ils pas en retard ?	Are they not late ? [friends ?
Où sont les amis de votre neveu ?	Where are your nephew's
Ils sont absents.	They are absent.
Avez-vous un verre[2] d'eau ?	Have you a glass[2] of water ?
Oui, mais elle est trop froide.[3]	Yes, but it (= she) is too cold.[3]
Ces chambres sont trop chaudes.	These rooms are too warm.

PRON.—1. ahss-eh, 2. vair, 3. fro'ahd.

ADDITIONAL EXERCISES.

26.

1. Vous (*plural*) êtes très fatigués. **2.** Ce couteau est trop mauvais. **3.** Ces officiers sont très polis. **4.** Ces chambres sont chaudes. **5.** La maison de votre ami est petite.

6. Ces soldats sont très grands. **7.** Sa mère est très riche. **8.** Les dames sont à la gare. **9.** Nos chevaux sont fatigués.

27.

1. il est ; **2.** nous sommes ; **3.** je suis ; **4.** elles sont ; **5.** tu es ; **6.** ils sont ; **7.** vous êtes ; **8.** elle est.

9. I am ; **10.** you are ; **11.** she is ; **12.** they are ; **13. thou art ; 14.** we are ? **15.** they (*f.*) are ; **16.** he is.

28.

Give the Fem. Singular, and Masc. and Fem. Plural of :

1. warm, *chaud* ; **2.** polite, *poli* ; **3.** large, *grand* ; **4.** tired, *fatigué* ; **5.** right, *droit* ; **6.** bad, *mauvais* ; **7.** small, *petit* ; **8.** ill, *malade* ; **9.** absent, *absent* ; **10.** left, *gauche* ; **11.** rich, *riche*.

29.

1. He is tall ; they (*f.*) are tall. **2.** She is short ; they (*m.*) are short. **3.** She is rich ; they (*f.*) are rich. **4.** We (*m.*) are tired ; we (*f.*) are tired. **5.** Your sister is polite ; your brothers are polite.

30.

1. The ink is bad. **2.** These horses are small. **3.** We are very ill. **4.** Our uncle's house is large. **5.** This room is warm. **6.** His letter is very polite. **7.** My niece is tired. **8.** These pens are very bad. **9.** The church is small. **10.** Your friends (*f.*) are absent.

FOURTH LESSON.

18. The *Interrogative* of *je suis*, etc., is formed as in English, but a hyphen (-) is placed between the Verb and the Pronoun ; as,

am I ?	suis-je ?	are we ?	sommes-nous ?
is he ?	est-il ?	are you ?	êtes-vous ?

PRON.—sweesh, ay *t'*ill, somm noo, ayt voo.

19. The *Negative* is always formed as explained in Rule 11 ; as,

I am not, *je ne suis* pas	am I not ? *ne suis-je* pas ?
she is not, *elle n'est* pas	are we not ? *ne sommes-nous* pas ?
they are not, *ils ne sont* pas	are you not ? *n'êtes-vous* pas ?

EXERCISE I.

1. She is not vain.[1]   2. These horses are not old.[2]   3. Are you not satisfied[3] ?   4. Is he not too young[4] ?   5. Am I not late ?   6. We (*f.*) are not tired.   7. Those ladies are pretty.[5] 8. Our rooms are not small. 9. Your neighbours[6] are very rich.

---

1. vain, 2. vieux, 3. satisfait, 4. jeune, 5. joli, 6. voisin.
PRON.—1. v*a*ng, 2. ve-*e*r, 3. sah-tiss-fay, 4. sh*e*rn, 5. sho-le, 6. vo'ah-z*a*ng.

---

20. *Questions* must be changed when translating, as follows :—

Has THE SOLDIER a gun ?=THE SOLDIER has HE a gun ?

Le soldat a-t-il un fusil ?

Have THE MEN the horses ?=THE MEN have THEY the horses ?

Les hommes ont-ils les chevaux ?

Is THE LAMP on the table ?=THE LAMP is SHE on the table ?

La lampe est-elle sur la table ?

The Question is only formed as above if the Subject is a Noun.

NOTE that in Questions the Subject comes immediately after the Verb in English. The Subject in the above Examples is printed in CAPITALS.

EXERCISE II.

1. Has the postman[1] brought[2] a letter ?   2. Have those officers bought your horses ?   3. Are not these flowers[3] very pretty ?   4. Is your sister at (the) church ?   5. Has this gentleman[4] two sons or three ?   6. Has the doctor[5] seen your friend ?   7. Are not the newspapers on the table ?   8. Is not the waiter[6] here ?   9. Is his house large ?

---

1. facteur, 2. apporté, 3. fleur, *f.*, 4. monsieur (*plur.* messieurs), 5. docteur, 6. garçon.   PRON.—1. fahk-ter, 2. ahpp-or-teh, 3. fler, 4. mer-se-er. may-*s*e-er, 5. dok-ter, 6. gahr-s*o*ng.

CONVERSATIONAL SENTENCES.

Monsieur S. est-il *à la maison?*	Is Mr. S. *at home?*
Oui, *monsieur,* il est dans le salon.[1]	Yes, *sir,* he is in the drawing-room.[1]
Les dames sont-elles *en haut*[2]?	Are the ladies *upstairs*[2]?
Non, elles ne sont pas *en haut.*	No, they are not *upstairs.*
Où avez-vous été[3] aujourd'hui[4]?	Where have you been[3] to-day[4]?
Nous avons été[3] à l'église de St. Paul.[5]	We have been to (the) St.[5] Paul's church.[5]
N'êtes-vous pas fatigués?	Are you (*plur.*) not tired?
Si, nous sommes bien[6] fatigués.	Yes, we are very[6] tired.
Voulez-vous une tasse[7] de café[8]?	*Will you have* a cup[7] of coffee[8]?
Oui, madame, *merci.*[9]	Yes, madam, *thank*[9] *you.*[9]

PRON.—1. sah-*long,* 2. *ahng* oh, 3. eh-teh, 4. oh-shoohr-dwe, 5. *der sang* pol, 6. be-*ang* (*bien* is often used instead of *très*), 7. tahss, 8. kah-feh, 9. ma[r]r-se.

ADDITIONAL EXERCISES.

31.

1. Nous ne sommes pas satisfaits.   2. N'est-elle pas jolie? 3. Nous n'avons pas rencontré leur voiture.   4. Ce monsieur est-il malade?   5. Cette chambre n'est-elle pas chaude?

6. Les livres sont-ils sur la table?   7. Ces plumes ne sont-elles pas mauvaises?   8. Votre docteur n'est-il pas très riche? 9. Le facteur a-t-il apporté nos lettres?

32.

1. sommes-nous?   2. es-tu?   3. êtes-vous?   4. est-elle?   5. sont-ils?   6. suis-je?   7. sont-elles?   8. est-il?

9. am I?   10. are they (*m.*)?   11. is he?   12. are we?   13. art thou?   14. are you?   15. is she?   16. are they (*f.*)?

33.

1. I am not;   2. we are not;   3. thou art not;   4. you are not;   5. he is not;   6. they are not;   7. are we not?   8. is he not?   9. are you not?   10. am I not?   11. are they not?   12. is he not?

34.

1. Is the table (the table is she) here?   2. Are not the letters (the letters are they not) there?   3. Are these houses (these houses are they) small?   4. Has not the doctor (the doctor has he not) written? 5. Has your friend (your friend has he) bought the carriage?

35.

1. Are these ladies vain?   2. Are not those flowers pretty? 3. Is not this officer young?   4. Have your sons brought the parcel?   5. Is not his sister's husband ill?

21. The *Past Tense* is generally changed into the *Perfect Tense* when translating; as,

PAST : The man saw : *into*	} L'homme a vu.
PERFECT : The man *has seen*.	
PAST : Did* you speak ? *into*	} Avez-vous parlé ?
PERFECT : *Have* you *spoken*?	
PAST : The lady did* not buy : *into*	} La dame n'a pas acheté.
PERFECT : The lady *has* not *bought*.	
PAST : Did* they not find ? *into*	} N'ont-ils pas trouvé ?
PERFECT : *Have* they not *found*?	

* " did " must be changed into " have " or " has."

(NOTE carefully that the PAST PARTICIPLE can only be used after an AUXILIARY, i.e. *have*, etc. *Je reçu, nous trouvé*, etc., is impossible French, just as *she written, they spoken*, etc., is bad English).

EXERCISE III.

1. I received (=I have received). **2.** My friend broke[1] the glass.[2] **3.** Did you hear[3] the noise[4] ? **4.** She lost[5] her umbrella. **5.** Did the doctor read[6] my note[7] ? **6.** He did not open[8] the parcel. **7.** Did they not see the fire[9] ? **8.** We did not open[8] the door.

1. brisé (*past participle*), 2. verre, *m.*, 3. entendu (*past part.*), 4. bruit, *m.*, 5. perdu (*past part.*), 6. lu (*past part.*), 7. note, *f.*, 8. ouvert (*past part.*), 9. incendie, *m.* PRON.—1. bree-zeh, 2. vair, 3. *ahng-tahng-*dü, 4. brwee, 5. pair-dü, 6. lü, 7. not, 8. oo-vair, 9. *ang-sahng-*de.

---

22. *of the, from the* are translated **du** instead of *de le*.
    to the, at the   „   „   **au**   „   *à le*.

of the doctor, **du** *docteur*	to the doctor, **au** *docteur*
from the postman, **du** *facteur*	at the postman, **au** *facteur*

NOTE.—**du** and **au** are only used before MASCULINE SINGULAR Nouns beginning with a Consonant; therefore they are never used instead of *de la, de l', à la, à l'*, thus:

of the hotel, *de l'hôtel*	to the hotel, *à l'hôtel*
from the house, *de la maison*	at the house, *à la maison*

EXERCISE IV.

1. from the garden ; **2.** to the doctor ; **3.** of the knife ; **4.** to the arm ; **5.** from the church ; **6.** at the hotel ; **7.** Did you receive the doctor's bill[1] ? **8.** Who found the gentleman's gloves ? **9.** The last[2] day of the month. **10.** The soldier's gun is here.[3] **11.** Did you see the doctor's carriage ?

---

1. compte, *m.*, 2. dernier, 3. ici. PRON.—1. kongt, 2. dair-ne-eh, 3. iss-e.

CONVERSATIONAL SENTENCES.

Avez-vous pris[1] une tasse de café ?	Did you take a cup of coffee ?
Non, j'ai pris une tasse de thé.	No, I had (=took) a cup of tea.
Le facteur a-t-il apporté une lettre pour[2] vous ?	Did the postman bring a letter for[2] you ?
Non, mais[3] il a apporté un paquet pour votre frère.	No, but[3] he brought a parcel for your brother.
Quel est le nom[4] du docteur ?	What is the doctor's name[4] ?
Pourquoi[5] ont-ils ouvert les fenêtres[6] de la chambre ?	Why[5] did they open the windows[6] of the room ?

PRON.—1. pree, 2. poor, 3. may, 4. nong, 5. poor-ko'ah, 6. fer-nay-tr.

ADDITIONAL EXERCISES.

36.

1. Votre oncle a-t-il reçu ma note ?   2. Les journaux sont-ils sur la table ?   3. Les chevaux du docteur sont-ils petits ? 4. Le mari de votre sœur est-il grand ?

5. Le facteur est-il malade ?   6. Les soldats de ces officiers sont-ils fatigués ?   7. Ces fleurs ne sont-elles pas jolies ?

37.

1. I saw=I have seen, we saw ;   2. he bought=he has bought, they bought ; 3. we lost=we have lost, she lost ; 4. she read=she has read, you read ; 5. you opened=you have opened.

38.

1. we did not receive=we have not received ;   2 they did not receive=they have not received; 3. he did not find ; 4. I did not find ;   5. you did not buy ;   6. she did not buy.

39.

1. did I see ?=have I seen ? 2. did you write ?=have you written ? 3. did we send ? 4. did she bring ? 5. did they break ? 6. did he hear ?   7. did the soldier see ?=the soldier has he seen ?

40.

1. did we not lose ?=have we not lost ?   2. did he not open ?= has he not opened ? 3. did you not receive ? 4. did I not break ? 5. did not the postman bring ?=the postman has he not brought ?

41.

1. from the chair, to the chair ;   2. of the hour, at the hour ; 3. of the month, at the month ;   4. the nephew's, to the nephew ; 5. of the room, to the room ; 6. from the hotel, at the hotel ; 7. of the fire, at the fire ; 8. from the price, at the price ; 9. of the man.

FIFTH LESSON.

23. **it** is translated by *il* if referring to a *Masculine Noun*, and *elle* if referring to a *Feminine Noun* ; as,

Where is your parcel ?	*Où est votre paquet?*
it is on the table.	Il *est sur la table.*
Where is his chair ?	*Où est sa chaise?*
It is here.	Elle *est ici.*

24. **they** is translated *ils* or *elles* according to the gender of the noun referred to ; as,

I have seen your pens ;	*J'ai vu vos plumes* ;
they are on the table.	elles *sont sur la table.*

EXERCISE I.

1. Have you heard his voice ? Yes, it is very strong.[1] 2. I read his letter ; it is very short.[2] 3. We bought this novel ; it is very interesting.[4] 4. Have you bought the house ? No ; it is sold.[5] 5. Where are the forks ? They are not good.[6]

---

1. fort, 2. court, 3. roman, 4. intéressant, 5. vendu, 6. bon, *m.,* bonne (*fem. irreg.*). PRON.—1. for, 2. koohr, 3. ro-mahng, 4. ang-téh-ress-ahng, 5. vahng-dü, 6. bong, bonn.

25. **of the**, *from the* are translated **des** instead of *de les.*
to the, *at the* „ „ **aux** „ *à les.*

des, aux are the only forms used in the Plural ; as,

of the hats, des *chapeaux*	to the hats, aux *chapeaux*
from the houses, des *maisons*	at the houses, aux *maisons*
of the churches, des *églises*	to the churches, aux *églises*
from the men, des *hommes*	to the men, aux *hommes*

EXERCISE II.

1. the pages[1] of the books ; 2. the feathers[2] of the birds[3] ; 3. the boys'[4] boots[5] ; 4. the girls'[6] shoes[7] ; 5. We gave[8] the money[9] to the waiters.[4] 6. They spoke[10] to the workmen's[11] wives.[12] 7. I wrote to our friend's brothers. 8. We sent the parcel to your uncle's sons. 9. They saw the soldiers from the windows of our house.

---

1. page, *f.,* 2. plume, *f.,* 3. oiseau, *m.,* 4. garçon, 5. botte, *f.,* 6. fille, 7. soulier, *m.,* 8. *given,* donné, 9. argent, *m.,* 10. *spoken,* parlé, 11. ouvrier, 12. femme (*prom.* fahmm).

PRON.—1. pahsh, 2. plüm, 3. wah-zoh, 4. gahr-song, 5. bot, 6. fee-e, 7. soo-le-eh, 8. donn-eh, 9. ahr-shahng, 10. pahr-leh, 11. oo-vre-eh, 12. fahmm.

CONVERSATIONAL SENTENCES

Votre leçon[1] est-elle difficile[2] ?	Is your lesson[1] difficult[2] ?
Non, elle est très facile.[3]	No, it is very easy.[3]
Mon parapluie est-il là ?	Is my umbrella there ?
Oui, il est dans cette chambre.	Yes, it is in this room.
Ses gants sont-ils bruns[4] ?	Are her gloves brown[4] ?
Non, ils sont noirs.[5]	No, they are black.[5]
Avez-vous vu sa montre[6] ?	Did you see her watch[6] ?
Oui, elle est très jolie.	Yes, it is very nice.
J'ai acheté ces bottes, mais elles sont très mauvaises.	I have bought these boots, but they are very bad.

1. ler-*song*. 2. diff-e-sill, 3. fah-sill, 4. br*ung*, 5. no'ahr, 6. m*ong*-tr.

ADDITIONAL EXERCISES.

42.

1. Où sont les chambres des garçons ?   2. N'avez-vous pas **entendu** les voix des messieurs ?   3. Il a apporté le compte du **docteur. 4.** Avez-vous vu mon journal ? Oui, il est sur la chaise. **5. N'avez-vous** pas perdu la lettre du voisin ? Non, elle est là.

6. Où sont mes fleurs ?   Elles sont sur la table.   7. La fenêtre est-elle ouverte ?   8. Vos voisins ne sont-ils pas absents ?   9. Sa femme n'est-elle pas malade ?

43.

1. Have you my hat ? No, it is there.   2. Where is her bird ? It is not here.   3. They have a knife, but it is bad.   4. We saw his house ; it is very large.   5. The workmen are not satisfied.

44.

1. Have you brought the chairs ? They are not good.   2. Where is the lamp ? It is broken.   3. Have you seen the table ? Is it not too small ?   4. I heard her voice ; it is very strong.   5. We saw your neighbour's garden ; it is very large.   6. We received the feathers ; they are very pretty.

45.

1. the ladies' umbrellas ; 2. the officers' gloves ; 3. to the gentlemen's horses ; 4. to the neighbours' gardens ; 5. the pages of the books ; 6. at the corners (*coin*) of the streets.

46.

1. Is not your friend's note (your friend's note is she not) very short ?   2. Have you brought the glasses ? No, they are broken. 3. Are not these novels interesting ?   4. Are these chairs good ? 5. Are not those letters interesting?

26. some (or *any*) is translated the same as OF THE, thus :

1. some bread, DU pain	3. some meat, DE LA viande
2. any money, DE L'argent	4. some friends, DES amis

PRON.—1. dü p*ang*, 2. der lahr-sh*ahng* (sh like s in *measure*), 3. der lah ve-*ahng*d, 4. day z'ah-me.

Have you ANY bread==Have you OF THE bread ?

Avez-vous du pain ?

They have bought SOME books==They have bought OF THE books.

Ils ont acheté des livres.

SOME is only translated as above if a Noun follows.

EXERCISE III.

1. some beer[1] ; 2. any cheese[2] ; 3. some ink ; 4. any glasses ; 5. some butter[3] ; 6. any salt[4] ; 7. some salad[5] ; 8. any water ; 9. some flowers ; 10. He has bought some pens and (some) pencils. 11. Did you find any money on the table ? 12. They had[6] some soup. 13. Did you hear any noise ?

---

1. bière, *f.*, 2. fromage, *m.*, 3. beurre, *m.*, 4. sel, *m.*, 5. salade, *f.* 6. eu (*past participle*).

PRON.—1. be-air, 2. fro-mahsh, 3. ber, 4. sell, 5. sah-lahdd, 6. ü.

27. any after NOT is simply translated DE or D' ; as,

We have not any bread.	Nous n'avons pas DE pain.
Have you not any friends ?	N'avez-vous pas D'amis ?

28. no before a Noun is translated the same as *not any* ; as,

They have no soup.	Ils n'ont pas DE soupe.
Have they no money ?	N'ont-ils pas D'argent ?

29. some or **any** must be expressed in French, even if omitted in English ; as,

He had bread and water.	Il a eu DU pain et DE L'eau.

EXERCISE IV.

1. We have not any soup. 2. Has he not any matches[1] ? 3. Have you no money ? 4. I have not any time.[2] 5. She has no gloves. 6. Have we not any sugar[3] ? 7. This gentleman has no sisters. 8. Have they not any beer ? 9. They have not received any letters. 10. The men had bread, cheese and wine. 11. Have you friends in (à) Paris ?

---

1. allumette, *f.*, 2. temps, *m.*, 3. sucre, *m.*

PRON.—1. ahll-ü-n-ett, 2. *tahna*, 3. sükr.

CONVERSATIONAL SENTENCES.

Avez-vous de la bière ?	Have you any beer ?
Oui, j'ai un verre de bière.	Yes, I have a glass of beer.
A-t-il des amis *à* Paris ?	Has he any friends *in* Paris ?
Je[1] *ne sais pas.*[1]	I[1] *do not know.*[1]
Son frère n'est-il pas *en haut* ?	Is not his brother *upstairs* ?
Il n'a pas de frères.	He has no brothers.
N'avez-vous pas de sel ici ?	Have you not any salt here ?
Si,[2] il est là.	Yes,[2] it is there.
Qui a ouvert la porte ?	Who has opened the door ?
Pourquoi n'avez-vous pas écrit à votre frère ?	Why have you not written to your brother ?

1. sher *ner* say pah, 2. se (*si* is used for *yes* in answer to a negative question).

:o:o:

ADDITIONAL EXERCISES.

47.

1. Avez-vous du pain, du fromage et du beurre ? 2. Nous n'avons pas d'eau. 3. J'ai de la soupe, de la viande, et de la salade. 4. Ils n'ont pas de sel. 5. N'a-t-elle pas de sucre dans son café ?

6. Il a du temps et de l'argent. 7. N'avez-vous pas d'amis ? 8. Ces dames n'ont pas de chapeaux. 9. Les messieurs n'ont-ils pas d'allumettes ?

48.

1. some paper ; 2. some soup ; 3. any ink ; 4. some workmen ; 5. any cheese ; 6. some salad ; 7. some water ; 8. any pens ; 9. some sugar ; 10. any money ; 11. some beer ; 12. some birds.

49.

1. Have you any letters ? 2. We have some sugar and (some) salt. 3. Have they any meat and (any) salad ? 4. He has some money. 5. Has she bought any pens ?

50.

1. some bread, no bread (*pas de pain*) ; 2. some water, no water ; 3. some soup, not any soup ; 4. some parcels, not any parcels ; 5. some matches, no matches ; 6. some ink, no ink.

51.

1. She sold some butter. 2. They did not sell any butter. 3. We gave some money to the boys. 4. I did not give any money to the waiter. 5. They had (=have had) some soup. 6. Had she not any soup ? 7. You saw some friends. 8. Did you not see any friends ?

RECAPITULATORY EXERCISES on Lessons 1 to 5.

————— :o: — -————

1.

a, the, my, his, her, its, our, your, their, this, that, } knife
　　which, what, what a　　　　　　　　　　　　 { *couteau*

the, my, his, her, its, our, your, their, these, those, } knives
　　which, what　　　　　　　　　　　　　　　　 { *couteaux*

*Practise in the same way the following words in the Singular
and Plural :*

street, *rue* ; hotel, *hôtel* ; church, *église* ; fire, *feu* ; voice, *voix* ;
uncle, *oncle* ; handwriting, *écriture.*

2.

1. a table, two tables ;　2. one month, three months ;　3. the
postman, the postmen ;　4. one hat, three hats ;　5. one arm, two
arms ;　6. this fire, these fires ;　7. his horse, his horses ;　8. the
price, the prices.

3.

1. I have ;　2. thou hast not ;　3. has he ?　4. has she not ?　5. we
have ;　6. have you not ?　7. they have ;　8. have they (*f.*) not ?

4.

1. am I ?　2. art thou not ?　3. he is ;　4. is she not ?　5. we are
not ;　6. are you ?　7. they are not ;　8. are they ?

5.

1. her address ;　2. this hotel ;　3. that handwriting ;　4. these
men ;　5. those women ;　6. that friend ;　7. this water ;　8. their
house.

6.

1. I received ;　2. we found ;　3. he wrote ;　4. I sent ;　5. she
lost ;　6. they brought ;　7. did you see ?　8. she did not hear ;
9. they did not read ;　10. did we not sell ?　11. you did not open ;
12. did they give ?

7.

1. he is absent, they (*f.*) are absent ;　2. our uncle is tired,
your aunt is tired ;　3. he is rich, they are rich ;　4. they are polite,
she is not polite ;　5. we (*f.*) are satisfied, the waiter is not
satisfied ;　6. you (*m.*) are young, you (*f. pl.*) are young.

8.

1. my sister's husband ; 2. the officer's horses ; 3. the neighbour's garden ; 4. the lady's carriage ; 5. the boys' books ; 6. the windows of the house ; 7. the men's sons.

9.

1. the school, of the school, to the school ; 2. the room, of the room, to the room ; 3. the garden, from the garden, at the garden ; 4. the addresses, of the addresses, to the addresses ; 5. the hotels, from the hotels, at the hotels.

10.

1. Is the book on the table ? 2. Are the boys in their room ? 3. Have the ladies the gloves ? 4. Has the soldier his gun ? 5. Is not your friend here ? 6. Has not the boy my pencil ?

11.

1. Where is the address ? It is on the table. 2. Have you my umbrella ? No, it is there. 3. Did you open the letter ? Is it not from your sister ? 4. Have you seen the flowers ? Yes, they are very pretty. 5. Where is the umbrella ? It is here.

12.

1. some cheese ; 2. some beer ; 3. any pens ; 4. some knives and (some) forks. 5. He has not any shoes. 6. They have not any cheese. 7. Have they not any sisters ?

13.

1. Our neighbour is very old. 2. Have you written to your friend ? 3. They have not heard the noise. 4. We sold those horses. 5. Did they not read the newspapers ? 6. You have a good fire. 7. The postman has not brought this letter.

14.

1. The flowers are very pretty. 2. Is your sister's friend (f.) tall ? 3. Are the workmen absent ? 4. I saw his brother's niece. 5. Why did you not speak to the men ? 6. Have you sent any money to the women ? 7. They have not any bread. 8. She bought some bread and (some) cheese.

15.

1. Did you give any money to the men ? 2. Has he sent the parcel to the ladies ? 3. Have you seen any birds in the garden ? 4. These pages are very interesting. 5. Are these boots good ? 6. She gave a note to the boy.

SIXTH LESSON.

The majority of *French Verbs* end in the *Infinitive* in **er**. **er** is the *Termination*, the rest of the word is the *Stem* ; as,

INFINITIVE.		STEM.	PRONUNCIATION.
(to) give	donner	donn...	donn-eh, donn
„ speak	parler	parl...	pahr-leh, pahrl
„ copy	copier	copi...	ko-pe-eh, ko-pe
, pass	passer	pass...	pahss-eh, pahss

30. The *Present Tense* of Verbs ending in **er** is formed by adding to the Stem the *terminations* printed in thick type, thus :

PRESENT TENSE of (*to*) *give*, **donner**.

I give	*je donn*e	we give	*nous donn*ons
thou givest	*tu donn*es	you give	*vous donn*ez
he } gives	*il* } *donn*e	they (*m.*) } give	*ils* } *donn*ent
she }	*elle* }	they (*f.*) }	*elles* }

PRON.—sher donn, tü donn, ill donn ; noo donn-*ong*, voo donn-eh, ill donn.

Notice that of the above terminations, only 'ons' and 'ez' are sounded.

EXERCISE I.

1. he speaks ; **2.** we copy ; **3.** you pass ; **4.** they accept[1] ; **5.** I visit[2] ; **6.** he shuts[3] ; **7.** they (*f.*) close[3] ; **8.** we speak ; **9.** she copies ; **10.** they pass ; **11.** I[*] accept ; **12.** she visits.

1. accepter, 2. visiter, 3. fermer (*to*) *close* or (*to*) *shut.*
PRON.—1. ahck-sep-teh, 2, ve-ze-teh, 3. fair-meh.

The Third Person Singular or Plural must be used after a Noun.

The boy copies, Le garçon copie. | The ladies speak, } Les dames parlent.

EXERCISE II.

1. He gives some bread and (some) butter to the men. **2.** The men speak to the postmen. **3.** Her son copies a letter. **4.** We speak to the men. **5.** You accept his money. **6.** They visit the house. **7.** She shuts the door. **8.** The men pass before[1] the house. **9.** We give (some) bread and (some) cheese to the workmen. **10.** They close the windows. **11.** He visits this school. **12.** They copy the bills.

* *je, le, ne,* and other words where the final *e* is the only vowel, become *j', l', n',* etc., if the next word begins with a vowel or an H mute ; as,
I accept, *j'accepte,* instead of *je accepte.* 1. devant (pron. **der-vahng**).

CONVERSATIONAL SENTENCES.

Quels sont les jours de la semaine[1] ?	What are the days of the week[1]?
Les jours de la semaine sont : dimanche,[2] lundi,[3] mardi,[4] mercredi,[5] jeudi,[6] vendredi,[7] samedi.[8]	The days of the week are : Sunday,[2] Monday,[3] Tuesday,[4] Wednesday,[5] Thursday,[6] Friday,[7] Saturday.[8]
Quelle heure est-il ?	What time (*hour*) is it ?
Il est une *heure.*	It is one *o'clock.*
Est-il deux heures ?	Is it two o'clock ?
Il n'est pas trois heures.	It is not three o'clock.
N'est-il pas quatre[9] heures ?	Is it not four[9] o'clock ?

PRON.—1. ser-main, 2. de-mahngsh, 3. lung-de, 4. mahr-de, 5. mair-krer-de, 6. sher-de, 7. vahng-drer-de, 8. sahmm-de, 9. kahttr.

:o:o:

ADDITIONAL EXERCISES.

52.

1. Je n'ai pas lu ce roman ; est-il intéressant ? 2. Où avez-vous acheté vos souliers ? 3. Nous avons trouvé les allumettes. 4. Ils ont eu du fromage et de la salade. 5. Elle donne du pain aux oiseaux. 6. Avez-vous vu les bottes de ces ouvriers ? 7. Les plumes de votre oiseau sont très jolies.

53.

1. il donne ; 2. nous parlons ; 3. vous copiez ; 4. elles passent ; 5. j'accepte ; 6. tu visites ; 7. elle ferme ; 8. ils parlent ; 9. nous fermons ; 10. vous acceptez ; 11. je donne ; 12. il passe.

54.

1. we give ; 2. he gives ; 3. they give ; 4. you give ; 5. I give ; 6. thou givest ; 7. she gives ; 8. they (*f.*) give ; 9. the postman gives ; 10. the workmen give.

55.

1. we speak ; 2. I copy ; 3. she passes ; 4. you speak ; 5. they copy ; 6. they (*f.*) pass ; 7. thou speakest ; 8. he copies.

56.

1. you accept ; 2. thou visitest ; 3. we shut ; 4. they close ; 5. I accept ; 6. he visits ; 7. she shuts ; 8. they (*f.*) close ; 9. I accept ; 10. we visit ; 11. you shut ; 12. she closes.

57.

1. He speaks to his nephew. 2. We give the shoes to the girls. 3. I accept your book. 4. They visit the house and the garden. 5. We pass the workmen's houses. 6. His wife shuts the door.

31. *I am giving, she is speaking, they are passing,* etc. (called the PROGRESSIVE FORM) must be changed before translating into *I give, she speaks, they pass,* etc. ; as,

My friend is copying=my friend copies.　　**Mon ami copie.**
The ladies are speaking=the ladies speak.　**Les dames parlent.**

EXERCISE III.

1. He is smoking[1] his pipe.[2]　2. We are cutting[3] the paper.
3. She is looking[4] for[4] the address.　4. They are lighting[5] the fire.　5. I am carrying[6] the parcel.　6. You are seeking[4] your friends.　7. He is wearing[6] boots.　8. I am speaking to my nephew.　9. She is giving some money to the workmen.

1. fumer,　2. pipe,　3. couper,　4. chercher (*to*) *seek* or *look for*,　5. allumer,
6. porter (*to*) *carry* or *wear.*

PRON, 1. fü-meh, 2. peep, 3. koo-pèh, 4. shair-sheh, 5. ahll-ü-meh, 6. por-teh.

32. *Questions* are formed by placing the *Pronoun* after the *Verb.*

In translating, the English construction is therefore changed thus :
does he give ? *or* is he giving ?　　　*into* gives he ?
do they cut ? *or* are they cutting ?　*into* cut they ?
do you visit ? *or* are you visiting ?　*into* visit you ?

NOTE that DO and DOES are not translated.

'The Verb and the Pronoun are connected by a hyphen, and -t- is inserted in the Third Person Singular ; as,

does he give ? *donne-t-il ?*　　|　do they speak ? *parlent-ils ?*
does she copy ? *copie-t-elle ?*　|　do we light ? *allumons-nous ?*
do you close ? *fermez-vous ?*　|　do I give ? *donné-je ?*

PRON.—dönn-till,　ko-pe-tell,　fair-meh voo,　pahrl-till,　ahll-ü-mong noo,
donn-ehsh.

Notice that an acute accent is placed over the *e* in the First Person Singular.
Is the boy copying ?=The boy copies he ?　**Le garçon copie-t-il ?**

EXERCISE IV.

1. Are they smoking cigars[1] or cigarettes[2] ?　2. Is she looking for a letter ?　3. Does he carry a walking-stick[3] ?
4. Are you lighting your pipe ?　5. Are those men wearing hats ?　6. Are they (*f.*) closing their windows ?　7. Do they accept those presents[4] ?　8. Are you looking for your bird ?
9. Does your friend speak to his neighbour ?

1. cigare, *m.*,　2. cigarette, *f.*,　3. canne, *f.*,　4. cadeau, *m.*
PRON.—1. se-gahr, 2. se-gahr-ett, 3. kahnn, 4. kah-doh.

CONVERSATIONAL SENTENCES.

The new words in these sentences are to be learnt.

Fumez-vous des cigares ?	Do you smoke cigars ?
Quelquefois,[1] mais générale-ment[2] je fume des cigarettes.	Sometimes,[1] but generally[2] I smoke cigarettes.
Portez-vous toujours[3] une canne ? [pluie.	Do you always[3] carry a walking-stick ?
Je porte quelquefois un para-	I sometimes carry an umbrella.
Que[4] cherchent-ils ? [souliers ?	What[4] are they looking for ?
Portent-ils des bottes ou des	Do they wear boots or shoes ?
Qui a allumé les feux ?	Who has lighted the fires ?
Nous allumons toujours le gaz[5] à cette heure.	We always light the gas[5] at this hour. [book ?
Coupe-t-il les pages de ce livre ?	Is he cutting the pages of that

1. kell-ker-fo'ah, 2. shèh-neh-rahl-mahng, 3. too-shoohr, 4. ker, 5. gahz.

:o:

ADDITIONAL EXERCISES.

58.

1. Il porte toujours un parapluie. 2. Ces dames portent des gants. 3. Les soldats fument des pipes. 4. Je fume toujours des cigarettes. 5. Passez-vous (or Dépassez-vous) générale-ment sa porte ? 6. Acceptent-ils de l'argent de votre fils ?

59.

1. she is passing=she passes ; 2. they are smoking=they smoke ; 3. I am cutting ; 4. we are looking for ; 5. he is lighting ; 6. you are carrying ; 7. the workmen are giving.

60.

1. parlez-vous ? 2. acceptent-ils ? 3. coupons-nous ? 4. fermé-je ? 5. donne-t-il ? 6. passes-tu ? 7. la femme cherche-t-elle ? 8. les messieurs visitent-ils ?

61.

1. is he wearing ?=wears he ? 2. do they light=light they ? 3. are you giving=give you ? 4. does he copy=copies he ? 5. are we closing ? 6. does she accept ? 7. are they visiting ? 8. am I copying ?

62.

1. Is he smoking a pipe ? 2. Are you wearing gloves ? 3. I am giving cigars to the men. 4. Do they carry umbrellas ? 5. Is your neighbour shutting the windows ? 6. Are the gentlemen visiting the school ? 7. Do you give presents to the girls ?

H F S 3

SEVENTH LESSON.

33. The *Negative* of all French Verbs is formed in the same way (see Rule 11), *do* and *does* not being translated.

In translating, the English construction is therefore changed thus :

I do not give *or* I am not giving *into* I give not

Does he not copy ? *or* Is he not copying ? *into* Copies he not ?

Your friend does not speak
(*or* is not speaking) } **Votre ami NE parle PAS**

Are not those men smoking ?
=Those men smoke they not ? } **Ces hommes NE fument-ils PAS ?**

EXERCISE I.

1. He does not find[1] the way.[2]   2. They do not pay[3] their debts.[4]   3. Are you not living[5] in[6] this house ?   4. Does she not often[7] sing[8] ?   5. Are they not looking for their bags ?
6. Why[9] do you not cut this string[10] ?   7. He is not living there.   8. Do I not sing well[11] ?

---

1. trouver, 2. chemin, *m.*, 3. payer, 4. dette, *f.*, 5. demeurer, 6. dans, 7. souvent, 8. chanter, 9. pourquoi, 10. ficelle, *f.*, 11. bien.

PRON.—1. troo-veh, 2. sher-m*a*ng, 3. pay-yeh, 4. dett, 5. der-mer-eh, 6. d*a*h*ng*, 7. soo-v*a*h*ng*, 8. sh*a*h*ng*-teh, 9. poohr-ko'ah, 10. fe-sell, 11. be-*ang*.

---------o:o---------

34. who ? *whom ?* QUI ? | what ? QUE ?

PRON.—kee, ker.—que before a *vowel* or an *h* mute becomes qu'

Who is speaking to the officer ? | **QUI parle à l'officier ?**
Whom did you see there ? | **QUI avez-vous vu là ?**
What do you copy ? | **QUE copiez-vous ?**
What have they bought ? | **QU'ont-ils acheté ?**

What is translated que before a Verb, and quel, etc., before a Noun.

EXERCISE II.

1. Who is shutting the door ?   2. Who has put[1] the matches on[2] the table ?   3. What are you copying ? 4. What did she accept ?   5. Whom are they looking for ?   6. Who opened the window ?   7. What did you say[3] ?   8. What is he carrying ?   9. Who is wearing gloves ?   10. What did we pay ?   11. Who has had the time ?   12. What is he giving to the postman ?   13. To whom did you write ?

---

1. mis. *past partic.*, 2. sur, 3. *said*, dit, *past part.* PRON. 1. mee. 2. sür. 3. dee.

CONVERSATIONAL SENTENCES.

The new words in these sentences are to be learnt.

Avez-vous appris[1] les nombres[2] depuis[3] un jusqu'à[4] quatre ?	Have you learnt[1] the numbers[2] from[3] one to[4] four ?
Oui, monsieur.	Yes, sir.
Prononcez[5] après[6] moi[7] : cinq[8], six, sept, huit, neuf, dix[8]	Pronounce[5] after[6] me[7] : five,[8] six, seven, eight, nine, ten[8].
Il est cinq heures.	It is five o'clock.
Est-il six heures ?	Is it six o'clock ?
Il n'est pas sept heures.	It is not seven o'clock.
N'est-il pas huit heures ?	Is it not eight o'clock ?
Est-il neuf heures ou[9] dix heures?	Is it nine or[9] ten o'clock ?

1. ahpp-ree, 2. nong-br, 3. (*depuis, since*) der-p'we, 4. (*jusque, till*) shüss-ker, 5. pro-nong-seh, 6. ah-pray, 7. mo'ah, 8. sangk, siss, sett, wit, nerf, diss, 9. oo.

------:o:------

ADDITIONAL EXERCISES.

63.

1. Que cherchez-vous là ? 2. Le docteur n'est-il pas votre oncle ? 3. Pourquoi (*why*) n'allument-ils pas le gaz ? 4. Pourquoi ne ferme-t-il pas les fenêtres ? 5. Parle-t-il quelquefois aux ouvriers ? 6. Il accepte toujours un cigare. 7. Je ne porte pas d'allumettes. 8. Donnez-vous toujours de l'argent au facteur ? 9. N'a-t-elle pas reçu de cadeaux ?

64.

1. I do not find ; 2. he is not singing ; 3. they do not live (reside) ; 4. we are not copying ; 5. you do not find ; 6. she is not speaking.

65.

1. do I not carry ? 2. dost thou not smoke ? 3. does he not cut ? 4. does she not look for ? 5. do we not find ? 6. do you not live (reside) ? 7. do they (*m.*) not pay ? 8. do they (*f.*) not pass ?

66.

1. is he not accepting ? 2. are we not visiting ? 3. am I not speaking ? 4. are they (*m.*) not giving ? 5. art thou not closing ? 6. is she not lighting ? 7. are you not wearing ?

67.

1. Who is smoking ? 2. Whom did you pass ? 3. What does he copy ? 4. What did you give ? 5. Who sent this parcel ? 6. To whom did you write ? 7. What is he smoking ? 8. What did they bring ? 9. Whom does he invite ? 10. What do they pay ?

35.   Some useful *Prepositions* are :

1. for, pour ; 2. in, dans ; 3. on, sur ; 4. under, sous ; 5. with, avec ;
6. without, sans.

PRON.—1. poor, 2. *dahng*, 3. sür, 4. soo, 5. ah-veck, 6 *sahng*.

EXERCISE III.

1. for her son ; 2. in the fire ; 3. on the chair ; 4. under
the table ; 5. with your knife ; 6. without that gentleman.

---

36. The *Past Participle* of Verbs ending in **er** is formed by
changing the *er* into é ; as,

(to) give, donner ; PAST PARTICIPLE : given, donné.

The PRONUNCIATION of these two words is the same, viz. ' donn-eh.'

We spoke *or* we have spoken.	*Nous* AVONS parlé.
She accepted *or* she has accepted.	*Elle* A accepté.
Did he wear *or* carry ? *or* has he worn *or* carried ? [closed.	A-*t-il* porté ?
They did not close *or* they have not	*Ils n'*ONT *pas* fermé.

The PAST PARTICIPLE can only be used after the Auxiliary Verbs *to
have* and *to be* (see Rule 21). The Auxiliaries are printed above in SMALL
CAPITALS.

EXERCISE IV.

1. I paid=I have paid ; 2. we visited; 3. she gave ; 4. he
did not find ; 5. did they pass ? 6. did you not accept ? 7. He
copied a letter. 8. They shut (*past*) the door. 9. We did not
speak to the doctor. 10. Did I not give money to the boy ?

---

37. Distinguish carefully between the *Present* and the *Past
Tense* in English.

do, does, am, is, and are are PRESENT ; did is PAST ; as,
they pass *or* they are passing, *ils passent.*
they passed *is translated* they have passed, *ils ont passé.*
I do not give *or* I am not giving, *je ne donne pas.*
I did not give *is translated* I have not given, *je n'ai pas donné.*
he does not find *or* he is not finding, *il ne trouve pas.*
did he not find ? *is translated* has he not found ? *n'a-t-il pas trouvé ?*
we do not carry *or* we are not carrying, *nous ne portons pas.*
we did not carry *is translated* we have not carried, *nous n'avons pas porté.*

EXERCISE V.

1. He does not light the fire. 2. Did they not light the gas ?
3. We do not carry umbrellas. 4. Did they not carry guns ? 5.
Are you not paying your debts ? 6. I paid your bill (account).

CONVERSATIONAL SENTENCES.

Quels sont les noms des mois ?	What are the names of the months ?
Les noms des mois sont : janvier[1], février, mars, avril[1], mai[2], juin, juillet, août[2], septembre[3], octobre, novembre, décembre.[3]	The names of the months are : January[1], February, March, April[1], May[2], June, July, August[2], September[3], October, November, December[3].
Il est une heure *et demie*[4]. [mie ?	It is *half*[4]-*past* one (o'clock).
N'est-il pas cinq heures et demie?	Is it not half-past five ?
Est-il neuf[5] heures[5] et demie ?	Is it half-past nine[5] ?
Il n'est pas dix[6] heures[6] et demie.	It is not half-past ten[6].

1. sh*ahng*-ve-eh, feh-vre-eh, mahrss, ah-vree, 2. may, shü-'*ang*, shü-'ee-yay, oo, 3. sep-*tahng*-br, ok-to-br, no-*vahng*-br, deh-*sahng*-br, 4. der-me, 5: nœver, 6. dee z'er.

——————:o:——————

ADDITIONAL EXERCISES.
68.

1. Qui demeure dans cette maison ? **2.** Le facteur n'a-t-il pas apporté une lettre pour vous ? **3.** Qui a envoyé ce paquet ? **4.** Que donnez-vous à cet homme ? **5.** Le docteur ne passe-t-il pas souvent notre maison ?

6. Qu'a-t-elle dit à la fille ? **7.** De qui avez-vous reçu ce cadeau ? **8.** À qui a-t-il payé le compte ? **9.** Qu'avez-vous coupé avec mon couteau ?

69.

1. for your sister ; **2.** in our garden ; **3.** on the paper ; **4.** under his chair; **5.** with a pencil ; **6.** without this money ; **7.** for which man ? **8.** under his address.

70.

1. we found ; **2.** they closed ; **3.** she accepted ; **4.** I sang ; **5.** thou lightedst ; **6.** you carried ; **7.** he looked for ; **8.** they (*f.*) wore ; **9.** I smoked ; **10.** the man spoke.

71.

1. did he accept ? **2.** they did not find ; **3.** did you pay ? **4.** did we not smoke ? **5.** she did not copy ; **6.** did they (*f.*) not sing ? **7.** I did not visit ; **8.** didst thou cut ?

72.

1. he does not smoke ; **2.** she did not give ; **3.** we are not closing ; **4.** I did not accept ; **5.** is she not singing ? **6.** did they not look for ? **7.** do we not light ? **8.** did they (*f.*) not carry ?

EIGHTH LESSON.

38.

ours, *le* (or *la*) *nôtre*	mine, *le mien, la mienne*
yours, *le* (or *la*) *vôtre*	thine, *le tien, la tienne*
theirs, *le* (or *la*) *leur*	his, hers, *le sien, la sienne*

The Plural is formed by changing *le* or *la* into *les*, and adding an *s* to the Singular.—PRON. of *Sing.* and *Plural*; noh-tr, voh-tr, ler; me-*ang* me-enn; te-*ang*, te-enn; se-*ang*, se-enn.

The above *Possessive Pronouns* take the *Gender* and *Number* of the word they stand for; as,

Your house and *his.*	*Votre maison et* la sienne.
Our horses and *yours.*	*Nos chevaux et* les vôtres.
His brother and *hers.*	*Son frère et* le sien.
He did not find his letters, but *mine.*	*Il n'a pas trouvé ses lettres, mais* les miennes.

EXERCISE I.

1. I have your key,[1] and you have mine. 2. Has she taken[2] my ticket[3] or hers? 3. We have their pictures,[4] and they have ours. 4. He has not lighted his lamp,[5] but[6] theirs. 5. Did you meet[7] my daughters,[8] or his? 6. I lost her watch[9] and mine. 7. They did not take my papers but hers. 8. Has he not spent[10] his money and yours?

---

1. clef *or* clé (both words *fem.* and both pron. kleh), 2. pris (*past part.*), 3. billet (*m.*), 4. tableau (*m.*), 5. lampe (*f.*), 6. mais, 7. rencontrer (*to*) *meet*, 8. fille, 9. montre (*f.*), 10. dépenser (*to*) *spend*.

PRON.—1. kleh, 2. pree, 3. bee'e-yay, 4. tah-bloh, 5. lahngp, 6. may, 7. rahng-kong-treh, 8. fee'e, 9. mong-tr, 10. deh-pahng-seh.

39. what? after a *Preposition* is translated QUOI? as,

Of what are you speaking?	De quoi parlez-vous?
What did he pay with?	Avec quoi a-t-il payé?

PRON.—ko'ah.—PREPOSITIONS always come before their object in French

what! in exclamations is also translated *quoi!* as,

What! you are here!	*Quoi! vous êtes ici!*

EXERCISE II.

1. On what have you written the address? 2. What did you say? 3. Which picture did they buy? 4. Whom did he meet at the concert[1]? 5. What did she send the things[2] in? 6. Why do you sing? 7. What did he find in the book?

---

1. concert (*m*), 2. chose (*f.*). PRON.—1. kong-sair, 2. shohz.

CONVERSATIONAL SENTENCES.

À quelle heure fermez-vous la maison ?	At what time do you shut the house ?
Nous fermons généralement à huit heures et demie.	We generally close at half-past eight.
N'a-t-elle pas allumé le gaz ?	Has she not lighted the gas ?
Non, mais elle a mis deux lampes sur la table.	No, but she has put two lamps on the table.
Pourquoi n'ont-ils pas envoyé les tableaux ?	Why have they not sent the pictures ?
Ils n'ont pas eu le temps.	They have not had (the) time.

ADDITIONAL EXERCISES.

73.

1. N'avez-vous pas trouvé vos amis dans le jardin ? 2. Pourquoi ne paye-t-il pas les dettes de son fils ? 3. Ne demeurent-ils pas avec leur oncle ? 4. Cette dame ne chante-t-elle pas bien ? 5. N'a-t-il pas rencontré les officiers et les soldats ?

6. Qu'ont-elles dit à leur mère ? 7. Qui cherchez-vous ici ? 8. Que donnent-ils à ces hommes ? 9. Qu'avez-vous reçu dans ce paquet ? 10. Vos voisins ont-ils un grand jardin ?

74.

1. my uncle and hers ; 2. our aunt and his; 3. their room and yours ; 4. your church and theirs ; 5. this hotel and mine.

75.

1. our books and theirs ; 2. his pens and mine ; 3. her gloves and yours ; 4. their guns and ours ; 5. your keys and his.

76.

1. in what ? 2. of what ? 3. to what ? 4. on what ? 5. under what ? 6. with what ? 7. what for ? 8. from what ? 9. What ! is he there ? 10. What ! you saw your friend ! 11. What ! they are here !

77.

1. I found your keys and mine. 2. We met our friends and yours. 3. Did you see her carriage and his ? 4. We did not receive your letter, but theirs. 5. Did they not accept our prices, but hers? 6. She is not looking for my pictures, but theirs. 7. We found our pipes and his (*plur.*). 8. Did you not meet your daughter and his ? 9. What did you carry the things on ? 10. What did he break the glass with ?

40. *Adjectives* generally follow the Noun in French ; **as,**

our absent friends=our friends *absent*, nos amis absents ;
a French (*francais*) town=a town *French*, une ville française ;
these black (*noir*) cows=these cows *black*, ces vaches noires.

(*Adjectives* agree with their *Noun* in *Gender* and *Number* ; see Rule 17)

PRON.—noh z'ah-me z'ahb-*sahng*, ün vill frahng-sayz, say vahsh no'ahr.

EXERCISE III.

1. an English[1] town ; 2. (some) German[2] officers ; 3. (some) French ships[3] ; 4. this round[4] table ; 5. those rich men ; 6. my right hand[5] ; 7. his left arm ; 8. Did they bring these yellow[6] flowers ? 9. Did you drink[7] red[8] wine[9] ?

1. anglais, 2. allemand, 3. vaisseau, 4. rond, 5. main (*f.*), 6. jaune, 7. *drunk,* bu (*past part.*), 8. rouge, 9. vin (*m.*).

PRON.—1. *ahng*-glay, 2. ahll-m*ahng*, 3. vaiss-oh, 4. *rong*, 5. m*ang*, 6. shohn, 7. bü, 8. roosh, 9. v*ang*.

41. *Past Participles* follow the same Rules as *Adjectives* ; **as,**

a broken window=a window *broken*, une fenêtre brisée.

The letter is *lost*.	La lettre est perdue.
The pictures are *sold*.	Les tableaux sont vendus.

PAST PARTICIPLES are invariable if coming after *to have* ; **as,**
The ladies have *written* the letters. | *Les dames ont* écrit *les lettres.*

EXERCISE IV.

1. a closed door ; 2. two lost children ; 3. The string is cut. 4. His debts are paid. 5. Are the windows open(ed) ? 6. The children are not yet[1] found. 7. Has he sold[2] his horses ? 8. His horses are not yet sold.[2] 9. Have they drunk the water?

1. encore, 2. vendu. PRON.—1. *ahng*-kor, 2. v*ahng*-dü.

Rule on the Gender of Things.

The Rule given in Lesson 1 for ascertaining the Gender of French Nouns must now be learned, as in future we shall only indicate the Gender of exceptions to that Rule. These exceptions should be learned as they occur ; but most of them are in accordance with the fuller Rule given in

HUGO'S " FRENCH GENDERS SIMPLIFIED."

This book (postfree 6½d.) includes a complete list of the exceptions.

CONVERSATIONAL SENTENCES.

Comment[1] prononce-t-on[2] les nombres cinq à dix suivis[3] d'une consonne[4] ?

Dans ce cas[5] on[6] ne prononce pas la consonne finale.[7]

Par[8] exemple : cinq francs, six schellings,[8] sept[9] pages, huit livres (sterling), neuf sous, dix centimes.[9]

Cent[10] centimes font[11] un franc ; cinq centimes font un sou.

How[1] does[2] one pronounce[2] the numbers five to ten followed[3] by a consonant[4] ?

In this case[5] one[6] does not pronounce the final[7] consonant.

For[8] example : five francs, six shillings,[8] seven[9] pages, eight pounds (sterling), nine sous, ten centimes.[9]

A hundred[10] centimes make[11] a franc ; five centimes make a sou.

---

1. kom-*ahng*, 2. pro-*nong*ss-*tong*, 3. swe-ve, 4. k*ong*-sonn, 5. kah, 6. *ong*, 7. fe-nahll, 8. pahr egg-*zahng*-pl, s*ang* fr*ahng*, see sher-l*ang*, 9. say-**pahsh**, wee lee-vr stair-l*ang*, ne*r* soo, dee s*ahng*-teem, 10. s*ahng*, 11. f*ong*.

ADDITIONAL EXERCISES.
78.

1. J'ai trouvé votre clef, mais pas la sienne. 2. Avez-vous vendu leur maison ? Non, mais j'ai vendu la nôtre. 3. Qui a pris mon billet ? 4. Je n'ai pas le vôtre. 5. Qu'a-t-elle dit à sa sœur ? 6. J'ai votre lampe ; la mienne est brisée. 7. À qui avez-vous envoyé la montre ? 8. N'a-t-elle pas payé ces comptes ? J'ai payé les miens.

79.

1. a black hat=a hat black ; 2. a warm room ; 3. the cold water (*f.*) ; 4. this red ink ; 5. his right arm ; 6. her left hand ; 7. these vain girls ; 8. (some) polite men ; 9. those French soldiers ; 10. what English towns ?

80.

1. a lost parcel ; 2. the broken stick ; 3. this tired horse ; 4. the invited ladies ; 5. The door is open(ed). 6. The lamps are broken. 7. Are the windows shut ? 8. My letter is lost. 9. Is their money spent ?

81.

1. Did you meet the French officers ? 2. We saw the German ship. 3. They are at an English hotel. 4. We wear black boots. 5. Did you take the red pencils ? 6. They have round hats. 7. He bought some yellow paper. 8. Have you a black bag ?

NINTH LESSON.

me, to me,	me		*us, to us,*	nous
thee, to thee,	te		*you, to you,*	vous
him, it (m.),	le	}	*them,*	les
her, it (f.),	la	}		
to him, to her,	lui		*to them,*	leur

PRON.—mer, noo ; ter, voo ; ler, lah, lay ; lwe, ler.

The above words are placed in French *immediately before the Verb*.

They are called PERSONAL PRONOUNS, and are the OBJECT of the Verb, which they *follow* in English, thus :

They break them.	Ils LES brisent.
The man speaks to us.	L'homme NOUS parle.
We are copying it.	Nous LE (*or* LA) copions.

EXERCISE I.

1. They carry it. 2. We give (to) them the flowers. 3. I am-smoking* it (*f.*). 4. She is-looking-for* us. 5. You find them. 6. He meets you. 7. The ladies are-speaking to us. 8. The doctor is-speaking to him. 9. The girl is-singing to her.†

*Several English words connected by hyphens are translated by one word in French.

43. *me, te, le, la* before a vowel (or *h* mute) become *m', t', l', l'*; as,

The man brings it (*f.*).	L'homme L'apporte.
His neighbours like him.	Ses voisins L'aiment.

PRON.—lom labpp-ort ; say vo'ah-*zang* laym.

EXERCISE II.

1. We invite[1] him. 2. I invite her. 3. She forgets[2] us. 4. They forget me. 5. We accept it. 6. They accept them. 7. The boy brings it (*f.*). 8. The ladies are-singing to them.† 9. They find it (*f.*). 10. Your sister is-copying it. 11. He likes[3] it. 12. We like them. 13. He brings us some bread and butter.

1. inviter, 2. oublier, 3. aimer. PRON.—1. *ang*-vee-teh, 2. oo-ble-eh, 3. ay-meh.

† In French an object must follow ; as, a song, *une chanson*.

EXERCISE III.

1. Your friends are-looking-for you. 2. We meet them. 3. Our aunt is-speaking to her. 4. You forget them. 5. Where is the letter ? He is-copying it. 6. Do the boys wear them ? 7. I give (to) them the money.

CONVERSATIONAL SENTENCES.

Apprenez[1] par[2] cœur[2] les nom-bres suivants : | Learn[1] by[2] heart[2] the following numbers :

Onze,[3] douze, treize, quatorze, quinze,[3] seize,[4] dix-sept, dix-huit, dix-neuf, vingt.[4]

Eleven,[3] twelve, thirteen, four-teen, fifteen,[3] sixteen,[4] seven-teen, eighteen, nineteen, twenty.[4]

[plaît.[5]

Fermez la porte, s'il[5] vous | Shut the door, if[5] you please.[5]

Avec plaisir,[6] madame. | With pleasure,[6] madam.

Où demeurez-vous ? | Where do you live ?

Nous demeurons à Londres.[7] | We live in (at) London.'

1. ahpp-rer-neh, 2. par ker, 3. ongz, dooz, trays, kahtt-orz, kangz, 4. saiz, diss-sett, deez-witt, deez-nerf, vang, 5. sill voo play, 6. play-zeer, 7. long-dr.

---o---

ADDITIONAL EXERCISES.

82.

1. La porte de sa maison est-elle fermée ? 2. Oui, ils ferment la maison à dix heures et demie. 3. Qui avez-vous rencontré dans la rue ? 4. Quel est le nom de ce monsieur ? 5. Quels sont les noms des jours ? 6. Quelle heure est-il ? 7. N'est-il pas une heure et demie ?

83.

1. They meet us ; 2. he pays me ; 3. I seek him ; 4. he breaks them ; 5. she meets her ; 6. we find you ; 7. you sing it (m.) ; 8. your friend copies it (f.)

84.

1. he speaks to me ; 2. we give to her ; 3. she sings to them ; 4. they forget us ; 5. they accept me ; 6. you like them ; 7. I invite her ; 8. she brings to me ; 9. her brother lights it (f.).

85.

1. I am-copying it (m.) ; 2. she is-singing to him ; 3. we are-seeking her ; 4. they are-bringing to us ; 5. we are-meeting him ; 6. you are-closing it (f.) ; 7. he is-forgetting us ; 8. we are-smoking them ; 9. I am-looking-for you ; 10. she is-lighting it (m.) ; 11. they are-accepting us ; 12. we are-meeting him. 13. Your brother is-looking-for you ? 14. His sister finds it (m.). 15. This postman brings (to) him his letters. 16. Your friend forgets us. 17. His uncle and (his) aunt invite me.

44. The Rule in Paragraph 42, of course, applies to *Question* also, as the following Examples show.

Does he speak to them?	LEUR parle-t-il?
Do they thank us?	NOUS remercient-ils?
Are you forgetting him?	L'oubliez-vous?
Does she invite you?	VOUS invite-t-elle?

(By Rule 42, *me, te, le*, etc., always come immediately before the Verb.)

EXERCISE IV.

1. Does he speak to you? 2. We do not praise[1] her. 3. Do you thank[2] them? 4. Is he looking-at[3] us? *translate:* regards[3] he us? 5. Do they strike[4] him? 6. Are you looking[3]-at[3] me? 7. We thank you. 8. Is your friend looking-for us? 9. They are-breaking it (*f.*). 10. Why do you hide[5] them? 11. Have you it? 12. We have them.

---

1. louer, 2. remercier, 3. (*to*) *look at, regard,* regarder, 4. frapper, 5. cacher. PRON.—1. loo-eh, 2. rer-mair-se-eh, 3. rer-gahr-deh, 4. frahpp-eh, 5. kah-sheh.

---

45. The Rule in Paragraph 42 also applies to *Negations*, thus:

I haven't it.	Je ne L'ai pas.
She is not speaking to him.	Elle ne LUI parle pas.
Do you not like them?	Ne LES aimez-vous pas?
Do they (*f.*) not invite her?	Ne L'invitent-elles pas?

As *me, te, le,* etc., must always immediately precede the Verb, the *ne* comes before these Pronouns.

EXERCISE V.

1. He does not copy it.* 2. Do you not thank us? 3. Are you not speaking to him? 4. We do not give (to) them the books. 5. Why do you not look-at me? 6. He does not hide it (*f.*). 7. Why does she not bring the letter to us? 8. My friend does not like them. 9. Does not his teacher[1] praise him? 10. Why do you not sing to them† ? 11. Do you not meet them every[2] day[2]? 12. Why does he not smoke those cigars? 13. He does not like them. 14. Why is this window not shut? 15. I am closing it.

---

1. maître, 2.=*all the days,* tous les jours. PRON. 1. maitr, 2. too lay shoobr.

*it is to be translated by *le* unless marked to the contrary, or referring to a Feminine Noun. † see remark page 38.

CONVERSATIONAL SENTENCES.

Est-il midi[1] ?	Is it twelve o'clock (noon[1]) ?
Il est minuit.[2]	It is twelve o'clock (midnight[2]).
Il est une heure cinq[3] or cinq minutes.[3]	It is five[3] minutes past[3] one o'clock.
Est-il deux heures dix[4] or dix minutes[4] ?	Is it ten[4] minutes past[4] two o'clock ?
Il n'est pas trois[5] heures un* quart.*[5]	It is not a[5] quarter past three o'clock.[5]
N'est-il pas quatre heures vingt[6] or vingt minutes[6] ?	Is it not twenty[6] minutes past[6] four o'clock ?
Il est cinq[7] heures vingt-cinq or vingt-cinq minutes.[7]	It is twenty-five[7] minutes past five o'clock.[7]

1. me-de, 2. min-we, 3. *sangk or sang* me-nüt, 4. diss *or* dee me-nüt, 5. tro'ah-z'er-*ung* kar, 6. *vang or vang* me-nüt, 7. *sangk-*er*-vangt-sang*k *or vangt-sang* me-nüt. * *or* et quart.

---o---

ADDITIONAL EXERCISES.

86.

1. Nous avons reçu votre lettre de vendredi dernier. 2. Qui a acheté le cheval noir de votre voisin ? 3. J'ai trouvé la lampe sur la table ronde. 4. Pourquoi n'a-t-elle pas allumé le feu dans ma chambre ? 5. Il nous parle tous les jours. 6. Qui demeure dans cette petite maison ? 7. Je ne le sais pas.

87.

1. is he copying it (*f.*) ? 2. do you praise them ? 3. we thank them ; 4. are they looking at us ? *translate:* regard they us ? 5. does he hide you ? 6. I strike him ; 7. is he spending it (*m.*)? 8. are they singing to her ?

88.

1. I do not speak to them ; 2. we are not carrying them ; 3. Do you not thank him ? 4. she is not hiding her ; 5. do you not forget us ? 6. we do not give (to) them the address ; 7. they do not pay the money to her ; 8. are they not meeting you every day(= *tous les jours*) ?

89.

1. The officer does not praise him. 2. Do not the ladies thank you ? 3. He is not looking at her. 4. Why does he strike them ? 5. I am not hiding it (*f.*). 6. Does not your neighbour speak to them ? 7. Is not the postman bringing any letters to you ? 8. We do not invite them.

TENTH LESSON.

Besides the Verbs ending in the *Infinitive* in er, of which there are about 4,000, there are about 50 Verbs ending in re, and 300 ending in ir, which belong to the *Regular Conjugations.*†

------:o:------

EXAMPLES of VERBS ending in *re*.

1. (to) sell, vendre, 2. (to) lose, perdre, 3. (to) give back, rendre, 4. (to) reply, répondre, 5. (to) expect or (to) wait for, attendre.

1. vahng-dr, 2. pair-dr, 3. rahng-dr, 4. reh-pong-dr, 5. ahtt-ahng-dr.

------:o:------

46. The *Present Tense* of Verbs ending in re is formed by adding to the Stem the *terminations* printed in thick type, thus :

PRESENT TENSE of (*to*) sell, vendre.

I sell,	*je vend*s	we sell,	*nous vend*ons
thou sellest,	*tu vend*s	you sell,	*vous vend*ez
he sells,	*il vend**	they sell,	*ils vend*ent

PRON.—sher vahng, tü vahng, ill vahng ; noo vahng-dong, voo vahng-deh, ill vahngd.

*There is no termination in the Third Person Singular, which consists of the Stem only. (The *Stem* of these Verbs consists of the part preceding re.)

EXERCISE I.

1. he loses ; 2. we give-back ; 3. you are-selling ; 4. they reply ; 5. I am-expecting ; 6. she is-selling ; 7. they lose ; 8. we are-replying ; 9. you are-waiting-for ; 10. your friend is-giving-back ; 11. the officer is-replying ; 12. these men are-losing ; 13. The man is-smoking a cigar. 14. Why do they not pay [for*] the watch ? 15. They reply to us always[1] by[2] return of post.[2] 16. Have you seen his house ? Yes, he is-selling it. 17. Enclosed[3] I return the sample[4] to you. 18. He expects us at five o'clock.

---

1. toujours, 2. par retour du courrier, 3. ci-inclus, 4. échantillon.

PRON.—1. too-shoohr, 2. pahr rer-toohr dü koohr-re-eh, 3. se-ang-klü, 4. ch-shahng-te-yong.

---

*Words in square brackets are not to be translated ; words in parentheses are required in French.

† The Regular Verbs are generally divided in the following way : 1st Conjugation ending in er, 2nd in ir, 3rd in oir, 4th in re. This is a very bad and arbitrary arrangement, which makes the Verbs needlessly difficult.

The re Verbs ought to be learnt next to the er Verbs, as they only differ slightly. The oir Verbs are placed by the best modern grammars among the *Irregular Verbs*, and this is the only correct way

(For fuller explanation see Hugo's "French Verbs Simplified.")

CONVERSATIONAL SENTENCES.

Il est six heures moins[1] (*less*) cinq *or* cinq minutes.	It is five[1] minutes to six o'clock.
Est-il sept heures moins dix *or* dix minutes[2] ?	Is it ten minutes to seven o'clock ?
Il n'est pas huit heures moins[3] un quart[3] (*or* le quart).	It is not a[3] quarter o[3] eight o'clock.
N'est-il pas neuf[4] heures[4] moins vingt *or* vingt minutes ?	Is it not twenty minutes to nine[4] o'clock[4] ?
Il est dix heures moins vingt-cinq *or* vingt-cinq minutes.	It is twenty-five minutes to ten o'clock.

1. mo'*ang* (*less*) sa*ng*k *or* sa*ng* me-nüt, 2. the pronunciation of these numbers is the same as shown on page 41, and explained in the Conversation on page 37, 3. mo-*ang* z'*ung*-kar, 4. ner-*ver*.

ADDITIONAL EXERCISES.

90.

1. Avez-vous trouvé la lettre de ce monsieur? 2. Non, mais je la cherche partout (*everywhere*). 3. Avez-vous oublié de (*to*) les inviter? 4. Où avez-vous trouvé l'adresse de mon fils? 5. Il ferme la porte tous les jours à dix heures et demie. 6. Ne parlent-ils pas de vous? 7. À quelle heure allume-t-il le gaz? 8. Les messieurs cherchent-ils les dames?

91.

1. il le vend; 2. nous le rendons; 3. vous l'attendez; 4. je lui réponds; 5. ils le perdent; 6. nous leur vendons; 7. vous lui rendez; 8. ils me donnent.

92.

1. I lose; 2. thou losest; 3. he loses; 4. we lose; 5. you lose; 6. they lose; 7. I am-replying—*translate:* I reply; 8. he is-replying; 9. she is-replying; 10. we are-replying; 11. you are-replying; 12. they are-replying.

93.

1. I am-expecting; 2. he is-selling; 3. we are-replying; 4. they are-giving-back; 5. you are-losing; 6. he is-smoking; 7. are they singing? 8. he does not strike; 9. is she not speaking? 10. he is-expecting it; 11. they are-selling them; 12. we reply to them; 13. I give (*to*) her a watch. 14. They bring us the newspaper every day. 15. Is she not speaking to him?

47. *Negations* and *Questions* of all Verbs are of course formed alike, as explained in Paragraphs 31, 32, and 33, thus :

are you selling ? *or* do you sell ?	vendez-vous ?
he does not lose *or* he is not losing	il NE perd PAS
do they not give back ? *or* are they not giving back ?	} NE rendent-ils PAS ?
does he wait for? *or* is he waiting for?	attend-il* ?

*No -t- is used in the 3rd person, because the verb does not end in a vowel.

EXERCISE II.

1. Does she sell ? 2. are you losing ? 3. are they replying ? 4. I do not give back; 5. she does not expect; 6. do we not sell ? 7. is she not giving-back ? 8. why do you not reply ?

EXERCISE III.

1. I am-waiting-for the train.[1] 2. Do they not sell postage[2] stamps[2] ? 3. Is he not losing his money ? 4. I lend[3] (to) them my dictionary,[4] and they do not return[5] it. 5. I met your brother to-day[6]; do you not expect him this evening[7]?

1. train, 2. timbre-poste* (m.), 3. *(to) lend,* prêter, 4. dictionnaire (m.), 5. =*give back,* 6. aujourd'hui, 7. soir.

PRON.—1. trang, 2. tang-br post, 3. pray-teh, 4. dick-se-on-air, 6. oh-shoohr-d'we, 7. so'ahr.

*Plural, *timbres-poste.*—Colloquially, *poste* is generally omitted.

48. The *Past Participle* of Verbs ending in re is formed by changing *re* into u ; as,

to sell, vendre ; PAST PARTICIPLE : sold, vendu.

they lost *or* they have lost	ils ont perdu
did he not wait ?	n'a-t-il pas attendu ?

EXERCISE IV.

1. I correspond[1] with you, and[2] he corresponded[1] with us. 2. He hears[3] them, and she heard[3] the noise. 3. They do not descend,[4] and they did not descend.[4] 4. Does he return[5] it ? Did he return[5] the money ? 5. Are you not waiting-for me ? Did you not expect your neighbour ? 6. Does the man not sell it ? 7. Did not the man sell the horses ?

1. correspondre, 2. et, 3. entendre, 4. descendre, 5. =*give back.*

PRON.—1. korr-ess-pong-dr, 2. eh, 3. ahng-tahng-dr, 4. dess-ahng-dr.

CONVERSATIONAL SENTENCES.

Vous avez appris les nombres depuis un jusqu'à vingt, *n'est-ce pas*[1] ? Oui,[2] monsieur.	You have learnt the numbers from one to twenty, *have you not ?* Yes, sir.
Apprenez par cœur les nombres suivants :	Learn by heart the following numbers :
Vingt[3] et un, vingt-deux,[3] vingt-trois,[4] vingt-quatre, vingt-cinq, vingt-six, vingt-sept, vingt-huit, vingt-neuf.	Twenty-one,[3] twenty-two,[3] twenty-three,[4] twenty-four, twenty-five, twenty-six, twenty-seven, twenty-eight, twenty-nine.

---

1. *literally : is it not*, nace-pah ; 2. *n'est-ce pas* here has no negative meaning ; see note 2 on page 23 ; 3. *vang-t'eh-ung*, *vangt-der* ; 4. *vangt-tro'ah*, etc. (notice that the *t* is sounded in numbers 21 to 29).

---o---

ADDITIONAL EXERCISES.

94.

1. Avez-vous pris du thé ou du café ? **2.** Le facteur lui a-t-il apporté une lettre ? **3.** Non, mais il a apporté un paquet pour vous. **4.** Vos leçons sont-elles très difficiles ? Non, madame, elles sont assez (*enough=rather*) faciles. **5.** Vos souliers ne sont-ils pas noirs ? Non, ils sont bruns. **6.** Avez-vous rencontré le mari de votre sœur ?

95.

1. do you sell ? 2. he does not lose ; 3. do they not reply ? 4. are you not giving-back ? 5. I do not correspond ; 6. thou dost not wait ; 7. do you not hear ? 8. she is not descending ; 9. do they not reply ? 10. are they not corresponding ?

96.

1. I have not been-waiting (=waited) ; 2. has he not descended ? 3. they have not been-selling (=sold) ; 4. have you not given back ? 5. he has been-corresponding (=corresponded) ; 6. has she lost ? 7. we have not heard ; 8. have you not replied ?

97.

1. he hears us ; 2. they do not sell them ; 3. she does not reply to them ; 4. Do-you-give-back the samples to her ? 5. Do they not expect us to-day ? 6. They do not correspond with us. 7. I always[b] lend[a] (to) him stamps, and he does not return them. 8. Why do you not reply to their letter ? 9. She does not sell her house to us. 10. Who is losing ?

ELEVENTH LESSON.

49. The Pronouns *me, le, lui*, etc., always come before the Verb, and in COMPOUND TENSES they are placed before the first Verb.

A COMPOUND TENSE in French consists of a PAST PARTICIPLE preceded by part of " *to have* " or " *to be.*"

He *has* written to us.	Il NOUS a écrit.
Have they spoken to him ?	LUI ont-ils parlé ?
We *have* not replied *or* we did not reply } to them.	Nous ne LEUR avons pas répondu.
Have you not sent *or* Did you not send } to me ?	Ne M'avez-vous pas envoyé ?

EXERCISE I.

1. They have written to you. 2. Have you spoken to her ? 3. We have not replied to them. 4. Have they not sent to us ? 5. I have brought (to) him the letters. 6. We have seen him to-day. 7. She did not give me the address. 8. Has he not returned the stamps to you ? 9. They have not found it.

EXAMPLES OF VERBS ending in *ir*.

1. (to) finish, **finir,**   2. (to) fill, **remplir,**   3. (to) obey, **obéir,**
     4. (to) choose, **choisir,**   5. (to) punish, **punir.**

PRON.—1. fe-neer, 2. r*ahng*-pleer, 3. o-beh-eer, 4. sho'ah-zeer, 5. pü-neer.

50. The *Present Tense* of Verbs ending in **ir** is formed by adding to the Stem the *terminations* printed in thick type, thus :

PRESENT TENSE of (*to*) *finish,* **finir.**

I finish,	*je fin***is**	we finish,	*nous fin***issons**
thou finishest,	*tu fin***is**	you finish,	*vous fin***issez**
he finishes,	*il fin***it**	they finish,	*ils fin***issent**

PRON.—Singular, fe-nee ;   Plural, fe-niss-*ong*, fe-niss-eh, fe-niss.
Paragraphs 31, 32, 33 also apply to ir Verbs.

EXERCISE II.

1. She does not fill the lamp. 2. Do these boys not obey ? 3. We do not choose these colours.[1] 4. Do you not punish your dog[2] ? 5. Why do they not finish their tasks[3] ? 6. Why do you not fill the inkstand[4] ? 7. He is finishing your coat[5] to-day. 8. My dog does not obey.

---

1. couleur (*f.*),   2. chien,   3. devoir,   4. encrier,   5. habit.
PRON.—1. koo-ler, 2. she-*ang*, 3. der-vo'ah*r*, 4. *ahng*-kre-eh, 5. ah-be.

CONVERSATIONAL SENTENCES.

Continuez[1] d'apprendre[1] les nombres suivants :

Trente,[2] trente et un,[2] trente-deux, etc. quarante,[3] quarante et un, quarante-trois, etc. cinquante,[4] cinquante et un, cinquante-quatre, etc. soixante,[5] soixante et un, soixante-cinq, etc. soixante-dix.[6]

Continue to learn the following numbers :

Thirty, thirty-one, thirty-two, etc. forty, forty-one, forty-three, etc. fifty, fifty-one, fifty-four, etc. sixty, sixty-one, sixty-five, etc. seventy.

PRON.—1. kong-te-nü-eh dahpp-*rahng*-dr, 2. trahngt, trahngt-eh-*ung*, 3. kah-*rahngt*, 4. sang-*kahngt*, 5. so'ahss-*ahngt*, 6. so'ahss-*ahngt*-diss.

---o---

ADDITIONAL EXERCISES.

(New words the same or nearly the same as in English are printed in *italics*.)

98.

1. N'est-il pas dix heures et demie ? 2. Non, il est presque (*nearly*) onze heures. 3. Qui attendez-vous ? 4. J'attends ma sœur par le train de Paris. 5. Quelle est la *date ?* 6. Je l'ai rencontré au mois de février à *Lyon*. 7. Nous avons reçu une *carte postale* de votre frère vendredi dernier.

99.

1. we have spoken to them ; 2. she answered (to) him ; 3. have you written to her ? 4. has he not sent to us ? 5. they have not seen me. 6. I have not given her the book.

7. He did not bring (=he has not brought) the paper to us. 8. Did they not speak (=have they not spoken) to him ? 9. We wrote (=we have written) to them. 10. Did she not lose it ? 11. They sent the parcel to you. 12. Have we not given back the umbrella to her ?

100.

1. I am filling ; 2. thou art filling ; 3. he is filling ; 4. we are filling ; 5. you are filling ; 6. they are filling ; 7. I am punishing; 8. we are punishing ; 9. he finishes ; 10. they are choosing ; 11. do you obey ? 12. are they obeying ? 13. does she finish ?

101.

1. I am not punishing ; 2. they are not obeying ; 3. are you not choosing ? 4. are we not finishing ? 5. She is finishing her letter 6. Are you not filling the glasses ? 7. They do not finish their lessons. 8. Does not this man punish the children ?

51. The *Past Participle* of Verbs ending in **ir** is formed by changing *ir* into **i**, thus:

(to) finish, **finir** ; PAST PARTICIPLE : finished, **fini**. PRON.—fe-nee.

They have obeyed (to) him.	Ils lui ont obéi.
I have not chosen it. I did not choose it.	Je ne l'ai pas choisi.
Have you not punished him ? Did you not punish him ?	Ne l'avez-vous pas puni ?

EXERCISE III.

1. Why have you not filled the bottle[1] ? 2. They have not yet[2] finished their work.[3] 3. We did not punish the thief.[4] 4. Has she chosen this hat ? 5. Do these boys not obey (to) their teacher ? 6. Have they not punished[b] him too[5a] much[5a]? 7. We obeyed (to) him with pleasure. 8. Did they not choose him at[6] first[6] ?

---

1. bouteille, 2. encore, 3. travail, 4. voleur, 5. trop, 6. d'abord. PRON.—1. boo-tay'e, 2. *ahng*-kor, 3. trah-vah'e, 4. vo-ler, 5. tro, 6. dah-bor.

:o:

The Interrogative of French Verbs can be formed in two ways : Either by placing the Pronoun after the Verb (see Paragraph 32), or by prefixing **est-ce que** (is it that). *Est-ce que* (pron. aiss-ker) corresponds to the English *do, does, did,* and should always be used in the *First Person Singular. Est-ce que* frequently expresses surprise.

Do you smoke ? *Fumez-vous ?* or *Est-ce que vous fumez ?*
Did they sing ? *Ont-ils chanté ?* or *Est-ce qu'ils ont chanté ?*
Do I sell ? *Est-ce que je vends ?*
Do I speak ? *Est-ce que je parle ?* (better than *parlé-je ?*)

52. Interrogative words (*how, when, where, why,* etc.,) always *begin* sentences like those in Par. 20, thus:

Pourquoi le soldat a-t-il un fusil ? NOT Le soldat pourquoi a-t-il un fusil ?

EXCEPTION.—If the sentence begins with **que,** the Verb comes next, thus :

What is the lady singing ?	*Que chante la dame ?* or *Qu'est-ce que la dame chante ?*

EXERCISE IV.

1. Why did the man speak to you ? 2. Where does the gentleman live ? 3. How did the lady sing ? 4. What did your neighbour send ? 5. Where are the soldiers ? 6. Why do the boys not copy their lessons ? 7. What did the postman say to you ? 8. What does your friend reply ?

CONVERSATIONAL SENTENCES.

Finissons[1] par les nombres dè soixante[2] et onze[2] jusqu'à cent.

Let[1] us finish[1] the numbers, from seventy-one[2] to a hundred.

Soixante et onze, soixante-douze, soixante-treize, soixante-dix-sept, soixante-dix-neuf.

Seventy-one, seventy-two, seventy-three, seventy-seven, seventy-nine.

quatre-vingts,[3] quatre-vingt-un,[4] quatre-vingt-deux, quatre-vingt-dix, quatre-vingt-onze, quatre-vingt-dix-neuf, cent.[5]

eighty,[3] eighty-one,[4] eighty-two, ninety, ninety-one, ninety-nine, a hundred.[5]

---

1. fe-niss-*ong*, 2. so'ah-*sahngt*-eh-*ongz*, 3. kahtt-tr-*vang*, 4. kahtt-tr-*vang-ung*, 5. *sahng*.

ADDITIONAL EXERCISES.

102.

1. Pourquoi n'avez-vous pas fini mon habit ?   2. N'a-t-elle pas rempli les encriers ?   3. Ne vous a-t-il pas répondu par retour du courrier ?   4. Ils ne m'ont pas envoyé les échantillons.   5. Pourquoi ne l'avez-vous pas remercié ?   6. Quelle est la couleur de son habit ?   7. Quels sont les jours de la semaine ?   8. Avez-vous appris par cœur les nombres depuis un jusqu'à cent ?   9. Que regardez-vous ?

103.

1. he has finished ;   2. they have not filled ;   3. we have chosen ;   4. have you not obeyed?   5. she has not punished ;   6. did you finish ?   7. she did not fill ;   8. he did not obey ;   9. did they not choose ?   10. did we not punish ?

104.

1. He is filling them.   2. They do not obey me.   3. We do not choose them.   4. Do you punish him ?   5. He is finishing it.   6. Has he not spoken to you ?   7. Have they not filled it ?   8. We have not replied to them.   9. Did they not give it back to you ?

105.

1. Where are your gloves ?   2. Where does your brother live ?   3. Where did the man hide the parcel ?   4. Why is your window open ?   5. Why did the doctor not take his umbrella ?   6. Why is that hat there ?   7. What is your sister looking for ?   8. What did the soldiers find ?

RECAPITULATORY EXERCISES on Lessons 6 to 11.

1.

1. I am speaking ;   2. thou dost not copy ;   3. is he smoking ?
4. he does not carry ;   5. does she not seek ?   6. we are singing ;
7. do you not live (reside) ?   8. they do not meet ;   9. are they
not spending ?

2.

1. Does your neighbour smoke cigars or cigarettes ?   2. Are
you looking for the butter ?   3. Does he wear a hat ?   4. She
is lighting the fire.   5. Are they not copying this letter ?
6. Why do you not shut the door ?

3.

1. Who is this gentleman ?   2. Whom did you see at the
hotel ?   3. What did she buy ?   4. What is he copying ?
5. What did you give to the postman ?   6. To whom did you
speak ?

4.

1. in the room ;   2. for her nephew ;   3. on your chair ;
4. under the table ;   5. with her pencil ;   6. without his
mother ;   7. to the boy ;   8. from the niece ;   9. the lady's glove ;
10. your brother's handwriting.

5.

1. he does not forget ;   2. he did not forget ;   3. do you
invite ?   4. did you invite ?   5. they do not like ;   6. they did
not like ;   7. do you light the fire ?   8. did you not light the gas ?

6.

1. your house or mine ;   2. their friends and ours ;   3. my
newspaper and hers ;   4. I met your brother and hers.
5. What are you selling ?   6. From what do you copy it ?
7. On what did she put it ?   8. Which horse did he buy ?

7.

1. a round hat ;   2. these round tables ;   3. an English
officer ;   4. a French town ;   5. a tired lady ;   6. (some) rich
men ;   7. warm water ;   8. our absent friends.

8.

1. They are carrying it. 2. Your friend is looking for you.
3. We do not forget them. 4. Do you give them the money?
5. Why do they not invite us? 6. She does not thank me.
7. Why do you not look at them? 8. Where are they hiding him?

9.

1. I do not lose; 2. art thou not selling? 3. he is not expecting; 4. we are not giving back; 5. are you waiting for?
6. they do not lose; 7. the boy does not answer; 8. why do the ladies not wait?

10.

1. I am waiting for my friend; 2. he did not sell the horses;
3. she does not reply to their letter; 4. did we not give back the umbrella? 5. they do not lose their money; 6. did you not sell the carriage?

11.

1. he sells it to his friends; 2. he wrote to me last week;
3. we gave them back the books; 4. she does not expect us to-day; 5. they did not correspond with us; 6. we are going down (=descending) the street.

12.

1. I do not obey; 2. thou dost not fill; 3. does he not choose? 4. we do not punish; 5. do you not finish? 6. do they not obey? 7. I did not fill; 8. did she not obey? 9. we did not punish; 10. have they not chosen?

13.

1. Is not my French dictionary on the table? 2. This gentleman is our uncle's doctor. 3. She did not thank us.
4. That ink is very bad. 5. They are at a German hotel.

14.

1. They closed the door at ten o'clock. 2. At what time do you light the gas? 3. Why did they not accept the money? 4. Who is losing? 5. Have you been to the concert? 6. Which picture did you choose? 7. What did you say to your teacher? 8. He brings me a letter every day.

TWELFTH LESSON.

53. Contrary to Rule 40, the following *Adjectives* come BEFORE the *Noun* in French :

    1. good bon, bad mauvais, wicked méchant ;
    2. new (different) nouveau, young jeune, old vieux ;
    3. large, tall grand, big gros, small, little petit ;
    4. beautiful, fine, handsome beau, nice joli, ugly, nasty vilain.

PRON.—1. bong, moh-vay, meh-sha*hng* ;   2. noo-voh, shern, ve-er ;
    3. gra*hng*, groh, per-te ;   4. boh, sho-le, ve-la*ng*.

IRREGULAR FEMININES : 1. *bonne*, 2. *nouvelle, vieille,* 3. *grosse,* 4. *belle.*
PRON.—bonn, noo-vell, ve-ay'e, grohss, bell.

Before Masculine Singular words beginning with a Vowel or *h* mute, *nouvel, vieil, bel* must be used ; as, a fine man, *un bel homme.*

EXERCISE I.

    1. a good thing ;   2. these fine apples[1] ;   3. her little cat[2] ;
4. a pretty bird[3] ;   5. what a small foot[4] !   6. an old fool[5] ;
7. those large rivers[6] ;   8. his nice ring[7] ;   9. a bad opinion[8] ;
10. these wicked men ;   11. a big parcel ;   12. our new house.

---

1. pomme, 2. chat, 3. oiseau, 4. pied, 5. fou, 6. fleuve *m.,* 7. bague, 8. opinion.
PRON.—1. pomm, 2. shah, 3. wah-zoh, 4. pe-eh, 5. foo, 6. flerv, 7. bahg,
   8. o-pe-ne-*ong.*

---:o:---

54. When the *Adjective* comes before the Noun, *some* or *any* is translated **de.**

They have some fine pictures.	Ils ont DE beaux tableaux.
He sells good wine.	Il vend DE* bon vin.

*some must be expressed in French, even if not in English (see Rule 22).

EXERCISE II.

    1. Here[1] is[1] some old wine.   2. Here[1] are[1] some beautiful rings.   3. There[2] is[2] a pretty bird.   4. There[2] are[2] some big parcels.   5. Here is a good cat.   6. There are some small houses.   7. Here are some good pens.   8. There is some good butter.   9. They sell good beer and (good) wine.

---

   1. voici, *here is* or *here are,*   2. voilà, *there is* or *there are.*
       PRON.—1. vo'ah-se,   2. vo'ah-lah.

EXERCISE III.

    1. Have you any good butter ?   2. We drank some bad wine. 3. They have bought some beautiful rings.   4. We have a bad opinion of you.   5. She wears a new hat every day.

CONVERSATIONAL SENTENCES.

Voici le reste des nombres cardinaux : cent un, cent dix, deux cents, quatre cents, huit[1] cent soixante,[1] mille,[2] deux mille soldats, en[3] mil huit cent soixante-dix, cent[4] mille, un million,[5] un milliard.[5]

Here are the rest of the cardinal numbers : one hundred and one, one hundred and ten, two hundred, four hundred, eight hundred and sixty, a thousand, two thousand soldiers, in the year one thousand eight hundred and seventy, a hundred thousand, a million, a milliard.

---

1. *Cent* does not take an *s* in the Plural—(a) if followed by another number ;—(b) in dates, as, *en quinze cent* ;—(c) if used instead of the ordinal number, as, *page deux cent.*—*Quatre-vingts* follows the same rules.

2. *Mille* never takes an *s*, and becomes *mil* in dates after Christ.

3. *En* (*ahng*), in the year. 4. *a*, *an*, *one* before 100 or 1,000 are not translated in French. Hyphens (-) are always used in the numbers 17 to 99, except 21, 31, 41, 51, 61, 71, where *et* is used. 5. mill-e-*ong*, mill-e-*ar*.

---o---

ADDITIONAL EXERCISES.

106.

1. Cette dame a acheté du thé et du café, du pain, du beurre et du fromage. 2. N'avez-vous pas encore lu le journal d'aujourd'hui ? 3. Où avez-vous rencontré monsieur le docteur ? 4. Voici vos gants. 5. Voilà nos amis. 6. Qui vous a dit cela (*that*) ? 7. Pourquoi ne l'avez-vous pas puni ? 8. Quelle opinion avez-vous de cet homme ?

107.

1. a fine picture ; 2. his bad opinion ; 3. a good thing ; 4. what an old horse ! 5. this young man ; 6. your big dog ; 7. his pretty sister ; 8. my new friend ; 9. these nice flowers ; 10. those large streets.

108.

1. fine horses ; 2. young birds ; 3. good apples ; 4. new books ; 5. bad cats ; 6. beautiful rivers ; 7. Have you any good pens ? 8. He has large hands. 9. She has small feet. 10. Haven't they fine rings ?

109.

1. Here are some pretty flowers. 2. Have you bought any old wine ? 3. There is a good boy. 4. They have not any German beer. 5. We have found some bad apples. 6. Have you any young dogs ?

55. *richer, taller,* etc., must be translated by *more rich, more tall,* etc. ;—*richest, tallest* by *the more rich, the more tall* ; as,

He is **taller** than you.	*Il est* plus *grand* que *vous.*
They are **younger** than we.	*Ils sont* plus *jeunes* que *nous.*
She is **more polite** than her sister.	*Elle est* plus *polie* que *sa sœur.*
She is **the tallest**.	*Elle est* la plus *grande.*
They (*f.*) are **the most polite**.	*Elles sont* les plus *polies.*

    1.—*in* after a superlative† is translated de ;

    2.—*than* before a number is translated de, *thus :*

The **richest*** man in the town.	*L'homme* le plus *riche* de *la ville.*
He has more **than six** horses.	*Il a* plus de six *chevaux.*

EXERCISE IV.

1. Our neighbours are richer than we. 2. Your garden is larger than ours. 3. Is not that tree[1] the highest[2] in the garden ? 4. These girls are the youngest in the school. 5. Her foot is smaller than his. 6. Is she not prettier than her sister ? 7. The poorest[3] woman in the town lives there.

---

1. arbre, *m.,* 2. haut, 3. pauvre. PRON.—1. ahr-br, 2. hoh, 3. poh-vr.

---

56. Learn the following words :

    good *bon,* better *meilleur,* the best *le meilleur,*

less *moins,* the least *le moins.* as...as *aussi...que,* so...as *si...que.*

    PRON.—may'e-yer, mo-*ang,* ler mo-*ang,* oh-se...ker, se...ker.

She is **less** pretty than her sister.	*Elle est* moins *jolie que sa sœur.*
This lady is **the least** polite.	*Cette dame est* la moins *polie.*
He is **as** tall **as** you.	*Il est* aussi *grand* que *vous.*
These pictures are **not so** beautiful **as** yours.	*Ces tableaux ne sont pas* si *beaux* que *les vôtres.*

EXERCISE V.

1. My watch is as good as his. 2. He is less active[1] than his brother. 3. This soldier is the best in the regiment.[2] 4. My hands are not so small as yours. 5. Her ring is the least beautiful. 6. His bag is the largest. 7. Here is the highest tree in the garden. 8. Is he not the best man in the world[3] ? 9. Are not these apples better than yours ? 10. My cigars are as good as his. 11. He has received less than ten francs to-day. 12. I gave her more than eight postage-stamps.

---

1. actif, 2. régiment, 3. monde, *m.*

    PRON.—1. ahk-teef, 2. reh-she-ma*hng,* 3. mongd.

---

† Forms like *larg*est, most *industrious* are called Superlatives.

**plus, le plus* before an Adjective do not alter its position (Rules 40, 53)

CONVERSATIONAL SENTENCES.

Quels sont les nombres ordi-naux[1] ? Ce[2] sont les suivants[3] : Le premier,[4] le second,[5] le troisième,[6] le quatrième, le cinquième, le sixième, le septième,[7] le huitième, le neuvième, le dixième, le onzième, le vingtième, le[8] vingt et unième,[8] etc.

Which are the ordinal num-bers? They are the following: The first, the second, the third, the fourth, the fifth, the sixth, the seventh, the eighth, the ninth, the tenth, the eleventh, the twentieth, the twenty-first, etc.

1. or-de-noh, 2. ser, 3. swe-*vahng*, 4. ler prer-me-eh, 5. ler-s'*gong* or ser-*gong*, 6. tro'ah-ze-ame, 7. ler-sett-e-ame, 8. *vang* t'eh-ü-ne-ame.

The *ordinal numbers* are formed from the cardinal numbers by adding *ième* ; if the cardinal number ends in *e*, the *e* is omitted in adding *ième*.

The 1st and the 2nd are irregular (the 2nd has also a regular form); and the 5th and the 9th slightly change the spelling.

———o———

ADDITIONAL EXERCISES.

110.

1. En mil huit cent quatre-vingt-quatorze. 2. Nous avons rencontré deux cents soldats. 3. Nous sommes à la page trois cent de ce livre. 4. Un million cinq cent mille francs. 5. En quinze cent. 6. Vous a-t-il apporté un nouveau livre ? 7. Votre jardin n'est pas si grand que le nôtre. 8. Mes bagues sont aussi jolies que les siennes. 9. Nous avons vu plus de (*than*) quinze cents soldats. 10. En mil huit cent.

111.

1. handsomer; 2. older; 3. the youngest (*f.*); 4. warmer; 5. colder; 6. the most beautiful (*f. pl.*); 7. more polite; 8. the best (*m.*), the best (*f.*), the best (*m. pl.*), the best (*f. pl.*); 9. the richest; 10. higher; 11. bigger; 12. worse (=more bad) (*f.*).

1. the best house; 2. their new school; 3. the oldest tree; 4. the vainest girl; 5. the prettiest garden; 6. the blackest ink; 7. our old dog; 8. this man is bigger; 9. her hands are smaller; 10. your rooms are nicer; 11. they are the richest.

112.

1. She is as vain as her sister. 2. He is less rich than his friend. 3. My coffee is as hot as yours. 4. Our tea is not so good as theirs. 5. Your niece is the most beautiful girl in the room. 6. The eldest women in the town are here. 7. This boy is the youngest in the family (*famille*). 8. The coldest day in the month. 9. You have read more than twelve pages.

THIRTEENTH LESSON.

57. The FUTURE of ALL VERBS is formed by adding to the INFINITIVE the following terminations :

ai, as, a, ons, ez, ont (same terminations as in *j'ai, tu as*, etc.)

I shall give,	je donnerai	we shall give,	nous donnerons
thou wilt give,	tu donneras	you will give,	vous donnerez
he will give,	il donnera	they will give,	ils donneront

PRON.—sher donn-*er*-reh, tü donn-*er*-rah, ill donn-*er*-rah ;
noo donn-*er*-rong, voo donn-*er*-reh, ill donn-*er*-rong.

The *e* in *re* Verbs is omitted when adding these terminations ;
avoir adds them to **aur**, and **être** to **ser** ; as,

I shall sell,	*je vendrai*	I shall finish,	*je finirai*
I shall have,	*j'aurai*	I shall be,	*je serai*

PRON.—sher *vahng*-dreh, sher fe-ne-reh, shoh-reh, sher ser-reh *or* s'reh.

Questions and *Negations* are formed as in the other Tenses :

will he speak ?	*parlera-t-il ?*	they will not have, *ils n'auront pas*
shall we finish ?	*finirons-nous ?*	will she not be ? *ne sera-t-elle pas?*

Students wanting more Exercises on the FUTURE should next go through the Additional Exercises.

EXERCISE I.

1. He will be here to-morrow.[1] **2.** We shall be there.[2] **3.** I shall speak to his father. **4.** He will sell his house. **5.** Will you have (the) time[3] to-morrow ? **6.** We shall finish our lessons[4] to-day. **7.** They will reply to our letter by return of post. **8.** Will you not punish your dog ? **9.** I shall not give the money to the man. **10.** Where will they live ? **11.** Will they not close the door ? **12.** She will choose this colour.

---

1. demain, 2. là, 3. temps, 4. leçon (*f.*).
PRON.—1. der-*mang*, 2. lah, 3. *tahng*, 4. ler-*song*.

EXERCISE II.

1. I shall speak to him to-morrow. **2.** We shall give the parcel back to them. **3.** He will not finish it before[1] this evening. **4.** Will they not invite us to the concert ? **5.** They will not reply to her. **6.** Will she not expect you ? **7.** You shall have it. **8.** We shall not find him at[2] home.[2] **9.** Will they not accept it ? **10.** She will bring you the things.[3]

1. avant, 2. à la maison, 3. chose.
PRON.—1. ah-*vahng*, 2. ah lah may-*zong*, 3. shohz.

CONVERSATIONAL SENTENCES.

Quelle est la date ?	What is the date ?
Le premier mars.	The first of* March.
Quel jour était-il ici ?	On* what day was he here ?
Il était ici lundi.	He was here on Monday.
Quand lui avez-vous écrit ?	When did you write to him ?
Le quinze† septembre.	On the 15th of September.
Quand l'avez-vous vu ?	When did you see him ?
Vendredi, le deux juin.	On Friday, the 2nd of June.
Quel jour de la semaine est-ce ?	What day of the week is this ?
Lundi, le vingt-cinq mai.	Monday, the 25th of May.

* of, on are not translated before *days, months* and *dates*.

† In dates, *two, three*, etc., are used instead of 2nd, 3rd, etc., the 1st (*le premier*) being the only exception.—Names of days and months do not begin with a capital letter in French.

---o---

ADDITIONAL EXERCISES.
113.

1. Je ne serai pas, ne seras-tu pas ? il ne sera pas ; 2. ne serons-nous pas ? vous ne serez pas, ne seront-elles pas ? 3. n'aurai-je pas ? *or* est-ce que je n'aurai pas ? tu n'auras pas, n'aura-t-elle pas ? 4. nous n'aurons pas, n'aurez-vous pas ? ils n'auront pas.

1. I shall be, wilt thou be ? he will not be, will she not be ? 2. We shall be, will you not be ? they will not be, will they (*f.*) be ? 3. I shall not have, thou wilt have, will he have ? she will not have ; 4. shall we have ? you will not have, will they have ? they will have.

114.

1. ne parlerai-je pas ? ne vendras-tu pas ? ne finira-t-il pas ? 2. nous ne parlerons pas, vous ne vendrez pas, ils ne finiront pas ; 3. je donnerai, tu oublieras, il n'invitera pas ; 4. nous demeurerons, vous apporterez, ils fermeront ; 5. n'attendrons-nous pas ? vous ne descendrez pas, n'entendront-ils pas ? 6. ne punirai-je pas *or* est-ce que je ne punirai pas ? tu ne rempliras pas, choisira-t-elle ?

1. I shall give, wilt thou copy ? he will not pass ; 2. shall we sing ? will you not carry ? they will not forget ; 3. I shall not reply, thou wilt not lose ; will he not give back ? 4. we shall not wait for, will you not hear ?

115.

1. I shall have it. 2. You will not be there. 3. Will she not pay us ? 4. They will not find you. 5. We shall not cut them. 6. Will they (*f.*) not expect him ? 7. We shall finish the pictures before the evening. 8. Will you not reply to their letter ? 9. They will not obey (to) your friend. 10. We shall not finish before ten o'clock. 11. Will he sell his ring ?

58. The IMPERATIVE is the same as the **Present**, except that the Pronouns *vous, nous, tu* are omitted ; thus :

speak	parlez	let us speak	parlons	speak (thou)	*parle**
do not } ne vendez		do not } ne vendons		do not sell „	ne vends
sell } pas		let us sell } pas			pas
finish	finissez	let us finish	finissons	finish „	*finis*

*the final s of *er* Verbs is omitted in the Imperative Singular.

The *Imperative* of (*to*) *have* and (*to*) *be* is irregular, thus :

have *ayez*   let us have *ayons*   have (thou) *aie*
be *soyez*   „ be *soyons*   be „ *sois*

The Imperative has only the above three Persons ; "let him speak" "let them speak," are rendered by the 3rd persons of the Subjunctive Present.

EXERCISE III.

1. Do not speak to the waiter. 2. Reply to his letter by return. 3. Let-us-invite our neighbours. 4. Fill the glasses. 5. Do not wait-for the train. 6. Look-at these pictures ; are they not pretty ? 7. Do not punish the little boy. 8. Don't sell your books. 9. Shut the window, if you please. 10. Do not spend more than five francs. 11. Cut some bread, if you please. 12. Do not bring your umbrella.

---

59. what? *which?* are translated **quel**, etc., if followed by the Verb *to be* and a *Noun* (see Rules 34 and 39) ; as :

What is your *opinion?*	Quelle est votre opinion ?
Which are their *friends?*	Quels sont leurs amis ?
What will be the *price?*	Quel sera le prix ?

60. which? *which one?* followed by **of** are translated *the which;* as,

lequel, laquelle, lesquels, lesquelles. PRON.—ler-kell, etc

Which (one) of these men ?	Lequel de ces hommes ?
Which of these ladies are singing ?	Lesquelles de ces dames chantent ?

EXERCISE IV.

1. What will be his position[1] ? 2. What will be their expenses[2] ? 3. What is her name ? 4. Which is your house ? 5. Which are your friends ? 6. What are their addresses ? 7. Which is his sister ? 8. What are your ideas[3] ? 9. Which of these soldiers have gained[4] the prizes[5] ? 10. Which of your daughters is singing ? 11. Which of the books is there?

---

1. position,   2. dépense,   3. idée,   4. *to gain*, gagner,   5. prix.

PRON.—1. po-ze-se-*ong*,   2. deh-p*ahng*ss,   3. e-deh.   4. gahnn-yeh,   5. pree.

CONVERSATIONAL SENTENCES.

L'entendez-vous sonner ?	Do you hear it striking ?
Oui, il sonne neuf heures.*	Yes, it is striking nine o'clock.
Non, c'est quatre heures.	No, that is four o'clock.
N'est-ce pas deux heures ?	Is that not two o'clock ?
Non, il est déjà trois heures.	No, it is already three o'clock.
Avoir faim,[1] avoir soif.[2]	(to) be hungry, (to) be thirsty.
N'ont-ils pas faim ?	Are they not hungry ?
Si, et ils ont soif aussi.	Yes, and they are thirsty too.
Vous aurez soif dans une heure, mais vous n'aurez pas faim.	You will be thirsty in an hour, but you will not be hungry.

*or neuf heures sonnent. 1. fang, 2. so'ahff.

ADDITIONAL EXERCISES.
116.

1, Qui nous invitera ? 2. Que lui répondrez-vous ? 3. Ils demeureront à Paris à l'avenir (in future). 4. Où nous attendrez-vous ? 5. Ne sera-t-elle pas trop fatiguée ? 6. Nous aurons plus de temps demain. 7. Choisirez-vous ma couleur où la sienne ? 8. Elle sera ici dans cinq minutes.

117.

1. Fermez la porte. 2. Ouvrez (open) la fenêtre. 3. N'attendons pas. 4. Ne dépensez pas tout (all) votre argent. 5. Ne perdez pas la lettre. 6. Ne fumez pas dans la chambre. 7. Ayez la bonté.[1] 8. Soyez[2] le bienvenu.[2] 9. Ne soyez pas en[3] retard.[3] 10. N'ayez pas peur.[4] 11. Soyons prêts.[5] 12. Ayons du courage. 13. Ayez pitié.

118.

1. Let us close the window. 2. Do not break the glass. 3. Reply to your father. 4. Do not sell this ring. 5. Let us wear our black hats. 6. Fill the lamp. 7. Wait for your friend. 8. Choose the day. 9. Let us finish the lesson. 10. Let us give back the books to the lady. 11. Do not pay more than ten francs. 12. Copy this letter, if you please.

119.

1, What is your name ? 2. Which is your house ? 3. Which are your letters ? 4. What is the date ? 5. What are your expenses ? 6. What will be my position ? 7. Which is the street where he lives ? 8. Which are your gloves ? 9. Which of your friends ? 10. Which of these letters ? 11. Which (pl.) of these ladies ? 12. Which (pl.) of these gentlemen ? 13. Which of those soldiers has won ? 14. Which of these ladies is singing ? 15. Which of those men are winning ?

---

1. kindness, 2. be=you are welcome, 3. late, 4. fear, 5. ready,

FOURTEENTH LESSON.

61. The CONDITIONAL of ALL VERBS is formed by changing the Terminations of the FUTURE to

ais, ais, ait ; ions, iez, aient.

The Stems of the Future and Conditional are therefore always the same.

I should give,	**je donnerais**	we should give,	**nous donnerions**
thou wouldst give,	**tu donnerais**	you would give,	**vous donneriez**
he would give,	**il donnerait**	they would give,	**ils donneraient**

PRON.—sher donn-er-ray, tü donn-er-ray, ill donn-er-ray ;

noo donn-er-re-ong. voo donn-er-re-eh, ill donn-er-ray.

Questions and *Negations* are formed in the usual way :

he would not be,	*il ne serait pas*	would he not sell ?	*ne vendrait-il pas ?*
would they have ?	*auraient-ils ?*	should we finish ?	*finirions-nous ?*

EXERCISE I.

1. We should forget his name. 2. He would be there in[1] time.[1] 3. I should not light the gas. 4. They would not lose the way. 5. Would you finish your work[2] before[3] the evening[4]? 6. They would not have the time. 7. She would be alone.[5] 8. We should break the window. 9. They would not be at[6] home.[6] 10. Would you have knocked[7] at the door ?

---

1. à temps, 2. travail, 3. avant, 4. soir, 5. seul, 6. à la maison, 7. frapper.

PRON.—1. ah t*ahng*, 2. trah-vah'e, 3. ah-v*ahng*, 4. so'ahr, 5. serl, 6. ah lah may-z*ong*, 7. frahpp-eh.

---

62. *who, whom, which, that,* when referring to a preceding word, are called RELATIVE PRONOUNS ; thus :

SUBJECT.—**who,** *which, that* **qui**

OBJECT.—**whom,** *which, that* **que** (*qu'* before a Vowel)

qui is used if the Verb comes immediately after these words in English ; **que** is used if there is another word between. PRON.—kee, ker.

EXERCISE II.

1. The lady who spoke to you is my niece. 2. The gentleman whom you saw[1] yesterday[2] is her uncle. 3. The house that he sold to you is very good. 4. The letter which is on the table is for your friend. 5. The newspapers that are here are French. 6. The bird that is in this cage[3] does not sing. 7. The pens which we have are very bad.

1.=*have seen* (vu), 2. hier, 3. cage. PRON.—1. vü, 2. e-air, 3. kahsh.

CONVERSATIONAL SENTENCES.

Avoir raison,[1] tort,[1] peur,[2] honte,[2] chaud,[3] froid.[3]	(To) *be* right, wrong, afraid, ashamed, warm, cold.
Qui a raison ?	Who is right ?
Vous avez tort.	You are wrong.
N'a-t-il pas froid ?	Is he not cold ?
Non, au[4] contraire[4] il a chaud.	No, on the contrary, he is warm.
J'aurais honte.	I should be ashamed.
N'aura-t-elle pas peur ?	Will she not be afraid ?
Les dames auraient froid.	The ladies would be cold.

1. ray-*zong*, tor ; 2. per, *hongt* ; 3. shoh, fro'ah ; 4. oh *kong*-trair.

ADDITIONAL EXERCISES.

120.

1. je ne serais pas ; ne serais-tu pas ? il ne serait pas ; 2. ne serions-nous pas ? vous ne seriez pas, ne seraient-ils pas ? 3. n'aurais-je pas ? *or* est-ce que je n'aurais pas ? tu n'aurais pas, n'aurait-elle pas ? 4. nous n'aurions pas, n'auriez-vous pas ? ils n'auraient pas.

1. I should be, wouldst thou be ? he would not be, would she not be ? 2. we should be, would you not be   they would not be, would they (*f.*) be ? 3. I should not have, thou wouldst have, would he have ? she would not have ; 4. should we have ? you would not have, would they have ?

121.

1. ne donnerais-je pas ? tu ne donnerais pas, ne finirait-il pas ? 2. nous ne fumerions pas, ne perdriez-vous pas ? elles n'obéiraient pas ; 3. je ne donnerais pas, ne rencontrerais-tu pas ? elle remplirait ; 4. descendrions-nous ? vous ne rendriez pas ; ne fermeraient-ils pas ?

1. I should carry, wouldst thou light ? he would not find, would she not copy ? 2. we should spend, would you meet ? they would not invite, would they (*f.*) not speak ? 3. I should not obey, would he choose ? she would not punish ; 4. we should not sell, would you wait ? they would give back, would they not reply ?

122.

1. l'oiseau qui chante ; 2. l'homme qui parle ; 3. les livres que vous avez ; 4. les hommes qui fument ; 5. l'argent qu'il dépense ; 6. les tableaux que vous regardez ; 7. le train qu'il attend ; 8. les enfants qui n'obéissent pas.

1. the boy who is singing ; 2. the prices which you pay ; 3. the colour that you are choosing ; 4. the books which you are giving back ; 5. the work that we are finishing ; 6. the books which are here ; 7. the men who are selling ; 8. the neighbours who are living there.

H F S 5

63. *whom, which, that,* may be omitted in English (when Object), but must always be expressed in French ; as,

The books you are looking for (*or* that you are looking for) are here.	Les livres **que** vous cherchez sont ici.
The pipe he is smoking (*or* **which** he is smoking) is very large.	La pipe qu'il fume est très grande.

EXERCISE III.

1. The man you saw is there. 2. The boys you meet are my nephews. 3. The horses they are selling are very old. 4. The pictures we are looking at are very pretty. 5. The shoes they are selling are good. 6. The things we shall return to them are on the table.

The following Rule is of no great importance to beginners. *In the Exercises it will always be pointed out when Rule 64 is to be applied.*

64. The PAST PARTICIPLE always takes the same Gender and Number as its object when it *follows* the Object in French. This occurs in three kinds of sentences :—

(*a*) In Questions beginning with *which, what,* followed by a Noun.

WHICH HOUSE have you bought ?	QUELLE MAISON avez-vous achetée ?
WHAT PICTURES did he sell ?	QUELS TABLEAUX a-t-il vendus ?
WHICH LADIES did they meet ?	QUELLES DAMES ont-ils rencontrées ?

(*b*) After the Relative Pronoun que (qu').

The lamp THAT I lighted	La lampe QUE j'ai allumée
The boys WHOM you saw	Les garçons QUE vous avez vus
The letters WHICH they lost	Les lettres QU'ils ont perdues

(*c*) After the Personal Pronouns in Paragraph 42, unless they mean to *me,* to *us,* to *him,* etc.

We met HER in the street.	Nous L'avons rencontrée dans la rue.
Did they not expect YOU (*m. plur.*) ?	Ne VOUS ont-ils pas attendus ?
I did not see YOU (*fem. sing.*).	Je ne VOUS ai pas vue.
Did you not lose THEM ? (the pens)	Ne LES avez-vous pas perdues ?
She saw US (*masc.*) yesterday.	Elle NOUS a vus hier.
BUT :—He gave (*to*) us the money.	Il nous a *donné* l'argent.

In the above examples the Object is printed in SMALL CAPITALS.

EXERCISE IV.

1. Which page have you read ? 2. I have found the postage stamps (that) you lost. 3. The postman has brought three letters for you ; have you received them ? 4. What animals did you see ? 5. Is the water which he brought you warm ? 6. His sister is very pretty ; have you not seen her ?

CONVERSATIONAL SENTENCES.

Quel âge[1] avez-vous ?	*How old are you ?*
J'ai vingt[2] ans.[2]	*I am twenty (years old).*
Quel âge a votre fils[3] ?	*How old is your son ?*
(or Quel âge votre fils a-t-il ?)	
Il *a* dix ans.	He *is* ten (years old).
Quel est votre âge ?	What is your age ?
Je suis *âgé[4] de[4]* vingt ans.	I am twenty years *old.*
Quel est l'âge de votre fille ?	What is the age of your daughter ?
Elle est âgée de dix ans.	She is ten years old.

1. ahsh, 2. *vang-t'ahng*, 3. fiss, 4. ah-sheh der.

---o---

ADDITIONAL EXERCISES.

123.

1. Garçon, apportez à cette dame une tasse de café.   2. Pourquoi n'avez-vous pas vendu votre maison ?   3. Mes dépenses sont trop grandes.   4. Voilà une bonne idée.   5. Il a une très belle position.   6. N'avez-vous pas perdu votre parapluie ?   7. Serez-vous à temps à la gare ?   8. Je lui parlerai demain.

124.

1. Do not speak to these boys. 2. Let-us-give some money to the woman. 3. Will you wait-for me? 4. They do not reply to our letters. 5. Why will you not finish your lessons to-day ? 6. Which one of these books will you choose? 7. Is your brother as tall as you ? 8. These birds do not sing so well (*bien*) as yours. 9. She has gained more than three prizes.

125.

1. Quelles dames avez-vous invitées ?   2. Voici vos plumes : je les ai trouvées sur la table.   3. Les garçons que vous avez choisis demeurent dans cette rue.   4. Quels noms avez-vous vus sur le papier ?   5. Voilà la dame que nous avons rencontrée hier.

6. I should-speak to her.   7. They would-not-wait-for us.   8. Would-you finish it before to-morrow ?   9. They would-not-be there.   10. I shall not have (the) time to-morrow.   11. Do not wait-for us more than an hour.

126.

1. Où est l'argent que vous avez trouvé ?   2. Voici les chaises que j'ai achetées.   3. Où sont les lettres qu'elle a reçues ? 4. L'oiseau qui chante est dans la cage.   5. Les échantillons qu'il nous a envoyés sont très jolis.   6. Les romans qu'elle a lus sont très intéressants. 7. La bague qu'il nous a vendue est très jolie.

8. The river which we saw is very large.   9. The trees which are in the garden are very high.   10. The wine you bought is very good.   11. The gentleman who is speaking is German.   12. The workmen who are in your house are very active.   13. There is the umbrella I lost yesterday.

FIFTEENTH LESSON.

65. The IMPERFECT (or PAST) TENSE of ALL VERBS is formed by adding to the STEM, ais, ais, ait ; ions, iez, aient.

I was giving,	je donnais	we were giving,	nous donnions
thou wast giving,	tu donnais	you were giving,	vous donniez
he was giving,	il donnait	they were giving,	ils donnaient

PRON.—donn-ay, donn-ay, donn-ay ; donn-e-*ong*, donn-e-eh, donn-ay.

Verbs ending in *ir* put iss before the above terminations ; avoir adds them to av, and être to ét ; as,

I was selling,	je vendais	I was finishing,	je finissais
I had,	j'avais	I was,	j'étais

PRON.—sher va*hng*-day, shah-vay, sher fe-niss-ay, sheh-tay.

EXERCISE I.

1. I was giving a lesson to-him. 2. She had two sisters. 3. They were alone.[1] 4. She was finishing the dress[2] for that lady. 5. They were listening-to[3] the music.[4] 6. We were waiting-for the train. 7. She was speaking to-us. 8. You were smoking a cigar. 9. They had the samples. 10. We were at home. 11. I was filling the lamp.

---

1. seul, 2. robe, 3. écouter, (*to*) *listen to*, 4. musique.
PRON.—1. serl, 2. rob, 3. eh-koo-teh, 4. mü-zick.

---

66. *I used to give* and *I gave* (and similar phrases),when meaning *I was giving* are always rendered by the *Imperfect ;* as,

She used to speak to me.	Elle me parlait.
They (*f.*) used to obey us.	Elles nous obéissaient.
Did you not listen to them ? or were you not listening to them?	Ne les écoutiez-vous pas ?

EXERCISE II.

1. They used to play[1] every day. 2. She was tearing[2] the papers. 3. We used to study[3] (the) French together.[4] 4. They were walking[5] to the market[6] with their baskets.[7] 5. Did they not play at[8] cards[8] yesterday evening ? 6. She won[9] always and I lost all[10] my money. 7. He was finishing my coat. 8. They did not succeed[11] in these things. 9. They were not here. 10. We had a little house. 11. Was she not very pretty ? 12. They had not the time.

---

1. jouer, 2. déchirer, 3. étudier, 4. ensemble, 5. marcher, 6. marché, 7. panier, 8. aux cartes, 9. gagner, 10. tout, 11. réussir.   PRON.—
1. shoo-eh, 2. deh-she-reh, 3. eh-tü-de-eh, 4. *ahng-sahng*-bl, 5. mahr-sheh, 6. mahr-sheh, 7. pah-ne-eh, 8. oh kahrt, 9. gahnn-yeh, 10. too, 11. reh-ü-seer.

CONVERSATIONAL SENTENCES.

Ma sœur a* vingt ans.	My sister is twenty years old.
Il n'avait pas peur.	He was not afraid.
Nous avions tort.	We were wrong.
De quoi parlait-elle ?	What was she speaking of ?
Vous avez bien¹ raison.	You are quite (=well) right.
Combien² a-t-il dépensé ?	How much has he spent ?
Il a dépensé tout son argent.	He has spent all his money.
À qui l'ont-ils montré ?	Whom have they shown it to ?
Il est arrivé hier matin.	He (is) arrived yesterday morn-
Nous ne serions pas à temps.	We should not be in time. [ing.
Qu'a-t-il dit cette fois ?	What did he say this time ?

* or est âgée de.   1. be-*ang*, 2. ko*ng*-be-*ang*.

---o---

ADDITIONAL EXERCISES.
127.

1. N'avais-je pas ? *or* est-ce que je n'avais pas ? tu n'avais pas, n'avait-il pas ?   2. nous n'avions pas, n'aviez-vous pas ? elles n'avaient pas ;   3. je n'étais pas, étais-tu ? elle n'était pas ; 4. n'étions-nous pas ? vous étiez, ils n'étaient pas.

1. I had, hadst thou ? he had not ; 2. we had, had you ? had they (*f.*) not? 3. I was not, wast thou ? was she not ? 4. we were not, were you not ? they were not.

128.

1. N'oubliais-je pas . *or* est-ce que je n'oubliais pas ? tu ne descendais pas, ne réussissait-il pas ?   2. nous chantions, ne correspondiez-vous pas ? ils ne réussissaient pas.

1. I was-tearing, wast-thou not waiting-for ? he was-finishing ; 2. we were-copying ; were you not succeeding ? they were-descending ; 3. I used-to-lend ; she did not succeed* ; did they not correspond* ? 4. we were-looking-at, were you not playing ? they (*f.*) were not succeeding.

129.

1. Qui déchirait ces lettres ?   2. Ils ne réussissaient pas.   3. Le panier n'était pas là.   4. Ils marchaient ensemble tout le temps. 5. Nous copiions† la liste.   6. N'avaient-ils pas perdu le chemin ? 7. Elle était seule à la maison.   8. Elles étaient très fatiguées.

1. She was filling the basket *with* (de) flowers. 2. Were you at the market yesterday ? 3. They were always losing. 4. Were they not playing together ? 5. She used to study more than you. 6. Had he not succeeded ? 7. The ladies were talking to the gentlemen. 8. Were they not corresponding with their friends ? 9. He was spending all his money. 10. They were finishing our coats.

* To be translated by the Imperfect.   † There are two i's, one in the stem, and one in the termination.

67. which and *whom* after a PREPOSITION (see Rule 35) are translated by *the which* ; as,

lequel, laquelle, lesquels, lesquelles.   PRON.—ler-kell, etc.
whom can also be rendered by **qui.**

whom and *which* are in this case Relative Pronouns, as they do not ask a question.

The house in which we live.	La maison dans laquelle nous demeurons.
The man with whom she danced.	L'homme avec lequel (*or* avec qui) elle dansait.

EXERCISE III.

1. The book in which he was studying is[1] a French grammar.[1] 2. The train by which she arrives[2] is always late.[3] 3. The lady with whom we were dancing[4] yesterday is not here. 4. The girls for whom you bought the boots. 5. The envelope[5] on which he wrote the address. 6. The man by[6] whom he sent the money.

1. grammaire, 2. arriver, 3. en retard, 4. danser, 5. enveloppe, 6. par.

PRON.—1. grahmm-air, 2. abr-ree-veh, 3. *ahng* rer-tahr, 4. d*ahng*-seh, 5. *ahng*-ver-lop, 6. pahr.

68. *of whom, of which* are generally translated by *dont* instead of *de qui* or *duquel, de laquelle, desquels*, etc.

The ladies of whom you were speaking.	Les dames dont (*or* de qui *or* desquelles) vous parliez.
The book from which he was copying it.	Le livre dont (*or* duquel) il le copiait.

All words beginning with *le, la, les* are contracted with **de** and **à** as usual.

EXERCISE IV.

1. Did you let[1] the rooms of which we were speaking ? 2. Where is the list[2] from which he was copying the names[3] ? 3. There is the man to whom I gave it. 4. The fire of which we heard[4] was very serious.[5] 5. We were speaking of our garden and not[6] of yours. 6. We lent it to our friends and not[6] to theirs. 7. To which one of these men did you send it ? 8. Of which (*plur.*) of these girls were you speaking ? 9. Did you give it to our waiter or to his ? 10. Have they heard[7] it from my servant[8] or from hers ?

1. louer, 2. liste, 3. nom, 4. *translate* have heard speak, 5. sérieux, 6. non *or* non pas, 7.=*learnt*, appris, 8. domestique (*masc.* or *fem.*).

PRON.—1. loo-eh, 2. list, 3. nong, 5. seh-re-er, 6. nong, nong pah, 7. ah-pree, 8. do-mess-tick

CONVERSATIONAL SENTENCES.

Il arrivera le dix-huit août.	He will arrive (on) the 18th (of) August.
Quel jour arriverons-nous ?	What day shall we arrive ?
Vendredi, le seize novembre,	(On) Friday, the 16th (of) November.
Avez-vous soif ?	Are you thirsty ?
Non, mais j'ai faim.	No, but I am hungry.
Et moi aussi.	So am I (=and I also).
N'ont-ils pas faim ?	Are they not hungry ?
Dix heures sonnaient.	Ten o'clock *was* striking.
Savez-vous quelle heure il est ?	Do you know what time it is ?

ADDITIONAL EXERCISES.

130.

1. Pourquoi déchiriez-vous la robe ? 2. Il ne nous écoutait pas. 3. Il gagne toujours aux cartes. 4. Les soldats marchaient le long de cette rue. 5. Ils ne réussiront pas. 6. Avez-vous acheté ce panier de pommes au marché ? 7. Etudions nos leçons ensemble ! 8. Jouiez-vous dans le jardin ?

131.

1. The room in which ; 2. the man to whom ; 3. the soldiers of whom ; 4. the chairs on which ; 5. the ladies to whom ; 6. the fire at which ; 7. the servants of whom ; 8. the streets through which ; 9. the fetter in which ; 10. the uncle of whom ; 11. the basket in which ; 12. the friend to whom.

132.

Note that *I had, I was*, etc., are generally translated by *j'avais* and *j'étais*, etc., not by the *Perfect Tense, I have had, I have been*, etc.

1. She had not, I was not, were you ? 2. they were not, had you ? was she not ? 3. had I not ? he was not, were we not ? 4. was I ? had they not ? you were not ; 5. I had, thou wast, had she ? it was not ; 6. we were, had you ? they (*f.*) were not.

133.

1. Have you read the book of which we were talking ? 2. Who is the gentleman to whom you have sent it ? 3. Where are the baskets in which we brought them ? 4. There is the lady to whom I lent my dictionary. 5. To which one of these boys did you give it ? 6. Of which (*plur.*) of these flowers were you speaking ? 7. We sent the address to his brother and to yours. 8. Have you received it from our friends or from theirs ? 9. Here is the grammar of which I was speaking.

RECAPITULATORY EXERCISES on LESSONS 12 TO 15.

1.

1. Here is a fine street. 2. She wears a black[1] hat. 3. There are your husband and (your) brother. 4. What a little foot she has! 5. Have you any matches ? 6. Yes, but I have not any tobacco.[2] 7. Is he as industrious[3] as you ? 8. He is much more active than we. 9. This officer is the tallest in his regiment. 10. We have bought more than six pounds[4] of ice.[5] 11. She is as pretty as her sister. 12. This lesson is less difficult[6] than yours.

2.

1. I shall have finished in two hours. 2. He will be there before the evening. 3. We shall not have the time. 4. I shall speak to them. 5. They will not reply to our letter. 6. We shall be there to-morrow morning.[7] 7. The ladies were absent. 8. Who will wait-for him ? 9. Where will you sell the postage-stamps? 10. I shall gain the first prize. 11. Speak more quickly.[8] 12. Do not spend all your money.

3.

1. Were you quite[9] alone ? 2. Why did you not drink this water ? 3. It was too warm. 4. Was this wine good ? 5. Yes, it was very good. 6. They will not finish before nine o'clock. 7. We shall not reply to them. 8. You will tear it. 9. She will not accept it. 10. He did not reply to us. 11. We shall pay his account[10] to-morrow. 12. She was looking-for her friends.

4.

1. What was his name ? 2. Which are our neighbours ? 3. Which one of these dogs will you sell ? 4. Do not speak so fast.[8] 5. Shut the doors and (the) windows. 6. Do not finish the dress to-day. 7. Do not smoke here, if[11] you please.[11] 8. Which are your houses ? 9. What will be the price ? 10. Let us have (some) courage. 11. Have the kindness.[12] 12. Do not be late.[13]

5.

1. He answered by return of post. 2. They were waiting-for him in this room. 3. I have not seen his handwriting. 4. Have you not forgotten our address ? 5. We did not see the fire. 6. At what time did you receive the letter ? 7. Why did she not give-back the money to him ? 8. There is his daughter.

---

1. noir, 2. tabac, 3. travailleur or laborieux, 4. livre (f.), 5. glace, 6. difficile, 7. matin, 8. vite, 9. tout, 10. compte, 11. s'il vous plaît, 12. bonté, 13. en retard. PRON.—1, no'ahr, 2. tah-bah, 3. trah-vah'yer or lah-bo-re-er, 4. leevr, 5. glass, 6. diff-e-sill, 7. mah-*tang*, 8. vitt, 9. too, 10. *kongt*, 11. sill voo play, bong-teh, 13. *ahna-rer-tahr*.

RECAPITULATORY EXERCISES ON THE VARIOUS TENSES.

6.

1. I am, I was (*imperf.*), I shall be, I should be; 2. is he? was he? will he be? would he be? 3. we are not, we were not, we shall not be, we should not be; 4. are you not? were you not? will they not be? would they not be?

7.

1. She has, she had (*imperf.*), she will have, she would have, 2. have you? had you? will you have? would you have? 3. we have not, we had not, we shall not have, we should not have; 4. have they not? had they not? will he not have?

8.

1. We are copying, we were copying, we shall copy, we should copy; 2. does he shut? was he shutting? will he shut? would he shut? would the servant shut? 3. I do not find, I was not finding, I shall not find, I should not find; 4. does that man work (=that man works he)? was that man working? will that man work? would that man work? 5. shut the door.

9.

1. He sells, he does not sell; does he sell? does he not sell? 2. I was corresponding, I was not corresponding; was I losing? was I not losing? 3. they will wait, they will not wait; will they wait? will they not wait? 4. we should lose, we should not lose; should we lose? should we not lose? 5. wait here; do not wait.

10.

1. You are finishing, you were finishing, you will finish, you would finish; 2. will she choose? would she choose? was she choosing? is she choosing? 3. they do not fill, they would not fill, the boys were not obeying; will not the boys obey? 4. fill the lamp; do not fill it (*fem.*); 5. let us wait here; do not lose it.

11.

1. She will not obey; was she obeying? would she not obey? 2. I am filling; the servant was not filling; were you not finishing? 3. they would not choose; shall we not finish? I do not choose; 4. will he obey? the boys were not obeying; I am choosing; would you finish?

12.

1. She was copying a letter; 2. I shall copy the names; 3. what are you copying? 4. we should not copy the list; 5. I am-waiting-for the train; 6. what was-he-selling? 7. will they not correspond with you? 8. you would not lose it; 9. we shall finish it to-morrow.

SIXTEENTH LESSON.

69. The PRESENT PARTICIPLE is formed by adding *ant* to the *Stem* ; Verbs ending in *ir* take *iss* before the *ant* ; as,

giving, donnant | *selling*, vendant | *finishing*, finissant

Irregular are : *having*, ayant   *being*, étant

PRON.—donn-*ahng*, vahng-*dahng*. fe-niss-*ahng*, ay-*yahng*, eh-*tahng*.

The INFINITIVE is used in French instead of the PRESENT PARTICIPLE after a *Preposition*, en (*in, on*) excepted ; as,

In smoking his pipe	En fumant sa pipe
On meeting their friends	En rencontrant leurs amis
BUT : After having spoken	Après avoir parlé

EXERCISE I.

1. In speaking to his friend ; 2. on returning the parcel ; 3. in finishing the dress ; 4. without replying to the letter ; 5. after having written ; 6. I have the pleasure[1] of informing[2] you ; 7. for having lost the money ; 8. in looking-for the street ; 9. without copying the letter ; 10. in lighting the gas[3] ; 11. having lost the way ; 12. in obeying (to) you ; 13. for having sold ; 14. on hearing the noise ; 15. without studying his lessons.

1. plaisir, 2. informer, 3. gaz. PRON.—1. play-zeer, 2. *ang*-for-meh, 3. gahz.

70. **this**, *that*, not followed by a Noun, are translated thus :

this ceci (ser-se), *that* cela (ser-lah) ; ça (sah) is a contraction of *cela*.

ce (or c' before a vowel) is generally used instead of *ceci* or *cela*, if connected with a tense of *to be*.

What is the price of **this**?	Quel est le prix de ceci ?
Did you buy **that**?	Avez-vous acheté cela ?
This will be easy.	Ce sera facile.
Is **that** not difficult ?	N'est-ce pas difficile ?

EXERCISE II.

1. Give this to your brother. 2. That costs[1] more than six shillings.[2] 3. Why did you not choose that ? 4. This is the best colour. 5. Was that not stupid[3] ? 6. This is too dear.[4] 7. That will be nice. 8. Do not show[5] (to) him this. 9. That is too good. 10. This smokes too much.[6] 11. Will that not be difficult ? 12. This was not easy.

1. coûter, 2. schelling. 3. stupide, 4. cher, 5. montrer, 6. *too much*, trop.
PRON.—1. koo-teh, 2. sher-*lang*, 3. stü-pid, 4. shair, 5. mong-treh, 6. tro.

71. The PAST DEFINITE* of Verbs ending in **er** is formed by adding to the *Stem* the terminations printed in thick type, thus:

I gave	*je donn*ai	we gave	*nous donn*âmes
thou gavest	*tu donn*as	you gave	*vous donn*âtes
he gave	*il donn*a	they gave	*ils donn*èrent

PRON.—donn-eh, donn-ah, donn-ah ; donn-ahm, donn-aht, donn-air.

Note that the terminations of the Singular are like those of " j'ai, tu as, il a."

EXERCISE III.

1. He spoke ; 2. I did not copy ; 3. didst thou close ? 4. we accepted ; 5. did you forget ? 6. they cut ; 7. we found ; 8. they did not give ; 9. did you not meet ? 10. we closed the door ; 11. they did not pay the account ; 12. he looked at me.

---

72. The PAST DEFINITE of Verbs ending in **re** and **ir** is formed by adding to the Stem is, is, it ; îmes, îtes, irent, thus :

I sold, etc.		*I finished, etc.*	
je vendis,	nous vendîmes	je finis,	nous finîmes
tu vendis,	vous vendîtes	tu finis,	vous finîtes
il vendit,	ils vendirent	il finit,	ils finirent

PRON.—Sing. *vahng*-dee, fin-ee ; Plur. *vahng*-deem, *vahng*-deet, *vahng*-deer.

Note that the terminations of the Singular are like those of the Present of verbs in " ir " ; the terminations of the Plural are the same as those of verbs in "er," the vowel being changed into " i."

EXERCISE IV.

1. We finished ; 2. he did not sell ; 3. I obeyed ; 4. we lost ; 5. they replied ; 6. did you choose ? 7. she gave back ; 8. I filled ; 9. you descended ; 10. they did not succeed.

---

73. The PAST DEFINITES of *avoir* and *être* have almost the same terminations, *i* being changed to *u*, thus :

I had, etc.		*I was, etc.*	
j'eus,	nous eûmes	je fus,	nous fûmes
tu eus,	vous eûtes	tu fus,	vous fûtes
il eut.	ils eurent	il fut,	ils furent

PRON.—shü, tü ü, ill ü ; noo *z'*üm, voo *z'*üt, ill *z'*ür. Singular : fü ; Plural : füm, füt, für.

EXERCISE V.

1. I was ; 2. he had ; 3. we were ; 4. they had ; 5. they (*f.*) were ; 6. we had ; 7. were you ? 8. hadst thou not ? 9. I had not ; 10. he was not ; 11. they were not ; 12. had they not ?

---

* This Tense is seldom used in conversation, but frequently occurs in reading. Students should continue to translate the Past by the *Perfect* or *Imperfect* (see Rules 21 and 66).

74. **this,** *that, these, those* are translated by CE (*c'*) if connected with a tense of *to be* and a *Noun* or *Pronoun* ; as,

That will be your room.	Ce sera votre chambre.
These (*those*) are my friends.	Ce sont mes amis.
Is this not your dog?	N'est-ce pas votre chien ?
That was yours.	C'était le vôtre.

PRON.—*c'est,* say ; *est-ce ?* aiss ; *ce sont,* ser *song* ; *sont-ce ?* song ss ; *c'était, c'étaient,* seh-tay ; *était-ce ? étaient-ce ?* eh-tayss.

EXERCISE VI.

1. This is my hat. 2. Is this your chair ? 3. These are my gloves. 4. Those are not his horses. 5. Is that not your ticket ? 6. Was that our music ? 7. Will that be your place ? 8. That was our regiment. 9. Is that not his shop[1] ? 10. Are those not their rings[2] ? 11. What songs[3] were those ?

---

1. boutique, 2. bague, 3. chanson. PRON.—1. boo-tick, 2. bahg, 3. shang-*song*.

75. **it** is generally translated by **ce** unless referring to a Noun just mentioned (see rule 23).

he, she, they are also rendered by **ce** if used with the Verb *to be* and a *Noun* or *Pronoun.*

It is not easy.	Ce n'est pas facile.
Is he a German ?	Est-ce un Allemand ?
They are Spaniards.	Ce sont des Espagnols.

PRON.—ahll-m*ahng,* ess-pahn-yol.

EXERCISE VII.

1. It was her husband. 2. Are they your gloves ? 3. It will not be his place. 4. It is good. 5. They are Germans. 6. Is he a Spaniard ? 7. Was it nice ? 8. They are not Frenchmen.

---

76. The *Pronouns* (rule 42) follow the Verb in the *Imperative,* unless the Verb is in the *Negative.*

They are connected with the Verb by a hyphen ; and *me* and *te,* when following the Verb, are changed into *moi* and *toi.*

Sell them	vendez-les	Do not sell them ne les vendez pas
Accept it	acceptez-le	Do not accept it ne l'acceptez pas
Speak to me	parlez-moi	Do not speak to me ne me parlez pas

EXERCISE VIII.

1. Give him the book. 2. Show us the way. 3. Lend them the money. 4. Return the letters to us. 5. Speak to me this evening. 6. Do not accept it. 7. Let us speak to them. 8. Do not give her the ring. 9. Do not sell them. 10. Reply to me. 11. Do not reply to them. 12. Do not forget us.

CONVERSATIONAL SENTENCES.

Que vous a-t-il dit ?	What did he say to you ?
Je n'ai pas compris[1] sa question.	I did not understand his question.
Que lui avez-vous répondu ?	What did you answer him ?
Où l'avez-vous trouvé ? [livres.	Where did you find it ?
Je l'ai trouvé dans un de ces	I found it in one of these books.
Qui avez-vous rencontré ce matin ?	Whom did you meet this morning ?
C'était le mari de ma cousine.[2]	It was my cousin's husband.
Pourquoi ne m'a-t-il pas écrit ?	Why has he not written to me ?

1. kong-pree, 2. koo-zeen.

---o---

ADDITIONAL EXERCISES.

134.

1. En me regardant. 2. Ils ne nous répondirent pas. 3. En fumant sa pipe. 4. Après avoir mangé.[1] 5. Il arriva le soir. 6. En passant le couteau. 7. Il me donna deux schellings pour avoir trouvé son chien. 8. Il nous répondit sans tourner[2] la tête. 9. En remplissant son verre. 10. Les Français rendirent les navires.[3] 11. Le roi visita la ville. 12. Nous avons le plaisir de vous informer.

1. eaten, 2. (to) turn, 3. ship.

135. (on the *Past Definite*).

1. she succeeded, did they succeed ? 2. we copied, did he not copy ? 3. I did not sell, you sold, did the man sell ? 4. you did not pass, the soldiers passed, did not the boy pass ? 5. did they have ? I had not, 6. were you not ? we were, thou wast not ; 7. he gave, she replied, he did not obey ; 8. I had, I was, I closed, I gave back, I filled ; 9. they had, they were, they spoke, they lost, they chose.

136.

1. On choosing the colour ; 2. without cutting the string ; 3. not being in (à) time ; 4. after having lighted the fire ; 5. Who gave you this ? 6. Do not lend him that. 7. That is not our opinion. 8. This will be very difficult without copying it. 9. It would be too late. 10. This will not cost much. 11. Are these your gloves ? 12. They are my neighbours. 13. Where are our hats ? They are not here. 14. That finishes well.

137.

1. Was it not his place ? 2. Were they your samples ? 3. This is not my handwriting. 4. Show it to your friend. 5. Do not give (to) her the parcel. 6. Let us finish it. 7. Do not lose them. 8. Send it to this address. 9. Show me your ring. 10. Do not show him the pictures. 11. Do not forget me.

SEVENTEENTH LESSON.

IRREGULAR VERBS.

The Irregular Verbs are easily learnt, their Terminations (*except sometimes in the Present*) being quite Regular. Example:—

77. INFINITIVE (to) see Voir

PRES. PARTICIPLE : seeing, voy*ant* | PAST PARTICIPLE : seen, **vu**
PRES. TENSE : I see, etc.,*je* vo*is*,*etc. | PAST DEF.: I saw, etc., *je* vis, etc.
FUTURE : I shall see, etc. *je* verr*ai*, etc.

PRON.—vo'ahr, vo'ah-*yahng*, vü, sher vo'ah, sher vee, sher vair-eh.

The above is all that need be learnt, if attention is paid to the rules below.

FULL CONJUGATION FOR REFERENCE.

PRESENT.	IMPERFECT.	PAST DEFINITE.	FUTURE.	CONDITIONAL.
I see	I was seeing	I saw	I shall see	I should see
je vo*is*	voy*ais*	v*is*	verr*ai*	verr*ais*
tu vo*is*	voy*ais*	v*is*	verr*as*	verr*ais*
il vo*it*	voy*ait*	v*it*	verr*a*	verr*ait*
nous voy*ons*†	voy*ions*	v*îmes*	verr*ons*	verr*ions*
vous voy*ez*†	voy*iez*	v*îtes*	verr*ez*	verr*iez*
ils voi*ent*	voy*aient*	v*irent*	verr*ont*	verr*aient*

IMPERATIVE : let us see, *voyons* ; see, *voyez* ; see (thou), *vois*.

† *i* is always changed to *y* before a sounded syllable.

EXERCISE I.

1. Do you see that man ? **2.** I shall see you to-morrow.
3. I saw him last[1] week.[1] **4.** Have you seen (rule 64) them ?
5. They saw (*past def.*) the steamer.[2] **6.** They do not see us.
7. On[3] seeing that. **8.** After having seen him. **9.** We used-to-see them every day. **10.** I should see them, if[4] they were there.

1. la semaine dernière, 2. vapeur (m.), 3. en, 4. si (s' *before* il *or* ils,—*not* elle). PRON.—1. lah ser-main dair-ne-air, 2. vah-per, 3. *ahng*, 4. see.

RULES FOR REFERENCE ONLY.

I. The Terminations are always regular, except in the *Present Tense*.

II. The Stems of the *Imperfect*, the *Imperative*, and the *Plural* of the *Present*, are the same as that of the *Present Participle*.

III. The Stems of the *Future* and *Conditional* are always alike.

From these Rules it follows that the PARTICIPLES, the PRESENT TENSE, and the FUTURE and PAST DEFINITE Stems, are all that need be learnt.

* If the first person ends in *s*, the second also ends in *s*, and the third in *t*.

78. *this, that,* meaning *this one, that one,* are translated thus :

	MASC.	FEM.		MASC.	FEM.
this one,	celui-ci	'celle-ci	these,	ceux-ci	celles-ci
that one,	celui-là	celle-là	those,	ceux-là	celles-là

PRON.—serl-we-se, sell-se ; serl-we-lah, sell-lah ; ser-lah, sell-lah.

These Pronouns always refer to a *Noun expressed before*, with which they agree in Gender ; as,

This house or that?	Cette maison-ci ou celle-là?
These horses or those?	Ces chevaux-ci ou ceux-là?
Here are two watches ; will you have this one or that one?	Voici deux montres ; voulez-vous celle-ci ou celle-là?

79. *-ci* (here), *-là* (there) may be added to the Noun to make a distinction between *this* and *that, these* and *those.*

This man and that woman	Cet homme-ci et cette femme-là
These boys or those girls	Ces garçons-ci ou ces filles-là

EXERCISE II.

1. Did you buy these books or those ? 2. What is the price of these watches ? 3. These cost a hundred francs,[1] and those two hundred francs. 4. I did not find your key, but this one. 5. This bottle is full[2] and that (one) is empty.[3] 6. Here are several[4] pieces[5] of money ; these are English and those are French. 7. Will[6] you have[6] these gloves or those ?

1. franc, 2. plein, 3. vide, 4. plusieurs, 5. pièce, 6. voulez-vous.
PRON.—1. frahng, 2. plang, 3. veed, 4. plü-ze-er, 5. pe-ess, 6. voo-leh voo.

80. Expressions like *his father's, their friends'*, must be translated by *that* (or *those*) *of his father, that* (or *those*) *of their friends.*

My umbrella or my brother's.	Mon parapluie ou celui de mon frère.
Your remarks and your friends'.	[amis. Vos observations et celles de vos

1. the one is translated like *that one.*
2. ci and là are left off before Relative Pronouns (rule 62), or de.

This lady and the one who wrote.	Cette dame et celle qui a écrit.
These children and those of whom we were speaking.	Ces enfants et ceux de qui (*or* dont) nous parlions.

EXERCISE III.

1. Is this your room or your sister's ? 2. He brought my gun and Henry's.[1] 3. We fetched[2] your umbrellas, but not (*non*) those gentlemen's. 4. Our garden is larger than our neighbour's. 5. These pictures are finer than those we saw yesterday. 6. Is this your carriage or your cousin's[3] (*f.*) ?

1. Henri, 2. chercher, 3. cousine. 1. hahna-re. 2. shair-sheh. 3. koo-zeen.

81.   INFINITIVE (to) read, **lire.**

PRES. PARTICIPLE : reading, lisant | PAST PARTICIPLE : read, **lu**
              PRON.—leer, le-*zahng*, lü.

PRES. TENSE : *Singular*—I read, *je* lis*   *Plural*—we read, *nous* **lisons**
     Rule I. The Stem of the Plural of the Present is the same as that
             of the Present Participle.

IMPERFECT : I was reading, *je* lisais | PAST DEFINITE : I read, *je* **lus**
     Rule II. The Stem of the Imperfect is the same as that of the
             Present Participle.

FUTURE : I shall read, *je* **lirai**   CONDITIONAL : I should read, *je* **lirais**
     Rule III. The Future and Conditional have always the same stem.

IMPERATIVE : read, *lisez* ; let us read, *lisons* (Familiar Form—read, *lis*).
     Rule IV. The Imperative is the same as the Present, without
             " vous," "nous" and " tu."

The rules on page 74 are repeated here singly. It suffices to learn the part
of the Verb printed in thick type, to conjugate the Verb in full, thus :

PRESENT.	IMPERFECT.	PAST DEFINITE.	FUTURE.	CONDITIONAL.
je lis*	*lisais*	*lus*	*lirai*	*lirais*
tu lis	*lisais*	*lus*	*liras*	*lirais*
il lit	*lisait*	*lut*	*lira*	*lirait*
nous lisons	*lisions*	*lûmes*	*lirons*	*lirions*
vous lisez	*lisiez*	*lûtes*	*lirez*	*liriez*
ils lisent	*lisaient*	*lurent*	*liront*	*liraient*

* If the first person ends *s*, the second ends in *s*, and the third in *t*.

EXERCISE IV.

1. Have you read this story[1] ?   2. Not[2] yet,[3] I am reading
this one.   3. Will-you-read the one (which) I was reading ?
4. Read this book or Henry's.   5. Let us read his letters and
his uncle's.   6. In which book were you reading ?   7. In the
one which is on the table.   8. Would you read my answer[3] or
my friend's ? 9. I shall read the one which is here. 10. These
pens are better than those which he brought (rule 64).

1. histoire,   2. pas encore,   3. réponse.   PRON.—1. iss-to'abr,   2. pah
z'ahng-kor,   3. reh-*pongss*.

82.   Like *lire* are conjugated the verbs formed from it :

(to) elect **élire.**   (to) re-elect **ré-élire,**   (to) read again **relire.**

EXERCISE V.

1. We shall elect a mayor.[1]   2. He was re-elected our
member[2] of Parliament.[2]   3. I was reading the letter again.
4. We shall not read the story again.   5. Who has been
elected ?   6. On reading it again.   7. Without being elected.

1. maire,   2. député.   PRON.—1. mair,   2. deh-pü-teh.

CONVERSATIONAL SENTENCES.

Laquelle de ces montres est la meilleure ?	Which of these watches is the best ?
Celle que vous avez dans la main. [voulez-vous ?	The one that you have in your (the) hand. [you have ?
Lesquelles de ces cigarettes Celles qui sont ici.	Which of these cigarettes will Those which are here.
A quelle heure avez-vous allumé les lampes ? [et demie.	At what time did you light the lamps ? [seven.
Je pense qu'il était sept heures	I think it was at half past

---o---

ADDITIONAL EXERCISES.

138.

1. Lequel de ces romans avez-vous lu ? Celui-ci ou celui-là ? 2. A-t-elle accepté votre cadeau[1] ou celui de votre cousin ? 3. N'a-t-il pas amené ses chiens et ceux de son voisin ? 4. Je vous verrai demain soir à huit heures un quart. 5. Ne l'oubliez pas, je vous attendrai.   (1. cadeau, *present*).

139.

1. I do not see, she did not see (*past def.*), 2. they used-to-see, let us see ; 3. on seeing us, after having seen them (64) ; 4. we shall see them, I should not see it ; 5. we see them, they do not see us ; 6. have you not seen her (64) ? do you see them ? 7. we should see her, they saw (*past def.*) it.

140.

1. This account or that ? 2. these flowers and those ; 3. this girl or that ; 4. these bottles and those ; 5. these hats or those ; 6. this glass and that one ; 7. these chairs and those tables ; 8. these pens or those pencils ; 9. this postman or that one ; 10. at this station or (at) that one : 11. with these knives or with those.

141.

1. Our house and our neighbour's ; 2. her uncle or her cousin's ; 3. my shoes and my friend's ; 4. his hands and Henry's ; 5. our postage stamps and our friends' ; 6. my carriage or our neighbours' ; 7. my stick and that which he has ; 8. your ticket or the one which I bought ; 9. our cigars or those which you smoke ; 10. their boots and those that you wear. 11. To your regiment or to the one (which is) in our town. 12. Her dress or her sister's.

142.

1. I am reading, he does not read ; 2. we were reading, they used to read ; 3. they read (*past def.*) it, he did not read (*past def.*) it, we did not read (*past def.*) them ; 4. I shall not read it, will he not read it ? 5. we should not read it, would they not read the books ? 6. let us read it, do not read his letter ; 7. in reading it (*f.*) ; after having read it ; 8. have they read it ?

EIGHTEENTH LESSON.

83. *that which*, and *what*, meaning *that which*, are translated :

ce qui when *Subject*, and ce que (*ce qu'*) when *Object*.

that which and *what* are generally *Object*; but they are *Subject* if followed immediately by the Verb in English.

I know what you have said.	Je sais ce que vous avez dit.
That is what he has done.	C'est ce qu'il a fait.
That which is on the table is mine.	Ce qui est sur la table est à moi.

EXERCISE I.

1. Did he show you what we found ? 2. She gave us what she bought. 3. That which you said is not right.[1] 4. That which is on the table is yours.[2] 5. All[3] that[3] he said is not true.[4] 6. I[5] know[5] what he has done.[6] 7. That is not what I saw. 8. I do not know what is in this box.[7]

---

1. juste, 2. à vous, 3. tout ce que, 4. vrai, 5. je sais, 6. fait, 7. boîte.

PRON.—1. shüst, 2. ah voo, 3. too ser ker *or* tooss ker, 4. vray, 5. sher say, 6. fay, 7. bo'ahtt.

Numbers are used instead of the names of the Tenses, thus :

1. Infinitive, 2. Present Participle, 3. Past Participle, 4. Present, 5. Imperfect, 6. Past Definite, 7. Future, 8. Conditional, 9. Imperative.

84.   1. to write écrire.

As explained on pages 74 and 76, if the parts printed in thick type are learned, the whole Verb is mastered.

2. writing, écrivant	3. written, écrit
4. I write, etc., j'écris tu écris, il écrit	4. we write, etc., nous écrivons vous écrivez, ils écrivent
5. I was writing, etc., j'écrivais, etc.	6. I wrote, etc., j'écrivis, etc.
7. I shall write, etc., j'écrirai, etc.	8. I should write, etc., j'écrirais, etc.
9. write, écrivez let us write, écrivons (Fam. form :—write, écris).	

PRON.—1. eh-kreer, 2. eh-kre-*vahng*, 3. eh-kree, 4. sheh-kree, noo z'eh-kre-*vong*, 5. sheh-kre-vay, 6. sheh-kre-vee, 7. sheh-kre-reh, 8. sheh-kre-ray, 9. eh-kre-veh, eh-kre-v*ong*.

EXERCISE II.

1. I am writing what you are dictating.[1] 2. Why did you not write to them ? 3. I shall write several letters after (the) dinner.[2] 4. He wrote (*past def.*) his name on a piece[3] of paper. 5. Was she not writing in her room ?

---

1. dicter, 2. dîner, 3. morceau.   PRON.—1. dick-teh, 2. dee-neh, 3. mor-soh

85. If the PERSONAL PRONOUNS (rule 42) are not the Subject or Object of a Verb, they are called *disjunctive*, and translated thus:

I, me	**moi**	we, us	**nous**
thou, thee	**toi**	you, you	**vous**
he, him	**lui**	they, them (*m.*)	**eux**
she, her	**elle**	they, them (*f.*)	**elles**

PRON.—mo'ah, to'ah, lwe, ell ; noo, voo, er, ell.

These disjunctive Pronouns are used *principally—*

1. after Prepositions, 2. in comparisons, 3. if standing alone; as,

for me, pour **moi**	from him, de **lui**
He is taller than **I**	Il est plus grand que **moi**
You and I, Vous et **moi**	He and they, Lui et **eux**

4. If the Verb used in English is not expressed in French, as in the following examples :

Who is there? I am	Qui est là ? **Moi**
Who has spoken? They have	Qui a parlé ? **Eux**
Whom have you seen? Him	Qui avez-vous vu ? **Lui**

EXERCISE III.

1. Have you anything[1] for him ? 2. I have received it from you. 3. We shall not continue[2] without them. 4. Who was singing? She was. 5. Who is passing before[3] the house ? He is. 6. Who has shown the town[4] to your friends ? I have. 7. Is he speaking of her ? 8. Have you received the money from them (*m.*) ? 9. She is not so old[5] as he. 10. We are richer than they. 11. My friend and I. 12. He and they (*f.*).

---

1. quelque chose, 2. continuer, 3. devant, 4. ville, 5. âgé.
PRON. 1. kell-ker shohz, 2. kong-te-nü-eh, 3. der-*vahng*, 4. vill, 5. ah-sheh.

---

86. *moi, lui, eux,* etc., are used after *ce* and a tense of *to be* ; as,

It is I, c'est moi	it is not we, ce n'est pas nous
was it he? était-ce lui?	was it not you ? n'était-ce pas vous?
is it they? est-ce eux?	it is they, ce sont eux *

* In the Third Person Plural, *sont* is used, except in Questions.

EXERCISE IV.

1. Who is there? It is I. 2. Was it not you ? No, it was she. 3. It will be he. 4. It is not they (*f.*). 5. It is not I. 6. It is your brother. 7. No, it was not he. 8. Is it not they ? 9. It is Henry. 10. Was it William[1] ? 11. Is it Mary[2] ?

---

1. Guillaume, 2. Marie. PRON.—1. ghe-yohm, 2. mah-re.

87. *mine, his,* etc., are generally translated by *à moi, à lui,* etc., after *to be,* if it has the meaning of "to belong to," thus:

This hat is mine.	Ce chapeau est à moi.
Those umbrellas are theirs.	Ces parapluies sont à eux.

à is also used in sentences like:

This fan is Louisa's.	Cet éventail est à Louise.
Is this pony William's?	Ce poney est-il à Guillaume?

EXERCISE V.

1. This money is mine. 2. Those pencils are not yours; they are Henry's. 3. Are not these ponies[1] ours? 4. No, they are theirs. 5. This purse[2] is William's. 6. Are these pears[3] Mary's? 7. Is this plate[4] mine? 8. No, it is this lady's.

1. poney, 2. porte-monnaie (m.), 3. poire, 4. assiette.
PRON.—1. po-nay, 2. port-mon-ay, 3. po'ahr, 4. ah-se-ett.

88.   1. to say, to tell **Dire**

2. saying, **disant**	3. said, **dit**
4. I say, etc., je dis	4. we say, *nous* **disons**
tu dis, il dit	*vous* **DITES**, *ils disent*
5. I was saying, etc., *je disais,* etc.	6. I said, etc., je dis, etc.
7. I shall say, etc., *je dirai,* etc.	8. I should say, etc., *je dirais,* etc.

9. say, **dites**, let us say, **disons**, (say thou, *dis*).

PRON.—1. deer, 2. de-*zahng,* 3. dee, 4. dee, de-*zong,* ditt, deez, 5. de-*zay,* 6. dee, 7. de-reh, 8. de-ray, 9. ditt.

EXERCISE VI.

1. He used-to-say that. 2. They will say so.[1] 3. I should not say so.[1] 4. What did you say to him? 5. Tell her what I said. 6. You do not say what they replied to you. 7. I shall tell you something to-morrow. 8. Tell me your name, if[2] you please.[2] 9. He only[3] said (*Past Def.*) yes. 10. What were you saying just[4] now[4]?

1. *so=it* le, 2. s'il vous plaît, 3. *only=not...but* ne...que, 4. tout à l'heure. PRON.—1. ler, 2. sill voo play, 3. ner ker, 4. too *t'*ah ler.

89. All Verbs formed from *dire* are conjugated in the same way.

The 2nd Person Plural Present, however, ends in *sez.* Example:

to contradict, *contredire* ; you contradict, *vous contrédisez.*

Exception: to curse. *maudire,* which doubles the *s* in the Present Participle *moudissant,* and the parts of the Verb formed from the Present Participle (Rule II, page 74).

CONVERSATIONAL SENTENCES.

Est-il chez[1] le libraire ?	Is he at the bookseller's ?
Non, mais je crois qu'il est chez le pharmacien.	No, but I believe that he is at the chemist's.
Avez-vous été chez le dentiste aujourd'hui ?	Have you been at the dentist's to-day ?
Oui, et aussi chez le médecin, mais il n'était pas chez[1] lui.	Yes, and also at the doctor's, but he was not at home.
Quand serez-vous chez vous la semaine prochaine ?	When will you be at home next week ?

1. chez (sheh) means *at the house of.*

ADDITIONAL EXERCISES.

143.

1. Ce qui est bon est généralement[1] cher ; mais ce qui est cher n'est pas toujours bon. **2.** Ce qui m'empêche[2] de[3] sortir,[3] c'est la maladie[4] de mon père. **3.** Ce que j'ai dans ce porte-monnaie est a lui. **4.** Tout ce qu'ils disent, est très invraisemblable.[5] **5.** Qui a été au concert avec vous ? Lui. **6.** Ne sont-ce pas les messieurs que nous avons rencontrés la semaine dernière ?

144.

1. What he says ; **2.** that which is here ; **3.** without them (m.) · **4.** who has written ? I have. **5.** they and you ; **6.** is it not she ? **7.** It is not Louisa.

8. we are writing, were you writing ? **9.** I shall not write, she would not write ; **10.** write, let us write ; **11.** they wrote (*past def.*), has she written ? **12.** she does not write, are you not writing ?

145.

1. On him ; **2.** without them ; **3.** for her ; **4.** under us ; **5.** smaller than they ; **6.** later than he ; **7.** as tired as we ; **8.** he and I ; **9.** who is smoking ? he is. **10.** it is not she ; **11.** was it not you ?

12. He says, he was not saying, did he say ? she said (*p.d.*) ; **13.** will he say ? would she not say ? tell (to) him, do not tell (to) him ; **14.** I do not say, they used to say, did you not say ? they said (*p.d.*) ; **15.** will-you-tell him ? we should tell them, do not speak to her.

146.

1. The paper is mine. **2.** Is this watch his ? **3.** This plate is hers. **4.** Those ponies are ours. **5.** This purse is William's. **6.** No, it is Mary's. **7.** Are those pears Henry's ? **8.** Did they tell you some (any) thing ? **9.** Tell us, if you please, what they answered. **10.** I do not know, I have forgotten it.

---

1. *generally*, sheh-neh-rahll-ma*hng*, 2. *prevents*, ahng-paish, 3. *from going out*, der sor-teer ; 4. *illness*, mah-lah-de, 5. *unlikely*, ang-vray-sang-blah-bl.

NINETEENTH LESSON.

90.   1. to take, **Prendre.**

2. taking, prenant	3. taken, pris
4. I take, etc., je prends	4. we take, *nous* **prenons**
tu prends, il prend	*vous prenez, ils prennent*
5. I was taking, etc., je *prenais*, etc.	6. I took, etc., je pris, etc.
7. I shall take, etc., je prendrai	8. I should take, je *prendrais*

9. take, *prenez* ; let us take, *prenons* ; (take thou, *prends*).

PRON.—1. pra*h*ngdr, 2. prer-n*a*hng, 3. pree, 4. pr*a*hng, prer-n*o*ng, prer-neh, prenn, 5. prer-nay, 6. pree, 7. pr*a*hng-dreb, 8. pr*a*hng-dray.

---

91. The principal *derivatives* of *prendre* are the following :

to learn, **apprendre**	to understand, **comprendre**
to surprise, **surprendre**	to undertake, **entreprendre**

EXERCISE I.

1. He does not understand your question.[1]   2. Why have you not learnt your lessons ?   3. Take a seat.[2]   4. I shall not undertake it.   5. Does[3] that surprise you ?   6. He took (*p.d.*) his hat.   7. Do you understand me ?   8. He does not take any tea.[4] 9. We shall surprise them to-morrow morning. 10. What[3] are you learning? (the) French or (the) German ?   11. At what time do you take your bath[5] ?   12. Take this money.

1. question, 2. siège (*m.*), 3. est-ce que, *see page 48*, 4. thé (*m.*), 5. bain. PRON.—1. kess-te-*ong*, 2. se-aysh, 3. ess ke*r*, 4. teh, 5. b*a*ng.

---

92. *Adverbs* are formed in French by adding *ment* to the Adjective, which ending corresponds to the English *ly*.

If the adjective does not end in a vowel, *ment* is added to the *feminine* form.

polite, *poli* ; politely, *poliment*	rare, *rare* ; rarely, *rarement*
happy, **heureux** (fem. *heureuse*) ; happily, **heureusement**	

EXERCISE II.

1. She writes politely.   2. They talk wisely.[1]   3. We are walking slowly.[2] 4. We rarely[3] see them. 5. She answered (*p.d.*) proudly.[4]   6. I shall work[5] actively.[6]   7. Write it carefully.[7] 8. Fortunately[8] he was there. 9. He passed (*p.d.*) us rapidly.[9]

1. *wise* sage, 2. *slow* lent, 3. *rare* rare, 4. *proud* fier, *fem.* fière, 5. travailler, 6. *active* actif, *fem.* active, 7. *careful* soigneux, *fem.* soigneuse, 8.=*happily*, 9. *rapid* rapide.   PRON.—1. sahsh, 2. l*a*hng, 3. rah*r*, 4. fe-air, 5. trah-v*a*h'e-yeh, 6. ah*c*k-tiff, 7. so'ahnn-ye*r*, 9. rah-pid.

93. The following words, called Adverbs of Quantity, take *de* (*d'*) after them if followed by a Noun :

1. assez	*enough*	5. moins	*less*
2. autant	*as much, as many*	6. peu	*little*
3. beaucoup	*much, many*	7. plus	*more*
4. combien	*how much, how many*	8. trop	*too much, too many*

PRON.—1. ahss-eh, 2. oh-*tahng*, 3. boh-koo, 4. kong-be-*ang*, 5. mo-*ang*, 6. per, 7. plü, 8. tro.

We have enough time.	Nous avons assez de temps.
How many rings has she?	Combien de bagues a-t-elle?
They have too much money.	Ils ont trop d'argent.

EXERCISE III.

1. Has he copied as many pages as I? **2.** How much sugar did you put[1] in my coffee? **3.** Do you eat[2] more meat than he? **4.** I have not enough paper for that. **5.** She has put too much salt in the soup.[3] **6.** We have less money than they. **7.** Have you many friends in this town? **8.** Give me a little bread. **9.** That has given me a[4] great deal[4] of trouble.[5] **10.** How many children have they?

---

1. mis, 2. manger, 3. soupe, 4.=*much*, 5. peine.
PRON.—1. mee, 2. ma*hng*-sheh, 3. soop, 5. pain.

94.   **1.** to send, **Envoyer.**

This Verb is quite regular except in the Stem of the *Future* and *Conditional*, thus :

2. sending, *envoyant* | 3. sent, *envoyé* | 4. I send, etc., *j'envoie** tu envoies, il envoie, nous envoyons, vous envoyez, ils envoient.

5. I was sending, etc., *j'envoyais*, etc.	6. I sent, etc., *j'envoyai*, etc.
7. I shall send, etc., j'enverrai, etc.	8. I should send, etc., *j'enverrait*, etc.

9. send, *envoyez* ; let us send, *envoyons* (send thou, *envoie*).

* *y* is changed to *i* whenever no sound follows.

renvoyer, *to send back*, is of course conjugated in the same way.

PRON.—1. and 3. ahng-vo'ah-yeh, 2. ahng-vo'ah-*yahng*, 4. *Singular and third Plural*: ahng-vo'ah ; ahng-vo'ah-yong, etc. 7. sha*hng*-vair-eh.

EXERCISE IV.

1. We are sending a parcel to Paris. **2.** When[1] will you send back my umbrella? **3.** Did you send the tickets to the hotel? **4.** I should send it back at[2] once.[2] **5.** Send us your account as[3] soon as[3] possible.[4] **6.** Do not send the things back. **7.** Will he send it by (the) post[5]?

---

1. quand, 2. tout de suite, 3. aussitôt que, 4. possible, 5. poste.
PRON.—1. ka*hng*, 2. too der switt. 3. oh-se-toh ker, 4. poss-eebl, 5. post

95. *Adverbs* are placed in French *immediately after the Verb*:

She closes the door gently.	Elle ferme doucement la porte.

1. Adverbs never come between the Subject and the Verb as in English.

He rarely reads the paper.	Il lit rarement le journal.

2. Adverbs come before the Past Participle in Compound Tenses.

They have sung well.	Ils ont bien chanté.

3. *aujourd'hui, hier, demain;* adverbs of place (*ici, là,* etc.), and adverbs of more than one word follow the Past Participle.

We have seen him to-day.	Nous l'avons vu aujourd'hui.
I have replied to their letter at once.	J'ai répondu à leur lettre tout de suite.

EXERCISE V.

1. This young-lady[1] learns her lessons well.[2] 2. We always take coffee[3] after (the) dinner. 3. The boys have often[4] seen it. 4. We received a letter from him yesterday. 5. I shall decline[5] the invitation[6] politely. 6. She often sings those songs. 7. My friends have dined[7] already.[8] 8. Has the postman been here this morning? 9. They sent it by return.

1. demoiselle, 2. bien, 3. café, 4. souvent, 5. refuser, 6. invitation, 7. dîner, 8. déjà. PRON.—1. der-mo'ah-zell, 2. be-*ang*, 3. kabff-eh, 4. soo-va*hng*, 5. rer-fü-zeh, 6. *ang*-ve-tahss-e-*ong*, 7. dee-neh, 8. deh-shah.

96. Sometimes two of the Pronouns in rule 42 occur in one sentence. · Both, of course, are placed *before* the Verb, LE or LA or L' or LES always following the other pronoun ; as,

I return it to you.	Je vous le rends.
He does not show it (*f.*) to me.	Il ne me la montre pas.
Do you not give them to us ?	Ne nous les donnez-vous pas ?

97. LUI and LEUR, however, come even after *le, la, les* ; as,

We give it to them.	Nous le leur donnons.
Did you not sell them to her ?	Ne les lui avez-vous pas vendus ?

In the IMPERATIVE their position is as in English.

Lend them to me.	Prêtez-les-moi.

EXERCISE VI.

1. Have you the newspaper? No, our neighbour has not given it back to me. 2. I shall not show them to him. 3. We shall not give it (*f.*) to them. 4. Send it to her. 5. Have they sold them to us? 6. Lend me your knife. 7. I lent it to your friend, but he did not give it back to me. 8. Why did you sell them to her? 9. Bring them to me.

CONVERSATIONAL SENTENCES.

Combien de chevaux a-t-il ?	How many horses has he ?
Je crois, qu'il en¹ a trois.	I believe that he has three.
Combien avez-vous payé votre chapeau ?	How much have you paid for³ your hat ?
Je l'ai payé dix francs.	I have paid ten francs for² it.
Combien de pages avez-vous lues ?	How many pages have you read ? [ing.
J'en ai lu trente ce matin.	I have read thirty this morn-
Qu'avez-vous appris par cœur ?	What have you learnt by heart?
J'ai appris ce que vous m'avez dit d'apprendre.	I have learnt what you told me to learn.

1. **en** (*ahng*) of it, of them, must be used in French when the noun is not expressed, 2. *for* in *pay for* is not translated.

ADDITIONAL EXERCISES.

147.

The French given here is the Adjective Masculine.

1. Correctly *correct*; 2. prettily *joli*; 3. frankly *franc*,¹ fem. *franche*²; 4. rarely *rare*; 5. truly *vrai*; 6. secretly *secret*,³ fem. *secrète*⁴; 7. false *faux*,⁵ fem. *fausse*⁶; 8. sweet *doux*,⁷ fem. *douce*⁸; 9. rapidly; 10. politely; 11. happily *heureux*,⁹ fem. *heureuse*.¹⁰

12. I am taking, thou art not learning, does he not surprise? 13. we understand, do you not undertake? they do not take; 14. I was learning, she was surprising, were they not understanding? 15. we shall undertake, will you take? they will not learn.

148.

1. Enough money; 2. too many children; 3. how much time? 4. many friends; 5. more room; 6. less butter; 7. little bread; 8. as many houses; 9. how many stamps? 10. too much noise; 11. much ink; 12. little water.

13. he is sending, she was sending, we shall send; 14. they would send back, send it back, I am sending it; 15. do you send? did you send? were you not sending? 16. they are sending, were you not sending? will you not send to them?

149.

1. He always smokes cigars. 2. We have often seen him. 3. Have you been there? 4. They found it at once. 5. I sent it by return. 6. They had already written the letter.

7. give it to me, do not give it to me, I will send them to her, will she not send it to us? 8. lend it to him, do not lend them to her; I shall show it to you, will you not show them to us? 9. did you return them to me? I returned them to her, will you bring it to me? we shall not bring them to you.

PRON.— 1. frahng, 2. frahngsh, 3. ser-kray, 4. ser-krate, 5. foh, 6. fohss, 7. doo, 8. dooss, 9. er-rer. 10. er-rerz

TWENTIETH LESSON.

98. If there is a *Negation* in the IMPERATIVE, the **Pronouns of** course *precede* the Verb in the usual order, thus :

Give it to me.	*Donnez*-le-moi.
Do not give it to me.	*Ne* me le *donnez pas.*
Lend them to her.	*Prêtez*-les-lui.
Do not lend them to her.	*Ne* les lui *prêtez pas.*

MOI if coming before the Verb is changed into ME.

EXERCISE I.

1. Here are the matches; give them to him. 2. This is my address; do not show it to them. 3. There is a knife; do not lend it to her. 4. Is this his purse? give it to him. 5. I lent him some money, but he did not return it to me.

99. **1.** to do *or* to make, **Faire.**

2. doing *or* making, faisant	3. done *or* made, **fait**
4. I make *or* I do, *je* **fais**	4. we make *or* do, *nous faisons*
tu fais, il fait	*vous* **FAITES,** *ils* **FONT.**
5. I was making *or* doing, *je faisais*	6. I made *or* did, *je* **fis**
7. I shall make *or* do, *je* ferai	8. I should make, *je ferais*
9. make, *faites* ;	let us make, *faisons* (make thou, *fais*).

PRON.—1. fair, 2. fer-*zahng*, 3. fay, 4. *Sing.* fay ; *Plur.* fer-*zong*, **fayt,** fong, 5. fer-zay, 6. fee, 7. fer-reh, 8. fer-ray, 9. fayt, fer-zong, **fay.**

EXERCISE II.

1. What are you doing? 2. I am doing what you told me. 3. You are always doing the same[1] thing. 4. What has he done this morning? 5. Let us do something[2] else.[2] 6. What was he doing? 7. Have you done that? 8. I shall not do it. 9. Would you do that? 10. These children are making too much noise. 11. Do it at once. 12. We were doing our lessons.[3] 13. How many mistakes[4] have you made (par. 64)?

1. même, 2. autre chose *or* quelque chose d'autre, 3. leçon (*f.*) *or* devoir, 4. faute. PRON.—1. maim, 2. oh-tr shohz, kell-ker shohz doh-tr, 3. ler-*song*, der-vo'ahr, 4. foht.

100. *each* and *every* followed by a Noun are translated CHAQUE.

each one, every one are translated CHACUN, fem. CHACUNE, according to the Noun they refer to. PRON.—shahck ; shahck-*ung*, shahck-*ün*. *each*, when meaning *each one*, is *chacun.*

Each lady, *chaque dame*	Every boy, *chaque garçon*
Each of these ladies	**Chacune** *de ces dames*

101. 1. to receive, Recevoir

2. receiving, recevant	3. received, reçu
4. I receive, je reçois	4. we receive, nous recevons
.tu reçois, il reçoit	vous recevez, ils reçoivent
5. I was receiving, je recevais	6. I received, je reçus
7. I shall receive, je recevrai	8. I should receive, je recevrais
9. receive, recevez; let us receive, recevons (receive thou, reçois).	

PRON.—1. rer-ser-vo'ahr, 2. rer-ser-va*h*ng, 3. and 6. rer-sü, 4. rer-so'ah, rer-ser-vong, rer-ser-veh, rer-so'ahv, 5. rer-ser-vay, 7. rer-ser-vreh, 8. rer-ser-vray.

EXERCISE III.

1. I receive a letter nearly[1] every day. 2. Each of those boys received a prize.[2] 3. You will receive an invitation from the mayor.[3] 4. Receive them politely. 5. Has he not received the money (which) we sent to him last week? 6. How many pounds have you received (64) for this sum[4] ? 7. The king[5] received (p.d.) the deputation.[6] 8. They will not receive the parcel before[7] the[8] day after to-morrow.[8]

1. presque, 2. prix, 3. maire, 4. somme, 5. roi, 6. députation, 7. avant, 8. après-demain. PRON.—1. press-ker, 2. pree, 3. mair, 4. somm, 5. ro'ah, 6. deh-pü-tahss-e-ong, 7. ah-va*h*ng, 8. ah-pray der-ma*n*g.

102. All Verbs ending in evoir are conjugated like recevoir.

The verbs in "evoir" are frequently called the third regular Conjugation. There are only seven, and besides "recevoir" the only one of importance is DEVOIR, to owe (it also means shall, ought to, must). The stem of "devoir" is the letter D.

1. to owe, devoir, 2. owing, devant, 3. owed, dû,*
4. I owe, je dois, ils doivent, 6. I owed, je dus, 7. I shall owe, je devrai.
* There is no accent in the Feminine and Plural forms.

FOR REFERENCE.

4. I owe, etc., je dois, tu dois, il doit; nous devons, vous devez, ils doivent
5. I was owing, etc., je devais, etc.; 8. I should owe, etc., je devrais, etc.
9. owe, devez; let us owe, devons (owe thou, dois).

EXERCISE IV.

1. How much do I owe you ? 2. He owes me twenty francs. 3. You must* shut the door. 4. Shall* I pay his account[1] ? 5. He must* do it. 6. You should* tell the truth.[2] 7. They do not owe him any money. 8. You must* not write to him. 9. Must* we not do our work[3] ? 10. They must not see him.

1. note (f.) or compte (m.), 2. vérité, 3. travail.
PRON.—1. not or kongt, 2. veh-re-teh, 3. trah-vah'e.

* translate must, shall, should by devoir, thus :

shall 1 or must I ? dois-je ? (do'ahsh)	he must not, il ne doit pas
I should not, je ne devrais pas	you should, vous devriez

103. *some, any,* not followed by a Noun, are translated by **en,** which is placed before the Verb like the Pronouns in rule 42.

Have you **any** cigars?	Avez-vous **des** cigares?
Yes, we have **some.**	Oui, nous **EN** avons.

1. en must be used in French, even if not expressed in English, thus:

How many sisters have you?	Combien de sœurs avez-vous?
I have three (*of them*).	J'EN ai trois.

2. *of it, of them, some (any) of it* or *of them,* are also **en:**

Are you not speaking **of it**?	N'EN parlez-vous pas?
Show us **some of them.**	Montrez-nous-EN.

EXERCISE V.

1. Here are some pears; will[1] you have[1] any? 2. There is the money; I spent[2] a shilling of it. 3. He brought his sketches[3]; he has shown me two (of them). 4. How many rings does she wear? 5. She wears three. 6. What is the colour of it? 7. What was the price of them? 8. What did she say of them? 9. Here is the pepper[4]; I have taken some of it.

1. voulez-vous, 2. dépenser, 3. croquis, 4. poivre.

PRON.—1. voo-leh voo, 2. deh-p*ahng*-seh, 3. kro-ke, 4. po'ah-vr.

104. *there, to it, to them,* are translated by **y,** which is put before the Verb, like the Pronouns in Rule 42.

(*there,* if pointing out something, is translated *là*).

Is he **there**?	Y est-il?
We shall add this *to them.*	Nous Y ajouterons ceci.
Add this **to it.**	Ajoutez-y ceci.

1. *y* and *en* follow the Pronouns which come before the Verb.
2. *en* comes last if *y* and *en* occur together.

We shall send *some there.*	Nous **y en** enverrons.
Add some to it. *Ajoutez-y-en.*	Give me some. *Donnez-m'en.*
	(instead of *moi en*).

3. y must be added, whenever it does not alter the sense.

Was he at the theatre? Yes, he was. | Etait-il au théâtre? Oui, il **y** était.

EXERCISE VI.

1. Did you put any ink in it? 2. Yes, I have put some in (it). 3. Have you been to Paris[1]? 4. Yes, I have (been there). 5. Did you eat some apples? 6. No, there are none (=it has not any of them there). 7. Have you put any oil[2] in the salad[3]? 8. I shall add[4] some to it.

1. Paris, 2. huile, 3. salade, 4. ajouter.

PRON.—1. pah-re, 2. weel, 3. sah-lahdd, 4. ah-**shoo-teh.**

CONVERSATIONAL SENTENCES.

Y[1] a-t-il[1] loin[2] d'ici au parc?	Is it far from here to the park?
Il y a à[3] peu près[3] dix minutes.	It is about[3] ten minutes.
N'y a-t-il pas assez de place pour nous?	Is there not sufficient room for us?
Non, il n'y a de place que[4] pour quatre.	No, there is only room for four.
Combien[5] de temps[5] y a-t-il que Monsieur X est parti?	How[5] long[5] is it since **Mr. H.** went?
Il n'y a que cinq minutes.	It is only five minutes.

1. literally: *there has it.* PRON.—1. e-ah-till, 2. lo'-*ang*, 3. ah per pray,
4. *ne...que* only, 5. lit *how much of time.*

ADDITIONAL EXERCISES.
150.

1. Ils étaient heureusement absents à ce moment. 2. **Quand me renverrez-vous les journaux que je vous ai prêtés?** 3. Nous les renverrons sans faute demain matin. 4. À qui est ce parapluie? 5. Il est à Guillaume. 6. N'est-il pas à vous?

151.

1. Sell it to me, do not sell it to me; 2. show them to her, do not show them to her; 3. let us give it back to them, do not let us give it back to them; 4. give it to him, do not give it to him; 5. each page, every picture; 7. each of these chairs, every one of my books.

8. he makes it, he was doing, he has not done it, he will do it; 9. we do not make, were you not doing it? 10. we shall not do it, would you not do it? 11. I do, thou wast not making, he did (*p.d.*); 12. we shall not make, would you not make? they have not made; 13. make it, do not do it, let us make it, do not let us do it.

152.

1. We have spoken of it. 2. He will give me some. 3. I will send you some. 4. They do not speak of it. 5. Will you have some?

6. I receive, he does not receive, we are receiving; 7. do you not receive? they receive, the ladies do not receive; 8. I was receiving, she received (*p.d.*), have you not received? 9. we shall receive, would you receive? do not receive them.

153.

1. I must speak to you. 2. Shall I shut the door? 3. Should you not accompany him? 4. We ought to (should) continue. 5. You must do it. 6. Shall (*devoir*) I not receive him?

7. I do not owe, he will not owe, do not owe; 8. shall I not? he ought not to, you should; 9. we used to owe, he will not owe, he owed; 10. I do not owe this money. 11. Does he not owe you twenty francs? 12. You must not speak to him.

TWENTY-FIRST LESSON.

105.   1. to drink, **Boire.**

2. drinking, **buvant**
4. I drink *or* am drinking, *je* **bois,**
            tu bois, il boit
5. I was drinking, *je buvais*
7. I shall drink, *je boirai*

3. drunk, **bu**
4. we drink, *nous* **buvons,**
            vous buvez, ils **boivent**
6. I drank, *je* **bus**
8. I should drink, *je boirais*

9. drink, *buvez* ;   let us drink, *buvons* (drink thou, *bois*).

1. bo'ahr, 2. bü-*vahng*, 3. and 6. bü, 4. bo'ah, bü-*vong*, bü-veh, bo-ahv,
5. bü-vay, 7. bo'ah-reh, 8. bo'ah-ray.

EXERCISE I.

1. I do not drink (any) beer. 2. They do not drink (any) wine. 3. She was drinking her coffee. 4. Do not drink this ; it is not very good. 5. I shall not drink any of it. 6. **Did** you drink any ? 7. We should drink tea and coffee.

---

106. *the whole* or *the whole of the* is translated, *all the.*

ALL MASC. *Sing.* tout, *Plur.* tous ; FEM. *Sing.* toute, *Plur.* **toutes.**
            PRON.—*Masc.* too, *Fem.* toott.

1. the whole, the whole of my, etc. *tout* le, *tout* mon, etc.

The whole town.   *Toute la ville.*
The whole of the book.   *Tout le livre.*

All my friends.   *Tous mes amis.*
All the ladies.   *Toutes les dames.*

2. *all* referring to a Noun in the Plural mentioned before is rendered by **tous** or **toutes.** (PRON.—tooss and toott.)

Where are the ladies ?
All are in this room.
Have you brought the journals ?
Yes, they are all here.

Où sont les dames !
Toutes sont dans cette chambre.
Avez-vous apporté les journaux ?
Oui, ils sont tous ici.

3. **everything** or **all** meaning *everything* is rendered by **tout,**
            which is invariable.

Everything is lost. *Tout est perdu.* | That is all. *C'est tout.*

EXERCISE II.

1. All these stamps are mine. 2. The whole house is full of smoke.[1] 3. Where are your friends ? Are they all here ? 4. Did you invite[2] the ladies ? 5. Yes, I have written to all. 6. Have you found everything ? 7. All his family[3] lives[4] in (=at) Paris. 8. They lost all their money. 9. That is all that (which) I have to ask you. 10. All these rules[5] are useful.[6] 11. Have you read the whole story[7] ? 12. Is this all ?

---

1. fumée, 2. inviter, 3. famille, 4. demeurer, 5. règle, 6. utile, 7. histoire,
PRON.—1. fü-meh, 2. *ang*-ve-teh, 3. fah-mee'e, 4. der-mer-eh, 5. raigl,
6. ü-till, 7. iss-to'ahr.

107.   **1. to be willing to** or **want to, Vouloir.**

2. being willing or wanting, **voulant**	3. been willing or wanted, **voulu**
4. I am willing or want, je **veux**	4. we want, nous **voulons**
tu **veux**, il **veut**	vous voulez, ils **veulent**
5. I was willing, je voulais	6. I wanted, je **voulus**
7. I shall be willing, je **voudrai**	8. I should want, je voudrais

9. IMPERATIVE is regular but seldom used, **veuillez** (will you kindly) being used instead of *voulez.*

PRON.—1. vool-wahr, 2. voo-*lahng*, 3. voo-*lü*, 4. ver, voo-*long*, voo-*leh*, verl, 9. ver'e-yeh.

EXERCISE III.

1. He does not want to* sing. 2. Are you willing to* fetch it? 3. She did not want to* learn it. 4. Will[1] you kindly[1] tell me? 5. I should be willing to* help[2] you. 6. Has he not been willing to* do it? 7. Will you narrate[3] us a story? 8. They do not want to see us. 9. He will be willing to pay you. 10. Are they not willing to help us?

---

1. veuillez, 2. aider, 3. raconter. PRON.—2. ay-deh, 3. rah-*kong*-teh.

     * *to* is part of *vouloir,* and is therefore not translated.

---

108. *Adverbs of Negation* always require *ne* before the Verb, as is shown in the following Examples:

Do you **never** sing?	**Ne** chantez-vous **jamais**?
We have **nothing** for you.	Nous **n'avons rien** pour vous.
I see **nobody** here.	Je **ne** vois **personne** ici.

1. *Personne, rien, jamais,* can come first; of course the *ne* precedes the Verb.

Nobody is here.	**Personne** n'est ici.
Never shall I do that.	**Jamais** je ne ferai cela.

2. Some more examples of Negations are:

She has **only** two friends.	Elle **n'a que** deux amis.
We have **no more** money.	Nous **n'avons plus** d'argent.
He drinks **neither** wine **nor** beer.	Il **ne** boit **ni** vin **ni** bière.

Wine and beer is du vin et de la bière; but after *ni, du* and *de la* are omitted.

EXERCISE IV.

1. He does not drink anything. 2. She never learns her lessons. 3. They had no more of it. 4. We were only three. 5. He is neither old[1] nor young. 6. I shall drink no more. 7. She has never seen me. 8. He is eating neither meat[2] nor fish.[3]

---

     1. vieux, 2. viande, 3. poisson (m.).

     PRON.—1. ve-er, 2. ve-*ahngd*, 3. po'ahss-*anc.*

109.   1. to be able to, (can), **Pouvoir.**

2. being able, **pouvant** | 3. been able, **pu**
4. I am able to or I can, *je* **peux** | 4. we can, *nous* **pouvons**
    tu peux, il peut | *vous pouvez, ils* **peuvent**
5. I was able or could, *je pouvais* | 6. I was able or could, *je pus*
7. I shall be able, *je* **pourrai** | 8. I should be able, *je pourrais*

PRON.—1. poo-vo'ahr, 2. poo-v*ahng*, 3. and 6. pü, 4. per, poo-v*ong*,
poo-veh, pèrv, 5. poo-vay, 7. poorr-eh, 8. poorray.

EXERCISE V.

1. I cannot speak to you to-day. 2. He could (*imp.*†) do it as[1] well as[1] you. 3. I shall be able to* be there before[2] six o'clock. 4. Would you be able to* go there this afternoon[3] ? 5. They cannot drink this tea, because[4] it is too strong.[5] 6. We were not able to* understand his question. 7. Have you not been able to* finish the letter ? 8. I shall not be able to* return the things (the) next[6] week. 9. Can they not come ?

---

1. aussi bien que *see rule 56*, 2. avant, 3. après-midi, 4. parce que, 5. fort, 6. prochain. PRON.—1. qh-se be-*ang* ker, 2. ah-v*ahng*, 3. ah-pray-me-de, 4. pahrss ker, 5. for, 6. pro-sh*ahng*,—*fem.* prochain,
   † In the Past Tense, the IMPERFECT of *vouloir* (Par. 107) and *pouvoir* is more generally used than the Perfect.
   * *to* is part of *pouvoir*, and is therefore not translated.

110. *every*, followed by a Noun, is generally translated by *tous les* (masc.) or *toutes les* (fem.) instead of *chaque*; as,

every day, *tous les jours* | every week, *toutes les semaines*
every year, *tous les ans* | every Monday, *tous les lundis*
        EVERYBODY, EVERYONE, tout le monde.

111. *some*, meaning *a few*, followed by a Noun, is *quelques* :

He bought some (a few) neckties. | *Il a acheté quelques cravates.*
    1. some one or some (ones), *quelqu'un, quelques-uns.*
Some of those girls. | *Quelques-*unes *de ces filles.*
Did you read these books ? | *Avez-vous lu ces livres ?*
I have read some (a few). | *J'en ai lu quelques-*uns

EXERCISE VI.

1. We meet them every Thursday. 2. They see a copy[1] every six months. 3. Everybody was saying so.[2] 4. Some of his friends were here. 5. We met some of the young ladies. 6. I have spent a few shillings. 7. Some one has broken the windows. 8. We have eaten some (a few) apples and (some) pears. 9. Has he not spoken to some of these men ?

---

1. exemplaire, 2.=*it.* PRON.—ex-*ahng*-plair.

CONVERSATIONAL SENTENCES.

Votre voisin est-il Français ?	Non, il est Espagnol, et sa femme est Allemande.
Avez-vous été en Amérique[1] ?	Non, mais nous avons été en Australie.[2]
Votre famille demeure-t-elle à Hambourg[3] ?	Non, elle demeure dans une petite ville d'Italie.[4]
Savez[5]-vous[5] que sa sœur est en Irlande[6] ?	Non, je pensais qu'elle était en Ecosse.[7]
Avez-vous visité tous les musées,[8] les galeries[9] de tableaux, etc. ?	Oui, nous avons visité toute la ville.
Son ami est-il Autrichien[10] ?	Non, je crois qu'il est Russe.[11]
Quelle est la capitale [2] de la France ?	Tout le monde sait[13] cela, c'est Paris.

1. ah-meh-reek, 2. oh-strah-le, 3. *ahng*-boor, 4. e-tah-le, 5. *do you know,*
6. eer-l*ahng*d, 7. eh-koss, *Scotland,* 8. mü-zeh, *museums,* 9. gah-ler-re,
10. oh-tree-she-*ang, Austrian,* 11. rüss, *Russian,* 12. kah-pe-tahll, 13. *knows.*

---o---

ADDITIONAL EXERCISES.
154.

1. All the week ; 2. the whole street ; 3. all the men ; 4. the whole of the lesson ; 5. all his children ; 6. the whole of their money ; 7. all the pictures ; 8. our whole journey[1] ; 9. all the wine ; 10. his whole life.[2]

11. I do not drink, he was drinking, will she drink it ? they would not drink it, do not drink ; 12. drink it, do not drink it, did you not drink it ? they are drinking ; 13. were you drinking ? he drank (*p.d.*); they will not drink, I should not drink it.

155.

1. Has he drunk all ? 2. I shall never learn that. 3. She did not buy anything. 4. We saw nobody. 5. I shall not give him more (of them). 6. Nobody asked me (it).

7. he is not willing to, I was not willing to, they did not want to (*p.d.*), we shall not want to ; 8. I should want to ; are they willing to ? she will not want to, will you kindly (*imperative*). 9. Do you want to ? were you willing to ? will you be willing to ? would you be willing to ?

156.

1. Every Sunday ; 2. every afternoon ; 3. some pens ; 4. some of these apples ; 5. a few pages ; 6. every gentleman ; 7. some of those books. 8. That is all. 9. Have you taken any (some) of these stamps ? 10. She bought a few pounds of fish.

11. I cannot, I was not able ; will he not be able ? we should be able ; 12. can you ? could you not ? will you be able ? would you not be able ? 13. they cannot, they were able, will they be able ? would they not be able ?

---

1. voyage (m.), 2. vie. PRON.—1. vo'ah-yahsh, 2. vee.

TWENTY-SECOND LESSON.

112.   1. to know, Savoir.

2. knowing, sachant	3. known, su
4. I know, *je* sais	4. we know, *nous* SAVons
tu sais, il sait	*vous savez, ils savent*
5. I knew, *je* savais	6. I knew, *je* sus
7. I shall know, *je* saurai	8. I should know, *je* saurais

9. know, sachez; let us know, sachons (know thou, *sache*).

PRON.—1. sah-vo'ahr, 2. sah-sha*hng*, 3. sü, 4. say, sah-v*ong*, sah-veh, sahv, 5. sah-vay, 6. sü, 7. soh-reh, 8. soh-ray, 9. sah-sheh, sah-sh*ong*.

Notice that the STEM in the *Plur. Present* and in the *Imperfect* is not *sach*, but *sav* by exception; in the *Imperative* the stem is *sach*.

EXERCISE I.

1. I know it. **2.** We used always to know our lesson. **3.** You will know it to-morrow. **4.** Don't you know where he lives? **5.** If I knew that he had done that, I should give (to) him a box[1] on the ear.[1] **6.** Does he not know the cab-man's[2] number[3]? **7.** He knew it, but he has forgotten it.

---

1. soufflet (literally, a blow on the cheek), **2.** cocher, **3.** numéro.
PRON.—1. soo-flay, 2. ko-sheh, 3. nü-meh-ro.

As explained in Rule 16, the Feminine of Adjectives is formed by adding **e** to the Masculine; but those ending in **e** do not change.

113. Some Adjectives undergo a further change, as follows:

		Masc.		Fem.
(a) Final *f* is changed to ve	... ...	*vif*	lively	vive
(b) „ *x* „ se	... ...	*jaloux*	jealous	jalouse
(c) „ *er, et* „ ère, ète	... ...	{ *cher*	dear	chère
		{ *secret*	secret	secrète
(d) Adjectives ending in eil, el, en *double*		*pareil,*	like	pareille
the final consonant and add e		*italien*	Italian	italienne
(e) Monosyllables ending in s or t also		*las*	tired	lasse
double the final consonant and add e		*net*	clean	nette

PRON.—(a) vif, veev; (b) shah-loo, shah-looz; (c) shair, shair; ser-kray, ser-krayt; (d) pah-ray'e, pah-ray'e; e-tah-le-*ang*, e-tah-le-enn; (e) lah, lahss; nay (or nett).

EXERCISE II.

Give the Feminine of the following words:

1. attentive *attentif*; **2.** Russian *russe*; **3.** complete *complet*; **4.** first *premier*; **5.** green *vert*; **6.** happy *heureux*; **7.** low *bas*; **8.** cruel *cruel*; **9.** Austrian *autrichien*; **10.** foolish *sot*.

PRON.—1. ah-ta*hng*-tif, 2. rüss, 3. kong-play, 4. prer-me-eh, 5. vair, 6. er-rer, 7. bah, 8. krü-ell, 9. oh-tree-she-*ang*, 10. so.

The following irregular feminines should be learned at once. The remainder are less important, and will be given in the Appendix.

Masc.	Fem.	Masc.	Fem.	Masc.	Fem.
blanc white	blanche	*faux* false	fausse	*long* long	longue
doux sweet	douce	*frais* fresh	fraîche	*public* public	publique
épais thick	épaisse	*franc* frank	franche	*sec* dry	sèche

114.   1. to hold, Tenir.

2. holding, tenant

3. held, tenu

4. I hold *or* I am holding, *je tiens tu tiens, il tient*

4. we hold, *nous tenons vous tenez, ils tiennent*

5. I was holding, *je tenais*

6. I held, *je tins, tu tins,* etc.

7. I shall hold, *je tiendrai*

8. I should hold, *je tiendrais*

9. hold, *tenez ;* let us hold, *tenons* (hold thou, *tiens*).

PRON.—1. ter-neer, 2. ter-*nahng*, 3. ter-nü, 4. te-*ang*, ter-*nong*, tėr-neh, te-enn, 5. ter-nay, 6. *tang*, *tang*, 7. te-*ang*-dreh, 8. te-*ang*-dray.

All compounds of *tenir* are conjugated in the same way, as, to contain, *contenir ;* to belong, *appartenir*.

EXERCISE III.

1. To whom does this belong? 2. This page contains all the information.[1] 3. The sailor[2] was holding the cable.[3] 4. These things used-to-belong to our neighbour. 5. Hold this, please. 6. These boxes contain nothing.

---

1. information,   2 matelot,   3 câble (*masc.*)
PRON.—1. *ang*-for-mah-se-*ong*, 2. mah-ter-lo, 3 kahbl.

---

115. VENIR (*to come*) is conjugated exactly like *tenir*. t being changed to v, thus :

1. to come, venir ;   2. coming, venant ;   3. come, venu.
4. I come, *je viens, ils viennent* ; 6. I came, *je vins, nous vînmes*, etc. ;
7 I shall come, *je viendrai*. PERFECT : I have come, *je suis venu*.

FOR REFERENCE.

4. *I am coming*, etc., je viens, tu viens, il vient ; nous venons, vous venez, ils viennent. 5. *I was coming, etc.*, je venais, etc. 8. *I should come, etc.*, je viendrais. 9. *come*, venez ; *let us come*, venons (*come thou*, viens).
Like *venir* are ; to become, *devenir* ; to come back, *revenir* ; to suit, *convenir*.

EXERCISE IV.

1. He will come back to-morrow. 2. Come here. 3. They used-to-come every day. 4. He comes from Paris. 5. Where do they come from[1] ? 6. I shall not come alone. 7. We should come with you, if we had (the) time. 8. He came (*p. def.*) at the end[2] of (the) last[b] month.[a] 9. That does not suit me.

---

1. Translate : From where do they come ?   2 fin (**fem.**).   PRON.—*fang*.

116. *être* (TO BE) is used in French before the following PAST PARTICIPLES instead of the English TO HAVE ; as,

1. allé gone, arrivé arrived, devenu become.
2. entré entered, parti gone away, revenu come back.
3. sorti gone out, resté remained, tombé fallen, venu come.

PRON.—1. ahll-eh, ahr-ee-veh, der-ver-nü ; 2. ahng-treh, pahr-te, rer-ver-nü ; 3. sor-te, ress-teh, *tong*-beh, ver-nü.

PAST PARTICIPLES following *to be* take the same Gender and Number as their Subject ; as,

She has not arrived.	*Elle n'est pas* arrivée.
Did the men come ?	*Les hommes sont-ils* venus ?
My sisters will have gone out.	*Mes sœurs seront* sorties.

EXERCISE V.

1. They have gone to a ball.[1] 2. She did not enter. 3. Have the girls gone away ? 4. Nobody had come. 5. The huntsmen[2] will have come back. 6. She would have remained with her aunt. 7. Has she not fallen down[3] the staircase[4] ? 8. Our friends (have) remained all the week.

---

1. bal, 2. chasseur, 3. en bas de, 4. escalier.
PRON.—1. bahll, 2. shahss-er, 3. *ahng* bah der, 4. ess-kahll-e-eh.

117. The PLURAL OF ADJECTIVES is formed from the Singular of the same Gender in the same way as the Plural of Nouns (see Rule 7), thus :

	Masc. Sing.	Fem. Sing.	Masc. Plur.	Fem. Plur.
small	petit	petite	petits	petites
bad	mauvais	mauvaise	mauvais	mauvaises
happy	heureux	heureuse	heureux	heureuses
legal	légal	légale	légaux	légales
tired	las	lasse	las	lasses
beautiful	beau	belle	beaux	belles

EXCEPTION.—*bleu* (blue) makes *bleus, bleues,* in the Plural.

EXERCISE VI.

1. They were reading (some) French newspapers. 2. The pictures (which) he bought (Rule 64) are very beautiful. 3. What beautiful blue flowers ! 4. My cousins were not present. 5. What large hands he has ! 6. I should[1] like to[1] see some black gloves. Have you any in[2] stock[2] ? 7. These rules are very difficult to (à) understand.

---

1. voudrais, 2. en magasin. PRON.—1. voo-dray, 2. *ahng* mah-gah-*zang*.

CONVERSATIONAL SENTENCES.

De qui avez-vous obtenu ces renseignements ?	Du chef[1] de gare[1] lui-même.[2]
Que contient cette malle[3] ?	Des effets[4] à mon usage.[5]
Ces bagages vous appartiennent-ils ? [soir ?	Non, ils appartiennent à cette dame.
Viendrez-vous nous voir demain	Oui, si le temps est beau.
Qu'est devenu votre ami, Monsieur F. ?	Il est parti aux États-Unis[6] d'Amérique.
Êtes-vous content de votre nouvelle maison ?	Oui, elle me convient beaucoup.

1. station-master, 2. himself, 3. trunk, 4. things, 5. use, 6. United States.

---o---

ADDITIONAL EXERCISES.

157.

1. This watch is very dear. 2. She is very jealous. 3. Is your sister not happy? 4. It is the first[a] street.[b] 5. These two houses are alike *(pareil)*. 6. Is not this lady Italian ? 7. That was a foolish[a] *affaire.*[b*] 8. The colour of-it is green.

9. I know, I did not know, I have known ; 10. he knew *(p.d.)*, she will not know, would he know it ? 11. we do not know, did you know *(impf.)* ? they will know it ; 12. he will not know, would you know ? they have known.

158.

1. a white hand ; 2. a sweet apple ; 3. (the) last week ; 4. (some) fresh water ; 5. a long[a] street[b] ; 6. (the) public *opinion* ; 7. a complete page ; 8. an Austrian town ; 9. a cruel *action* ; 10. a lively *conversation*; 11. a secret *correspondance* ; 12. a complete *édition.*

13. he does not hold, I was holding, we held *(p.d.)* ; 14. have you been-holding (=held) ? I shall not hold, would they not hold ? 15. let us hold, do not hold it, I am holding them ; 16. it contains, it belonged, did it not contain ?

159.

1. She did not come-in. 2. Why did they *(f.)* not come ? 3. They will have gone out. 4. They had not arrived. 5. I should have gone out. 6. The men have not come back.

7. is he coming ? we were not coming, have they not come ? 8. she becomes, we shall not come back, would they not come ? 9. they are not coming, were you coming ? do not come ; 10. come with me, has he become ? have they not come back ? do they not come ?

160.

Give the Fem. Sing., Masc. Plural and Fem. Plural of :
French, Russian, Austrian, lively, unhappy *(malheureux)*, last, discreet *(discret)*, similar *(pareil)*, low *(bas)*, foolish, white, dry.

---

*The French word only is given, when nearly the same as in English.

TWENTY-THIRD LESSON.

118.   1. to go, **Aller.**

2. going, **allant**	3. gone, **allé**
4. I am going, *je* **vais**	4. we go, *nous allons*
tu **vas,** *il* **va**	*vous allez, ils* **vont**
5. I was going, *j'allais*	6. I went, *j'allai*
7. I shall go, *j'irai*	8. I should go, *j'irais*

9. go, *allez* ; let us go, *allons* (go thou, *va*).

    PERFECT TENSE : I *have* gone, *je* **suis** *allé* or *allée.*

PRON.—1. ahll-eh, 2. ahll-*ahng*, 3. ahll-eh, 4. vay, vah, ahll-*ong*, ahll-eh, *v*ong, 5. shahll-ay, 6. shahll-eh, 7. shee-reh, 8. shee-ray.

I am about to or *I am going to,* etc., are rendered by *je vais,* etc., *to* not being translated ; as,

He *is going to* write to him.	*Il* **va** *lui écrire.*
We're they not *going to* play ?	*N'*allaient-*ils pas jouer ?*

EXERCISE I.

1. Where are you going ? **2.** He was going to the theatre. **3.** We shall go to Paris to-morrow. **4.** Why does he not go with you ? **5.** He will not go alone. **6.** Let us go together. **7.** Do not go in the street. **8.** Are these men going to the market? **9.** They are not going to sing. **10.** We are about to commence. **11.** I am not going to buy it. **12.** She was not going to do it.

119. *myself, ourselves,* etc., following a Verb in English, **are** translated in French like *me, us,* etc. (see Rule 42).

    himself, herself, themselves are translated by **se (or s').**

These words precede the Verb in the usual way.

I flatter **myself**	*Je* me *flatte*
He does not warm **himself**	*Il ne* se *chauffe pas*
We were amusing **ourselves**	*Nous* nous *amusions*
Were they not dressing **themselves?**	*Ne* s'*habillaient-ils pas ?*
Do not flatter **yourself**	*Ne* vous *flattez pas.*

EXERCISE II.

1. Warm yourself in this room. **2.** He is flattering **himself** too much. **3.** Why are you not dressing yourself ? **4.** Are they not amusing themselves ? **5.** Does he not dress himself (in) the evening ? **6.** Amuse yourself well at the theatre. **7.** Were they not warming themselves ? **8.** We were not flattering ourselves. **9.** Do not warm yourselves too much. **10.** Were the ladies not dressing themselves ?

120. When **shall** or **will** comes before a Verb, the FUTURE is used when the meaning is future, i.e. is equivalent to *I am going to*, etc.; as,

I shall not speak to them.	Je ne leur parlerai pas.
Will they come to-morrow ?	Viendront-ils demain ?

121. When **should** or **would** comes before a Verb, the CONDITIONAL is used when meaning that something would happen *conditionally on something else happening* ; as,

I should not accompany him.	Je ne l'accompagnerais pas.
Would they arrive in time ?	Arriveraient-ils à temps ?

122. When **shall** and **should** express *compulsion* or *duty*, i.e., are equivalent to *must, am to, have to, ought to*, etc., DEVOIR must be used (see page 87) ; as,

Shall I shut the window ?	Dois-je fermer la fenêtre ?
They shall (=must) not do it.	Ils ne doivent pas le faire.
She should (=ought to) have it.	Elle devrait l'avoir.

123. When **will** and **would** mean *to want to, to intend to, to be willing to*, VOULOIR must be used ; as,

Will he (is he willing to) sell it ?	Veut-il le vendre ?
They would not (=did not want to)	Ils n'ont pas voulu venir.
I will not give it to you. [come.	Je ne veux pas vous le donner.

REMARKS.

As *shall, will, should, would* do not always convey the same idea, the exact meaning must be known before the phrase can be translated correctly.

Shall and *should* are generally employed in the first person (i.e. with *I* and *we*) ; *will* and *would* in the other persons. This rule, however, is often broken, especially in questions.

When *shall, will* are FUTURE, and *should, would* CONDITIONAL, they are very seldom emphasized.

EXERCISE III.

(*Italics* indicate that the word is emphasized).

1. She *will* not accompany us. 2. You *should* not say that 3. We shall wash ourselves. 4. The children *would* not amuse themselves. 5. *Shall* they not inform him ? 6. *Should* we not accompany her home ? 7. They would not come without informing us of-it. 8. They *would* not come with us. 9. I *will* not speak to him. 10. *Shall* I go there without you ? 11. She *shall* not keep[1] that. 12. I *will* write it myself.[2] 13. They will not find him at home. 14. He *would* not apologise.[3]

---

1. garder. 2. moi-même. 3. s'excuser.
PRON.—1. gahr-deh, 2. mo'ah-mame, 3. sex-kü-zeh.

124. 1. to run, Courir.

2. running, courant | 3. run, couru
4. I am running, *je* cours | 4. we run, *nous* courons
    tu cours, il court | *vous courez, ils courent*
5. I was running, *je courais* | 6. I ran, *je* courus
7. I shall run, *je* courrai | 8. I should run, *je* courrais
9. run, *courez* ; let us run, *courons* (run thou, *cours*).

PRON.—1. koo-reer, 2. koo-*rahng*, 3. koo-rü, 4. koohr, koo-*rong*, koo-reh, koohr, 5. koo-ray, 6. koo-rü, 7. koor-reh, 8. koor-ray, 9. koo-reh, koo-*rong*, koohr.

EXERCISE IV.

1. The horses are running. 2. Do not run so[1] fast.[2] 3. He was running the whole time. 4. Let us run after[3] them. 5. Why are you running? 6. The boys will run this evening. 7. Why are you always running? 8. I should not run, if I were in[4] your place.[4]

1. si, 2. vite, 3. après, 4. à votre place.
PRON.—1. se, 2. vitt, 3. ah-pray, 4. ah votr plahss.

Verbs followed by myself, herself, etc., are called REFLECTIVE, because the action done reflects back on to the doer; thus,

He amuses *himself* ('*He* amuses *me*' is not reflective).

125. The COMPOUND TENSES of *Reflective Verbs* are formed in French with *être*.

The *Past Participle* therefore takes the Gender and Number of the word it refers to; as,

Has she amused herself? | S'est-elle amuséE?
We (*m.*) have warmed ourselves. | Nous nous sommes chaufféS.
The ladies had not yet dressed themselves. | Les dames ne s'étaient pas encore habilléES.

It will he noticed that the Verb "to have" is translated by the corresponding part of "to be."

EXERCISE V.

1. We have not amused ourselves. 2. They would have dressed themselves. 3. The boys had not washed[1] themselves. 4. H s she not been-flattering herself? 5. They have established[2] themselves. 6. He had not been-hurrying[3] himself.[3] 7. Why has she not dressed herself? 8. The girls will not have dressed themselves in time.

1. laver, 2. établir, 3. se dépêcher.
PRON.—1 lah-veh, 2. eh-tah-bleer, 3. ser deh-pay-sheh.

CONVERSATIONAL SENTENCES.

Comment[1] ! vous n'avez pas encore répondu à sa lettre ?

Pas encore ; mais je vais le faire tout[2] de suite.[2]

Pourquoi vous êtes-vous habillé si[3] élégamment[4] ?

Je vais à une soirée[5] qui commence à huit heures.

Quand pensez-vous aller à la campagne[6] ?

Probablement la semaine prochaine, s'il fait beau temps.[7]

Vous (*f. plur.*) êtes-vous bien amusées au théâtre hier soir ?

Oui, assez bien ; on[8] jouait une très belle comédie. [Et vous ?

Comment vous portez[9]-vous ?

Merci, je me porte très bien ;

1. *how* or *what*, 2. at once, 3. so, 4. elegantly, 5. evening party, 6. country, 7. weather, 8. one, people, they, 9. *se porter* to be. PRON.—1. kom-*ahng*, 2. too der switt, 3. see, 4. eh-leh-gahmm-*ahng*, 5. so'ah-reh, 6. *kahng*-pahn-yer, 7. t*ahng*, 8. *ong*, 9. por-teh.

---o---

ADDITIONAL EXERCISES.
161.

1. I am going to speak to him. **2.** He was about to[1] go[2] away.[2] **3.** They were not going to buy it. **4.** Are you not about to go[3] out[3] ? **5.** We were going to punish them. **6.** Is he not going to sing ?

7. I am not going to, art thou going to ? he is going to ; 8. is she not going to ? we are going to, are you not going to ? 9. they are going to, are they (*f.*) not going to ? I was about to ; 10. she was not about to, are they not about to ? they were not going to.

162.

1. I was warming myself before[4] the fire. **2.** They are flattering themselves too[5] soon.[5] **3.** You will enjoy (amuse) yourself. **4.** We shall not excuse ourselves. **5.** Wash yourself. **6.** Are the boys dressing themselves ?

7. I wash myself, dost thou wash thyself ? he does not wash himself : 8. is she washing herself ? we are washing ourselves, do you not wash yourself ? 9. the children are washing themselves, does not your brother wash himself ? 10. I was washing myself, he was not flattering himself, was she amusing herself ?

163.

1. I shall run faster[6] than you. **2.** They would run as[7] long[7] as we. **3.** Is he running after me ? **4.** Let us run a little[8] faster. **5.** Do not run all the time. **6.** The horses were running as fast as possible.[9]

7. I shall amuse myself, will he not dress himself ? we shall flatter ourselves ; 8. will you not warm yourself ? they will not dress themselves ; 9. I should warm myself, would he not enjoy himself ? you would not flatter yourself.

---

1. *to* in *I am going to* or *I am about to* is not translated ; 2. partir, 3. sortir, 4. devant, 5. trop tôt, 6. vite, 7. aussi longtemps, 8. peu, 9. possible

TWENTY-FOURTH LESSON.

126. All the verbs of importance *which are very irregular* have now been given. To conjugate the remainder, it is sufficient to learn the following forms :

Infinitive.	Pres. Part.	Past Part.	Present.	Past Def.
to follow, suivre	suivant	suivi	je suis	suivis
to suffice, suffire	suffisant	suffi	je suffis	suffis
to laugh, rire	riant	ri	je ris	ris

PRON.—swee-vr, swe-*vahng*, swe-ve, swee, sü-fe-*zahng*, sü-fe, sü-fe, reer, re-*ahng*, ree, ree.

By learning the above parts, and the FUTURE STEM when *irregular,* the rest of the Verb can always be formed (see Rules on pages 74, 76).

RULE ON FORMATION OF PRESENT TENSE (*repeated*).

If the *First Person Singular* ends in s, the *Second* also ends in s, and the *Third* in t. The Stem of the *Plural* is found by taking ant from the *Present Participle.*

4. I follow, *je suis, tu suis, il suit*
5. I was following, *je suivais*
7. I shall follow, *je suivrai*

4. we follow, *nous suivons, vous suivez, ils suivent*
8. I should follow, *je suivrais*

EXERCISE I.

1. Why are you laughing? 2. He does not follow us. 3. It did not suffice (*imperf.*). 4. Do not laugh so loud (*haut*). 5. I do not follow you. 6. That will not suffice. 7. He will laugh if he sees that. 8. Has he been following you?

---

127. Many Verbs are *reflective* in French without being so in English, thus :

1. *to dispute,* quarrel, se disputer; 2. *to be* (in health) se porter;
3. *to rest,* se reposer; 4. *to exclaim,* cry out, s'écrier.

PRON.—1. ser diss-pü-teh, 2. ser por-teh, 3. ser rer-po-zeh, 4. seh-kre-eh.

They are not disputing.
How are you? *or* How do you do?
She has rested.

Ils ne se disputent pas.
Comment vous portez-vous?
Elle s'est reposée.

EXERCISE II.

1. They are quarrelling every day. 2. You rest too often. 3. Why did you cry out? 4. He is not well. 5. She did not quarrel with her sister. 6. Have you (*plur.*) rested? 7. I am not well. 8. We are very well. 9. How is your cousin to-day? 10. The soldiers were fighting.[1] 11. They *would* not fight. 12. We must apologize.[2]

---

1. to fight, *se battre,* 2. to apologize, *s'excuser.*
PRON.—1. ser bahtt-r, 2. sex-kü-zeh.

128. **to** *between two Verbs* is generally translated **de**, unless *to* means *in order to*, when it is rendered by *pour*; as,

I advise you to speak to him.	*Je vous conseille de lui parler.*
We did it (in order) to satisfy them.	*Nous l'avons fait pour les satisfaire.*

EXERCISE III.

1. I forgot to write to him. 2. We waited at the station (in order) to meet them. 3. I regretted[1] having (=to have) spoken. 4. He said so[2] to calm[3] you. 5. She tries[4] to help[5] me. 6. They are studying to pass an examination.[6] 7. We work[7] to earn[8] money. 8. He recollects[9] having (=to have) written this.

---

1. regretter, 2.=it, 3. calmer, 4. essayer, 5. aider, 6. examen, 7. travailler, 8. gagner, 9. se souvenir. PRON.—1. rer-grett-eh, 3. kahll-meh, 4. ess-ay-yeh, 5. ay-deh. 6. eg-zah-m*ang*, 7. trah-vah'e-yeh, 8. gahnn-yeh, 9. soo-ver-neer.

---

129. After certain Verbs (for complete list, see 'Hugo's French Verbs Simplified'), **to** must be translated **à** instead of *de*. The most important of these Verbs are:

1..aimer, to like,	2. apprendre, to learn,
3. avoir, to have,	4. inviter, to invite.

PRON.—1. ay-meh, 2. ah-pr*ah*ngdr, 3. ah-vo'ahr, 4. *ang*-vee-teh.

I like to do that.	*J'aime à faire cela.*
He has nothing to say.	*Il n'a rien à dire.*

---

130. **to** is not translated at all, after certain Verbs of an auxiliary nature (for complete list, see 'French Verbs Simplified'); as,

1. aller, to go. 2. devoir, must *or* ought to. 3. laisser, let *or* allow to. 4. pouvoir, can *or* be able to. 5. vouloir, want to *or* be willing to.

They wanted to see you.	*Ils voulaient vous voir.*
Is he not able to come?	*Ne peut-il pas venir?*

EXERCISE IV.

1. He is learning to write. 2. Are you not going to commence? 3. They invited us to come with them. 4. Allow me to pass. 5. We have to obey. 6. Were they not able to help you? 7. The soldiers were not able to cross[1] the river. 8. Have they not to do this? 9. The ladies will want to dance. 10. Do you like skating (=to skate)[2]? 11. Have you nothing to do? 12. They must try it.

---

1. traverser, 2. patiner. PRON.—1. trah-vair-seh, 2. pah-te-neh.

131.	Infinitive.	Pres. Part.	Past Part.	Present.	Past Def.
to feel	sentir	sentant	senti	je sens	je sentis
to go out	sortir	sortant	sorti	je sors	je sortis
to go away	partir	partant	parti	je pars	je partis
to sleep	dormir	dormant	dormi	je dors	je dormis
to serve	servir	servant	servi	je sers	je servis
to lie	mentir	mentant	menti	je mens	je mentis

EXERCISE .V.

1. Do you feel the draught[1] ? 2. She does not feel (herself) well. 3. Why did you (*pl.*) go out without me ? 4. They will go away before six o'clock.[2] 5. Has your cousin (*f.*) gone out ? 6. At what time[2] will she come[3] back[3] ? 7. You will feel it to-morrow. 8. Let us go out together. 9. They are serving in the same regiment. 10. He does not sleep well. 11. Do not lie. 12. The dinner[4] was served upstairs.[5]

1. courant d'air, 2. heure, 3. revenir, 4. dîner, 5. en haut.

PRON.—1. koo-*rahng* dair, 2. er, 3. rer-ver-neer, 4. dee-neh, 5. *ahng* ho.

132. The Preposition *chez* means literally *at* or *to the place of*, thus:

at my place,	chez moi	at my aunt's,	chez ma tante
at his house,	chez lui	to the doctor's,	chez le docteur
to their place,	chez eux	at our house,	chez nous
	from my butcher's,	de chez mon boucher.	

home, *at home* is also frequently rendered by *chez moi*, *chez lui*, etc., instead of *à la maison*.

She is not at home.	Elle n'est pas chez elle.
Are they at home ?	Sont-ils chez eux ?
They are going home.	Ils vont chez eux (*or* à la maison).

133. TO, AT, IN before the name of a town, village, or place, are translated by à, and before the name of a country by en ; as,

He lives in Paris.	Il demeure à Paris.
Are you going to London ?	Allez-vous à Londres ?
She is in France.	Elle est en France.
They are going to Switzerland.	Ils vont en Suisse.

EXERCISE VI.

1. He is going home. 2. She was coming out of the butcher's. 3. He is writing a letter to Germany. 4. Are they not in Paris ? 5. We met them at our aunt's. 6. Is he not at home ? 7. She was not at home ; she was at her neighbours'. 8. We met them as[1] they were coming[2] away[2] from home.

1. comme, 2. sortir, PRON.—1. komm, 2. sor-teer.

CONVERSATIONAL SENTENCES.

Quelle méthode suivez-vous pour apprendre cette science ?

Je suis la méthode que mon professeur m'a recommandée.

Cet argent vous suffira-t-il pour faire vos achats[1] ?

Je pense en avoir assez pour ce que j'ai à acheter.

Pourquoi ces hommes se disputent-ils ?

Parce qu'ils ont trop bu.

N'oubliez pas de venir nous voir le[2] plus tôt[2] possible.

J'essayerai[3] de venir mercredi prochain dans l'après-midi.[4]

Allez-vous partir bientôt[5] pour le continent ?

Je compte[6] y aller dans une quinzaine[7] de jours.[7]

1. purchases, 2. the most soon=as soon as, 3. (to) try, 4. afternoon, 5. soon, 6. count—intend, 7. fifteen of days=fortnight.

---o---

ADDITIONAL EXERCISES.

164.

1. They were following their friends. **2.** Rest a little. **3.** Why do you laugh so loud ? **4.** How is (*se porter*) your friend ? **5.** Do not apologize (=excuse yourself). **6.** I do not follow him.

7. I follow, he does not follow, do we follow ? **8.** you do not follow, do the men not follow ? she was following ; **9.** he followed (*p. def.*), he will not follow, would he follow ? **10.** follow me, do not follow us, let us follow them ; **11.** it suffices, it did not suffice (*imperf.*), it will suffice ; **12.** are you laughing ? were you not laughing ? you would not laugh.

165.

1. I shall try to write to-day. **2.** We did it (in order to) help them. **3.** Do you like to work ? **4.** Are you willing to accompany us ? **5.** We have nothing to do. **6.** She was singing in order to amuse us.

7. I go out, thou wast going out, he will not go out ; **8.** should we go out ? you (*plur.*) have not gone out, let us go out ; **9.** do not go away, is he going away ? they were going away ; **10.** I shall not go away, would she not go away ? she has not gone away ; **11.** is she sleeping ? do not sleep, have they been sleeping? **12.** he will not sleep, the children were not sleeping, let us sleep.

166.

1. Is he not at home ? **2.** We were at their place. **3.** We are not going home. **4.** He was at my brother's. **5.** Do you live in France or in Germany ? **6.** We have a house in Paris.

7. Are you going to Switzerland ? **8.** He sent a parcel to England. **9.** They went away to Germany. **10.** she serves, are you serving ? I was serving ; **11.** we have served have you not served ? they will serve ; **12.** do you not feel ? have you felt it? I should not feel it.

TWENTY-FIFTH LESSON.

134. Notice the following peculiarities of Verbs ending in *er :*

(*a*) those in ger and cer change g into ge, and c into ç (cedilla), before a termination beginning with *a, o,* or *u.*

This is done to preserve the same sound as in the Infinitive.

(*b*) e and é are changed into è, if occurring before a **single** consonant followed by mute *e, es,* or *ent.*

juger we judge, *nous jugeons*	*commencer* he began, *il commença*
acheter I buy, *j'achète*	*espérer* he hopes, *il espère*

E is always mute except in the termination EZ, and in the Infinitive termination ER.

(*c*) Some Verbs in ler and ter double the l and t before mute *e, es, ent.* The most important are :

épeler to spell, **appeler** to call, **rappeler** to recall, **renouveler** to renew, **jeter** to throw, **cacheter** to seal, **feuilleter** to turn over the leaves.

(*d*) Verbs in yer generally change y to i before mute *e, es, ent.*

épeler he spells, *il épelle*	*jeter* they throw, *ils jettent*
payer I pay, *je paie* or *paye*	*essuyer* he wipes, *il essuie*

EXERCISE I.

1. He commences, we do not commence ; 2. do you judge ? they were judging ; 3. we buy, he does not buy ; 4. has he led[1] ? will you lead ? 5. he was repeating,[2] does he not repeat ? 6. he will not pay you, do not pay him ; 7. He is sealing his letter. 8. They will renew their order.[3]

1. mener, 2 répéter, 3. commande. PRON.—1. mer-neh, 2. reh-peh-teh, 3. kom-*ahng*d.

135. The following Verbs in *frir* and *vrir* are all conjugated alike :

Infinitive.	Pres. Part.	Past Part.	Present.	Past Def.
to cover	couvrir	couvrant	couvert	je couvre*	je couvris
to offer	offrir	offrant	offert	j'offre	j'offris
to open	ouvrir	ouvrant	ouvert	j'ouvre	j'ouvris
to suffer	souffrir	souffrant	souffert	je souffre	je souffris

to discover, *découvrir*, is conjugated like *couvrir.*

PRON.—koo-vreer, koo-vr*ahng*, koo-vair, off-reer, oo-vreer, soo-freer, etc.
* If the First Person ends in E, the Second ends in ES, and the Third in E.

EXERCISE II.

1. Do you open the shop[1] at eight o'clock ? 2. He is suffering a[2] great deal.[2] 3. She was offering me a chair. 4. What have you discovered ? 5. Open the door. 6. Do not cover the things. 7. Has he offered you anything[3] ? 8. I shall open the doors and (the) windows.

1. boutique, 2. beaucoup, 3. quelque chose.

136. IMPERSONAL VERBS and expressions are only used in the *Third Person Singular* ; as,

It is raining, il pleut	It is not necessary, il ne faut pas
It is fine, il fait beau	It was cold, il faisait froid

137. THERE IS, *there are*, etc., are translated by *it there has*, etc.

There is, there are, il y a	there was, there were, il y avait
there will be, il y aura	there would be, il y aurait
there is not, il n'y a pas	are there not? n'y a-t-il pas?

Voilà is the translation of *there is*, *there are*, when anything is pointed out.

EXERCISE III.

1. There are some persons[1] who say that. **2.** Are there not any chairs for us ? **3.** There will not be anything[2] to do. **4.** Is there a post-office[3] in this street ? **5.** There were no pictures on the wall.[4] **6.** Are there any mice[5] in your kitchen[6] ? **7.** Were there no cigars in my case[7] ?

---

1. personne, fem., even if referring to a male, 2. *not...anything*, ne...rien (see Rule 108), 3. bureau de poste, 4. mur, 5. souris (f.), 6. cuisine, 7. étui.

---

138. PREPOSITIONS never come at the end (see Rule 39) ; as,

Where do you come from ?	D'où venez-vous ?
What is he speaking of ?	De quoi parle-t-il ?
The man he is writing to.	L'homme à qui il écrit.

139. **before** is translated by *devant*, if meaning *in front of* ; in other cases by *avant*, which refers chiefly to *time* ; as,

He was waiting before the door.	Il attendait devant la porte.
They left before us.	Ils sont partis avant nous.

140. **même** (-self) ; *mêmes* (-selves) ; are added to MOI, LUI, etc. (Rule 85), connected by a hyphen, when *myself, ourselves*, etc. are not reflective.

The queen herself.	La reine elle-même.

EXERCISE IV.

1. What are you writing on ? **2.** The children they were playing with. **3.** He goes away before five o'clock. **4.** The paper he is reading in. **5.** We were here before you. **6.** The table was before us. **7.** The gentleman he is speaking to. **8.** Which parcel did you put it in ? **9.** He came himself. **10.** They gave it to the ladies themselves.

141. *to put*: 1. **mettre,** 2. **mettant,** 3. **mis,** 4. **je mets,** 6. **je mis.**

PRESENT TENSE in full : *mets, mets, met ; mettons, mettez, mettent.*

PRON.—may, may, may ; mett-*ong,* mett-eh, mett.

The **t** of the termination in the 3rd person *Sing. of the Pres.* is omitted, whenever the *Stem* ends in *d* or *t.* All verbs ending in *mettre* are conjugated in the same way ; as, *admettre* to admit, *omettre* to omit, *permettre* to permit, *promettre* to promise. Examples :—

He does not permit	Il ne permet pas
Do we not admit ?	N'admettons-nous pas ?

EXERCISE V.

1. Do you not admit them ? 2. He **did** not promise it. 3. We shall not permit it. 4. Why have they omitted them ? 5. He will not admit it. 6. They promised (*p.def.*) it to me. 7. Do not omit to tell (it) them. 8. Would he not permit it ?

---

142. **Whose** when Interrogative is translated *à qui......*?

Whose carriage is that ?	A qui est cette voiture ?

de qui is used when the following word refers to a person, thus :

Whose doctor is he ?	De qui est-il le médecin ?

143. **What,** when *subject,* must be translated *qu'est-ce qui...*? **what,** when *object* is translated *que* or *qu'est-ce que...*?

What is causing that noise ?	Qu'est-ce qui fait ce bruit ?
What have you bought ?	Qu'est-ce que vous avez a-cheté ? or *Qu'avez-vous acheté?*

144. All Verbs ending in *indre* are conjugated alike :

1. *to fear* **craindre,** 2. *fearing* **craignant,** 3. *feared* **craint**

4. I fear, **je crains**	4. we fear, *nous* **craignons**
tu crains, il craint	*vous craignez, ils craignent*
5. I feared, **je craignais**	6. I feared, **je craignis**
7. I shall fear, **je craindrai**	8. I should fear, **je craindrais**

9. fear, *craignez* ; let us fear, *craignons* (fear thou, *crains*).

PRON.—1. kr*ang*-dr, 2. krain-y*ahng,* 3. kr*ang,* 4. kr*ang,* krain-y*ong,* krain-yeh, krain-yer, 5. krain-yay, 6. krain-yee, 7. kr*ang*-dreh, 8. kr*ang*-dray.

EXERCISE VI.

1. Whose hat was this ? 2. What are you painting[1] ? 3. Whose friend is he ? 4. What smells[2] so strong ? 5. Why is he complaining[3] ? 6. What amuses you ? 7. Whose gloves are these ? 8. They do not fear anything.[4] 9. Everybody[5] feared (*imperf.*) him. 10. Why did you complain[3] ? 11. Who will paint the picture ? 12. Why does he not put[6] out[6] the lamp ?

---

1. peindre, 2. sentir, 3. se plaindre, 4. rien, 5. tout le monde, 6. ~~eztinguish,~~ éteindre.

145. The INDEFINITE PRONOUN " on " is much used in French.

(1) Its literal translation is *one* used indefinitely.

One does not say that.	On *ne dit pas cela.*

(2) *we, you, they, people,* if not referring to a definite person or persons, are rendered by *on* (the Verb being always made singular).

What are they playing at the theatre this evening?	Que *joue-t-on au théâtre ce soir?*
Where do they sell stamps?	Où *vend-on des timbres-poste?*
People like to enjoy themselves.	On *aime à s'amuser.*

(3) The English Passive Voice is frequently rendered by *on.*

It is said. On *dit.*	It is announced. On *annonce.*
French spoken here.	*Ici* on *parle français.*
It is easily understood.	On *comprend cela facilement.*

On after *et* or *si* is changed into *l'on*; if they ask you, *si l'on vous demande*; but not if the next word commences with an *l.*

EXERCISE VII.

1. There is a knock=One knocks.[1] 2. You are wanted= One demands[2] you. 3. People are speaking of you. 4. One likes to be at[3] home.[3] 5. Someone (=one) was singing in the street. 6. No smoking allowed=One smokes not here. 7. It is said that she is going to die.[4] 8. If they ask for your address.

---

1. frapper,   2. demander,   3. chez soi (one's self),   4. mourir.

---

146. BETTER is translated by *meilleur* if ADJECTIVE, and by *mieux* if ADVERB.

better is an Adverb when it describes how a thing is done.

This apple is better.	Cette pomme est meilleure.
She sings better than he.	Elle chante mieux que lui.

The same distinction applies to *le meilleur,* and *le mieux.*

REMARKS.—*pire* worse (Adjective) is sometimes used for *plus mauvais*
   moindre less   „   „   „   „   „ *plus petit*
   pis worse (Adverb) „   „   „   „   „ *plus mal.*

147. DEMI *half* is made *feminine* if coming *after,* but not before a *Feminine* Noun; as;

It was two hours and a half.	C'était deux heures et demie.
I shall come in half an hour.	Je viendrai dans une demi-heure.

EXERCISE VIII.

1. These books are better than those. 2. She writes better than you. 3. He bought a pound and a half of butter. 4. His umbrella is the best. 5. He is working worse than yesterday. 6. She eats less every day. 7. This boy works best of all.

H F S 3

TWENTY-SIXTH LESSON.

148. The Present of the Subjunctive is formed from the PRESENT PARTICIPLE by changing *ant* into :

e, es, e; ions, iez, ent*

that I (*may*) *give, etc.*	*that we* (*may*) *give, etc.*
que je donne	que nous donnions
que tu donnes	que vous donniez
qu' il donne	qu' ils donnent

FURTHER EXAMPLES : that I (may) sell, finish, put, etc.

que je	*que tu*	*qu'il*	*que nous*	*que vous*	*qu'ils*
vende	vendes	vende	vendions	vendiez	vendent
finisse	finisses	finisse	finissions	finissiez	finissent
mette	mettes	mette	mettions	mettiez	mettent

EXERCISE I.

Form the Present of the Subjunctive of the following :

1. *fermer, attendre, remplir* ; 2. *partir* (Rule 131), *écrire* (84), *lire* (81) ; 3. *savoir* (112), *voir* (77), *dire* (88). 4. that I may pass ; 5. that he may not speak ; 6. that we may lose ; 7. that you may not give back ; 8. that they may succeed ; 9. that she may obey ; 10. that he may write ; 11. that they may not know ; 12. that you may sell.

149. The only irregular *Present Subjunctives* are :

acquérir,	que j'acquière	prendre,	que je prenne
aller,	„ j'aille	recevoir,†	„ je reçoive
s'asseoir,	„ je m'asseye	seoir,	qu'il siée
boire,	„ je·boive	tenir,	que je tienne
falloir,	qu'il faille	venir,	„ je vienne
mourir,	que je meure	valoir,	„ je vaille
mouvoir,	„ je meuve	vouloir,	„ je veuille

The *First Person Singular only* need be learned, as all the Singular, and the 3rd Person Plural, have the *same Irregular Stem*.

EXAMPLE :—aller, *that I* (*may*) *go*, etc. que j'aille, que tu ailles, qu'il aille ; que nous allions, que vous alliez, qu'ils aillent.

150. The following four are quite irregular :

	que je	*que tu*	*qu'il*	*que nous*	*que vous*	*qu'ils*
avoir	aie	aies	ait	ayons	ayez	aient
être	sois	sois	soit	soyons	soyez	soient
faire	fasse	fasses	fasse	fassions	fassiez	fassent
pouvoir	puisse	puisses	puisse	puissions	puissiez	puissent

* These are the endings of the Present Indicative of ER Verbs, with an " i " added in the First and Second Persons Plural.

† All Verbs in " evoir " are conjugated like " recevoir."

EXERCISE II.

Form the Present of the Subjunctive of the following :

1. *aller, faire, boire* ; 2. *pouvoir, prendre, venir* ; 3. *avoir, être, vouloir* ; 4. that I (may) come ; 5. that he (may) not be able ; 6. that we may be willing ; 7. that you may not hold ; 8. that they may not go ; 9. that we may come back ; 10. that you may not receive ; 11. that they may do it.

---

151. The Third Person of the PRESENT SUBJUNCTIVE is used for the Third Person IMPERATIVE (see remark to Rule 58) ; as,

let him have,	qu'il ait	let them be,	qu'ils soient
let him speak,	qu'il parle	let them finish,	qu'ils finissent

152. The Imperfect Subjunctive of ALL Verbs (without exception) is formed from the PAST DEFINITE by changing the final letter of the *1st Person Singular* into :

sse, sses, ^t, ssions, ssiez, ssent

In the 3rd Person Sing., the vowel preceding the *t* takes a circumflex accent.

EXAMPLES :

that I had or *that I might have*		*that I was* or *that I might be*	
que j'eusse	que nous eussions	que je fusse	que nous fussions
que tu eusses	que vous eussiez	que tu fusses	que vous fussiez
qu'il eût	qu'ils eussent	qu'il fût	qu'ils fussent

that I gave, finished, received *or* that I might give, finish, receive.

que je	*que tu*	*qu'il*	*que nous*	*que vous*	*qu'ils*
donnasse	donnasses	donnât	donnassions	donnassiez	donnassent
finisse	finisses	finît	finissions	finissiez	finissent
reçusse	reçusses	reçût	reçussions	reçussiez	reçussent

REMARK.—In deference to custom, we have placed que before the Subjunctive, and given an English translation. Both practices, however, are misleading. Que is not always followed by the Subjunctive, and *may* and *might* are frequently an entirely incorrect translation of this mood.

EXERCISE III.

Form the Past of the Subjunctive of the following :

1. *avoir, être, fermer* ; 2. *attendre, remplir, lire* (81) ; 3. *pouvoir* (109), *tenir* (114), *prendre* (90) ; 4. that I replied *or* might reply ; 5. that she might not succeed ; 6. that they might not have ; 7. that she might come (115) ; 8. that we might speak ; 9. that you might be ; 10. that he might write (84).

153. 1. to be necessary, **Falloir.**

3. been necessary, fallu	4. it is necessary, il faut
5. it was necessary, il fallait	6. it was necessary, il fallut
7. it will be necessary, il faudra	8. it would be necessary, il faudrait

The Verb following *falloir*, unless *Infinitive*, must be in the *Subjunctive*.

154. The *Subjunctive* is used in RELATIVE SENTENCES :—(1) if following a *Superlative* ; (2) if following *seul, premier, dernier:*

The largest horse (that) I saw.	*Le plus grand cheval que j'aie vu.*
The only man who knows it.	*Le seul homme qui le sache.*

155. The *Subjunctive* must be used after certain CONJUNCTIONS, the most important of which are :

afin que so that, *avant que* before, *en cas que* in case,
jusqu'à ce que until, *pour que* in order that, *quoique* although.

We shall go, although it is late.	*Nous irons, quoiqu'il soit tard.*
I shall wait until he comes.	*J'attendrai jusqu'à ce qu'il vienne.*

EXERCISE IV.

1. It is the only thing he sells. 2. The best book that I have ever read. 3. The finest picture that he has painted. 4. Give it to the first man who comes. 5. Wait until I am ready. 6. Although he is rich, he is not happy. 7. We shall speak to them before they have finished it. 8. He has come, so that we may-be-able-to speak of-it.

156. The *Subjunctive* is used after Verbs used *negatively* or *interrogatively.*

Is it probable that she will* come ?	*Est-il probable qu'elle vienne ?*
He does not believe they will* start.	*Il ne croit pas qu'ils partent.*

After 'dire,' 'savoir,' and 'informer,' the Subjunctive is not employed ; as. 'Je ne sais pas ce qu'il a dit.'

157. The *Subjunctive* is used after IMPERSONAL VERBS and expressions, except those denoting certainty or probability ; as,

It is necessary for me to start.	*Il faut que je parte.*
It is just that he should* be punished.	*Il est juste qu'il soit puni.*
It is better that he should* come.	*Il vaut mieux qu'il vienne.*

EXERCISE V.

1. Do you think (that) he will* be at home ? 2. I do not believe[1] (that) she wants to dance. 3. Do you not hope that we shall* pass the examination ? 4. I did not think (*imperf.*) he would* come. 5. Is it necessary that we should* start ? 6. Is it not likely (=probable) that he will* see it ? 7. Don't you know that he will be there ? 8. He did not say that he could (*imperf.*) do it. 9. Is it possible that the money is his ? 10. I do not expect (=think) that he will receive a prize.

---

* see Rule 158.—I believe, *je crois* (from *croire*).

158. The *Subjunctive* has only two Tenses. The *Present Subjunctive* is always used unless the first Verb is *Imperfect* or *Conditional*. After these two the *Imperfect Subjunctive* is used.

From this Rule it follows that *he is, was, will be, should be, would be, may be, might be*, etc., can only be translated by **soit** or **fût**.

159. The *Subjunctive* is used after certain VERBS, followed by *que*, the most important of which are:

vouloir to want, wish; *falloir* to be necessary; *désirer* to desire; *craindre* to fear; *regretter* to regret; *douter* to doubt.

I regret she is here.	*Je regrette qu'elle soit ici.*
We want them to be there.	*Nous désirons qu'ils soient là.*
He does not want me to see it.	*Il ne veut pas que je le voie.*

160. A few of these Verbs governing the *Subjunctive* also require **ne** before the following verb, unless the first verb is *Interrogative* or *Negative*. The principal are:

avoir peur, craindre, trembler to be afraid, to fear; *empêcher* to prevent; *prendre garde* to take care; also—*à moins que* unless.

He fears that you know it.	*Il craint que vous ne le sachiez.*
BUT: Does he fear that you know it?	*Craint-il que vous le sachiez?*

EXERCISE VI.

1. We regret that he did not find us. 2. She fears that he will come. 3. Is it necessary *for us to wait* (=that we wait)? 4. I doubted whether (=that) they would come. 5. I am afraid he will wait for you. 6. We feared (*imperf.*) that you would not receive it. 7. We wish (*conditional*) they had not commenced it. 8. I wish (*conditional*) she were not here.

161. *falloir* is frequently used for *must, have to*, and other words denoting compulsion. In this case the English must be changed thus:

I *shall have to* do it=it will be necessary that I do it
Il faudra que je le fasse.

Are you not not *obliged to* wait=is it not necessary that you wait?
Ne faut-il pas que vous attendiez?

He *must* start=it is necessary that he start. Il faut qu'il parte.

EXERCISE VII.

1. Must you do it? 2. You will have to write to him. 3. He would not have to finish it. 4. We must know it. 5. It is not necessary *for us to* (=that we) copy the address. 6. It was not necessary (*imperf.*) *for them to speak* (=that they spoke).

162. When *want, wish,* etc. are followed in *English* by an *Object* and an *Infinitive,* the construction must be changed, thus :

I want *you to go* there with him=I want *that you* go there with him.
Je veux que vous y alliez avec lui.

They wished *him to come*=They wished *that he* came.
Ils voulaient qu'il vînt.

163. *shall I? shall we?* are frequently rendered thus :

Shall we copy it? *Voulez-vous que nous le* copiions?
Shall I not finish that? *Ne voulez-vous pas que je* finisse *cela?*

EXERCISE VIII.

1. Does he want *her to* (=that she) read it? 2. They want me to speak to him. 3. Will he want you to write to them? 4. She wishes you to accept this. 5. They will not want us to keep it. 6. Does she not wish us to stay there? 7. We do not want them to hear us. 8. Did you want (*imperf.*) *me to do* (=that I did) it for you? 9. Shall I do it for him? 10. Shall we not go there? 11. Shall I not send it to him? 12. Shall we fetch it? 13. Shall I shut the window?

REMARKS ON THE SUBJUNCTIVE MOOD.

The SUBJUNCTIVE should be used as explained in the foregoing Rules, *no matter what the English wording is.* It is always preceded by que, although que is not always followed by the Subjunctive. If therefore the second Verb in English does not follow, *"that,"* the construction must be entirely changed before translating. Thus :

CHANGE	INTO	
We deny his having been here	We deny that he has been here	*Nous nions qu'il ait été ici*
It is not fair for her to say that	It is not fair that she says that	*Il n'est pas juste qu'elle dise cela*
I prefer you not to wait	I prefer that you do not wait	*Je préfère que vous n'attendiez pas*

The SUBJUNCTIVE generally denotes doubt when *certainty* is expressed, the Indicative should be employed.

We have given in a simple and condensed form the Rules on the Subjunctive, as laid down by the best modern authorities. But—in spite of what grammarians may say—this mood is avoided by Frenchmen in conversation as much as possible, it being often pedantic even when grammatically correct.

Vouloir and *falloir* are the principal Verbs after which the Subjunctive must be used unless an Infinitive can be substituted. This can always be done when the SUBJECT in both sentences would be *the same.* Thus : *I* am sorry *I* am late, *Je regrette d'être* (to be) *en retard;*—but *I* am sorry *you* are late, *Je regrette que vous soyez en retard.*

APPENDIX.

IRREGULAR PLURALS & FEMININES (*contd. on page 116*).

The following NOUNS ending in *al* take *s* in the Plural :
bal (dancing ball), *carnaval* carnival, *chacal* jackal,
nopal (a flower), *régal* treat, *serval* tiger-cat.

The following NOUNS ending in *ou* add *x* :
bijou jewel, *caillou* flint, chou cabbage, genou knee, *hibou* owl,
joujou plaything, *pou* louse.

The following NOUNS ending in *ail* change *ail* into *aux* :
bail lease, *corail* coral, *émail* enamel, *soupirail* loophole, *ventail* folding-
door, *travail* labour, work.—*travail* (report of a minister) is regular.
The Plural of *ail* garlic, is *aulx* or *ails* ; the Plural of *bétail* cattle, is *bestiaux*

aïeul *ancestor*	aïeux *ancestors*, or aïeuls *grandfathers*
ciel *heaven*	cieux *heavens* ,, ciels *skies of pictures*, or *bed-testers*
œil *eye*	yeux *eyes* ,, œils-de-bœuf *oval windows*

The following ADJECTIVES have irregular Feminine forms :

absous	*absolved*	absoute	hébreu	*Hebrew*	hébraïque
bas	*low*	basse	jumeau	*twin*	jumelle
beau*	*fine*	belle	long	*long*	longue
bénin	*benign*	bénigne	malin	*malicious*	maligne
blanc	*white*	blanche	mou*	*soft*	molle
bon	*good*	bonne	muet	*dumb*	muette
caduc	*decrepit*	caduque	muscat	*muscatel*	muscade
coi	*quiet*	coïte	nouveau*	*new*	nouvelle
dissou	*dissolved*	dissoute	nul	*no*	nulle
doux	*sweet*	douce	oblong	*oblong*	oblongue
épais	*thick*	épaisse	préfix	*prefixed*	préfixe
exprès	*express*	expresse	public	*public*	publique
faux	*false*	fausse	roux	*red*	rousse
favori	*favorite*	favorite	sec	*dry*	sèche
fou*	*foolish*	folle	sot	*stupid*	sotte
frais	*fresh*	fraîche	sujet	*subject*	sujette
franc	*free*	franche	tiers	*third*	tierce
gentil	*genteel*	gentille	traître	*treacherous*	traîtresse
gras	*fat*	grasse	turc	*Turkish*	turque
grec	*Greek*	grecque	vieux*	*old*	vieille
gros	*big*	grosse	violet	*violet*	violette

* Before a Masculine Noun commencing with a *vowel* or an *h* mute, *bel, fol,
mol, nouvel, vieil* are used instead of *beau, nouveau*, etc.

The following ADJECTIVES in *al* take *s* in the Plural :
bancal, fatal, final, glacial, initial, jovial, labial, matinal, naval, pascal.

*In most Grammars, this list is lengthened by inserting Adjectives never
used in the Plural ! This once more proves that the writers simply
copy each other, without attempting to simplify or improve the Rules.*

COMPLETE CONJUGATIONS OF THE REGULAR AND AUXILIARY VERBS.

FOR REFERENCE ONLY.

1. INFINITIVE.

to speak parler	to sell vendre	to finish finir	to have avoir	to be être

2. PRESENT PARTICIPLE.

speaking parlant	selling vendant	finishing finissant	having ayant	being étant

3. PAST PARTICIPLE.

spoken parlé	sold vendu	finished fini	had eu	been été

4. PRESENT INDICATIVE.

I speak, etc.	*I sell, etc.*	*I finish, etc.*	*I have, etc.*	*I am, etc.*
je parle	je vends	je finis	j'ai	je suis
tu parles	tu vends	tu finis	tu as	tu es
il parle	il vend	il finit	il a	il est
nous parlons	nous vendons	nous finissons	nous avons	nous sommes
vous parlez	vous vendez	vous finissez	vous avez	vous êtes
ils parlent	ils vendent	ils finissent	ils ont	ils sont

5. IMPERFECT or PAST.

I was speaking.	*I was selling.*	*I was finishg, etc.*	*I had, etc.*	*I was, etc.*
je parlais	je vendais	je finissais	j'avais	j'étais
tu parlais	tu vendais	tu finissais	tu avais	tu étais
il parlait	il vendait	il finissait	il avait	il était
nous parlions	nous vendions	nous finissions	nous avions	nous étions
vous parliez	vous vendiez	vous finissiez	vous aviez	vous étiez
ils parlaient	ils vendaient	ils finissaient	ils avaient	ils étaient

6. PAST DEFINITE.

I spoke, etc.	*I sold, etc.*	*I finished, etc.*	*I had, etc.*	*I was, etc.*
je parlai	je vendis	je finis	j'eus	je fus
tu parlas	tu vendis	tu finis	tu eus	tu fus
il parla	il vendit	il finit	il eut	il fut
nous parlâmes	nous vendîmes	nous finîmes	nous eûmes	nous fûmes
vous parlâtes	vous vendîtes	vous finîtes	vous eûtes	vous fûtes
ils parlèrent	ils vendirent	ils finirent	ils eurent	ils furent

7. FUTURE.

speak (I shall speak)	sell (I shall sell)	finish (I shall finish)	have (I shall have)	be (I shall be)
je parlerai	je vendrai	je finirai	j'aurai	je serai
tu parleras	tu vendras	tu finiras	tu auras	tu seras
il parlera	il vendra	il finira	il aura	il sera
nous parlerons	nous vendrons	nous finirons	nous aurons	nous serons
vous parlerez	vous vendrez	vous finirez	vous aurez	vous serez
ils parleront	ils vendront	ils finiront	ils auront	ils seront

8. CONDITIONAL.

speak (I shld. speak)	sell (I should sell)	finish (I shld. finish)	have (I should have)	be (I should be)
je parlerais	je vendrais	je finirais	j'aurais	je serais
tu parlerais	tu vendrais	tu finirais	tu aurais	tu serais
il parlerait	il vendrait	il finirait	il aurait	il serait
nous parlerions	nous vendrions	nous finirions	nous aurions	nous serions
vous parleriez	vous vendriez	vous finiriez	vous auriez	vous seriez
ils parleraient	ils vendraient	ils finiraient	ils auraient	ils seraient

9. IMPERATIVE.

speak	sell	finish	have	be
speak (thou) parle	sell (thou) vends	finish (thou) finis	have (thou) aie	be (thou) sois
qu'il parle	let him sell qu'il vende	qu'il finisse	let him have qu'il ait	let him be qu'il soit
let us speak parlons	let us sell vendons	let us finish finissons	let us have ayons	let us be soyons
speak parlez	sell vendez	finish finissez	have ayez	be soyez
qu'ils parlent	qu'ils vendent	qu'ils finissent	qu'ils aient	qu'ils soient

10. PRESENT SUBJUNCTIVE.—QUE (that) is usually prefixed in conjugating the Subjunctive.

speak (I may speak)	sell (I may sell)	finish (I may finish)	have (I may have)	be (I may be)
je parle	je vende	je finisse	j'aie	je sois
tu parles	tu vendes	tu finisses	tu aies	tu sois
il parle	il vende	il finisse	il ait	il soit
nous parlions	nous vendions	nous finissions	nous ayons	nous soyons
vous parliez	vous vendiez	vous finissiez	vous ayez	vous soyez
ils parlent	ils vendent	ils finissent	ils aient	ils soient

11. PAST or IMPERFECT SUBJUNCTIVE.—QUE is usually prefixed in conjugating.

speak (I might speak)	sell (I might sell)	finish (I might finish)	have (I might have)	be (I might be)
je parlasse	je vendisse	je finisse	j'eusse	je fusse
tu parlasses	tu vendisses	tu finisses	tu eusses	tu fusses
il parlât	il vendît	il finît	il eût	il fût
nous parlassions	nous vendissions	nous finissions	nous eussions	nous fussions
vous parlassiez	vous vendissiez	vous finissiez	vous eussiez	vous fussiez
ils parlassent	ils vendissent	ils finissent	ils eussent	ils fussent

NOUNS and **ADJECTIVES** ending in *eur* (derived from a *Present Participle*) change into *euse*; as,

> danseur *dancer* danseuse | menteur *liar* menteuse
> (except seven seldom used words.)

Those in *teur* change into *trice*; as,

> acteur *actor* actrice | inventeur *inventor* inventrice
> (except chanteur *singer* chanteuse, and a few seldom used words.)

Those ending in *érieur*, and *majeur, meilleur, mineur* add *e*; as, supérieur *superior* supérieure | extérieur *exterior* extérieure.

Adjectives ending in *gu* take a diaresis over the ө to show that the *u* is pronounced, thus; *aigu* acute *aiguë*; (*aigue* would be pronounced **aig**).

In COMPOUND NOUNS, both parts are made Plural except in the following cases :

(1) No change is made if the Compound is formed from a *Verb* and *Adverb*; as, *passe-partout* "latch-key" and "latch-keys."

(2) Only the *Noun* changes if formed with *Noun* and *Verb*, or *Noun* and *Preposition*.

> passe-port *passport* passe-ports, sous-officier *sub-officer* sous-officiers.
> porte-monnaie, *purse*, does not change in the Plural.

(3) Only the *first Noun* changes if the parts are joined by a Preposition. chemin de fer *railway* chemins de fer ; hôtel de ville *town hall* hôtels de ville

EXCEPTIONS :

Monsieur Messieurs, Madame Mesdames, Mademoiselle Mesdemoiselles.

ADVERBS are formed from Adjectives ending in *ant* or *ent* by changing the termination *nt* to *mment*; as,

> constant *constantly* constamment | prudent *prudently* prudemment
> PRON.—*kong*-stah-ma*hng* prü-dah-ma*hng*.

Two exceptions : lent *slowly* lentement | présent *presently* présentement.

The following **ADVERBS** take an *acute accent* over the ө preceding *ment* :

aveugle	*blindly*	aveuglément	impuni	*with impu-*	impunément
commun	*commonly*	communément		*nity*	
conforme	*conformably*	conformément	obscur	*darkly*	obscurément
confus	*confusedly*	confusément	opiniâtre	*obstinately*	opiniâtrément
diffus	*diffusely*	diffusément	précis	*precisely*	précisément
énorme	*enormously*	énormément	profond	*deeply*	profondément
exprès	*expressly*	expressément	uniforme	*uniformly*	uniformément
immense	*immensely*	immensément			

---

beau, fou, mou, nouveau form the **ADVERB** from their Feminine

> *bellement, follement, mollement, nouvellement*

QUITE IRREGULAR is : gentil *nicely* gentiment.

LIST OF THE IRREGULAR VERBS.

(for Reference only.)

The Verbs can be conjugated in full from the following table (see our Rules on the formation of Tenses, pages 74, 83, 106, 108, 110, 111).

This List does not include Compound Verbs conjugated like those from which they are derived, nor the 16 seldom used Defective Verbs given in a separate list in Hugo's "French Verbs Simplified."

All Verbs ending in **indre** are conjugated like *craindre* (Par. 144).

INFINITIVE.	PRES. PARTIC.	PAST PARTIC.	PRESENT.	PAST DEF
absoudre *to absolve*	absolvant	absous (absoute f.)	absous	(not used)
acquérir* *to acquire*	acquérant	acquis	acquiers†	acquis
aller *to go* (see Paragraph 115)				
assaillir *to assail*	assaillant	assailli	assaille	assaillis
s'asseoir* *to sit down*	s'asseyant	assis	assieds	assis
battre *to beat* (regular except PRESENT SING., which is "bats, bats, bat")				
bénir *to bless*			béni or bénit (otherwise regular)	
boire *to drink* (see Par. 105)				
bouillir *to boil*	bouillant	bouilli	bous	bouillis
conclure *to conclude*	concluant	conclu	conclus	conclus
conduire *to conduct*	conduisant	conduit	conduis	conduisis
confire *to preserve*	confisant	confit	confis	confis
connaître *to know*	connaissant	connu	connais	connus
contredire *to contradict* (Par 89)				
coudre *to sew*	cousant	cousu	couds	cousis
courir *to run* (124)				
couvrir *to cover* (135)				
craindre *to fear* (144)				
croire *to believe*	croyant	cru	crois	crus
croître *to grow*	croissant	crû	croîs	crûs
cueillir* *to gather*	cueillant	cueilli	cueille	cueillis
cuire *to cook* (conjugated like "conduire")				
déchoir* *to decay*	(not used)	déchu	déchois	déchus
devoir *to owe* (102)				
dire *to say, tell* (88)				
dormir *to sleep* (131)				
échoir* *to fall due*	échéant	échu	il échoit	il échut
écrire *to write* (84)				
envoyer *to send* (94)				
exclure *to exclure* (conjugated like "conclure")				
faire *to do, make* (99)				
falloir *to be necessary* (153)				
fuir *to run away*	fuyant	fui	fuis	fuis
haïr *to hate*	haïssant	haï, hais, haïssons. haïs, haïmes		
instruire *to instruct* (conjugated like "conduire")				
lire *to read* (81)				
mandire *to curse* (89)				
mentir *to tell lies* (131)				
mettre *to put* (141)				

INFINITIVE.	PRES. PARTIC.	PAST PARTIC.	PRESENT.	PAST DEF.
moudre *to grind*	moulant	moulu	mouds	moulus
mourir* *to die*	mourant	mort	meurs†	mourus
mouvoir* *to move*	mouvant	mu	meus†	mus
naître *to be born*	naissant	né	nais	naquis
nuire *to hurt*	nuisant	nui	nuis	nuisis
\ffrir *to offer* (135)				
ouvrir *to open* (135)				
paraître *to appear* (conjugated like "connaître				
partir *to start* (131)				
plaire *to please*	plaisant	plu	plais	plus
pleuvoir* *to rain*	pleuvant	plu	il pleut	il plut
pourvoir *to provide*	pourvoyant	pourvu	pourvois	pourvus
pouvoir *to be able* (109)				
prendre *to take* (90)				
prévaloir *to prevail* (like "valoir," except that it is regular in Subjunctive)				
prévoir *to foresee*	prévoyant	prévu	prévois	prévis
recevoir *to receive* (101)				
repaître *to feed* (conjugated like "connaître")				
se repentir *to repent* (conjugated like "mentir," Paragraph 131)				
résoudre *to resolve*	résolvant	résolu *or* résous.	résous.	résolus
rire *to laugh* (126)				
rompre *to break* (regular except 3rd PERS. PRES. SING., which is "rompt")				
saillir *to project* (conjugated like "assaillir," but used only in the Third Pers.)				
savoir *to know* (112)				
sentir *to feel* (131)				
servir *to serve* (131)				
sortir *to go out* (131)				
souffrir *to suffer* (135)				
suffire *to suffice* (126)				
suivre *to follow* (126)				
se taire *to be silent* (conjugated like "plaire ")				
tenir *to hold* (114)				
traire *to milk*	trayant	trait	trais	(not used)
tressaillir *to startle* (conjugated like "assaillir")				
vaincre *to conquer*	vainquant	vaincu	vaincs†	vainquis
valoir* *to be worth*	valant	valu.	vaux. vaux, vaut.	valus
venir *to come* (115)				
vêtir *to clothe*	vêtant	vêtu	vêts	vêtis
vivre *to live*	vivant	vécu	vis	vécus
voi- *to see* (77)				
vouloir *to be willing* (107)				

---

* These Verbs are irregular in the Future Stem, thus : j'acquerrai, je m'assiérai, je cueillerai, je décherrai, il écherra, je mourrai, je mouvrai, il pleuvra, je vaudrai.

† acquiers, acquiers, acquiert ; acquérons, acquérez, acquièrent.
  meurs, meurs, meurt ; mourons, mourez, meurent.
  meus, meus, meut ; mouvons, mouvez, meuvent.
  vaincs, vaincs, vainc ; vainquons, vainquez, vainquent.

VOCABULARY OF WORDS

occurring more than once in the Exercises.

The Numbers indicate the Paragraphs in which the full Conjugations of Irregular Verbs, and the various ways of translating PRONOUNS, etc., are given.

For the Numbers, Days, and Months, see pages 27 to 55.

—o—

A, an, 1
to be able to, 109
about to, 118
absent, *absent*
to accept, *accepter*
to accompany, *accompagner*
account, *compte*, m.
active, *actif*
to add, *ajouter*
address, *adresse*, f.
to admit, 141
after, *après*
afternoon, *après-midi*, f.
all, *tout* (106)
to allow to, *laisser*
almost, *presque*
alone, *seul*
already, *déjà*
although, 155
always, *toujours*
to amuse, *amuser*
and, *et*
animal, *animal*, m.
answer, *réponse*, f.
any, 26, 27, 29, 54, 103
anything, *quelque chose* 108
to apologise, *s'excuser*
apple, *pomme*, f.
are, 15, 31
arm, *bras*, m.
to arrive, *arriver*
as...as, 56
as much, as many, 93
as soon as, *aussitôt que*
to ask, *demander*
at, 22, 25, 133
at once, *tout de suite*
aunt, *tante*, f.
BAD, *mauvais*
badly, *mal*

bag, *sac*, m.
basket, *panier*, m.
to be, 15, *se porter*
beautiful, 53, 117
because, *parce que*
to become, 115
been, *été*
beer, *bière*, f.
before, 139, 155
to begin, *commencer*
to belong, 114
best, better, 56, 146
big, *gros, grosse*
bill, *compte*, m.
bird, *oiseau*, m.
black, *noir*
blue, *bleu, bleus*
book, *livre*, m.
boot, *botte*, f.
bottle, *bouteille*, f.
box, *boîte*, f.
boy, *garçon*, m.
bread, *pain*, m.
to break, *briser*
to bring, *apporter*
brother, *frère*, m.
but, *mais*
butter, *beurre*, m.
to buy, *acheter*
by, *par*
TO CALL, *appeler*
can, 109
cane, *canne*, f.
carriage, *voiture*, f.
to carry, *porter*
cat, *chat*, m.
chair, *chaise*, f.
chamber, *chambre*, f.
cheese, *fromage*, m.
child, *enfant*, m. or f.
to choose, *choisir*
church, *église*, f.

cigar, *cigare*, m.
to close, *fermer*
coat, *habit*, m.
coffee, *café*, m.
color, *couleur*, f.
to come, 115
to come back, 115 [*cer*
to commence, *commen-*
to complain, *se plaindre*
concert, *concert*, m. [144
to contain, 114
to continue, *continuer*
to copy, *copier*
to correspond, *corres-*
to cost, *coûter* [*pondre*
could, 109
cousin, *cousin, cousine*
to cover, 135
cow, *vache*, f.
to cut, *couper*
TO DANCE, *danser*
daughter, *fille*, f.
day, *jour*, m.
dear, *cher*
debt, *dette*, f.
to descend, *descendre*
to desire, *désirer*
dictionary, *dictionnaire*
did, 21, 51, 99 [*masc.*
difficult, *difficile*
to dine, *dîner*
dinner, *dîner*, m.
to discover, 135
to dispute, *se disputer*
to do, 99
do, does, 32, 33, 51, 99
doctor, *médecin, docteur*
dog, *chien*, m.
done, *fait*
door, *porte*, f.
to doubt, *douter*
dress, *robe*, f.

to dress, *habiller*
to drink, 105
EACH, 100
easy, *facile*
to eat, *manger*
empty, *vide*
end, *fin* f.
English, *anglais*
enough, 93
to enter, *entrer*
envelope, *enveloppe* f.
evening, *soir* m.
ever, *jamais*
every, *chaque*, 100, 110
everybody *tout le monde*
everything, *tout*
examination, *examen* m.
to exclaim, *s'écrier*
to expect, *attendre*
expense, *dépense* f.
TO FALL, *tomber*
family, *famille* f.
fast, *vite*
father, *père* m.
to fear, 144
feather, *plume* f.
to feel, 131
to fetch, *chercher*
a few, *quelques*
to fight, *se battre*
to fill, *remplir*
to find, *trouver*
fine, 53, 117
to finish, *finir*
fire, *feu* m., *incendie* m.
first, *premie--*
at first, *d'abord*
fish, *poisson* m.
to flatter, *flatter*
flower, *fleur* f.
to follow, 126
foot, *pied* m.
for, *pour*
to forget, *oublier*
fork, *fourchette* f.
franc, *franc* m.
French, *français*
Frenchman, *Français*
friend, *ami, amie*
from, *de*, 22, 25
full, *plein*
TO GAIN, *gagner*

garden, *jardin* m.
gas, *gaz* m,
gentleman, *monsieur* m.
German, *allemand*
Germany, *Allemagne*
girl, *fille* f.
to give, *donner*
to give back, *rendre*
glass, *verre* m.
glove, *gant* m.
to go, 118
to go away, 131
to go out, 131
good, *bon, bonne*
grammar, *grammaire* f.
great, *grand*
a great deal, *beaucoup*
gun, *fusil* m.
HAD, *eu*, 65, 73
half, 147
hand, *main* f.
handwriting, *écriture* f.
handsome, 53, 117
happy, *heureux*
hat, *chapeau* m.
to have, 5
he, *il*, 75, 85
to hear, *entendre*
to help, *aider*
her, 9, 10, 42, 85
hers, 38, 87
herself, 119, 140
here, *ici*
here is, here are, *voici*
to hide, *cacher*
high, *haut*
him, 42, 85
himself, 119, 140
his, 9, 10, 38, 87
to hold, 114
home, at home, 132
to hope, *espérer*
horse, *cheval* m.
hotel, *hôtel* m.
hour, *heure* f.
house, *maison* f.
how, *comment*
how much, how many 93
husband, *mari*
I, *je*, 85
idea, *idée* f.
if, *si*

ill, *malade*
in, *dans, en*, 55, 133
to inform, *informer*
ink, *encre* f.
inkstand, *encrier* m.
invitation, *invitation* f.
to invite, *inviter*
it, 23, 42, 75, 103
its, 9, 10
JOURNAL, *journal* m.
to judge, *juger*
TO KEEP, *garder*
key, *clef* f.
kindly, *veuillez*
king, *roi* m.
knife, *couteau* m.
to knock, *frapper*
to know, 112
LADY, *dame* f.
young lady, *demoiselle* f.
lamp, *lampe* f.
large, *grand*
last, *dernier*
late, *en retard*
to laugh, 126
to learn, 91
least, 146
left, *gauche*
to lend, *prêter*
less, 93, 146
lesson, *leçon* f.
let, 58, 151
to let, *louer*
letter, *lettre* f.
to light, *allumer*
to like, *aimer*
list, *liste* f.
to listen, *écouter*
little, *petit*, 93
to live, *demeurer*
to look at, *regarder*
to look for, *chercher*
to lose, *perdre*
loud, *haut*
TO MAKE, 99
man, *homme* m.
many, 93
market, *marché* m.
match, *allumette* f.
mayor, *maire* m.
me, 42, 76, 85
meat *viande* f.

to meet, *rencontrer*
mine, 38, 87
mistake, *faute* f.
money, *argent* m.
month, *mois* m.
more, *plus*, 93
morning, *matin* m.
the most, *le plus*
mother, *mère* f.
much, 93
music, *musique* f.
must, 102
my, 9, 10 ; myself, 119
NAME, *nom* m.
nearly, *presque*
to be necessary, 153
neighbour, *voisin*, -e
neither, 108
nephew, *neveu* m.
never, 108
new, *nouveau*, 53
newspaper, *journal* m.
next, *prochain*
nice, *joli*
niece, *nièce* f
no, *non*, 28
no more, 108
nobody, 108
noise, *bruit* m.
nose, *nez* m.
not, 11, 19
note, *note* f.
nothing, 108
TO OBEY, *obéir*
o'clock, *heure(s)* f.
of, 22, 25, 103
of which, of whom, *dont*
to offer, 135
officer, *officier* m.
often, *souvent*
old, *vieux*, 53
to omit, 141
on, *sur*, 69
one, *un, une*, 145
only, 108, 154
to open, 135
opinion, *opinion* f.
order, *commande* f.
ought to, 102
our, 6 ; ours, 38, 87
ourselves, 119, 140
to owe, 102

PAGE, *page* f.
to paint, *peindre*, 144
paper, *papier* m.
parcel, *paquet* m.
to pass, *passer*
to pay (for), *payer*
pear, *poire* f.
pen, *plume* f.
pencil, *crayon* m.
people, 145
to permit, 141
picture, *tableau* m.
piece, *pièce* f, *morceau* m
pipe, *pipe* f.
place, *place* f.
plate, *assiette* f.
to play, *jouer*
if you please, *s'il vous plaît*
pleasure, *plaisir* m.
polite, *poli*
pony, *poney* m.
poor, *pauvre*
position, *position* f.
possible, *possible*
poste, *poste* f.
postage-stamp, *timbre-poste* m.
postman, *facteur* m.
pound, *livre* f.
to praise, *louer*
present, *cadeau* m.
present, *présent*
pretty, *joli*
price, prize, *prix* m.
probable, *probable*
to promise, 141
to punish, *punir*
purse, *porte-monnaie* m.
to put, 141
QUARREL, *se disputer*
question, *question* f.
TO READ, 81
ready, *prêt*
to receive, 101
red, *rouge*
regiment, *régiment* m.
to regret, *regretter*
to remain, *rester*
to repeat, *répéter*
to reply, *répondre*
to rest, *se reposer*

to return, *rendre*
rich, *riche*
right, *droit*
ring, *bague* f.
river, *fleuve* m.
room, *chambre* f.
round, *rond*
to run, 124
SALAD, *salade* f.
salt, *sel* m.
same, *même*
sample, *échantillon* m
satisfied, *satisfait*
to say, 88
school, *école* f.
to seal, *cacheter*
to see, 77
to seek, *chercher*
to sell, *vendre*
to send, 94
to send back, 94
serious, *sérieux*
servant, *domestique* m.f.
to serve, 131
several, *plusieurs*
shall, 57, 102, 122
she, *elle*, 75, 85
shilling, *schelling* m.
ship, *vaisseau* m.
shoe, *soulier* m.
shop, *boutique* f.
short, *court*
should, 61, 102, 122
to show, *montrer*
to shut, *fermer*
to sing, *chanter*
sister, *sœur* f.
to sleep, 131
small, *petit*
to smoke, *fumer*
so...as, *si...que*
so that, *afin que*
soldier, *soldat* m.
some, 26, 29, 54, 103, 111
something, *quelque*
son, *fils* m.   [*chose*
song, *chanson* f.
soup, *soupe* f.
Spaniard, *Espagnol* m.
to speak, *parler*
to spell, *épeler*
to spend, *dépenser*

stamp, *timbre-poste* m.
to start, *partir*, 131
station, *gare* f. *station* f.
stick, *canne* f.
story, *histoire* f.
street, *rue* f.
to strike, *frapper*
strong, *fort*
to study, *étudier*
to succeed, *réussir*
to suffer, 135
sugar, *sucre* m.
to suit, 115
sum, *somme* f.
to surprise, 91
TABLE, *table* f.
to take, 90
tall, *grand*
task, *devoir* m.
tea, *thé* m.
teacher, *maître* m.
to tear, *déchirer*
to tell, 88
than, *que, de* (55)
to thank, *remercier*
that, 13, 62, 70, 74, 78
that which, 83
the, 2, 3, 4 ; the one, 80
theatre, *théâtre* m.
thee, 42, 76, 85
their, 6
theirs, 38, 87
them, 42, 85, 103
themselves, 119, 140
there, *là*, 104
there is, there are, 137
these, 13, 74, 78
they, 24, 75, 85, 145
thine, 38, 87
thing, *chose* f.
to think, *penser*
this, 13, 70, 74, 78
those, 13, 70, 74, 78

thou, *tu*
to throw, *jeter*
thy, 9, 10
thyself, 119
ticket, *billet* m.
time, *temps* m.
time (of day), *heure* f.
tired, *fatigué*
to, *à*, 128, 129, 130, 133
to the, 22, 25
to it, to them, 103
to-day, *aujourd'hui*
to-morrow, *demain*
together, *ensemble*
too, *trop* 93
town, *ville* f.
train, *train* m.
tree, *arbre* m.
trouble, *peine* f.
to try, *essayer*
UGLY, *vilain*
umbrella, *parapluie* m.
uncle, *oncle* m.
under, *sous*
to understand, 91
to undertake, 91
unless, *à moins que*
until, 155
upstairs, *en haut*
us, to us, *nous*
used to, 66
useful, *utile*
VAIN, *vain*
very, *très*
to visit, *visiter*
voice, *voix* f.
TO WAIT (for) *attendre*
waiter, *garçon* m.
to walk, *marcher*
to want to, 107
warm, *chaud*
to warm, *chauffer*
was, 65, 73

to wash, *laver*
watch, *montre* f.
water, *eau* f.
way, *chemin* m.
we, *nous*, 145
to wear, *porter*
week, *semaine* f.
well, *bien*
were, 65, 73
what, 12, 34, 39, 59, 83,
when, *quand*   [143
where, *où*
which, 12, 59, 60, 62, 67,
who, 34, 62   [68
whole, 106
whom, 34, 62, 67, 68
whose, 68, 142
why, *pourquoi*
wicked, *méchant*, 53
wife, *femme* f.
will, 57, 107, 123
to be willing to, 107
to win, *gagner*
window, *fenêtre* f.
wine, *vin* m.
to work, 107
to wish to, 107
with, *avec*
without, *sans*
work, *travail* m.
to work, *travailler*
workman, *ouvrier*
world, *monde* m.
worse, worst, 146
would, 61, 123
to write, 84
YEAR, *an* m.
yes, *oui* (page 23, note)
yesterday, *hier*
yet, *encore*
you, to you, *vous*, 145
young, *jeune*
your, 6 ; yours, 38, 87
yourself, -ves, 119

FRENCH
PRONUNCIATION
SIMPLIFIED

A COLLECTION OF

EASY ANECDOTES AND DIALOGUES

With Literal Translation and

Imitated Pronunciation of Every Word

Including Complete

RULES OF FRENCH PRONUNCIATION

———

PHILADELPHIA

DAVID McKAY, Publisher

604-8 S. Washington Square

INSTRUCTIONS FOR
READING THE IMITATED PRONUNCIATION
of the Anecdotes on pages 4 to 28.

NEARLY ALL FRENCH VOWELS ARE PRONOUNCED SHORT, unless there is a Circumflex Accent over them. The exceptions to this very important rule are explained in Hugo's "Complete Guide to French Pronunciation."

We are compelled to imitate the usual French sound of I, O, by the English letters E, O, these being the nearest English approach to the French sounds ; but the ordinary French I is not pronounced so long as the E in ' we,' nor the ordinary French O so long as the O in 'go.' The exact sound is between the vowel sounds in 'we' and 'wit,' 'go' and 'got.'

Still less is the French A like A in the English 'part,' 'charm.' It has the same sound ; but in French the A must be pronounced AS SHORT AND SHARP AS POSSIBLE, never in the least lengthened or prolonged. Its pronunciation must be INSTANTANEOUS.

Bear constantly in mind that:

1. **ah** must always be pronounced very short and sharp.

2. *ng* in italics must on no account be pronounced ; these letters merely indicate that the preceding vowel is to be pronounced nasally.

3. *r* in italics must not be pronounced at all ; it is merely inserted to ensure the correct pronunciation of the preceding vowel.

4. **sh** in thick type always represents the sound of S in 'leisure.'

5. **ü** represents a sound that never occurs in the English language ; this sign is used because the sound is identical with that of ü in German.

Students who know no German must avoid pronouncing this ü like an English U ; the sound more nearly approaches the English EE. Instructions for pronouncing the French U properly are given on page 33

Letters printed in italics, and followed by an apostrophe, are only pronounced because a vowel sound follows,—see page 45. Full explanation of this linking of words (called in French the *liaison*) is given in our 'Complete Guide,' post free 1s. 1d.

SIMPLE ANECDOTES, etc.,

WITH LITERAL TRANSLATION AND IMITATED PRONUNCIATION.

FRENCH :   N'avez-vous pas reçu ma lettre ?
Imitated Pronunciation : nah-veh   voo   pah rer*-süt mah   lettr ?
Literal Translation :   Have   you   not received my   letter ?

Si ; vous me demandiez si j'étais complètement
see   voo   mer der-mahng-de-eh se sheh-tayt kong-plate-mahng*
Yes; you   me   asked   if I was   completely

rétabli. — Alors, pourquoi n'avez-vous pas
reh-tah-blee   ah-lor   poohr-ko'ah nah-veh voo   pah
well-again. — Then,   why   have you   not

répondu ? — Mais, vous avez oublié d'envoyer
reh-pong-dü   may   voo   z'ah-veh z'oo-blee-eh dahng-vo'ah-yeh
answered ?   But   you   have forgotten   to send

une enveloppe affranchie pour la réponse.
ün   ahng-ver-lopp   ah-frahng-she   poohr   lah reh-pongss
an   envelope   stamped   for   the reply.

Un prédicateur dit dans un sermon que
ung   preh-de-kah-ter   dee   dahng z'ung sair-mong   ker
A   preacher   said   in   a   sermon   that

Saint François avait converti en un jour
sang   frahng-so'ah ah-vay kong-vair-te ahng ung shoohr
Saint   Francis   had   converted   in   one   day

cinquante mille hommes dans une île déserte.
sang-kahngt   mill   omm   dahng z'ün eel   deh-zairt
     fifty   thousand men   in   an island desert(ed).

---

*ng and r in italics not to be pronounced.

†ü must be pronounced like EE with rounded lips,—not like an
     English U.

‡sh=S in 'pleasure.'

Monsieur le rédacteur, vous avez annoncé ma
mer-se-er ler reh-dahck-ter voo z'ah-veh z'ah-nong-seh mah
Mr. the editor, you have announced my

mort dans votre journal. Cette nouvelle est
mor dahng votr shoohr-nahll set noo-vell ay
death in your newspaper. This news is

fausse, et vous devez la démentir dans
fohss eh voo der-veh lah deh-mahng-teer dahng
false, and you must it contradict in

votre prochain numéro. — Le lendemain on
votr pro-shang nü-meh-ro ler lahng-der-mang ong
your next number. The next-day one

lisait ceci : Nous regrettons extrêmement
le-zay ser-se noo rer-grett-ong ex-tray-mer-mahng
read this : We regret extremely

que la nouvelle qui annonçait la mort
ker lah noo-vell ke ah-nong-say lah mor
that the news which announced the death

du capitaine Joubert soit sans fondement.
dü kah-pe-tane shoo-bair so'ah- sahng fongd-mahng
of(the) captain Joubert (should)be without foundation.

Pourquoi me regardes-tu comme ça, petit ?—Parce
poohr-ko'ah mer rer-gahr-der-tü komm sah per-te pahrss
Why me dost thou look at like that, little(one) ? Be-

que maman dit que vous buvez comme un poisson,
ker mah-mahng dee ker voo bü-veh komm ung po'ah-song
cause mamma says that you drink like a fish,

et je veux voir comment les poissons boivent.
eh sher ver vo'ahr komm-ahng lay po'ah-song bo'ahv
and I want to see how the fish drink.

L'institutrice :   Lucie,   quel   est   le   pluriel   de
lang-ste-tü-triss   lü-see   kell   ay   ler*   plü-re-ell   de*r*
The governess :   Lucy,   what   is   the   plural   of

"bébé."—Lucie   (sans   hésitation) :   Jumeaux !
beh-beh   lü†-see   *sahng*   z'eh-ze-tah-se-*ong*   shü-moh‡
"baby." — Lucy   (without   hesitation) :   Twins !

J'ai beaucoup souffert de névralgies, dernièrement
sheh   boh-koo   soo-fair de*r* nehv-rahl-she dair-ne-air-ma*hng*
I have much   suffered from neuralgia,   recently.

—Dans la tête, je suppose ? - Comment avez-vous
dahng lah tate sher   sü-poz   komm-*ahng* ah-veh voo
In   the head, I   suppose ?   How   have you

deviné ?—Cela attaque toujours le point faible.
de*r*-vee-neh   ser-lah   ah-tahck   too-shoohr ler po'*ang*   fay-bl
guessed ?   That   attacks   always   the point weak.

La morale de la fable.—Tu vois, mon enfant,
lah mo-rahll de*r* lah fahbl   tü   vo'ah mo*ng* n'ah*ng*-fa*hng*
The moral of the fable. Thou seest, my   child,

le loup a mangé l'agneau parce qu'il n'a pas
ler loo ah ma*hng*-sheh lahn-yoh   parss   kill   nah pah
the wolf has eaten   the lamb because   it   has not

été sage. — J'ai bien compris. Si l'agneau
z'eh-teh sahsh   sheh   be-*ang*   kong-pree   se   lahn-yoh
been wise. I have well understood. If   the lamb

avait été sage, c'est nous qui l'aurions mangé.
ah-vay t'eh-teh sahsh   say   noo   ke   loh-re-*ong* ma*hng*-sheh
had been wise, it is   we   who it would-have eaten.

---

*ng and r in italics not to be pronounced.

†ü must be pronounced like EE with rounded lips,—not like an
English U.

‡eh=S in ' treasure.'

Maintenant, mon petit garçon, répondez à
m*a*ng-ter-n*a*hng   m*o*ng   per-te   gahr-*s*ong   reh-*p*ong-deh   z'a*b*
    Now,   my   little   boy,   reply   to

cette question. Si votre père me devait
  set   kess-te-*o*ng   se   votr   pair   mer   der-vay
this   question.   If   your   father   me   owed

deux mille francs et promettait d*ə* me payer
der   mill   fr*a*hng   eh   pro-met-ay   der   mer   pay-yeb
two   thousand   francs   and   promised   to   me   pay

cent francs par mois, combien me devrait-il
s*a*hng   fr*a*hng   par   mo'ah   kong-be-*a*ng   mer   der-vray   *t*'ill
hundred francs   per   month,   how much   me   would he owe

au bout de six mois ? — Deux mille
oh   boo   der   see   mo'ah   der   mill
at-the   end   of   six   months ?   Two   thousand

francs, monsieur. -Et l'enfant avait raison.
fr*a*hng   mer-se-e*r*   eh   l*a*hng-f*a*hng   ah-vay   ray-*z*ong
francs,   sir.   And   the child   was right (had reason).

À mon avis, Laurent est un âne.—Pardon, mais
ah   m*o*ng   *n*'ah-ve   loh-r*a*hng   ay   *t'*ung   *n*'ahn   pahr-d*o*ng   'may
At(in) my   opinion,   Laurent   is   an   ass.   Pardon,   but

je ne puis vous permettre de parler ainsi
s*h*er ner   pwe   voo   pair-mettr   der   pahr-leb   *a*ng-se
I   not   can   you   permit   to   speak   thus

de lui. Il m'a prêté cinquante francs l'autre
der lwe   ill mah   pray-teh   s*a*ng-k*a*hngt   fr*a*hng   lohtr
of him.   He to-me has lent   fifty   francs   the other

jour. — C'est justement pourquoi je le dis.
shoohr   say   s*h*üst-m*a*hng   poohr ko'ah   s*h*er   ler   dee
day.   That is   just   why   I   it   say.

Un paysan alla un jour chez un professeur
ung pay'e-zahng ahll-ah ung shoohr sheh *z'ung* pro-fess-*er*
A countryman went one day to-the-house-of a professor

de musique, et lui demanda le prix de ses leçons.
der mü-zick eh lwe der-*mahng*-dah ler pree der say ler-*song*
of music, and to-him asked the price of his lessons.

Trente francs le premier mois, dit le professeur,
trah*ng*t frah*ng* ler prer-me-eh mo'ah dee ler pro-fess-er
Thirty francs the first month, said the professor,

et vingt francs le second.—Très bien, répondit
eh vang frah*ng* ler ser-*gong* tray be-*ang* reh-*pong*-de
and twenty francs the second. Very well, replied

le paysan, je commencerai au second mois.
ler pay'e-*zahng* sher kom-*ahng*-ser-reh oh ser-*gong* mo'ah
the countryman, I shall-begin at-the second month.

Un monsieur dînant dans un restaurant demanda
ung mer-se-er dee-*nahng* da*ng z'ung* ress-toh-*rahng* der-*mahng*-dah
A gentleman dining in a restaurant asked

à quelqu'un assis près de lui d'avoir la bonté de
ah kell-*kung* ah-see pray der lwe dah-vo'ahr lah *bong*-teh der
some one seated near him to have the kindness to

lui passer la moutarde.—Monsieur, dit celui-ci, me
lwe pahss-eh lah moo-tahrd mer-se-*er* dee ser-lwe-se mer
to-him pass the mustard. Sir, said the-latter, me

prenez-vous pour un garçon ?—Oh ! non, monsieur,
prer-neh voo poohr *ung* gahr-*song* oh *nong* mer-se-er
do you take for a waiter? Oh ! no, sir,

fut la réponse, je vous prenais pour un gentleman
fü lah reh-*pong*ss sher voo prer-*nay* poohr *ung* gentleman*
was the reply, I you took for a gentleman.

     * This word retains its English pronunciation when used in French.

Savez-vous nager, mon garçon? — Un peu,
sah-veh voo nah-sheh mong gahr-song ung per
Know you (how to) swim, my boy? A little,

monsieur.—Où avez-vous appris?—Dans l'eau.
mer-se-er oo ah-veh voo z'ah-pree dahng loh
sir. Where have you learnt? In the water.

Pourquoi avez-vous une ficelle attachée à
poohr-ko'ah ah-veh voo z'ün fe-sell ah-tah-sheh ah
Why have you a string tied to

votre doigt?—Ma femme l'a attachée ce matin
votr do'ah mah fahmm lah ah-tah-sheh ser mah-tang
your finger?— My wife it has tied-on this morning

pour me rappeler que j'avais une lettre à
poohr mer rah-per-leh ker shah-vay z'ün lettr ah
to me remind that I had a letter to

expédier pour elle.—Ah! et vous l'avez mise dans
ex-peh-de-eh poohr ell ah eh voo lah-veh meez dahng
send-off for her. — Ah! and you it have put in

la boîte?—Non, elle a oublié de me la donner.
lah bo'ahtt nong ell ah oo-ble-eh der mer lah donn-eh
the box? — No, she has forgotten to me it give.

Un juge, agacé par la volubilité d'un témoin,
ung shüsh ah-gah-seh pahr lah vol-ü-bil-e-teh dung teh-mo'ang
A judge, irritated by the volubility of a witness,

lui dit avec impatience : Ne bavardez pas tant.
lwe dee ah-veck ang-pah-se-ahngss ner bah-vahr-deh pah tahng
to-him said with impatience : Chatter not so.

Taisez-vous, et répondez à ma question
tay-zeh voo eh reh-pong-deh z'ah mah kess-te-ong
Silence yourself,* and reply to my question.

* =keep silent.

Je fume beaucoup, disait le charcutier, et
sher füm boh-koo dee-zay ler shahr-kü-te-eh eh
I smoke much, said the pork-butcher, and

pourtant je ne fume ni pipe, ni cigares, ni
poohr-tahng sher ner füm ne peep ne se-gahr ne
nevertheless I (not) smoke neither pipe, nor cigars, nor

cigarettes. — Que fumez-vous alors? demanda
se-gah-rett ker fü-meh voo ah-lor der-mahng-dah
cigarettes. — What smoke you then? asked

son ami.—Des jambons! répondit le charcutier.
song n'ah-me day shahng-bong reh-pong-de ler shahr-kü-te-eh
his friend.—(some) Hams! answered the pork-butcher.

Le petit garçon : Voulez-vous me donner
ler per-te gahr-song voo-leh voo mer donn-eh
The little boy : Will you me give

quatre sous, monsieur?—Le vieux monsieur :
kah-tr soo mer-se-er ler ve-er mer-se-er
four halfpennies, sir? — The old gentleman :

Vous voulez quatre sous, parce que vous
voo voo-leh kah-tr soo pahrss ker voo
You want four halfpennies because you

n'avez encore rien mangé aujourd'hui, pro-
nah-veh z'ahng-kor re-ang mahng-sheh oh-shoohr-dwe pro-
not have yet anything eaten to-day, pro-

bablement ?—Le petit garçon : Non, monsieur,
bah-bler-mahng ler per-te gahr-song nong mer-se-er
bably ? — The little boy : No, sir,

c'est parce que mon père n'a encore rien bu.
say pahrss ker mong pair nah ahng-kor re-ang bü
it is because my father not has yet anything drunk.

Un missionnaire écrit d'Afrique : Les membres de
ung miss-e-on-air eh-kree dah-frick lay m*ahng*-br der
A missionary writes from Africa : The members of

ma congrégation refusent d'abandonner leurs
mah k*o*ng-greh-gah-se-*ong* rer-füz dah-b*ahng*-donn-eh ler
my congregation refuse to give-up their

habitudes de cannibalisme, mais je suis heureux
z'ah-be-tüd der kah-ne-bah-leez-m may sher swe z'er-rer
habits of cannibalism, but I am happy

de dire que, grâce à mes efforts, ils ont appris
der deer ker grahss ah* may z'eff-or ill z'ong t'ah-pree
to say that, thanks to my efforts, they have learnt

à manger avec une fourchette et un couteau.
z'ah m*ahng*-sheh ah-veck ün foohr-shett eh *ung* koo-toh
to eat with a fork and a knife.

Une dame qui écrivait une lettre s'aperçut qu'un
ün dahmm ke eh-kre-vay t'ün lettr sah-pair-sü k*ung*
A lady who was-writing a letter noticed that a

jeune homme lisait la lettre par-dessus ses
shern omm le-zay lah lettr pahr-der-sü say
young man was-reading the letter over her

épaules. Elle ajouta alors : J'aurais encore
z'eh-pohl elle ah-shoo-tah ah-lor shoh-ray z'*ahng*-kor
shoulders. She added then : I should-have still

beaucoup à vous dire, mais Monsieur Lesimple
boh-koo p'ah voo deer may mer-se-er ler-s*ang*pl
much to you tell, but Mr. Simple

est derrière moi qui lit tout ce que j'écris.—
ay dair-e-air mo'ah ke iee too ser ker sheh-kree
is behind me who reads all that which I write.—

Pardon, madame, dit-il, je n'ai rien lu.
pahr-d*ong* mah-dahmm dee t'ill sher neh re-*ang* lü
Pardon, madam, said he I not have anything read.

Un voyageur quelque peu distrait cherchait
ung vo'ah-yah-sher kell-ker per diss-tray shair-shay
A traveller some little absent-minded was-looking-fo:

la clé de sa malle. Comme il ne pouvait la
lah kleh der sah mahll komm ill ner poo-vay lah
the key of his trunk. As he not could it

trouver nulle part, il dit à sa femme: Je
troo-veh nül pahr ill dee t'ah sah fahmm sher
find anywhere, he said to his wife: I

dois l'avoir enfermée dans la malle. C'est très
do'ah lah-vo'ahr ahng-fair-meh dahng lah mahll say tray
must it have locked-up in the trunk. That is very

ennuyeux, car c'est la seule clé que j'aie.
z'ahng-n'we-yer kahr say lah serl kleh ker shay
annoying, for it is the only key that I have.

Lui: À propos, voulez-vous me permettre de
lwē ah pro-po voo-leh voo mer pair-mettr der
He: By-the-way, will you me permit to

vous amener mon ami, Lebrun, demain soir?
voo z'ah-mer-neh mong n'ah-me ler-brung der-mang so'ahr
to-you bring my friend Brown to-morrow evening?

C'est le célèbre organiste, vous savez.—Maîtresse
say ler seh-laybr or-gah-nist voo sah-veh may-tress
He is the celebrated organist, you know. — Mistress

de la maison: Je serai très heureuse de le voir.
der lah may-zong sher ser-reh tray z'er-rerz der ler vo'ahr
of the house: I shall-be very happy to him see.

Dites-lui d'apporter son instrument avec lui!
ditt lwe dah-por-teh song n'ang-strü-mahng ah-veck lwe
Tell (to-)him to bring his instrument with him!

Un monsieur envoya un jour son domestique
ung mer-se-er *ahng*-vo'ah-yah *ung* shoohr *song* do-mess-tick
A gentleman sent one day his servant

voir l'heure au cadran solaire dans le jardin.
vo'ahr ler oh kah-dr*ahng* so-lair d*ahng* ler shahr-d*ang*
to-see the time at-the sun-dial in the garden.

Au bout d'une demi-heure le serviteur rentra,
oh boo dün der-me er ler sair-ve-ter r*ahng*-trah
At-the end of a half-hour the servant came-in-again,

portant dans ses bras le cadran. Voici
por-t*ahng* d*ahng* say brah ler kah-dr*ahng* vo'ah-se
carrying in his arms the sundial. Here-is

le cadran, Monsieur, dit-il à son maître.
ler kah-dr*ahng* mer-se-er dee t'ill ah *song* maytr.
the dial, sir, said he to his master.

Voyez vous-même quelle heure il est ; moi,
vo'ah-yeh voo-mame kell er ill ay mo'ah
See yourself what time it is; [as for]me

je ne comprends rien à ces sortes d'horloges.
sher ner k*ong*-pr*ahng* re'*ang* ah say sort dor-losh
I not understand anything at(=about) these sorts of clocks

Le docteur: Je vois maintenant d'où vient votre
ler dock-ter sher vo'ah m*ang*-ter-n*ahng* doo ve-*ang* votr
The doctor : I see now from where comes your

maladie. La boisson est votre faible.—Le malade:
mah-lah-de lah bo'ahss-*ong* ay votr faybl ler mah-lahdd
illness. Drinking is your weak(point). The patient :

Au contraire, docteur, c'est justement mon fort.
oh k*ong*-trair dock ter say shüst m*ahng* m*ong* for
To-the contrary, doctor, it is just my strong(point).

Deux petits garçons trouvèrent une noix. Cette
der per-te gahr-*song* troo-vair *t'*ün no'ah set
Two little boys found a walnut. This

noix m'appartient, dit l'ün, car j'ai été le
no'ah mah-pahr-te-*ang* dee *lung* kahr sheh eh-teh ler
nut to-me belongs, said the one, for I have been the

premier à la voir.—Non, répondit l'autre, elle
prer-me-eh ah lah vo'ahr *nong* reh-*pong*-de lohtr ell
first to it see. — No, replied the other, it

doit m'appartenir, puisque je l'ai ramassée.
do'ah mah-pahr-*ter*-neer pweesk sher leh rah-mahss-eh
must to-me belong, since I it have picked-up.

Un jeune homme survint et les mit d'accord.
ung shern omm sür-*vang* · eh lay mee dah-kor
A young man came-up and them put of(==in) agreement.

Il prit la noix, la cassa et dit : Voici une
ill pree lah no'ah lah kahss-ah eh dee vo'ah-se ün
He took the nut, it broke and said : Here-is a

coquille pour celui qui a été le premier à
ko-kee'yer poohr ser-lwe ke ah eh-teh ler prer-me-eh ah
shell for him who has been the first to

voir la noix, et voilà l'autre pour celui
vo-ahr lah no'ah eh vo'ah-lah lohtr poohr ser-lwe
see the nut, and there-is the other for him

qui l'a ramassée. Quant à l'amande, je la
ke lah rah-mahss-eh *kahng* *t'*ah lah-*mahng*d sher lah
who it has picked-up. As to the kernel, I it

garde, comme rémunération pour mon jugement.
gahrd komm reh-mü-neh-rah-se-*ong* poohr *mong* shüsh-*mahng*
keep as remuneration for my judgment.

La jolie demoiselle : Quel est le prix de cette
lah sho-le der-mo'ah-zell kell ay ler pree der set
The pretty young lady : What is the price of this

paire de gants ? — Le commis (galamment)
pair der gahng ler komm-ee gah-lah-mahng
pair of gloves ? — The assistant (gallantly) :

Un baiser. — La jolie demoiselle : Très bien ;
ung bay-zeh lah sho-le der-mo'ah-zell tray be-ang
A kiss. — The pretty young lady : Very well ;

veuillez m'en donner trois paires. J'enverrai
ver'e-yeh mahng donn-eh tro'ah pair shahng-vair-eh
kindly to-me of-them give three pairs. I shall-send

ma grand'mère vous payer cet après-midi.
mah grahng-mair voo pay-yeh set ah-pray me-de
my grandmother you to-pay this afternoon.

Un facteur distribue le courrier. Voici, dit-il,
ung fahck-ter diss-tree-bü le koohr-e-eh vo'ah-se dee t'ill
A postman is-distributing the post. Here-is, says he,

une lettre pour mademoiselle Julie Duval.—Mais
ün lettr poobr mah-der-mo'ah-zell shü-le dü-vahll may
a letter for Miss Julia Duval. — But

comment pouvez-vous déjà savoir le nom de
komm-ahng poo-veh voo deh-shah sah-vo'ahr ler nong der
how can you already know the name of

cette demoiselle ? réplique le concierge étonné.
set der-mo'ah-zell reh-plick ler kong-se-airsh eh-tonn-eh
that young lady ? replies the hall-porter astonished.

Elle n'est dans la maison que depuis hier.
elle nay dahng lah may-zong ker der-pwe z'e-air
She not is in the house but since yesterday.

Professeur : Pourquoi riez-vous continuellement?—
pro-fess-er   poohr-ko'ah ree-eh voo   kong-té-nü-ell-mahng
    Professor :   Why   do you laugh   continually ?

Élève : Vous faites des questions si drôles, monsieur!
eh-lave   voo   fate day kess-te-ong se   drohl   mer-se-er
Pupil :   You   put (make) questions so funny,   sir.

Madame Bertrand (à son fils) : Je croyais que
mah-dahmm bair-trahng ah song fiss sher kro'ah-yay ker
  Madame   Bertrand (to her son) : I   thought   that

vous disiez que c'était le petit garçon d'à côté
voo dee-ze-eh ker seh-tay ler per-te gahr-song dah koh-teh
you   said   that it-was the little boy next door(of at side

qui faisait tout le bruit.—Petit Bertrand : C'est
ke fer-zay too ler brwe   per-te bair-trahng   say
who was-making all the noise.— Little Bertrand : It is

vrai, maman. Je le battais avec une canne.
vray mah-mahng sher ler bah-tay ah-veck ün kahnn
true, mamma. I him was-beating with a   stick.

Toto : Bonjour, mon oncle. Je vous souhaite
to-to bong-shoohr mong n'ongkl sher voo   soo'ayt
Toto : Good day, my   uncle. I to-you wish

une bonne et heureuse année. Maman m'a
ün bonn eh er-erz   ahnn-eh   mah-mahng mah
a good and happy   year. Mamma to-me has

dit que si vous me donnez un louis, je
dee ker se voo mer donn-eh z'ung loo-ee sher
said that if you to-me give   a sovereign, I

dois prendre bien soin de ne pas le perdre.
do'ah prahng-dr be-ang so'ang der ner pah ler pairdr
am-to take   well care to not it lose.

Quel terrible orage nous avons eu la nuit passée !
kell tairr-ribl o-rahsh noo z'ah-vong z'ü lah n'we pah-seh
What(a) fearful storm we have had last night(the night past)

—Vraiment?—Comment! vous n'avez pas entendu?
vray-mahng komnt-ahng voo nah veh pah z'ahng-tahng-dü
Indeed? — What! you have not heard?

—Non! Le petit faisait sa première dent.
nong ler per-te fer-zay sah prer-me-air dahng
No. The child was cutting(made) its first tooth.

L'autre jour un jeune homme alla voir un
loh-tr shoohr ung shern omm ahll-ah vo'ahr ung
The other day a young man went to see an

auteur. Il lui dit: Monsieur, j'ai composé
n oh-ter ill lwe dee mer-se-er sheh kong-po-zeh
author. He to him said : Sir, I have composed

deux poèmes. Permettez - moi de vous les
der po-ame pair met-eh mo'ah der voo lay
two poems. Permit me to to you them

lire. — Il en lut un Il allait lire l'autre.
leer ill ahng lü t'ung ill ahll-ay leer lohtr
read. — He of them read one. He was going to read the other.

L'auteur lui dit : Ne vous donnez pas la
loh-ter lwe dee nèr voo donn eh pah lah
The author to him said : (Not) yourself give not the

peine. Je préfère l'autre. — Le jeune
pain sher preh-fair loh-tr ler shern
trouble. I prefer the other — The young

homme comprit, et se retira aussitôt.
omm kong-pree eh ser rer-te-rah oh se-toh
man understood, and (himself) withdrew immediately.

Explique-moi, Robert, ce que c'est qu'un veuf.
ex-pleek   mo'ah   ro-bair   ser ker   say   kung   verf
Explain   to-me,   Robert,   what   (it)is (that)a widower.

—Robert réfléchit un instant, puis tout à
ro-bair   reh-flch-shee   ung n'ang-stahng   p'we   too   t'ah
Robert   reflects   an   instant,   then   sudden-

coup : Un veuf, c'est le mari d'une veuve,
koo   ung verf   say   ler   mah-re   -dün   verv
ly :   A widower,   it is   the   husband   of a   widow.

Eh bien, madame ! quelle est votre opinion
eh   be-*ang*   mah-dahmm   kell   ay   votr   o-pe-ne-*ong*
Well,   madam !   What   is   your   opinion

de ce tableau ? — Ce ne peut pas être
der   ser   tah-bloh   ser   ner   per   pah   z'ay-tr
of   this   picture ?   — It   cannot   be

le chef-d'œuvre dont tout le monde parle.
ler   shay-der-vr   dong   too   ler   mongd   parl
the   masterpiece   of which everyone (all the world)is speaking,

— Qu'est-ce qui vous fait penser cela?—
kess   ke   voo   fay   p*ahng*-seh   ser-lah
— What is it   that   you   makes   think   that ?—

Je trouve qu'il est si simple que
sher   troov   kill   ay   se   sang-pl   ker
I   find   that it   is   so   simple   that

n'importe qui peut voir du premier
nang-port   kee   per   vo'ahr   dü   prer-me-eh
anybody   (no matter who) can see at (from)   the   first

coup d'œil exactement ce qu'il représente.
koo   der'e   egg-zahck-ter-m*ahng*   ser   kill   rer-preh-z*ahng*t
glance (stroke of eye)   exactly   what   it   represents.

Le touriste : Vous devez avoir de bon lait ici.—
ler   too-rist   voo   der-veh z'ah-vo'ahr der bong lay iss-e
The tourist :   You   must   have   good milk here.—

Le paysan : Vous pouvez en être sûr, monsieur.
ler pay'e-zahng voo   poo-veh z'ahng n'aytr sür   mer-se-er
The peasant : You   may   of it be sure,   sir.

Nous ne sommes qu'à quarante milles de Londres.
noo ner somm kah kah-rahngt mill der long-dr
We are only (at)   forty   miles from London.

Le littérateur allemand, Lessing, était si
ler lit-eh-rah-ter ahl-mahng   lessing   eh-tay se
The man of letters German,   Lessing,   was so

distrait qu'un soir il frappa à sa propre
dis-tray kung so'ahr ill frah-pah ah sah propr
absent-minded that one evening he knocked at his   own

porte et demanda si le professeur était
port eh der-mahng-dah se ler pro-fess-er eh-tay
door and   asked   if the professor   was

chez lui. La nuit était fort noire, et
sheh lwe lah n'we eh-tay for   no'ahr   eh
at-home. The night was very dark(strong black)and

la servante, ne reconnaissant pas son
lah sair-vahngt ner rer-konn-ess-ahng pah song
the servant,   recognizing   not her

maître, répondit négativement. — Ah !
may-tr reh-pong-de neh-gah-teev-mahng   ah
master,   replied   negatively. — Ah !

n'importe, dit Lessing ; je reviendrai demain.
nang-port dee lessing sher rer-ve-ang-dreh der-mang
it matters not, said Lessing ; I will come again to-morrow.

Entre bohêmes.—Mais pourquoi avez-vous refusé
ahng-tr   bo-ame   may   poohr-ko'ah ah-veh **voo** rer-fü-zeh
Between Bohemians. — But   why   have **you** refused

de donner votre adresse à ce monsieur ? Est-ce
der donn-eh votr ah-dress ah ser mer-se-er   ess
to   give   your   address to that gentleman?   Is he

un créancier ?—Non, mais il peut le devenir.
ung kreh-*ahng*-se-eh n*o*ng may z'ill per ler der-ver-neer'
a   creditor ? — No, but   he may .it become.

Un touriste (au guide) : Est-ce que nous approchons
ung too-rist oh gheed ess ker noo z'ah-pro-sh*o*ng
A   tourist (to the guide) : Is it that we are approaching

de la cataracte ?—Le guide : Oui, monsieur, c'est
der lah kah-tah-rahkt ler gheed oo'e mer-se-er say
the   cataract ? — The guide : Yes, sir,   it is

tout près, et si ces dames veulent bien se taire
too pray eh! se say dahmm verl be-*ang* ser tair
quite near, and if these ladies will kindly themselves silence

un instant, vous entendrez le bruit formidable.
ung n'*ang*-stahng voo z'*ahng*-tahng-dreh ler br'we   for-me-dahbl
an   instant,   you   will hear the noise formidable.

Ce doit être terrible pour une grande cantatrice
ser do'ah t'ay-tr tairr-ibl poohr ün gr*ahng*d k*ahng*-tah-triss
It   must be dreadful for a   great   singer

de savoir qu'elle a perdu la voix. — C'est bien
der sah-vo'ahr kell ah pair-dü lah vo'ah say be-*ang*
to know   that she has lost her(the)voice.—It is well(much)

plus terrible encore quand elle ne le sait pas.
plü tairr-ibl *ahng*-kor k*ahng* t'ell ner ler say pah
more terrible still when she   it knows not.

Un conférencier : N'est-ce pas drôle? On
ung kong-feh-rahng-se-eh   ness   pah   drohl   ong
A   lecturer :   Is it   not   funny?   They

me paie souvent autant pour une courte
mer   pay   soo-vahng   oh-tahng   poohr   ün   koohrt
me   pay   often   as much   for   a   short

conférence que pour une longue.—Son ami :
kong-feh-rahngss   ker   poohr   ün   long-g   song n'ah-me
lecture   as   for   a   long (one).—His friend :

Je croyais qu'on vous aurait payé davantage.
sher kro'ah-yay   kong   voo   z'oh-ray   pay-yeh dah-vahng-tahsh
I   believed   that one   you   would have paid   more.

Au théâtre.—Un monsieur s'installe aux fauteuils
oh teh-ahtr   ung   mer-se-er   sang-stahll   oh   foh-ter'e
At the theatre.—A   gentleman   himself instals in the armchairs

d'orchestre et place son chapeau sur le
dor-kestr   eh   plahss   song   shah-poh   sür   ler
of orchestra   and   places   his   hat   on   the

fauteuil voisin. Un nouveau spectateur
foh-ter'e   vo'ah-zang   ung   noo-voh   spek-tah-ter
armchair(=stall) neighbouring. A   new   spectator

survient et demande : Cette place est-elle
sür-ve-ang   eh   der-mahngd   set   plahss   ay t'ell
comes up   and   asks :   This   place   is it

occupée ? — Oui, monsieur, je la garde
ok-ü-peh   oo'e   mer-se-er   sher   lah   gahrd
engaged ? — Yes,   sir,   I   it am keeping

pour un monsieur qui ne peut pas venir.
poohr   ung   mer-se-er   ke   ner   per   pah   ver-neer
for   a   gentleman   who (not)   can   not   come.

L'avocat (au juge) : J'admets que mon client
lah-vo-kah   oh   shüsh   shahd-may   ker   mong   kle-ahng
The lawyer (to the judge) :   I admit   that   my   client

ait appelé le plaignant "bœuf," mais vu le
ay   t'ah-per-leh ler   plane-yahng   berf   may   vü   ler
(have) called the   plaintiff   " ox,"   but seeing(seen)the

prix de la viande, je considère cela plutôt
pree   der lah   ve-ahngd   sher   kong-se-dair   ser-lah   plü-toh
price   of (the)   meat,   I   consider   that · rather

comme un compliment que comme une insulte.
komm   ung kong-ple-mahng   ker   komm   ün   ang-sült
as   a   compliment   than   as   an   insult.

Un homme d'esprit disait un jour qu'il vieillissait,
ung   n'omm   dess-pree · de-zay t'ung shoohr kill   ve-ay'e-say
A   man   of wit   said   one day that he was growing old

quand un jeune impertinent, à tête creuse,
kahng   t'ung   shern   ang-pair-te-nahng   ah   tayt   krerz
when   a   young impertinent fellow, at (with) head hollow,

lui dit : Que donneriez-vous pour être aussi
lwe   dee   ker   donn-er-re-eh   voo   poohr   aytr   oh-se
to him said : What   would you give   to   be   as

jeune que moi ?—Ma foi, répondit le monsieur,
shern   ker   mo'ah   mah   fo'ah   reh-pong-de ler   mer-se-er,
young   as   I ?— My faith, replied   the gentleman,

je me résignerais même à être aussi sot.
sher mer   reh-zeen-yer-ray   mame   ah   aytr   oh-se   soh
I myself should resign   even   to   be   as foolish.

Pierre   qui   roule   n'amasse   pas   mousse.
pe-air   ke   rool   nah-mahss   pah   mooss
Stone   which   rolls   gathers   not   moss.

Un duel sérieux.—Oui, dit le brave Duval, un des
ung dü-ell seh-re-*er*   oo'*e* dee l*er* brahv dü-vahll *ung* day
A   duel serious. — Yes, said the brave Duval, one of the

adversaires tira en l'air et l'autre tomba mort.
z'ahd-vair-sai*r* te-rah *ahng* lair eh lohtr t*o*ng-bah mor
adversaries fired in the air and the other fell dead.

Premier vagabond : J'ai eu la nuit dernière un
pr*er*-me-eh vah-gah-b*o*ng sheh ü lah nwe dair-ne-air *ung*
First tramp : I have had the night last a

cauchemar épouvantable.— Deuxième vagabond :
kohsh-mahr eh-poo-*vahng*-tahbl der-ze-ame vah-gah-b*o*ng
nightmare dreadful. — Second tramp :

Vraiment ?—Oui. J'ai rêvé que je travaillais.
vray-*mahng* oo'*e* sheh ray-veh ker sher trah-vah'e-yay
Truly (=indeed) ?—Yes. I (have) dreamed that I was working.

Comment faites - vous pour gagner toujours?
komm-*ahng* fate voo poohr gahn-yeh too-shoohr
How do you(manage) to win always ?

— Un de mes amis qui connaît les
 ung der may z'ah-me ke konn-ay láy
— One of my friends who knows the

chevaux m'indique sur lequel je dois
sher-voh *mang*-deek sür ler-kell sher do'ah
horses to-me indicates on which I am to

parier. — Et vous suivez exactement son
pah-re-eh eh voo swe-veh z'eg-zahk-ter-m*ahng* s*o*ng
bet. — And you follow exactly his

conseil ? — Non, je fais tout le contraire.
k*o*ng-say'e n*o*ng sher fay too ler k*o*ng-trair
advice ? — No, I do just(=all) the contrary.

Le visiteur : Madame Durand est-elle chez elle?
ler ve-ze-ter mah-dahmm dü-ra*hng* ay *t*'ell sheh *z*'ell
The visitor : Mrs. Durand is she at-home?

—La domestique : Non, monsieur.—Le visiteur :
  lah do-mess-tick *n*ong mer-se-*e*r ler ve-ze-ter
—The servant : No, sir. — The visitor :

Voulez-vous monter lui demander quand. elle y
voo-leh voo *m*ong-teh lwe der-m*a*hng-deh k*a*hng *t*'ell e
Will you go-upstairs[and]to-her ask when she in

sera?—La bonne (y allant) : Oui, monsieur.
ser-rah lah bonn e ahll-*a*hng oo'*e* mer-se-*e*r
will-be?—The servant (there going) : Yes, sir.

Le professeur (à la classe) : Une seule goutte de
ler pro-fess-*e*r ah lah. klahss ün serl goot der
The professor (to the class) : One single drop of

ce poison versée sur la langue d'un chat suffit
ser po'ah-*z*ong vair-seh sür lah l*a*hng-g *d*ung shah sü-fee
this poison poured on the tongue of a cat suffices

pour tuer l'homme le plus fort de la terre!
poohr tü-eh lomm ler plü for der lah tair
to kill the man the most strong of the earth!

En cour d'assises.—Le juge : Êtes-vous coupable
*a*hng koohr dahss-eez ler shüsh ate voo koo-pahbl
In court of assizes. The judge : Are you guilty

ou non?—L'accusé : Je ne le sais pas encore ; je
oo *n*ong lah-kü-zeh sher ner ler say pah *z*'*a*hng-kor sher
or not? The accused : I it know not yet ; I

vous répondrai après avoir entendu les témoins.
*v*oo reh-*p*ong-dreh ah-pray *z*'ah-vo'ahr *a*hng-tahng-dü lay teh-mo'*a*ng
*y*ou shall answer after having heard the witnesses

Le contentement consiste, en grande partie, à
ler kong-tahngt-mahng   kong-sist   ahng   grahngd   pahr-te   ah
(The)   contentment   consists to a (in) large extent(part) in

ne pas désirer ce qùi est hors de notre portée.
ner pah deh-ze-reh ser ke ay hor der notr por-teh
not desiring that which is out of our reach.

Un officier anglais reçut une balle dans la
ung n'off-iss-e-eh ahng-glay rer-sü t'ün bahll dahng lah
An officer English received a ball in the

jambe. Il fut transporté chez lui. Deux
shahngb ill fü trahngs-por-teh sheh lwe der
leg. He was carried to-the-home-of him. Two

médecins furent appelés. Sonder la plaie fut
meh-der-sang für t'ah-per-leh song-deh lah play fü
doctors were called. To probe the wound was

la seule chose faite. Cela fut répété tous les jours
lah serl shohz fate ser-lah fü reh-peh-teh too lay shoohz
the only thing done. This was repeated all the days

pendant une semaine. — Que cherchez-vous?
pahng-dahng t'ün ser-mane ker shair-sheh voo
during a week. — What seek you?

demanda enfin l'officier. — Les médecins ré-
der-mahng-dah ahng-fang loff-iss-e-eh lay meh-der-sàng reh-
asked at last the officer. — The doctors

pondirent: Nous cherchons la balle.—C'est trop
pong-deer noo shair-shong lah bahll say tro
answered : We seek the ball. — That is too

fort, dit l'officier : elle est dans ma poche.
for dee loff-iss-e-eh ell ay dahng mah posh
strong(bad), said the officer ; it is in my pocket.

Un gamin comprend toujours qu'il est mal de
ung gah-*mang* *kong*-prahng too-shoohr kill ay mahll der
A youngster understands always that it is wrong(bad) to

chercher querelle lorsqu'il sort battu du combat.
share-sheh ker-rell lors-kill sor bah-tü dü *kong*-bah
(seek) quarrel when he comes out beaten from the fight.

Un vieil avare, après avoir entendu un· éloquent
ung ve-ay'e *y*'ah-vahr ah-pray *z*'ah-vo'ahr ahng-tahng-dü *ung* n'eh-lo-*kahng*
An old miser, after having heard an eloquent

sermon sur la charité, s'écria : Ce sermon dé-
sair-*mong* sür lah shah-re-teh seh-kre-ah ser sair-*mong* deh-
sermon on charity, exclaimed : That sermon de-

montre si clairement la nécessité de faire
*mong*tr se klair-*mahng* lah neh-sess-e-teh der 'fair
monstrates so clearly the necessity to make(give)

l'aumône que j'ai. presque envie de mendier.
loh-mohn ker sheh press-ker ahng-ve der m*ahng*-de-eh
alms that I have almost inclination to beg.

Je vous serai éternellement reconnaissante. Vous
sher voo ser-reh eh-tair-nell-m*ahng* rer-konn-ess-*ahng*t voo
I to you shall be eternally grateful. You

avez ˙secouru mon mari lorsqu'il se noyait;
z'ah-veh ser-koo-rü m*ong* mah-re lor-skill ser no'ah-yay
have rescued my husband when he (himself) was-drowning ;

vous lui avez sauvé la vie.—Je vous en prie,
voo lwe ah-veh soh-veh lah vee sher voo *z*'ahng pree
you to him have saved the life.— I you pray,

madame, ne parlez pas d'une telle bagatelle.
mah-dahmm ner pahr-leh pah dün tell bah-gah-tell
madam, speak not of a such trifle.

La bonne (hors d'haleine) : Monsieur, il y a un
lah bonn   hor   dah-lane   mer-se-er   ill e ah *ung*
The servant   (out of breath) :   Sir, it there has(=there is) a

cambrioleur dans le salon !—Le savant (distrait) :
kahng-bre-o-ler d*ahng* ler sah-lo*ng*   ler sah-v*ahng* diss-tray
burglar in the drawing-room !—The man of science(absent-minded)

Impossible de le recevoir. Je suis très occupé.
ang-poss-eebl der ler rer-ser-vo'ahr sher swe   tray z'ok-ü-peh
Impossible to him receive.   I   am   very   busy.

Oh ! docteur, si vous saviez comme je souffre !—
oh   dok-ter se voo sah-ve-eh   komm sher soofr
Oh !   doctor, if you   knew   how   I   suffer ! —

Où souffrez-vous ?—Dans l'estomac, docteur. Ce
oo   soof-reh   voo   d*ahng* less-to-mah   dok-ter   ser
Where suffer   you ?— In   the stomach, doctor. This

matin, en m'éveillant, j'avais bien soif. Comme
mah-t*ang* *ahng* meh-vay'e-y*ahng* shah-vay be-*ang* so'ahf   komm
morning in (myself) waking, I was   very thirsty.*   As

il ne faisait pas encore bien clair et que mes
ill ner fer-zay pah z'*ahng*-kor be-*ang* klair eh ker   may
it was (made) not   yet   very light and as(that) my

idées n'étaient pas très nettes, j'ai pris le
z'e-deh   neh-tay   pah   tray   net   sheh pree ler
ideas   were   not   very clear,   I have taken the

verre d'eau qui était sur ma table de nuit, et
vair   doh   ke eh-tay sür mah tahbl der n'we eh
glass of water which was on my   table of night, and

je l'ai vidé. Mon œil de verre était dedans !
sher leh ve-deh mong n'er'e der   vair   eh-tay der-d*ahng*
it have emptied. My eye of glass   was   therein !

* literally, had well thirst.

Les enfants et les fous s'imaginent que vingt
lay z'ahng-fahng eh lay foo se-mah-sheen ker vang
(The) children and (the) fools imagine that twenty

francs et vingt ans ne peuvent jamais finir.
frahng eh vang t'ahng ner perv shah-may fe-neer
francs and twenty years can never finish.

Logique de paysan.—Le paysan (au médecin):
lo-shick der pay'e-zahng ler pay'e-zahng oh meh-der-sang
Logic of countryman.—The countryman (to the physician):

Comment! vous demandez des honoraires pour
komm-ahng voo der-mahng-deh day z'o-no-rair poohr
What! you ask (for) some fees for

les soins que vous avez donnés à
lay so'ang ker voo z'ah-veh donn-eh ah
the cares that you have given to

ma défunte femme? Est-ce que vous l'avez
mah deh-fungt fahmm ess ker voo lah-veh
my deceased wife? Is it that you her have

guérie? — Le docteur: Non. — Le paysan:
gay-re ler dock-ter nong ler pay'e-zahng
cured? — The doctor: No. — The countryman.

Vous l'avez peut-être tuée? — Le docteur:
voo lah-veh per-t'aytr tü-eh ler dock-ter
You her have may-be killed? — The doctor:

Non. — Le paysan: Eh bien, alors, pour
nong ler pay'e-zahng eh be-ang ah-lor poohr
No. — The countryman: Well, then, for

quel motif demandez-vous des honoraires?
kell mo-tif der-mahng-deh voo day z'o-no-rair
what reason demand you some fees?

REMARKS ON HUGO'S PHONETICALLY IMITATED PRONUNCIATION.
(for reference only)

If learners pronounce each syllable in the Imitated Pronunciation as if it were an English syllable, any Frenchman will understand them ; but as there are a few sounds in French which do not occur in the English language at all, the following instructions should be borne in mind :—

sh (in **thick type**) must be pronounced like s in 'measure' or 'leisure.' Examples :

âge	général	joli	rouge	rougi	j'avais
ahsh	shay-nay-rahll	sho-le	roosh	roo-she	shah-vay
age	general	pretty	red	blushed	I had

ü represents a sound which does not occur in English, but which can be produced with absolute correctness by following the instructions on page 3. We occasionally imitate this sound by EE.

lu	vu	du	mu	accumula	salut
lü, lEE	vü, vEE	dü, dEE	mü	ah-kü-mü-lah	sah-lü
read	seen	of-the	moved	accumulated	safety

r (in **thick type**) should be pronounced more strongly than in English.

alarme	fermé	sorte	père	fortune	par
ah-lahrm	fair-may	sort	pair	for-tün	pahr
alarm	shut	sort	father	fortune	by

r (printed in *italics*) must on no account be pronounced at all.

le	reçu	appartenir	premier	petit
ler	rer-sü	ah-pahr-ter-neer	prer-me-ay	per-te
the	received	to belong	first	little

[At first, it may be wondered why this *r* is inserted, if it is not to be pronounced. Its insertion is necessary, because it affects the sound of the preceding vowel. For example, *ce* and *se* are pronounced like the English word 'sir,' less the sound of the R. We therefore imitate these words as 'se*r*.' If the *r* were omitted, the vowel sound would be quite different.]

ng (printed in *italics*) must also on no account be pronounced at all. Its insertion is necessary, as in the case of the italic *r*, to indicate the pronunciation of the preceding vowel. The vowel before *ng* must be made nasal.

son	tante	vin	brun	entendre	oncle
song	ta*hng*t	va*ng*	bru*ng*	ah*ng*-tah*ng*-dr	o*ng*kl
his	aunt	wine	brown	to hear	uncle

[In French nasal syllables, it is most important not to let the NG be heard. For example, the French word *son* is not pronounced like the English word ' song.' It is like the ' so' in ' song,' pronounced nasally. To reproduce the exact sound, begin saying ' song,' pronouncing the word through the nose ; but leave off before the NG is reached.]

ah is to be pronounced like the A in ' charm,' not drawn out, but PRONOUNCED SHORT, and as quickly as possible. It is never like the A in ' ham.'

a	bal	animal	fatal	Paris	car	vache
a	bahll	ah-ne-mahll	fah-tahll	pah-re	kahr	vahsh
has	ball	animal	fatal	Paris	for	cow

[Vowels are generally pronounced short in French, unless there is a circumflex accent over them.]

eh should be pronounced like AY, but sharper, and less broad.

bébé	été	espéré	était	répétait
beh-beh	eh-teh	ess-peh-reh	eh-tay	reh-peh-tay
or bay-bay	ay-tay	ess-pay-ray	ay-tay	ray-pay-tay
baby	summer	hoped	was	repeated

[In the Imitated Pronunciation, we usually employ ' eh' to indicate é (with Acute Accent), and ' ay' to indicate è (with Grave Accent). The difference between these two sounds is not always perceptible to English ears ; and as beginners are inclined to pronounce ' eh' like the vowel sound in ' sir,' ' fur,' we sometimes in elementary lessons substitute ' ay,' to ensure an approximately correct pronunciation. Advanced students must not assume this to imply that the sound is that of the Grave Accent.]

LINKING OF FINAL CONSONANTS.

When a word beginning with a Vowel or a silent H follows (IN THE SAME PHRASE) a final Consonant, this Consonant, even if otherwise not pronounced, is sounded, the two words being thus linked together. Thus, *ils* (they) is pronounced 'ill,' and *ont* (have) is pronounced '*ong.*' But the phrase *ils ont* (they have) is pronounced 'ill *z'ong,*' and the phrase *ont-ils* (have they) '*ong t'*ill.' In our Imitated Pronunciation, letters thus linked on are printed in *italics,* followed by an apostrophe.

GENERAL REMARKS.

When first brought out, Hugo's system of indicating the pronunciation was the *only one* by which a beginner could reproduce the sounds, with even approximate correctness, without the aid of a teacher. This system has since been extensively copied, in many cases without acknowledgment, but as in so doing, a few alterations (none of them alterations for the better) had to be made in order to prevent the piracy being of too glaring a nature, Hugo's phonetic pronunciation remains the best.

Our Imitated Pronunciation is only intended for self-taught students ; we freely admit that a few of the sounds can be acquired more accurately if heard. A French sound can only be imitated perfectly in type, if it is a sound that occurs in the English language. But it stands to reason that sounds which never occur in English can only be imitated approximately in English syllables.

For this reason, certain grammarians, who have not cared to go to the trouble of indicating the pronunciation in their own text-books, have called our phonetic method a ' makeshift.'

To a slight extent, this is true. It could not possibly be otherwise, in the case of sounds that are peculiar to the French language. But as we have repeatedly proved, by actual experiment, that entire beginners using our Imitated Pronunciation can in every case reproduce the sounds with sufficient correctness to be understood, without having heard them, we can justly claim that it is not merely by far the best makeshift obtainable— it is of inestimable value to students learning without a teacher.

Rules of French Pronunciation.

:o:

1.--Remarks on the Vowels.

The French Vowels are pronounced thus, but short and sharp :

A is pronounced **ah** (as in the English *cart, master*)
E   ,,   **ay** (,,   ,,   ,,   *day, play*)
I   ,,   **ee** (,,   ,,   ,,   *see, need*)
O   ,,   **oh** (,,   ,,   ,,   *go, home*)

U has no corresponding sound in English. The only way of producing the sound is to try to pronounce the English EE (as in *see*) with *rounded lips* ; that is, with the lips in the same position as when in the act of whistling.

The sounds given above are merely the NAMES of the letters ; it is most important to distinguish between the NAME given to each letter, when standing alone, and the SOUND given to that letter, when it forms part of a word.

(For example, the English letter A is always CALLED "ay" ; but when it forms part of a word, it is pronounced in various ways,— compare its sounds in *cat, far, ball, care, take, local, any.*)

The French Vowel sounds will be dealt with fully in due course. Meanwhile, we restrict our Examples to words in which the SOUND of the Vowel is the same as the NAME of that Vowel. The French Vowel sounds are usually

much shorter than in English.

:o:

EXAMPLES OF THE FRENCH VOWEL SOUNDS.

FRENCH WORD :	a	la	ta	sa	papa	ma	car
PRONUNCIATION :	ah*	lah	tah	sah	pah-pah	mah	kahr
ENG. TRANSLATION :	has	the	thy	his	papa	my	for

* the 'ah' must always be pronounced short and sharp,—not drawn out.

IMPORTANT RULE.—Consonants are seldom pronounced in French when they are the last letter of a word.

des	mes	ses	les	tes	carnet	valet	dater
day	may	say	lay	tay	kahr-nay	vah-lay	dah-teh
some	my	his	the	thy	pocket-book	valet	to date

si	lit	mis	riz	ami	pris	gris	Paris	vit
see	lee	mee	ree	ah-me	pree	gree	pah-re	vee
if	bed	put	rice	friend	taken	grey	Paris	saw

oh!	gros	dos	trop	abricot	coloris	poli
oh	groh	doh	tro	ah-bree-ko	ko-lo-re	po-le
oh!	big	back	too	apricot	tint	polite

bu*	tu	su	nu	salut	paru	dodu	plu
bü	tü	sü	nü	sah-lü	pah-rü	do-dü	plü
drunk	thou	known	bare	safety	appeared	plump	rained

*The French U is always pronounced like the English EE (as in *tree*), but
with rounded lips. This sound is represented in Hugo's Imitated Pronunciation by ' ü.' The exact sound of the first four words given above
can be obtained thus · Round the lips as if about to whistle. When practising this sound, it is even advisable to whistle a note or two first. Then,

without moving the lips in the least,

try to say the English words *bee, tea, sea, knee*. If the lips are kept quite
still, according to instructions, the result is a perfect French U. It will be
found impossible to pronounce an English E with the lips in this position.

Y (which is called in French *i grec*, meaning "Greek i") is
pronounced exactly like a French I.

y	Ivry	lyre	Vitry	synode	type	bicyclette
ee	eev-ree	leer	vee-tree	se-nod	teep	be-se-klett
there	Ivry	lyre	Vitry	synod	type	bicycle

E at the end of a syllable* is pronounced like U in *fur* ; as,

arsenal	retenu	retard	demi	venu	petit	tenu
ahr-ser-nahll	rer-ter-nü	rer-tahr	der-me	ver-nü	per-te	ter-nü
arsenal	retained	delay	half	come	small	held

This sound is as nearly as possible like that of U in *fur*, I in
sir, or E in *her*. But it must be pronounced short and sharp ;
and the R must on no account be sounded at all. This R is merely
introduced in our Imitated Pronunciation to indicate how the
preceding vowel is to be pronounced.

E at the end of words of one syllable is also pronounced like ʊ in *fur*. Examples :

de	le	ne	te	me	se
de*r*	le*r*	ne*r*	te*r*	me*r*	se*r*
of	the	not	thee	me	himself

E is not pronounced at the end of words of more than one syllable.† Examples :

porte	plume	classe	pire	donne	malade	parle	liste
port	plüm	klahss	peer	donn	mah-lahdd	pahrl	list
door	pen	class	worse	gives	ill	speaks	list

†Theoretically, such final E's as these form part of a distinct syllable. In serious music, a separate note is always provided for such cases ; *ma mère*, for example, is sung as three syllables:—*ma mè-re*. But in ordinary conversation, all such words are pronounced as imitated above, not as por-ter, plü-n er, etc. This latter pronunciation, though correct in theory, is pedantic, being unnaturally and painfully correct.

In rapid speaking, the unaccented E is frequently dropped, even in monosyllables. Thus, *je ne te le donne pas* (I do not give it to you) may sound as if spelt je-n-te-l-donn-pâ.

The Æ in *ne* is elided in preference to any other E, because *ne* is never an emphasized word ; and the E in *que* is seldom elided. But it is not possible—it is not even advisable—to give any rules on this point. The foreigner must be prepared to find such E's ignored by natives ; but he himself should only adopt the practice very sparingly, if at all. The more mute E's he pronounces. the more easily will he be understood.

In careless, hasty speaking, many natives often even omit a preceding consonant also, and pronounce *votre livre*, for example, as *vot' liv.'* Foreigners should avoid this slovenly practice.

When a final unaccented E is heard, it must of course be pronounced AFTER the preceding consonant, although this is not done in English. For example, the English words ' theatre ' and ' possible ' are pronounced as if spelt ' theater,' ' possibel.' In America, they even adopt the spelling ' theater.' But in French, *théâtre, table, possible,* must be pronounced teh-ahtr, tahbl, poss-eebl ; or—with greater, but with somewhat unnatural correctness—' teh-ah-trer, tah-bler, poss-ee-bler.' It would be quite wrong to let the least vowel sound, or even breath, be heard between the T and the R, or the B and the L, in French.

*Remarks on the division of words into syllables.

I.—A single consonant between two vowels begins the syllable :

te-nu, a-mi, pro-mis, fi-ni, do-du, fu-ma, va-let, a-lors, pa-ru, re-tard

II.—If there are two consonants, one belongs to each syllable, as :

por-te, har-nais, car-net, par-la, sor-ti, don-na, ar-se-nal, par-tir

III.—R and L are not separated from a preceding consonant, as :

li-vre, or-dre, ar-bre, fi-a-cre, of-fre, pos-si-ble, ta-ble, ou-bli, sou-ple

———— :o: ————

When the CIRCUMFLEX ACCENT is placed over a Vowel, it makes the pronunciation of that Vowel broad-and long, without actually altering its sound. Examples :

âme	tête	île	côte	dû	grêle	sûr	bête
ahm	tate	eel	koht	dü	grail	sür	bait
soul	head	island	coast	owed	hail	sure	beast

The ACUTE ACCENT, which is only placed over E, gives that Vowel a sound similar to the Interjection *eh*, or to the EY in *they*. This sound (*é*) is produced with the mouth nearly closed ; as,

été	café	dé	porté	répété	sérénade	donné
eh-teh	kah-feh	deh	por-teh	reh-peh-teh	seh-reh-nahdd	donn-eh
been	coffee	thimble	carried	repeated	serenade	given

The GRAVE ACCENT also gives to E a sound similar to the E in *they* ; but this sound is produced with the mouth more open ; as,

très	près	élève	zèle	répète	père*	frère*
tray	pray	eh-lave	zayl	reh-pate	pair	frair
very	near	pupil	zeal	repeats	father	brother

As already mentioned, FINAL CONSONANTS are seldom pronounced. ER and EZ, when final, are pronounced like *é*. Before other mute consonants, E takes the sound of *è*. Examples :

nez	porter	fermer	ces	mes	valet	carnet
neh	por-teh	fair-meh	say	may	vah-lay	kahr-nay
nose	to carry	to shut	these	my	valet	pocket-book

IMPORTANT RULE.

C, F, L, R, are pronounced when final ; other consonants are mute. . Examples :

avec	bref	sel	mer	bloc	canif	fatal	par
ah-veck	breff	sell	mair	block	kah-niff	fah-tahll	pahr
with	brief	salt	sea	block	penknife	fatal	by

caduc	tarif	il	sur	lac	actif	vil	car
kah-dük	tah-riff	ill	sür	lahck	ahck-tif	vill	kahr
decrepit	tariff	he	on	lake	active	vile	for

EXCEPTION.—The final R is silent in words ending in ER, except monosyllables. Examples :

vider	prêter	passer	drapier	mer	ver	fer
ve-deh	pray-teh	pahss-eh	drah-pe-eh	mair	vair	fair
to empty	to lend	to pass	draper	sea	worm	iron

The Diphthongs.

AI and **EI** both sound like AY in *play*, thus :

mais	veine	aimé	laid	vrai	peine	reine	paire*
may	vain	ay-meh	lay	vray	pain	rain	pair
but	vein	loved	ugly	true	trouble	queen	pair

* R sometimes modifies the sound of the preceding Vowel, in French as well as in English. Thus, *père* and *paire* are pronounced like the English word 'pear' or 'pair,' NOT like 'payer.'

OU sounds like the OO in *shoot*, thus :

ou	où†	trou	poupée	toux	loué	fou	roue	trouve
oo	oo	troo	poo-peh	too	loo-eh	foo	roo	troov
or	where	hole	doll	cough	let	fool	wheel	finds

†The grave accent only alters the sound of E (see page 35) ; but it is occasionally used over A and U, to distinguish between words spelt alike, but with different meanings.

AU and **EAU** both sound like the O in *go*, thus :

mauvais	cadeau	couteaux	faux	beau	peau	maux
moh-vay	kah-doh	koo-toh	foh	boh	poh	moh
bad	present	knives	false	beautiful	skin	evils

EU and **ŒU** sound nearly like the **u** in *fur*, thus :

neuf	œuf	sœur	mieux	pleure	peu	fleur
ne**rf**	e**rf**	se**r**	me-e**r**	ple**r**	pe**r**	fle**r**
nine	egg	sister	better	weeps	little	flower

We imitate this sound by an **e** in **thick type** ; but it is difficult to indicate in type the slight difference between this sound and that of the unaccented **E** (see page 34). These sounds can best be acquired from a competent teacher ; but anyone who pronounces them as imitated by us will be understood.

OI sounds like wah, pronounced short, thus :

loi	soif	trois	boit	moineau	foi	moi	foire
lo'ah	so'ahf	tro'ah	bo'ah	mo'ah-noh	fo'ah	mo'ah	fo'ahr
law	thirst	three	drinks	sparrow	faith	me	fair

REMARK.—This sound can be imitated in English syllables either as ' wah ' or ' o'ah.' We prefer the latter, because the use of ' wah ' sometimes involves a rather puzzling combination of consonants, such as ' trwah ' for *trois*. We therefore imitate this sound as ' tro'ah ' ; but the learner must be careful not to sound the ' tro ' as a separate syllable. ' Tro'ah ' must be pronounced as *one syllable, short and sharp*, with the stress on the **AH**. To pronounce it as two syllables (' tro-ah,' rhyming with the interjectional oh ! ah !) would be entirely wrong.

————:0:————

THE CONSONANTS.

Nearly all the Consonants (that is, all letters except **a, e, i, o, u, y**) are pronounced as in English.

J, which is pronounced exactly like the **s** in the English words ' measure,' ' treasure,' ' leisure,' is the ONLY Consonant which is always pronounced quite differently in the two languages. Examples :

je	joue	déjà	joli	jaune	jaloux	jour	jeune
sher	shoo	deh-shah	sho-le	shohn	shah-loo	shoohr	shern
I	cheek	already	pretty	yellow	jealous	day	young

☞The following points connected with the pronunciation of the Consonants in French must be carefully noted.

H is generally silent ; and even in those words where it is supposed to be pronounced, the aspiration is nothing like so
strong as in English.

R is pronounced more strongly than in English.   In London,
and other parts of Southern England, the R, unless it begins a
syllable, is frequently, though incorrectly, ignored.   For
instance, ' door ' is pronounced very much like ' daw,' ' farm '
like ' fahm,' and so on.   But French people sound the R
strongly, and somewhat gutturally, except of course in
words where it is not pronounced at all (see page 36).

S between two vowels is pronounced like a z ; in other cases, it
has the sharp hissing sound of ss.*   Examples :

rose	aise	brisé	abusif	loisir	paisible	plaisir	rusé
rohz	ayz	bre-zeh	ah-bü-zeef	lo'ah-zeer	pay-zeebl	play-zeer	rü-zeh
rose	glad	broken	abusive	leisure	peaceable	pleasure	artful

sou	valse	soulier	absurde	sel	souper	ses
soo	vahlss	soo-le-eh	ahb-sürd	sel	soo-peh	say
halfpenny	waltz	shoe	absurd	salt	supper	his

*This is precisely the distinction that is usually, *although far from
always*, made in English, as will be seen by comparing the pronunciation
of the following words : like z—rose, easy, miserable, lose
like s—song, silent, instant, parts, rest.

G before E, I, or Y sounds like a French J (that is, like s in the
English word ' measure ') ; in all other cases, it sounds like G
in the English word ' go.'   Examples :

G soft, like the French J

âge	tige	origine	gilet	général	plage	piège
ahsh	teesh	o-re-sheen	she-lay	sheh-neh-rahll	plahsh	pe-aysh
age	stem	origin	waistcoat	general	beach	snare

G hard, as in English

gare	argot	aigu	grave	gloire	gradé	goutte
gahr	ahr-go	ay-gü	grahv	glo'ahr	grahd	goot
station	slang	acute	grave	glory	grade	drop

In English also, G before E, I, or Y takes the sound of J ; but in a few words, it retains the hard sound, even before E or I (gear, begin, gimlet) ; whereas in French, G before E, I, or Y is ALWAYS pronounced like a French J.

C before E, I, or Y sounds like ss ; in all other cases, it sounds like c in the English word 'cat.' Examples :

like S

cime	ces	ici	ce	bicyclette	racine	cela	ceci
seem	say	iss-e	ser	be-se-klett	rah-seen	ser-lah	ser-se
summit	these	here	this	bicycle	root	that	this

like K

écrit	clou	coude	cas	cri	avec	colis	sec	curieux
eh-kree	kloo	kood	kah	kree	ah-veck	ko-lee	seck	kü-re-er
written	nail	elbow	case	cry	with	package	dry	curious

This also is an English rule, if we except the modern pronunciation of words like *Celtic*, *Cicero* [now often pronounced 'keltick,' 'kickero'].

From the two foregoing rules, it follows that CC must be pronounced like *k-s*, and GG like *g-j*, if E or I follows, Thus, although *succursale* (branch) is pronounced 'sü-kür-sahll,' and *àggraver* (to make heavier) ' ah-grah-veh,' *accepté* (accepted) is pronounced ' ahck-sep-teh,' and *suggérer* (to suggest) süg-sheh-reh.'

It will be noted that the second C and G are soft (like S, J) because an E immediately follows. The first C and G are hard (like K, G), because the next letter is not E, I, or Y.

The Cedilla.

As already explained, the French C is pronounced like the English C, inasmuch as it takes the sound of SS before E, I, or Y, and the sound of K in all other cases. The only difference is that in a few French words, C takes the sound of SS before A, O, and U, whereas this is never the case in English.

This fact is indicated by putting a *cedilla* (a sign like a comma) under the C. Thus, CO is pronounced "ko," but ço is pronounced "so." Examples :

ça	reçu	aperçu	reçoit	perçoir	reçoive	plaça
sah	rer-sü	ah-pair-sü	rer-so'ah	pair-so'ahr	rer-so'ahv	plah-sah
that	received	perceived	receives	piercer	receive	placed

Double Letters.

GU is pronounced like G in *go*. Examples :

guêpe	Guy	guide	guichet	fatigué	fatigue	guitare
.gape	ghee*	gheed	ghee-shay	fah-te-gheh	fah-teeg	ghe-tahr
wasp	Guy	guide	booking-office	tired	fatigue	guitar

* GH to be pronounced like the G in 'big' or 'gave.'

QU is pronounced like K. Examples :

qui	que	quel	quoi	musique	piquet	qualité	quatre
kee	ker	kell	ko'ah	mü-zick	pe-kay *	kah-le-teh	kahttr
who	that	which	what	music	picket	quality	four

PH is pronounced like F. Examples :

philosophe	paragraphe	téléphone	phase	phare
fe-lo-sof	pah-rah-grahf	teh-leh-fon	fahz	fahr
philosopher	paragraph	telephone	phase	lighthouse

CH is pronounced like the English SH. Examples :

chaise	cheval	vache	chapeau	pêcheur	bêche	mioche
shayz	sher-vahll	vahsh	shah-poh	pay-sher	baysh	me-osh
chair	horse	cow	hat	fisherman	spade	urchin

TH is pronounced like T. Examples :

thé	thème	thermomètre	pathétique	théâtre	théoriste
tèh	tame	tair-mo-maytr	pah-teh-tick	teh-ahtr	teh-o-rist
tea	theme	thermometer	pathetic	theatre	theorist

EXCEPTIONS.—In words derived from the Greek, CH usually has the sound of K. These are easily identified, as in most cases there is a similar English word in which CH also has the sound of K (*orchestre, chaos, chromatique, chronomètre, chrysanthème*). There are also some unimportant words (derived from Latin), in which QU is pronounced like KW (*équilatéral, equateur, aquatique*, etc.).

THE FRENCH NASAL SOUNDS.

INTRODUCTORY REMARKS.—Every Vowel, or combination of Vowels, has a nasal sound in French, whenever M or N follows. The pronunciation is exactly the same, whether the next letter is M or N; the words *nom* and *non*, for instance, are ABSOLUTELY IDENTICAL in sound.

It is impossible to indicate the *exact* pronunciation of the French nasal sounds by English syllables, for the simple reason that the sounds do not occur in the English language at all. The syllables *ahng, ang, ong, ung*, which are employed in Hugo's Imitated Pronunciation to represent the four French nasal sounds, are only APPROXIMATELY correct; the pronunciation can best be acquired from the lips of an educated native or a competent teacher. Learners who have no opportunity of hearing these sounds must bear in mind that the *ng* in the Imitated Pronunciation is ON NO ACCOUNT TO BE PRONOUNCED. It is merely inserted to show that the preceding vowel has a nasal sound.

————:o:————

Pronunciation of the French Nasal Sounds.

AM and AN are pronounced something like AU in *aunt*; as,

lampe	tant	danser	sans	tambour	grand	champ
lah*ng*p	t*ah*ng	dah*ng*-seh	sah*ng*	tah*ng*-boohr	grah*ng*	shah*ng*
lamp	so much	to dance	without	drum	large	field

EM and EN have the same sound as AM, AN.

argent	enfant	pensée	client	entrant	lentement
ahr-shah*ng*	ah*ng*-fah*ng*	pah*ng*-seh	kle-*ah*ng*	ah*ng*-trah*ng*	lah*ng*t-mah*ng*
money	child	thought	customer	entering	slowly

IM and IN are pronounced something like ANG in *fang*; as,

grimper	fin	inclusif	impossible	timbre	vint	vin
grang-peh	fang	ang-klü-ziff	ang-poss-eebl	tang-br	vang	vang
to climb	end	inclusive	impossible	stamp	came	wine

OM and **ON** are pronounced something like ONG in *wrong*.

non	nom	plomb	content	garçon	tombé	chanson
no*ng*	no*ng*	plo*ng*	ko*ng*-tah*ng*	gahr-*song*	to*ng*-beh	sha*h*ng-*song*
no	name	lead	content	waiter	fallen	song

UM and **UN** are pronounced something like the UNG in *lung*, or the URN (with the R silent) in *turn*. Examples :

un	lundi	parfum	emprunté	humble	commun	brun
u*ng*	lung-de	pahr-*fung*	ah*ng*-pru*ng*-teh	u*ng*-bl	komm-*ung*	br*ung*
a	Monday	perfume	borrowed	humble	common	brown

YM and **YN** have the same sound as IM, IN. Examples :

nymphe	cymbale	lynx	lymphe	syntaxe	tympan
na*ng*f	*sang*-bahll	la*ng*ks	la*ng*f	*sang*-tahks	ta*ng*-pah*ng*
nymphe	cymbal	lynx	lymph	syntax	drum of the ear

As already shown, there are four distinct nasal sounds **in the French** language, distributed among the six vowels, thus :

O when nasal is something like o in *song*
U ,, ,, ,, u in *hung*
A ,, ,, ,, au in *aunt*
I ,, ,, ,, a in *bang*
E when nasal has the same sound as A.
Y ,, ,, ,, ,, I.

We now come to the NASAL DIPHTHONGS.

AIM, AIN, EIM, EIN, all are pronounced like **IN.**
(That is to say, the A or E is altogether ignored.)

faim	feindre	sein	saint	plein	plainte	grain	peint
fa*ng*	fa*ng*-dr	sa*ng*	sa*ng*	pla*ng*	pla*ng*t	gra*ng*	pa*ng*
hunger	to feign	bosom	saint	full	complaint	grain	painted

In the syllables OIN and UIN, the o and u are pronounced in the usual way, and the IN is nasal ; but the combination must be pronounced as *one syllable*, not as two, thus :

loin	juin	joindre	soin	foin	joint	guindé
lo'*ang*	shü'*ang*	sho'*ang*-dr	so'*ang*	fo'*ang*	sho'*ang*	*gang*-deh
far	June	to join	care	hay	joined	hoisted

When IEN is at the end of a word or syllable, the E takes the nasal sound of I. In other words, the combination is pronounced as if spelt I-IN.

chien	bien	vient	tiendrai	italien	rien	BUT	{ client
she-*ang*	be-*ang*	ve-*ang*	te-*ang*-dreh	e-tah-le-*ang*	re-*ang*		{ kle-*ahng*
dog	well	comes	shall hold	Italian	anything		{ client

Important Exceptions.

There is no nasal sound if the M or N is doubled, or if a vowel immediately follows in the same word. Compare the following :

Nasal.

un	bon	plein	inconstant	impossible	an	brun
ung	*bong*	pl*ang*	*ang*-kong-stahng	*ang*-poss-eebl	*ahng*	br*ung*
a, one	good	full	inconstant	impossible	year	brown

Not Nasal.

une	bonne	pleine	inutile	imiter	âne	brunâtre
ün	⁻bonn	plain	e-nü-teel	e-me-teh	ahn	brü-nahtr
a, one	good	full	useless	to imitate	donkey	brownish

———— :o: ————

The Diaresis, or Tréma.

A diaresis (¨) indicates that the Vowel over which it is placed forms part of a separate syllable. Thus, *ciguë, naïf, Saül* (hemlock, artless, Saul), are pronounced respectively see-gü, nah-eef, sah-ül. Without the diaresis, the pronunciation would be seeg, nafe, sole.

THE LIQUID SOUNDS.

[Hugo's Phonetic Pronunciation imitates the Liquid Sounds as exactly as possible ; but as they do not occur in English at all, the imitation can only be approximately correct. · The Liquid Sounds can best be acquired from the mouth of an educated native.]

ILL generally has what is called a ' liquid ' sound. It is impossible to indicate the sound properly in English syllables; the nearest approach to it is ee-ye, or ee-yer, with a strong stress upon the ee.

fille	famille	billet	haillons	briller	travailler
fee-ye*	fah-mee-ye	bee-yay	hah'e-*yong*	bree-yeh	*t*rah-vah'e-yeh
daughter	family	ticket	tatters	to shine	**to work**

*The vowel sound printed in thick type must be pronounced clearly and distinctly. The following ' ye ' must be pronounced faintly, something like the IA in ' Amelia.'

Some Frenchmen pronounce the consonant L in liquid syllables, making the foregoing words more like 'feel-yer,' 'fah-meel-yer,' etc. This is, perhaps, the better way ; but it is far more usual to omit the L sound altogether.

ILL is not liquid in words beginning with ' ill,' ' mill,' or 'vill.'

ville	village	mille	million	illustré	illusion
vill	vill-ahsh	mill	mill-e-*ong*	ill-üs-treh	ill-ü-ze-*ong*
town	village	thousand	million	illustrated	illusion

IL is liquid when it is final, and a Vowel precedes, thus :

travail	soleil	fauteuil	sommeil	éventail	gouvernail
*t*rah-vah'e	so-lay'e	foh-ter'e	somm-ay'e	eh-*vahng*-tah'e	goo-vair-nah'e
work	sun	arm-chair	sleep	fan	helm

GN sounds very much like the *ni* in ' union ' or 'companion,' but this sound cannot be indicated exactly in type.

agneau	signal	grogner	compagnon	désigner
ahn-yoh	seen-yahll	grohn-yeh	*k*ong-pahn-y*ong*	deh-zeen-**yeh**
lamb	signal	to grumble	companion	to point out

GNE when final has a similar sound to GN.

campagne	Boulogne	cygne	règne	montagne
kahng-pahn-*yer*	boo-lon-*yer*	seen-*yer*	rayn-*yer*	*mong*-tahn-*yer*
country	Boulogne	swan	reign	mountain

Some Frenchmen pronounce the final GNE more like ' ing,' **thus :** k*ahng*-pah'ing, etc.

——— :o: ———

THE LINKING OF WORDS.

If a word beginning with a Vowel or a silent H follows a final Consonant, this Consonant (even if otherwise mute) is pronounced, the two words being thus *linked* together. When linked on to the following word, s and x are pronounced like *z*, D is pronounced like *t*, F like *v*, and G like *k*. Examples :

vous êtes ;	ils ont ;	est-elle ?	un grand homme ;
voo z'ayt	ill z'*ong*	ay *t*'ell	*ung* gr*ahng* *t*'omm
you are	they have	is she	a great man

pas encore ;	neuf heures ;	vous avez oublié ;
pah z'*ahng*-kor	ne*r* v'er	voo z'ah-veh z'oo-ble-eh
not yet	nine hours	you have forgotten

cinq élèves ;	sang impur ;	parleront-ils ?
s*ang* k'eh-layv	s*ahng* k'*ang*-pür	pahr-ler-*rong* *t*'ill
five pupils	blood impure	will they speak ?

The joining of final mute Consonants to the following word **should** only be done *when no pause can be made between the two words.* For instance, the sentence ' we have written to our friends to-day ' groups itself naturally in three phrases : ' we have written,' ' to our friends,' and ' to-day.' No one would think of saying: we have [*pause*] written to our [*pause*] friends to-day.

This being so, the corresponding French would be pronounced :

nous	avons	écrit	à	nos	amis	aujourd'hui
noo	z'ah-*vong*	z'eh-kree	ah	noh	z'ah-me	oh-shoohr-dwe

Learners must not suppose that linking is always either compulsory or inadmissible. This is not so; *it is to a great extent a matter of taste.* Common sense teaches us to link together words which have a close connection; beyond this, little can be said.

The quicker a Frenchman speaks, the more he links; the slower he speaks, the less he links. If he were dictating the foregoing sentence to a class of children, and paused with exceptional frequency, he could not possibly say: noo z'ah-vo*ng* [*pause*] z'eh-kree. It would then be: noo z'ah-vo*ng*, eh-kree. Conversely, it is not actually incorrect (though very unusual) to say in rapid speaking: noo z'ah-vo*ng* z'eh-kree *t*'ah noh z'ah-me z'oh-shoohr-dwe.

Foreigners should link very sparingly, at all events until they have acquired some degree of fluency in the language.

—————:o:—————

MISCELLANEOUS REMARKS.

When the same consonant occurs twice consecutively in a word, it is only pronounced once, thus:

donner	passer	effroi	effort	lutté	poussé	apporté
donn-eh	pahss-eh	eff-ro'ah	eff-or	lü-teh	poo-seh	abpp-or-teh
to give	to pass	fright	effort	struggled	pushed	brought

NOTE.—Such words as the above are divided into syllables according to the ordinary rules (see page 35), thus: don-ner, pas-ser, ef-froi, etc. But the consonant is NOT pronounced twice, any more than in the English words *commence, effort, abbey, sinner,* etc.

Y between two vowels is pronounced like *i-y* or *i-i*; in other words, it is pronounced in both syllables. Examples:

royal	payer	effrayé	tuyau	essuyant	balayeur
ro'ah-yahll	pay-yeh	eff-ray-yeh	twe-yoh	ess-we-ya*hng*	bah-lay-yer
royal	·to pay	frightened	tube	wiping	sweeper

ENT is silent when it is the termination of a Verb.

ENT is the termination of the Third Person Plural of every **Tense** except the Future.

ils négligent	ils résident	ils expédient
ill neh-gleesh	ill reh-zeed	ill z'ex-peh-de
they neglect	they reside	they send off

négligent	résident	expédient
neh-glee-sh*ahng*	reh-ze-d*ahng*	ex-peh-de-*ahng*
negligent	resident	expedient

TI, when it does not begin a word, is usually pronounced like SI, especially if it occurs between two vowels.   Examples :

nation	révolution	portion	patience	action
nah-se-*ong*	reh-vo-lü-se-*ong*	por-se-*ong*	pah-se-*ahng*ss	ahck-se-*ong*
nation	revolution	'portion	patience	share, stock

IMPORTANT REMARK.—The words to which the foregoing rule applies can easily be identified, as they are in nearly every case spelt alike in French and English, *the* TI *in the English words being pronounced like* SH.

EXCEPTIONS.—In the Terminations *stion, tié, tier, tière, tième,* the T is pronounced as in English, thus :

question	portière	trentième	pitié	quartier	amitié
kess-te-*ong*	por-te-air	tra*hng*-te-ame	pe-te-eh	kahr-te-eh	ah-me-te-eh
question	carriage	door	thirtieth	pity	quarter	friendship

The **T** is also pronounced as in English when it is the last letter of the stem of a Verb ; as,

Nous portions	nos portions.—	Nous acceptions ces
noo por-te-*ong*	noh por-se-*ong*	noo z'ahck-sep-te-*ong* say
We were-carrying	our portions.	We accepted these

acceptions du mot.—	Nous exceptions l'exception.
z'ahck-sep-se-*ong* dü mo	noo z'eck-sep-te-*ong* leck-sep-se-*ong*
meanings of-the word.	We excepted the exception.

FRENCH
IDIOMS

SIMPLIFIED

A Collection of Practical

CONVERSATIONAL SENTENCES

Introducing Numerous Examples of

ALL THE IMPORTANT IDIOMS

AND

PECULIARITIES OF FRENCH CONSTRUCTION

PHILADELPHIA

DAVID McKAY, Publisher

604-8 S. Washington Square

PREFACE.

This work will be found invaluable to all who have mastered the principal rules of French grammar, and wish to attain fluency in COLLOQUIAL CONVERSATION, especially as regards Idioms in every-day use.

Though intended as a continuation of HUGO'S " FRENCH GRAMMAR SIMPLIFIED," it forms an equally good second course to any grammar, as no previous acquaintance with any particular series of rules is required, the English being given in full throughout, side by side with the corresponding French.

As this book is only intended for students who already possess a fair knowledge of French, we have not thought it necessary to devote much space to explanatory foot-notes, even in cases where the French is not a literal translation of the English. The learner who finds himself unable to understand the construction of any of the Idioms given ought to be working at the rules of grammar, rather than at such text-books as this.

Students are advised to go steadily through the book page by page, first putting the French into English, and afterwards the English into French, not resting satisfied until they can translate every sentence correctly into French, without hesitation.

Still greater fluency will be attained by practising each idiom in its various forms, varying the Number, Tense, Mood, and Person whenever possible.

EXAMPLES OF IMPORTANT IDIOMS,
peculiarities of French construction, etc.

---

to be right, avoir raison* ;   to be wrong, avoir tort*

I am right. You are wrong.	J'ai raison.[1] Vous avez tort.
The absent are always in the	Les absents ont toujours tort.
This time he is right. [wrong.	Cette fois il a raison.
They are quite right.	Ils ont tout à fait raison.
You were right, weren't you ?	Vous aviez raison, n'est-ce pas?
We shall be wrong again.	Nous aurons encore tort.

*These idioms (to have reason, have wrong) are only applied to persons ;
' this bill is not right' would be rendered as ce compte n'est pas juste.

---

to be (referring to health), aller or se porter

How are you ?	Comment allez-vous[2] ?
How do you do ?	Comment vous[3] portez-vous[3] ?
I am very well, thank you.	Je vais très bien, merci.
I was not well yesterday.	Je n'allais pas bien hier.
How is your father ?	Comment se porte votre père ?
He is very well.	Il se porte très bien.
He is quite well again.	Il est tout à fait rétabli.[4]
She recovered quickly.	Elle s'est remise[5] rapidement

---

to believe so, croire que oui

I believe so.	Je crois que oui.
We believe not.	Nous croyons que non.
I am afraid not.	Je crains[6] que non.
They hope so.	Ils espèrent que oui.
He hopes not.	Il espère que non.
I fear so.	Je crains que oui.
Who said so ?—He did.[0]—I did.[0]	Qui a dit cela ?—Lui.—Moi.
I did not think so.	Je croyais[7] que non.[7]

EXPLANATORY NOTES, SHOWING THE LITERAL TRANSLATION.

0 not to be translated ; 1 the same, or nearly the same, as in English :
2 do you go ? 3 do you carry yourself? 4 re-established ; 5 se remettre,
to become well again ; 6 fear ; 7 believed that not.

to be hungry, **avoir faim** ;	to be thirsty, avoir soif
Are you hungry ?	Avez-vous[2] faim[2] ?
I am not thirsty.	Je n'ai pas soif.[3]
We were very hungry.	Nous avions bien[4] faim.
They will be thirsty, after running (=having run) so fast.	Ils auront soif, après avoir[5] couru si vite.
The assistants seemed to be hungry.	Les employés avaient[6] l'air[6] d'avoir faim.
They were not very thirsty.	Ils n'avaient pas très soif.
I rarely feel thirsty.	J'ai rarement soif.
Your dog seems to be hungry.	Votre chien semble avoir faim.

2 have you hunger ? 3 thirst ; 4=indeed ; 5 the Verb following any Preposition (except en) must be in the Infinitive, and après is followed by the Compound Infinitive ; 6 had the appearance.

to be cold, **avoir froid*** ;	to be warm, avoir chaud*
I am cold.—He is not warm.	J'ai froid.—Il n'a pas chaud.
Are you warm enough ?	Avez-vous assez chaud ?
We shall be hot, after running[2] for such a long time.	Nous aurons chaud, après avoir couru si longtemps.
You look cold.	Vous avez l'air[3] d'avoir froid.
We are not very cold.	Nous n'avons pas très froid.
The children were nice and warm.	Les enfants avaient bien[4] chaud.

2 =having run,—see note 5 above ; 3 appearance ; 4=very, indeed.

*These idioms are not applied to THINGS. 'This room is cold' would be translated Cette pièce est froide ; 'The water was very hot,' L'eau était très chaude, and so on.

to have just read, venir de lire	
He has just arrived.	Il vient d'arriver.[2]
They have just come in again.	Ils viennent de rentrer.
We had just gone out.	Nous venions de sortir.
The boat had just started.	Le bateau venait de partir.
They had just begun.	Ils venaient de commencer.
I have just finished it.	Je viens de le finir.
He has just telegraphed to them.	Il vient de leur télégraphier.
I have just sent it to him.	Je viens de le lui envoyer.

2 literally : he comes from arrive(ing).

to the right, on the right, **à droite** ;	to the left, on the left, **à gauche**
Turn to the left.	Tournez à gauche.
Don't turn to the right.	Ne tournez pas à droite.[2]
My room is the second on the left.	Ma chambre est la deuxième à gauche.
Take the third turning to the right.	Prenez la troisième (rue) à droite.
You must turn to the left, after passing the church.	Vous devez tourner à gauche, après avoir dépassé[3] l'église.
Am I to turn to the right, or go straight on ?	Dois-je tourner à droite, ou marcher tout[4] droit[4] ?
We were told to go straight on.	On nous a dit de marcher tout droit.

2 Feminine Form, because **main** (hand) is Feminine ; 3 'to pass,' in the sense of 'go past,' ' pass by,' is **dépasser** ; 4 all straight.

---

to be fine (referring to the weather), **faire beau**	
It is (=makes) fine to-day.	Il fait beau aujourd'hui.
It was finer yesterday.	Il faisait plus beau hier.
It will be windy to-morrow.	Il fera du vent[2] demain.
The weather is bad.	Il fait mauvais[3] temps.[3]
It has been very close all day.	Il a fait très lourd toute la journée.[4] [montagne.
It was very damp on the mountain.	Il faisait très humide sur la
It thundered nearly all night.	Il a fait[5] du tonnerre[5] presque toute la nuit.
It is still lightening a little.	Il fait encore quelques[6] éclairs.[6]
It will be rather dusty.	Il fera assez[7] de poussière.[7]

We are going to have a storm..	Nous allons avoir de l'orage.
It is raining. It was snowing.	Il pleut. Il[8] tombait de la
Was it freezing ?	Gelait il ? [neige.[8]
It wasn't thawing.	Il ne dégelait pas.
It will rain to-morrow.	Il pleuvra demain.
There is not much mud.	Il n'y a pas beaucoup de boue.

2 wind ; 3 bad time ; 4 daytime ; 5 made some thunder ; 6 a few lightnings ; 7 enough dust ; 8 it (=there) was falling some snow.

so am I, so could I, so shall I, so ought I, etc., et moi aussi

I smoke too much.—So does he.	Je fume trop.—Et[2] lui aussi.[2]
They generally arrive too late.	Ils arrivent généralement trop tard.
So do you.—So do I.	Et vous aussi.—Et moi aussi.
So does your husband, I believe.	Votre mari aussi, je crois.
You can understand it, can't you ?	Vous pouvez le comprendre, n'est-ce pas ? [aussi.
Yes.—So can we.—So can he.	Oui.—Et nous aussi.—Et lui
We shall start this evening.	Nous partirons ce soir.
So shall I.—So will she.	Et moi aussi.—Et elle aussi.

2 literally, and he also ; the et can be omitted from such expressions.

---

neither do (can, will, must, etc.) they, ni eux non plus

I do not smoke much.	Je ne fume pas beaucoup.
Neither does my cousin.	Mon cousin non plus. [fois.
We formerly smoked a great deal.	Nous fumions beaucoup autre-
So did you, didn't you ?	Et vous aussi, n'est-ce pas ?
I could not understand what they were saying.	Je ne pouvais pas comprendre ce qu'ils disaient.
Neither could we.	Ni nous non plus.
Neither could our friends.	Nos amis non plus.

---

it (=the weather) is warm, il fait chaud

It is very hot to-day.	Il fait[2] très chaud aujourd'hui.
It wasn't so cold yesterday.	Il ne faisait pas si froid hier.
I think it will be warm to-morrow.	Je pense qu'il fera[3] chaud demain.
Wasn't it cold this morning ?	Ne faisait-il pas froid ce matin ?
It would be much warmer, if it were not so windy.	Il ferait beaucoup plus chaud, s'il[4] ne faisait pas tant de vent.[4]
It isn't very warm this evening.	Il ne fait pas très chaud ce soir. [née.[5]
It has been hot all day.	Il a fait chaud toute la jour-
It is never very cold here.	Il ne fait jamais très froid ici.

2 makes ; 3 will make ; 4 if it made not so much wind ; 5 daytime.

on Tuesday, **mardi**   on Tuesdays, **le mardi**

They both came on Monday.	Ils sont venus tous les deux lundi. [jeudi.
They generally come on Thursdays.	Ils viennent généralement le
I was at the office on Saturday.	J'étais au bureau samedi.
He always comes to see me on Sundays.	Il vient toujours me voir le dimanche.
She arrived on January 15th.	Elle est arrivée le 15 janvier
He died on Christmas Eve.	Il est mort la veille de la Noël.
I was born on October 1st.	Je suis né le 1er octobre.

how often=how many times per ... ? combien de fois par ... ?

How many times a week does he come here ?	Combien de fois par semaine vient-il ici ?
He comes two or three times a month.	Il vient deux ou trois fois par mois.
How often do you meet him ?	Combien de fois par mois[2] le rencontrez-vous ?
How often have you been to Switzerland ?	Combien de fois avez-vous été en Suisse ?
How much does he earn a week ?	Combien gagne-t-il par semaine ?
How often do they write to you ?	Combien de fois par mois[2] vous écrivent-ils ?

2 or par semaine, or par an.

how far is it ... ?=how much is there ... ? combien y a-t-il ... ?

How far is it from here to the station ?	Combien y a-t-il d'ici à la gare ?
How far was it from the station to the hotel ?	Combien y avait-il de la gare à l'hôtel ?
How far did he have to walk ?	Jusqu'où[2] a-t-il dû[3] marcher ?
How far (=to what point) can we trust him ?	Jusqu'à quel point pouvons-nous nous fier à lui ?
How far in this book have you read ? or How far have you got in this book ?	Jusqu'à[4] quelle page[4] de ce livre avez-vous lu ? or Où[5] en[5] êtes-vous de ce livre-ci ?

2 as far as where ; 3 been obliged to ; 4 up to what page ? 5=whereabouts.

to send for=send to fetch, **envoyer chercher**
to go and fetch, **aller chercher**

I have sent for a taxi.	J'ai envoyé chercher un taxi.
We ought to send for a doctor.	Nous devrions envoyer chercher un docteur.
Go and fetch an ambulance.	Allez chercher une ambulance.
Why didn't you send for the police ?	Pourquoi n'avez-vous pas envoyé chercher la police ?
Has anyone gone for a cab ?	Quelqu'un est-il allé chercher un fiacre ?
I shall go and fetch them.	J'irai les chercher.
Who has gone for it ?	Qui est allé le chercher ?
I am going to send for some.	Je vais en envoyer chercher.
Have they sent for any ?	En ont-ils envoyé chercher ?
Nobody has gone for any.	Personne n'est allé en chercher.

How long has he been here ? **Depuis combien de temps est-il ici ?**

How long have you been learning French ?	Depuis[2] combien de temps[2] apprenez-vous[3] le français ?
How long have they been waiting for us ?	Depuis combien de temps nous attendent-ils ?
How long did they wait for them ?	Combien de temps les ont-ils attendus ?
How long has he been in Paris ?	Depuis combien de temps est-il[4] à Paris ?
How long did he stay in London ?	Combien de temps est-il resté à Londres ?
How long has she been working ?	Depuis combien de temps travaille-t-elle ?
How long had you been listening ?	Depuis combien de temps écoutiez-vous ?
How far was it from his office to the workshop ?	Combien y avait-il de son bureau à l'usine ?

2 since how-much time ?   3 do you learn ? [the Present Tense is employed in all such sentences, because the action is still continuing at the time of speaking] ;   4 Present Tense, because he is spoken of as still being in Paris.

a month ago, il **y a un mois**

We saw them a week ago.	Nous les avons vus il[2] y a[2] une semaine.
She was here two hours ago.	Elle était ici il[2] y a[2] deux heures. [Rome.
A year ago we were in Rome.	Il y a un an, nous étions à
So were we. So was I.	Et[3] nous aussi. Et[3] moi aussi.
He died a long time ago.	Il est mort il y a longtemps.
It is a very long time since she died.	Il y a bien longtemps qu'elle est morte.
That happened several months ago.	Cela s'est passé il y a plusieurs mois.

2 it there has=there is or there are ; 3 the **et** is often omitted from such phrases as these.

It is six months since I met him.	Il y a six mois que je ne* l'ai rencontré.[2]
It is not long since she wrote to me.	Il n'y a pas longtemps depuis qu'elle m'a écrit.
It is nearly a year since we saw her.	Il y a près d'un an que nous ne l'avons vue.
Has your husband been in good health since I saw him last ?	Votre mari est-il en bonne santé depuis que je ne l'ai vu ?
How long ago did you move ? or „ „ is it since you moved ?	Depuis combien de temps avez-vous déménagé ?
We moved about three months ago.	Nous avons déménagé il y a environ trois mois.

2 literally, there are six months that I have not met him.
*ne is employed without pas, with a Perfect Tense following il y a ... que or depuis que (since).

this way, **par ici***   that way, **par là***   which way ? **par où* ?**

They went in that direction.	Ils sont allés par[2] là.[2]
Which way have they gone ?	Par où sont-ils allés ?
This way, please.	Par ici, s'il vous plaît.
Don't go that way.	Ne passez pas par là.
Have the kindness to come this way.	Ayez la bonté de venir par ici.

2 or **dans cette direction,** or **de ce côté-là.** *by here, by there, by where?

he is twelve years old, il a douze ans

How old are you ?	Quel âge[1] avez-vous ?
His eldest brother is twenty.	Son frère aîné a vingt ans.[2]
I am twenty-seven.	J'ai vingt-sept ans.
She will be eighteen next month.	Elle aura[3] dix-huit ans le mois prochain.
Her sister was fifteen last February.	Sa sœur a[4] eu quinze ans[4] en février dernier.
I was thirty-five when I married.	J'avais trente-cinq ans quand je me suis marié.
He is older than I thought.	Il est plus âgé que je (ne le) pensais.

1 the same as in English ;   2 years ;   3 will have ;   4 has had fifteen years.

Are they ill ? **Sont-ils malades ?**   Yes, they are. **Oui, ils le sont.**

Was she tired ?	Etait-elle fatiguée ?
Yes, she was.	Oui, elle l'était.
No, she wasn't.	Non, elle ne l'était pas.
I don't think she was.	Je[2] crois qu'elle ne l'était pas.
Will they be ready in time ?	Seront-ils prêts à temps ?
Yes, they will.	Oui, ils le seront.
No, they will not.	Non, ils ne le seront pas.
Are you cold ?	Avez-vous froid ?
Yes, (I am).	Oui, (j'ai froid).
Is he warm ?	A-t-il chaud ?
No, (he isn't).	Non, (il n'a pas chaud).

2 I believe that she was (it) not.

what is the matter ?=what is there ?   qu'y a-t-il ?

What is the matter ?	Qu'est-ce qu'il y a ? or Qu'y a-t-il ?
What was the matter ?	Qu'est-ce qu'il y avait ?
Do you know what is the matter here ?	Savez-vous ce qui se passe[2] ici ?
Nothing is the matter over there.	Il n'y a rien là-bas.
What has been the matter here ?	Qu'est-ce qu'il y a eu ici ?

2 to happen, occur, take place, se passer

a pennyworth of bread, **pour deux sous de pain**

I bought a franc's worth of stamps.	J'ai acheté pour un franc de timbres.
Give me two pennyworth of milk.	Donnez-moi pour quatre sous de lait.
I think it will be quite sufficient if you buy two francs' worth.	Je pense que si vous en achetez pour deux francs, ce sera bien suffisant.
We are going to buy five shillingsworth of flowers.	Nous allons acheter pour cinq schellings de fleurs.
Did you sell him a shillingsworth of it?	Lui en avez-vous vendu pour un schelling?

he ought to have done it, **il aurait dû le faire**

You ought to pay this.	Vous devriez payer ceci.
I ought to have paid* the bill before.	J'aurais dû payer la note auparavant.
He ought not to wait for them.	Il ne devrait pas les attendre.
They ought to have waited longer for me.	Ils auraient dû m'attendre plus longtemps.
Ought he to buy one (of them)?	Devrait-il en acheter un?
You ought not to have thrown it away⁰ so quickly.	Vous n'auriez pas dû le jeter si vite.

You might fall.	Vous pourriez tomber.
You might have fallen.*	Vous auriez pu tomber.
He could not come.	Il ne pouvait (pas²) venir.
He would not pay me.	Il ne voulait pas me payer.
He might have taken it.	Il aurait pu le prendre.
We might lose the way.	Nous pourrions perdre le chemin.
They might have broken it.	Ils auraient pu le briser.
I might have forgotten it.	J'aurais pu l'oublier.

* literally: I should-have ought-to pay, you would-have been-able-to fall, etc.; note that the Auxiliary Verb is put in the Compound Tense in French, whereas the Principal Verb (that is, the Verb that follows the Auxiliary) is made Compound in English. 0 not to be translated.

2 pas is frequently omitted from the Negative Form of pouvoir; but as this is never compulsory, it is better for students always to insert the pas.

to get something done=have it done, cause it to be done
faire faire quelque chose

Get it done without delay.	Faites-le[2] faire[2] sans retard.
Have it done at once.	Faites-le faire tout de suite.
I am having them mended.	Je suis en train[3] de les faire raccommoder.
I shall have this repaired.	Je ferai réparer ceci.
Get the documents copied.	Faites copier les documents.
He is having a new bicycle made.	Il se[4] fait faire une nouvelle bicyclette.
We must have this room re-painted.	Nous devons faire repeindre cette pièce. [ceci ?
When will you get this printed ?	Quand ferez-vous imprimer
Where can I get my watch cleaned ?	Où puis-je faire nettoyer ma montre ?

2 make it do=cause it to be done, have it done, get it done;   3=the course ;   4 to himself=for himself.

---

in (=occupying, during) an hour, **en une heure**
in an hour's time, in an hour from now, **dans une heure**

We could finish the work in two hours.	Nous pourrions finir le travail en deux heures.
I shall be able to begin in an hour.	Je pourrai commencer dans une heure.
It is said that he wrote the novel in six weeks.	On dit qu'il a écrit le roman en six semaines.
We are going to Scotland in a fortnight.	Nous irons en Ecosse dans une quinzaine[2] (de jours).[2]
One can now get from Europe to America in less than[3] a week.	On peut se rendre maintenant d'Europe en Amérique en[4] moins d'une semaine.
He will leave England in less than[3] a month.	Il quittera l'Angleterre en[4] moins d'un mois.
We shall be at your service in five minutes.	Nous serons à vous dans cinq minutes.
You could cycle there in twenty minutes.	Vous pourriez y[5] aller à bicyclette[6] en vingt minutes

2 fifteen of days ;   3 before a Numeral, THAN is rendered by de ;   4 en is employed before moins ;   5 go there by bicycle.

to end by ..., finir par

He ended by losing his temper.	Il a fini par se[2] mettre en colère.[2]
They at length consented to it.	Ils ont fini par y consentir.
In the end, I did what he asked (me to do).	J'ai fini par faire ce qu'il m'a demandé.
You will end by breaking it.	Vous finirez par le casser.
At last we succeeded.	Nous avons fini par réussir.
We shall buy a new one in the end.	Nous finirons par en acheter un nouveau.
They finally turned him out.	Ils ont fini par le[3] mettre à la porte.[3]

2 put(ting) himself in anger ; 3 put(ting) him to the door.

---

five metres long, cinq mètres de long(ueur)*

Our garden is sixty feet long, and[2] about twenty feet wide.	Notre jardin a soixante pieds de longueur* sur environ vingt pieds de largeur.*
The steeple is about a hundred metres high.	Le clocher a à peu près cent mètres de hauteur.*
These walls are more than eight feet thick.	Ces murs ont[3] plus de huit pieds d'épaisseur.[3]
How deep is this well ? or What is the depth of this well ?	Quelle est la profondeur[4] de ce puits ?
There are mines in this district more than a thousand feet deep.	Il y a des mines dans cette localité de plus de mille pieds de profondeur.
The table in our dining room is twelve feet long.	La table de notre salle à manger a douze pieds de longueur.*
This lake is half a mile wide.	Ce lac a un demi-mille de largeur.*

2=BY, rendered as ON ; 3 have more than eight feet of thickness ; 4 depth.

*The Adjectives long, large, haut (long, broad, high) can be substituted, in all such phrases, for the Nouns longueur, largeur, hauteur (length, width, height); but épais, profond (thick, deep) cannot replace épaisseur, profondeur (thickness, depth).

to set store on, value, care about..., tenir à

We don't particularly care about it.	Nous n'y[3] tenons[2] pas beaucoup. [ment.[4]
I set great store on that.	J'y tiens tout[4] particulière-
He specially wanted to speak to you.	Il tenait spécialement à vous parler.
He values your good opinion.	Il tient à votre bonne opinion.
They are very anxious to settle this matter in a friendly way.	Ils tiennent à régler cette affaire à l'amiable.
She thinks a great deal of their friendship.	Elle tient beaucoup à leur amitié.

2 hold; 3 to it; 4 all particularly.

to look like, avoir l'air de

You look well.	Vous avez bonne mine.[2]
They looked very tired.	Ils[3] avaient l'air d'être[3] très fatigués.
She looks very ill.	Elle a l'air malade.
He looks a disagreeable man.	Il a l'air / d'un homme désagréable.
You do not look pleased.	Vous n'avez pas l'air content.
Do I look (as if I were) angry?	Est-ce que j'ai l'air d'être en colère?

2 you have good mien (=appearance); 3 they had the look of being.

to use, make use of ..., se servir de

I generally use scissors.	D'habitude je me sers de ciseaux.
We prefer to use these tools.	Nous préférons nous servir de ces outils.
He will use his pen-knife to cut the string.	Il se servira de son canif pour couper la ficelle.
The knife he was using did not cut very well.	Le couteau dont il se servait ne coupait pas très bien.
Use a gimlet.	Servez-vous d'une vrille.
Don't make use of this.	Ne vous servez pas de ceci.
Weren't you using his bicycle?	Ne vous serviez-vous pas de sa bicyclette?

like a friend, as a friend, en ami

He came as a friend.	Il est venu en ami.
He acted like an honorable man.	Il a agi en honnête homme.
She was disguised as a gipsy.	Elle était déguisée en bohémienne.
A soldier was posted as a sentinel at the entrance.	Un soldat fut placé en sentinelle à l'entrée.
At the fancy ball, I was dressed in sailor's costume.	Au bal masqué, j'étais habillé en marin.
He talked to them like a father.	Il leur a parlé en père.
They were both dressed as civilians.	Ils étaient tous les deux habillés en civil.

only to us, ne ... qu'à nous

I have only to speak to him.	Je n'ai qu'à lui parler.
She only wrote to me.	Elle n'a écrit qu'à moi.[2]
It is only to them that we spoke.	Ce n'est qu'à eux[2] que nous avons parlé. [minutes.
We have only ten minutes left.	Il[3] ne nous reste que[3] dix
He had only six francs left.	Il ne lui restait que six francs.
They have only brought one trunk. [done.	Ils n'ont apporté qu'une malle. [faire.
Only one thing remains to be	Il ne reste qu'une chose à

2 the Disjunctive Pronouns must be used in such sentences, where the Pronoun is the emphasized word ; 3 there not to-us remains but.

to have a mind to, be strongly inclined for, avoir envie de

I am inclined to go to France.	J'ai envie d'aller en France.
What are you so anxious for ?	De quoi avez-vous envie ?
We feel sleepy.	Nous avons envie[2] de dormir.[2]
He has a mind to borrow some money from us.	Il a envie de nous[3] emprunter de l'argent.
If you feel inclined to read, here is a book.	Si vous avez envie de lire, voici un livre.
Greedy people want everything they see.	Les gourmands ont envie de tout ce qu'ils voient.

2 envy (=inclination, desire, liking) to sleep ; 3 to borrow something from somebody, emprunter quelque chose à quelqu'un.

at (*or* to) my house, **chez moi** ;   from his house, **de chez lui**

They were coming from their milliner's.	Elles venaient de chez leur modiste.
Where do you come from[2] ?	D'où venez-vous ?
From my house.	De chez[3] moi.
He is at home all day long.	Il est chez lui toute la journée.[4]
You will find that book at the bookseller's.	Vous trouverez ce livre chez le libraire. [heures.
She was at home at five o'clock.	Elle était chez elle à cinq
We have[0] just[0] come from our uncle's.	Nous venons de chez notre oncle.
It is not far from our house to the station.	Il n'y a pas loin de chez nous à la gare.
It is rare among the French.	C'est rare chez les Français.
I am going to dine at their house to-morrow.	Je vais dîner chez eux demain.

0 not translated ; 2 Prepositions can never be the last word in a French sentence ; 3 to *or* at the place (house, shop, office, etc.) of ; 4 daytime.

to call on some one, **passer chez quelqu'un**
to call for some one, **passer prendre quelqu'un**

He is going to call at the doctor's.	Il va passer chez le docteur. [matin.
Call on me to-morrow morning.	Passez[2] chez moi[2] demain
He will call for you with a carriage.	Il passera vous prendre[3] en voiture.[3]
Why don't you call on your friends ?	Pourquoi ne passez-vous pas chez vos amis ?
I left a parcel at his place ; call for it.	J'ai laissé un paquet chez lui ; passez le prendre.
We often call on our customers.	Nous passons souvent chez nos clients.
They will be at their office ; call there.	Ils seront à leur bureau ; passez-y. [prendre ?
When will you call for me ?	Quand passerez-vous me
I sometimes call at their house on Sundays.	Je passe quelquefois chez eux le dimanche.

2 pass at-the-place-of me ; 3 to-take in carriage.

to delay, be a long time in ..., **tarder à**

Do not be long before you start, or you will miss the train.	Ne tardez pas à partir, ou vous manquerez le train.
Why was he so long in coming?	Pourquoi tardait-il[2] tant à venir?
I delayed writing to you, because I was busy.	J'ai tardé à vous écrire, parce que j'étais occupé.
Send off the packages without further delay.	Expédiez les colis sans plus tarder.
Do not let us delay calling on him.	Ne tardons pas à passer chez lui.
You are too long in finishing that work.	Vous tardez trop à finir cet ouvrage.
He is a long time writing to us.	Il tarde beaucoup à[3] nous donner de ses nouvelles.[3]
We ought not to wait any longer before we claim the money.	Nous ne devrions pas tarder plus longtemps à réclamer l'argent.

2 did he delay? 3 in giving us his news; a simpler rendering would be : à nous écrire.

---

to undertake ..., **se charger de**

Will you undertake the sale of this house?	Voulez-vous vous charger[2] de la vente de cette maison?
Here is some money; see to the payments.	Voici de l'argent; chargez-vous des paiements.
I have entrusted him with a commission.	Je l'ai chargé d'une commission.
He had taken on himself to write to you.	Il s'était chargé de vous écrire.
We will willingly undertake it.	Nous nous en chargerons volontiers.
The conductor will see to our luggage.	Le conducteur se chargera de nos bagages.
Would you undertake the responsibility of taking him to London?	Vous chargeriez-vous de le conduire[3] à Londres?
Can you undertake it?	Pouvez-vous vous en charger?

2 se charger de, to load one's self with=take on one's self, undertake the task of; 3 conduct.

2

from day to day, de jour en jour

He sells his goods from door to door.	Il vend sa marchandise[2] de porte en porte.
We expect him every minute.	Nous l'attendons de[3] minute en minute.[3] [jour.
She is expecting us every day.	Elle nous attend de jour en
Why do you put off your departure from month to month ?	Pourquoi remettez-vous votre départ de mois en mois ?
I am making progress every day. [to month.	Je fais des progrès de jour en jour. [en mois.
You postpone that from month	Vous renvoyez cela de mois

2 marchandise, one particular 'line' of goods ; in a general sense, marchandises (plural) is used ; 3 or à chaque instant, or d'un moment à l'autre.

to have the toothache, avoir mal aux dents

Take a rest ; you have got[0] a headache.	Reposez-vous[2] ; vous avez mal[3] à la tête.[3]
I have had a bad foot since the day before yesterday.	J'ai[4] mal au pied depuis avant-hier.
That draught has given me a sore throat.	Ce courant[5] d'air[5] m'a donné mal à la gorge.
It is impossible to work when one has a headache.	Il est impossible de travailler quand on a mal à la tête.
If you have the toothache, go to the dentist's.	Si vous avez mal aux dents, allez chez le dentiste.

2 repose yourself ; 3 pain in the head ; 4 Present Tense, because the pain still continues at the time of speaking ; 5 current of air.

to make game of ..., laugh at ..., se moquer de

Why do you make game of him ? [that.	Pourquoi vous moquez-vous de lui ?
There is nothing to laugh at in	Il n'y a pas à s'en moquer.
When we speak to her, she laughs at us. [opinion.	Quand nous lui parlons, elle se moque de nous.
I don't care a straw for their	Je me moque de leur opinion.
It is rude to laugh at people.	Il est impoli[1] de se moquer des gens.
What are you making fun of ?	De quoi vous moquez-vous ?

to make a mistake in the..., to take the wrong..., **se tromper de**

You are making a mistake in the number.	**Vous** vous trompez de numéro.
I took the wrong turning ; I am short-sighted.	Je me suis trompé de rue ; je suis myope.
He had taken the wrong hat.	Il s'était trompé de chapeau.
To make mistakes like this is ridiculous.	Se tromper ainsi est ridicule. [trompé ?
How had you made a mistake ?	**Comment vous** étiez - vous
If you pay attention, you will not go wrong so often.	Si vous faites attention, vous ne vous tromperez pas si souvent.

to remember or recollect something
se souvenir de quelque chose* or se rappeler quelque chose*

He has a good memory ; he remembers everything.	Il a bonne mémoire ; il[2] se souvient de tout.[2]
What ! you cannot remember his name ?	**Comment !** vous ne pouvez vous[3] rappeler son nom[3] ?
Remember it.	Rappelez-vous-le.[4]
Will you remember your promise ?	Vous[5] souviendrez-vous de votre promesse[5] ?
What address did they give you ? Do you remember it ?	Quelle adresse vous a-t-on donnée ? Vous[6] la rappelez-vous[6] ?
She remembered all my questions.	Elle[7] se souvenait de[7] toutes mes questions.
We remember the important things.	Nous[8] nous rappelons les[8] choses importantes.
I recollected the experience.	Je me suis rappelé l'aventure.

*There is no more difference in meaning between these expressions than between ' remember ' and ' recollect ' in English. Note carefully that although **se souvenir** takes **de** after it, **de** must not be used with **se rappeler**. The latter phrase means literally ' to recall TO one's self.'

2 or il se rappelle tout ; 3 or vous souvenir de son nom ; 4 or souvenez-vous-en ; 5 or vous rappellerez-vous votre promesse ? 6 or vous en souvenez-vous ? 7 or elle se rappelait ; 8 or nous nous souvenons des.

to see to, look after, veiller à

Look after my business while I am away.	Veillez à mes affaires pendant[2] mon absence.
I shall constantly study your interests. [thing.	Je veillerai continuellement à vos intérêts.
He told me to see after every-	Il m'a dit de veiller à tout.
The principal ought to see to the good management of his firm.	Le patron devrait veiller à la bonne marche de sa maison
We superintended his studies.	Nous avons veillé à ses études.
We must see that they do not do it. [them.	Il[3] faut[3] veiller à ce qu'ils ne le fassent[4] pas. [pas.
Be careful that he does not lose	Veillez à ce qu'il ne les perde[4]
She will see that he does not go out.	Elle veillera à ce qu'il ne sorte[4] pas. [tout.
Rely on me ; I see to everything.	Comptez sur moi ; je veille à

2 during ; 3 it is-necessary-to=I, we, you, he, she, or they must ; 4 the Verb following veiller à is Subjunctive, preceded by ce que.

to be worth while, valoir la peine

That play is worth seeing.	Cette pièce vaut[2] la peine d'être vue.[2]
It would be worth mending,— worth while to mend it.	Cela vaudrait la peine de le raccommoder.
I told you it was not worth while.	Je vous ai dit que cela n'en[3] valait pas la peine.
It is not worth troubling about.	Cela ne vaut pas la[4] peine de s'en occuper.[4]
Why get angry ? it is not worth while.	Pourquoi vous[5] fâcher[5] ? cela n'en[3] vaut pas la peine.
If it was worth the trouble, you did well to act.	Si cela en[3] a valu la peine, vous avez bien fait d'agir.
I went there because the journey was worth the trouble.	J'y suis allé, parce que le voyage en[3] valait la peine.
It is not worth while to put one's self out for him.	Il ne vaut pas la peine qu'on se dérange pour lui.

2 is worth the trouble of be(ing) seen ; 3 of it ; 4 the trouble to occupy one's self of-it (=with it) ; 5 anger yourself.

to mean=wish to say, vouloir dire

Explain clearly what you mean (=want to say).	Expliquez bien ce que vous voulez dire.
What does this mean? *or* What is the meaning of this?	Que veut dire ceci? *or* Qu'est-ce que ceci veut dire?
What did that mean? *or* What was the meaning of that?	Que voulait dire cela? *or* Qu'est-ce que cela voulait dire?
I do not know what they meant (=wished to say).	Je ne sais pas ce qu'elles (*or* ils) voulaient dire.
What do you mean by that?	Que voulez-vous dire par là?
All this does not mean anything.	Tout ceci ne veut rien dire.
This news means no good.	Cette nouvelle ne veut rien dire de bon.
He did not mean to say anything wrong.	Il n'a rien voulu dire de mal.

to be (worth) better, valoir mieux

It would be better to take our umbrellas.	Il vaudrait mieux prendre nos parapluies.
This is better than that.	Ceci vaut mieux que cela.
Do you think that is worth more?	Pensez-vous que cela vaille[2] mieux?
Would it not be better to go there sooner?	Ne vaudrait-il pas mieux y aller plus tôt?
It would have been better for you to go there alone.	Il aurait mieux valu que vous y alliez seul.
We were told it was preferable to wait here.	On nous a dit qu'il valait mieux attendre ici.
It is better than to get (ourselves) wet.	Cela vaut mieux que de nous mouiller.
Do not use that ink; this is much better.	Ne vous servez pas de cette encre; celle-ci vaut beaucoup mieux.
It will be better to tell the truth.	Il vaudra mieux dire la vérité

2 Subjunctive, after an Interrogative Form.

to get rid of, se débarrasser de

I cannot rid myself of him, *or* get rid of him.	Je ne peux pas me³ débarrasser² de lui.
How does one get rid of a cold ?	Comment se débarrasse-t-on d'un rhume ?
We shall easily relieve ourselves of it.	Nous nous en débarrasserons facilement.
Throw off your overcoat, if you are warm.	Débarrassez-vous de votre pardessus, si vous avez chaud,
It is difficult to get rid of troublesome people.	Il est difficile de se débarrasser des importuns.
This parcel is too heavy ; relieve me of it.	Ce paquet est trop lourd ; débarrassez-m'en.
I should like first to get rid of mine.	Je voudrais d'abord me débarrasser du mien.

What is it all about² ?	De quoi s'agit-il³ ?
He told us that a good stroke of business was in question.	Il nous a dit qu'il s'agissait d'une bonne affaire.
My interests were at stake.	Il s'est agi de mes intérêts.
It will be a matter of making haste.[4]	Il s'agira de se dépêcher.
You were speaking very seriously ; what was the point under discussion ? [to me.	Vous parliez bien sérieusement ; de quoi s'agissait-il ?
If it is a question of money, apply	S'il s'agit d'argent, adressez-vous à moi.
Investigations must be made.	Il s'agit de faire des recherches.
Convincing him will be the chief thing.	Il s'agira de le convaincre.
Let it come to a question of fighting, and he will be quite ready.	Qu'il s'agisse de se battre, et il sera tout prêt.
It was a question of taking a long journey.	Il s'agissait d'un long voyage.
The gentleman in question has just gone away.	Le monsieur dont il s'agit vient de partir.

2 *or* What is in question ? What is under discussion ? What is the subject of conversation ? What is the point at issue ? etc. 3 literally, of what does it act itself ? 4 ⇒we shall have to make haste.

what has become of him ?   qu'est-il devenu ?

Do you know what has become of her ?	Savez-vous ce[2] qu'elle est devenue[2] ? [soldats.
All my sons became soldiers.	Tous mes fils sont devenus
What will become of them, when they get to France ?	Que deviendront-ils à leur arrivée[3] en France ?
We became ill through it.	Nous en[4] sommes devenus malades.
I fear that she will become dissatisfied about it.	Je crains qu'elle n'en[4] devienne[5] mécontente.
What has become of them ?	Que sont-ils devenus ?

2 what she is become ; 3 arrival ; 4 from it, on account of it ; 5 the Verb following **craindre** que must be Subjunctive, and **ne** may precede it.

to apply to=address one's self to, s'adresser à

Apply to the housekeeper.	Adressez-vous au concierge.
We shall apply at the booking-office.	Nous nous adresserons au guichet.
It is here you have to apply for information.	C'est ici qu'il faut s'adresser pour les renseignements.
He applied to me.	Il s'est adressé à moi.
You can apply to him on my behalf.	Vous pouvez vous adresser à lui de ma part.
Let them apply on the first floor.	Qu'ils s'adressent au premier étage.
They told us they would apply at the office.	Ils nous ont dit qu'ils s'adresseraient au bureau.
People always apply to me here.	On s'adresse toujours à moi ici.

We should not be able to hear well.	Nous ne pourrions pas bien entendre.
Neither would the others.	Les autres non plus.
How many times a year do you send in[6] your account ?	Combien de fois par an envoyez-vous votre compte ?
These articles are not pretty ; I don't want them. [take.	Ces articles ne sont pas jolis ; je n'en ai pas envie.
They have only one course to	Ils n'ont qu'un parti à prendre.

to think of=have an opinion concerning, penser de

What do you think of my French?	Que pensez-vous de mon français?
What was his opinion about that gentleman?	Que pensait-il de ce monsieur?
You may think whatever you please about me.	Pensez de moi ce qu'il vous plaira.
We don't think badly of it.	Nous n'en pensons pas de mal.
Tell me what you thought of it.	Dites-moi ce que vous en avez pensé.
Whatever they may think about it, they never speak of it.	Quoiqu'ils en pensent, ils n'en parlent jamais.
One must always think well of others.	Il faut toujours bien penser des autres.

to think of=bear in mind, think over, penser à

What are you thinking about now?	A quoi pensez-vous maintenant?
He was always thinking of his business.	Il pensait toujours à ses affaires.
We shall remember to write to him to-morrow.	Nous penserons à lui écrire demain.
Have they thought about what you said to them?	Ont-ils pensé à ce que vous leur avez dit?
My grocer did not think to send on⁰ my order.	Mon épicier n'a pas pensé à expédier ma commande.
Would you have thought of it, if I had not spoken to you about it?	Auriez-vous pensé à cela, si je ne vous en avais pas parlé?
I was thinking about him when he came in.	Je pensais à lui, quand il est entré.
Our appointment is for noon; think of it (=don't forget it).	Notre rendez-vous est à midi; pensez-y.

Let him talk; we do not care.	Laissez-le dire; nous nous en moquons. [cela.
You sneer at all that.	Vous vous moquez de tout

he has died, he is dead, **il est mort**

She died very young.	Elle est morte bien jeune.
We thought he would die from his fall.	Nous pensions qu'il serait[2] mort[2] de sa chute.
The doctor said that the patient would soon be dead.	Le docteur disait que le malade serait bientôt mort.
My father died ten years ago. [grief.	Il y a dix ans que mon père est mort.
I should have died through	J'en[3] serais mort de chagrin.
Take care of her, or she will soon be dead.	Soignez-la, ou elle sera bientôt morte.
At what period did that general die ?	A quelle époque ce général est-il mort ?

2 would be dead ; 3 from it.

to be born, **naître**

We were all born in France. [London.	Nous sommes* tous nés en France. [dres.
Their brothers were born in	Leurs frères sont nés à Lon-
When she was born, I was travelling.	Quand elle est née, je me[2] trouvais en voyage.[2]
He would have been born richer, if his father had worked.	Il serait né plus riche, si son père avait travaillé.
When were they born ?	Quand sont-ils nés ?
My son was born on the fifth of January in the same year.	Mon fils est né le cinq janvier de la même année.
Where were these girls born ?	Où ces fillettes sont-elles nées?
She was born in Italy.	Elle est née en Italie.

*The Compound Tenses of the Irregular Verb **naître** (to BE born) are formed with **être**. Consequently, **il est né** does not mean 'he is born,' but 'he has been-born.' 2 found myself on a voyage.

We shall dress like Spaniards.	Nous nous habillerons en Espagnols.
We were unable to get rid of our bicycles.	Nous ne pouvions nous débarrasser de nos bicyclettes.
I cannot walk, as I have a bad foot.	Je ne peux pas marcher, car j'ai mal au pied.

to hurt, faire mal à

We have hurt (=caused pain to) that man.	Nous avons fait[2] mal à[2] cet homme.
You will hurt your cousin, if you push him.	Vous ferez mal à votre cousin, si vous le poussez.
He hurt us by accident.	Il nous a fait mal par mégarde.
Did he happen to hurt his arm in jumping ?	Se serait[3]-il fait mal au bras en sautant ?
His shoulder hurts him when he leans on it.	Son épaule lui fait mal quand il s'appuie dessus.
When did she hurt her hand ?	Quand s'est-elle fait mal à la main ?

2 made (=caused) pain to ;　3 the Conditional here suggests a possibility.

to frighten, faire peur à

I scared him with a pistol.	Je lui[2] ai fait peur[2] avec un pistolet.
Our threats do not frighten them.	Nos menaces ne leur font pas peur.
She will not frighten us.	Elle ne nous fera pas peur.
The darkness made the children afraid.	L'obscurité faisait peur aux enfants.
It is difficult to scare a good soldier.	Il est difficile de faire peur à un bon soldat.　　[peur ?
Why do you frighten us ?	Pourquoi nous faites-vous
How will they frighten them ?	Comment leur feront-ils peur?
Nothing (of what) you say scares me.	Rien de ce que vous dites ne me fait peur.

2 to-him have made (=caused) fear.

There is no question of drawing back now.	Il ne s'agit pas de reculer maintenant.
Let me know when you want any help.	Avertissez-moi quand il s'agira de vous aider.
The thing to be done would be to send him away.	Il s'agirait de le renvoyer.
The noise almost always gave us a headache.	Le bruit nous donnait presque toujours mal à la tête.

to have to deal with..., **avoir affaire à**

You will have to reckon with me, if you behave badly.	Vous aurez affaire à moi, si vous vous conduisez mal.
It is the chief clerk with whom we have to deal.	C'est au chef de bureau auquel nous avons affaire.
I am dealing with an intelligent man.	J'ai affaire à un homme intelligent.
Come with us ; we have to deal with an artful man.	Venez avec nous ; nous avons affaire à un rusé.
They had them to deal with.	Ils ont eu affaire à eux.
Distrust the people you will have to negotiate with.	Méfiez-vous des personnes auxquelles vous aurez affaire.
Whom have you just been dealing with ?	A qui venez-vous d'avoir affaire ?

he thinks he can do it=he thinks to be able to do it
il croit pouvoir le faire

I think I can understand it.	Je crois pouvoir le comprendre.
He said he could not accept your offer.	Il a dit ne pouvoir accepter votre offre.
She believed she would arrive much too late.	Elle a cru arriver beaucoup trop tard.
We believe we can see what they are doing from here.	Nous croyons voir ce qu'ils font d'ici.

in a position to, **à même de**

He is not in a position to pay his debts.	Il n'est pas à même de payer ses dettes.
I am in a position to travel all the year round.⁰	Je suis à même de voyager toute l'année.
Will you be competent to do this work ?	Serez-vous à même de faire ce travail ?
We were unable to come to your house.	Nous n'étions pas à même de venir chez vous.
That lady thinks that she can understand everything.	Cette dame pense être à même de tout comprendre.
We are not in a position to be of service to you.	Nous ne sommes pas à même de vous rendre service.

to be fast, to gain (speaking of clocks, etc.), avancer
to be slow, to lose   „   „   „   retarder

My watch is five minutes slow.	Ma montre retarde[2] de[3] cinq minutes.
This clock gained far too much (*or* was much too fast).	Cette pendule avançait[4] beaucoup trop.
The cathedral clock is slow by the station clock.	L'horloge de la cathédrale retarde sur celle de la gare.
How fast is your watch?	De[3] combien avance votre montre?
I have had our clock repaired; it no longer loses.	J'ai fait réparer notre pendule; elle ne retarde plus.
You always arrived late; your watch was slow.	Vous arriviez toujours en[5] retard[5]; votre montre retardait.
On the contrary, it was fast.	Au contraire, elle avançait.
You have set your clock by a watch that is slow.	Vous avez réglé votre pendule sur une montre qui retarde.

2 delays;   3=by;   4 advanced;   5 in delay.

---

to begin, start, **se mettre à**

It is high time they set to work to do something.	Il est temps qu'ils se mettent à faire quelque chose.
It is lack of politeness to start speaking all together.	C'est manque de politesse de se mettre à parler tous ensemble.
Why would you start off laughing?	Pourquoi vous mettriez-vous à rire?
Let us start off on our journey.	Mettons-nous[2] en route.
She began to write directly I asked her.	Elle[3] s'est mise[3] à écrire dès que je le lui ai demandé.
He began to sing, to show off[0] his voice.	Il s'est mis à chanter, pour montrer sa voix.
This man was setting about his work.	Cet homme se[4] mettait à[4] son travail.
The train was just moving off.	Le train se[5] mettait en marche.[5]

2 let us put ourselves;   3 elle a commencé is a simpler, and equally correct construction in such cases;   4 or commençait;   5 put itself in motion: le train partait would be equally correct.

to go bankrupt, faire faillite

He went bankrupt (=made failure) at the end of six months.	Il a fait faillite au bout de six mois.
This is the third time they have gone bankrupt.	C'est la troisième fois qu'ils font faillite.
It was a bad year ; numerous merchants failed.	C'était une mauvaise année ; de nombreux négociants ont fait faillite.
We had charged him with having been a bankrupt.	Nous l'avions accusé d'avoir fait faillite.
That firm has failed already.	Cette maison a déjà fait faillite.
You will not go bankrupt with such a capital.	Vous ne ferez pas faillite avec un tel capital.

to strike work, faire grève or se mettre en grève

They went on strike without any plausible reason.	Ils[2] ont fait grève[2] sans motif plausible.
Everybody suffers when the coalmen go out on strike.	Tout le monde souffre quand les charbonniers font[3] grève.[3]
We shall gain nothing by[4] striking work.	Nous ne gagnerons rien à faire grève.
Strike, if you think proper ; personally, I am against it.	Faites grève si vous voulez ; moi, je m'y oppose.[5]
I shall work, even if a strike takes place.	Je travaillerai, même si l'on fait grève.

2 or ils se sont mis en grève ; 3 or se mettent en grève ; 4 to gain by, gagner à ; to lose by, perdre à ; 5 to oppose something, s'opposer à quelque chose.

You ought to turn to the left.	Vous devriez tourner à gauche.
Afterwards, take the first turning on the right.	Ensuite, prenez la première rue à droite.
They make fun of everything.	Ils se moquent de tout.
In the end, he will have to give me back my money.	Il faudra qu'il finisse par me rendre mon argent.
He does not particularly want to keep it.	Il ne tient pas à le garder.

to go away, s'en aller

We told him to go away.	Nous lui avons dit de[2] s'en aller.[2]
They went away without saying a word.	Ils[3] s'en sont allés[3] sans mot dire.
Our guests will leave to-morrow.	Nos invités s'en iront demain.
I am going to do some errands.	Je m'en vais faire des courses.
Do not go away without me.	Ne vous en allez pas sans moi.
If he goes away, let us know.	S'il s'en va, prévenez-nous.
Why would they go away so soon ?	Pourquoi s'en iraient-ils si tôt ?
Let them go home.	Qu'ils s'en aillent chez eux.
I should not be sorry to see him go away.	Je ne serais pas fâché de le voir s'en aller.
Go away ! Be off !	Allez-vous-en !

2 or de partir ; this Verb, which means ' to depart, start off,' can usually be substituted for s'en aller ; 3 or ils sont partis ; the Compound Tenses of partir are formed with être.

to suit or fit* (speaking of clothes), aller bien

Your new suit fits (or suits) you very well.	Votre nouveau complet vous va très bien.
All that that dressmaker used to make fitted them well.	Tout ce que faisait cette couturière leur allait bien.
This black hat would suit you well.	Ce chapeau noir vous irait bien.
His trousers are too short ; they fit him badly.	Son pantalon est trop court il lui va mal.
She is easy to fit ; everything suits her well.	Elle est facile à habiller ; tout lui va bien.
This dress will always fit her badly.	Cette robe lui ira toujours mal.
If it did not suit you, I should tell you so.	Si cela ne vous allait pas bien je vous le dirais.

*As a rule, no attempt is made in French to indicate the slight difference between ' suiting ' and ' fitting,' as applied to what a person is wearing. If a distinction is thought necessary, ' your costume suits (=becomes) you ' might be rendered as votre costume vous habille (or sied) bien, and ' your costume fits you ' as votre costume vous va bien.

to take place, be held, occur, **avoir lieu**

The performance only took place once a[3] day.	La représentation n'**avait**[2] **lieu**[4] qu'une fois par jour.
When will the examination be held ?	Quand l'examen[4] aura - t - il lieu ?
These meetings will be held on Sundays.	Ces réunions **auront** lieu **le** dimanche.
The review of the troops took place on the appointed day.	La revue **des troupes** a eu lieu au jour fixé.[1]
The meeting was held fort-nightly.	La réunion **avait lieu tous**[5] les quinze jours.[5]
The performance has not taken place yet.	La représentation **n'a pas en-**core eu lieu.

1 nearly the same as in English ; 2 had place=took place ; 3=**PER,** **par** ; 4 pronounced : eg-zah-ma*ng* ; 5 all the (=every) fifteen days.

---

to make enquiries, **se renseigner**

Where do you make enquiries ?	Où peut-on se renseigner[2] ?
We obtained information at the station.	Nous nous sommes renseignés à la gare.
Enquire of the manager.	Renseignez-vous auprès **du** directeur.
When does one enquire ?	Quand se renseigne-t-on ?
They will make enquiries between now and to-morrow.	Ils se renseigneront d'ici à demain. [suite.
They used to enquire at once.	Ils se renseignaient tout de
I must obtain information before settling this affair.	Je dois me renseigner avant de terminer cette affaire.
Apply to an agent, if you wish to obtain information.	Adressez-vous à un agent, si vous voulez vous renseigner.

2 where can one inform one's self ?

That man begs from door to door,—at every door.	Cet homme mendie de porte en porte.
A sore throat prevents me from speaking.	Le mal de gorge m'empêche de parler.
My wife was thirty in 1914.	Ma femme avait (*or* était âgée de) trente ans en 1914.

to take (into one's possession), prendre ;   to take=carry, convey, porter
              to take (living beings)=lead, conduct, mener

Will you take a cup of tea ?	Voulez-vous prendre une tasse de thé ?
I will take a glass of wine, if you have any.	Je prendrai un verre de vin, si vous en avez.
They have taken too much.	Ils en ont trop pris.
Take these letters to the post.	Portez ces lettres à la poste.
When did you take your trunk to the cloak-room ?	Quand avez-vous porté votre malle à la consigne ?
He took the dog to its master.	Il a mené le chien à son maître.
Did you take the lady to her carriage ?	Avez-vous mené la dame à sa voiture ?
This street will take you to the station.	Cette rue vous mènera à la gare.
Our teachers will take us round the museums.	Nos professeurs nous mèneront visiter[1] les musées.

to take away [things]=carry away, emporter
to take away [living beings]=lead away, emmener

Who told you to take that away ?	Qui vous a dit d'emporter cela ?
He has carried off my hat.	Il a emporté mon chapeau.
I asked him to take his horse away.	Je l'ai prié d'emmener[2] son cheval.
Take me (away) with you.	Emmenez-moi avec vous.
The police were taking him off to the station.	La police l'emmenait au poste.
I shall take everything of value away from here.	J'emporterai d'ici tout ce qui a de la valeur.

He is in a position to be well informed.	Il est à même d'être bien renseigné.
When am I to set about this work ?	Quand dois-je me mettre à cet ouvrage ?
He does not care whether his clothes fit him well or badly.	Que ses vêtements lui aillent bien ou mal, il s'en moque.

1 nearly the same as in English ·   2 pronounced : *ahnq-mer-neh.*

to feel sleepy, avoir sommeil ;   to be ashamed, avoir honte

I am never ashamed of my actions.	Je n'ai jamais* honte de mes actions. [meil² ?
What ! you are sleepy already ?	Quoi ! vous avez déjà som-
We shall not be ashamed of going out with him.	Nous n'aurons pas* honte de sortir avec lui.
I always feel sleepy about ten o'clock in the evening.	J'ai toujours sommeil vers³ les dix heures du soir.
He was so shy that he felt ashamed of it.	Il était si timide qu'il en avait* honte.
When we are sleepy, we go to bed.	Quand nous avons sommeil,² nous allons nous coucher.⁴

*As the H in honte (shame) is not mute, the final consonant of the preceding word must not be linked on.

2 slumber ; 3 towards ; 4 to lie down, go to bed, se coucher ; [to rise, get up, se lever].

---

to sleep, dormir   to fall asleep, s'endormir
he is asleep=he sleeps, il dort

Children sleep soundly.	Les enfants dorment profondément.
We were asleep when you knocked.	Nous dormions quand vous avez frappé.
The smoke will send us to sleep.	La fumée nous endormira.
Don't go to sleep at the table.	Ne vous endormez pas à table.
Shake her, that she may not fall asleep.	Secouez-la, afin qu'elle ne s'endorme² pas.
If he is asleep, wake him up.	S'il dort, réveillez-le.
He fell asleep in the train.	Il s'est endormi dans le train.

2 afin que governs the Subjunctive.

That suit fits him like a glove.	Ce complet lui va comme un gant.
My uncle will take us with⁰ him⁰ to the theatre.	Mon oncle nous emmènera au théâtre.
Wait until to-morrow before taking them away.	Attendez à demain avant de les emporter.
Have you a headache ?	Avez-vous mal à la tête ?

he has five francs left, il lui reste cinq francs

How much time did they have left ?	Combien leur[2] restait-il[2] de temps ?
We shall not have much room left.	Il ne nous restera pas beaucoup de place. [heure.
There is only half an hour left.	Il ne reste plus qu'une demi-
I have only two tickets left.	Il ne me reste que deux billets.

2 remains to them.

---

it concerns you, cela vous regarde

The question does not concern us.	La question ne nous regarde pas. [ment.
This chiefly concerns you.	Ceci vous regarde principale-
It was no business of mine.	Cela ne me regardait pas.

---

that's enough, cela suffit (or c'est assez)

Will that be enough for you ?	Cela vous suffira-t-il ?
It would be enough for me.	Cela me suffirait.
Ten metres of cord will suffice.	Dix mètres de corde suffiront.

How long have you been here ?	Depuis combien de temps êtes-vous ici ?
They were making fun of him.	Ils se moquaient de lui.
It is very cold this afternoon.	Il fait très froid cet après-midi.
We expect them every moment.	Nous les attendons à chaque instant. [attendre ?
How long can he wait ?	Combien de temps peut-il
Buy me a pennyworth of tobacco when you go out.	Achetez-moi (pour) deux sous de tabac quand vous sortirez.
We see them from time to time.	Nous les voyons de temps en temps.
The walls of this church are more than a metre thick.	Les murs de cette église ont plus d'un mètre d'épaisseur.
Do you know what has become of him ?	Savez-vous ce qu'il est devenu ?
This is what is in question.	Voici ce dont il s'agit.

to dispense with, do without, se passer de

I cannot do without this assistant.	Je ne peux pas me passer de cet employé.
We could very well manage without those expenses.	Nous nous passerions bien de faire ces dépenses.
He is so poor that he goes without a new suit.	Il est si pauvre qu'il se passe d'un nouveau complet.
How did you manage without it?	Comment vous en êtes-vous passé?
Until now, I have got on all right without a motor-car.	Jusqu'ici, je me suis passé d'automobile.
My brother cannot do without his smoke.	Mon frère ne sait se passer de fumer.

it doesn't matter, n'importe, cela ne fait rien

What does it matter?	Qu'importe?
It doesn't matter much.	Peu[2] importe.[2]
It was immaterial to me.	Cela m'était indifférent.
It is all the same to us.	Cela nous est égal.[3]
That will not matter to him.	Cela[4] ne lui fera rien.[4]
What does that matter to you?	Qu'est-ce que cela vous fait?
What does what they said about me matter?	Qu'importe ce qu'ils ont dit de moi?
It doesn't matter much to them.	Cela leur importe peu.

2 it matters little; 3 equal; 4 that will not make anything to him.

This house is twenty metres high.	Cette maison a vingt mètres de haut.
The street is twelve metres wide.	La rue a douze mètres de large. [teau.
You must use a hammer.	Il faut vous servir d'un mar-
How old is she?	Quel âge a-t-elle?
She will be eighteen in November.	Elle aura dix-huit ans au mois de Novembre.
They have managed without it.	Ils s'en sont passés.
Has the child fallen asleep?	L'enfant s'est-il endormi?
He ended by ruining himself.	Il a fini par se ruiner.

to owe anyone a grudge,2 **en vouloir à quelqu'un**

Why have you such a strong feeling against your sister ?	Pourquoi en voulez-vous tant à votre sœur ?
I have good reasons for owing her a grudge.	J'ai de bonnes raisons de lui en vouloir.
You would do better to overlook all that ; on her part, she cherishes no ill feeling against you.	Vous feriez mieux de passer sur tout cela ; pour sa part, elle ne vous en veut pas.
Why should she bear any malice against me ?	Pourquoi m'en voudrait-elle ?

to say in vain, uselessly, **beau dire**

It doesn't matter what you say and do ; you won't convince him.	Vous aurez beau dire et beau faire ; vous ne le convaincrez pas.
It is no use for him to get angry ; it doesn't do any good.	Il a beau se fâcher ; cela ne sert3 à rien.
We tried in vain ; we could not finish it.	Nous avons eu beau faire ; nous n'avons pu le finir.
The wind may blow as much as it likes ; it won't blow that tree down.	Le vent a beau souffler ; il ne fera pas tomber4 cet arbre.

2 more literally, to wish something to somebody ; 3 serves ; 4 fall.

When will you take us for a walk ? [here.	Quand nous emmènerez-vous faire une promenade ?
Let them be taken away from	Qu'on les emmène d'ici.
The burglars carried off all our silver.	Les cambrioleurs ont emporté toute notre argenterie.
The factories do not take back those who have gone out on strike.	Les usines ne reprennent pas ceux qui ont fait grève (or qui se sont mis en grève).
What was the matter with you2 ? did you fall asleep ?	Qu'aviez-vous ? vous êtes-vous endormi ?
Aren't you ashamed to get up so late ?	N'avez-vous pas honte de vous lever3 si tard ?

2 =what (complaint) had you ? 3 to rise, get up, se lever.

there is, il y a	there must be il doit y avoir
there has been, il y a eu	can there be ? peut-il y avoir ?

What is there to do (=be done) ?	Qu'y a-t-il à faire ?
There was nothing to be said.	Il n'y avait rien à dire.
Will there not be enough meat for all ?	N'y aura-t-il pas assez de viande pour tous ?
There would not be much room.	Il n'y aurait pas beaucoup de place.
There must be another exit.	Il doit y avoir une autre sortie.
There[2] must have been[2] some accident.	Il a dû y avoir quelque accident.
There has been a mistake somewhere.	Il y a eu une erreur quelque part.
There cannot be any danger.	Il ne peut pas y avoir de danger.
Hadn't there been a misunderstanding ?	N'y avait-il pas eu un malentendu ?

2=there has been obliged to be ; in all such sentences, the Auxiliary Verb is the Compound Tense in French, whereas the Principal Verb is Compound in English.

---

to be necessary to, falloir

Is it necessary to[2] go out[2] ?	Faut-il sortir ?
Will it be necessary to speak to him ?	Faudra-t-il lui parler ?
It would not be necessary to tell them.	Il ne faudrait pas le leur dire.
I should send it to them, if it were necessary.	Je le leur enverrais, s'il le fallait.
Has it been necessary to mend it?	A-t-il fallu le réparer ?
It is necessary for me to start at once, to arrive in time.	Il faut que je parte tout de suite, afin d'arriver à temps.
Isn't it necessary for you to write to him ?	Ne faut-il pas que vous lui écriviez?

2=for me, you, us, him, her, or them to go out ; falloir que, followed by the Subjunctive, need only be employed when the person has to be indicated distinctly, thus : faut-il que je sorte? faut-il que nous sortions ? faut-il que vous sortiez? etc.

to suspect, **se douter de**

He suspected something.	Il s'est douté de quelque chose.
That is what he suspected.	C'est ce dont il se doutait.
She would never have suspected it.	Elle ne s'en serait jamais doutée.
Nobody will suppose that.	Personne ne se doutera de cela.
I don't think he had the least idea of it.	Je ne pense pas qu'il s'en soit[2] douté.

2 The Subjunctive is generally employed if the preceding Verb is negative or interrogative.

---

six shillings a pound,* **six schellings la livre**
a hundred francs a month,* **cent francs par mois**

Seven francs a metre seems to me very dear.	Sept francs le mètre me semble fort cher.
These apples cost two francs a dozen.	Ces pommes coûtent deux francs la douzaine.
I go there two or three times a year.	J'y vais deux ou trois fois par an.
They pay me five francs a lesson.	Ils me paient cinq francs par leçon.
I am going to offer him three shillings a pound for it.	Je vais lui en offrir trois schellings la livre.
She earns two hundred francs a week.	Elle gagne deux cents francs par semaine.

* 'A,' meaning PER, should be rendered as le or la before Nouns denoting WEIGHT, MEASURE, or NUMBER, and as par before Nouns denoting a period of time, and all other Nouns. It is always safe for foreigners to follow this simple rule; when Frenchmen depart from it, as they occasionally do, it is because they MAY, not because they must.

I think not.	Je pense que non.
They thought so.	Ils pensaient que oui.
How long have they been working? [back.	Depuis quand travaillent-ils ?
Do not be long before you come	Ne tardez pas à revenir.
They had the thief arrested.	Ils ont fait arrêter le voleur.
Get the luggage registered.	Faites enregistrer les bagages.

to interfere with, mix in, se mêler de

He always interferes with my affairs.	Il se[2] mêlé[2] toujours de mes affaires.
Attend to your own business.	Mêlez-vous de vos affaires.
Do not let us meddle in other people's quarrels.	Ne nous mêlons pas des querelles d'autrui.
He has been dabbling a great deal in politics for some time.	Il se mêle beaucoup de politique depuis quelque temps.

it is dark, il fait nuit   it is getting dark, il se fait nuit

Night comes on very early now.	Il[3] fait[3] nuit maintenant de bonne heure.
Yes, darkness settles in about five o'clock.	Oui, l'obscurité se fait vers cinq heures.
The day does not break until six o'clock.	Il ne fait jour qu'à six heures.
The fog came on about noon, and it was almost like night.	Le brouillard tomba[4] vers midi, et la nuit se fit presque complètement.
It will be daylight at four o'clock soon.	Il fera bientôt jour à quatre heures.

2 mixes himself ;   3 it makes ;   4 fell.

We shall be able to send them to you without delay.	Nous serons à même de vous les envoyer sans délai.
I am anxious to finish this work to-day.	Je tiens à finir cet ouvrage aujourd'hui.
The judge ordered the prisoner to be taken away.	Le juge ordonna d'emmener l'accusé.
The parcels were not heavy ; I took them away.	Les paquets n'étaient pas lourds ; je les ai emportés.
To strike increases the dearness of food.	Faire grève augmente la cherté des vivres.
You would fall asleep to hear his stories.	Vous vous endormiriez à entendre ses histoires.
It didn't matter to your friend.	Cela n'a rien fait à votre ami.
That wouldn't matter to us.	Cela ne nous ferait rien.

that may be, cela se peut, or cela peut être

That cannot be.	Cela ne se peut pas, *or* Cela ne peut pas être.
[be. I don't know whether that can	Je ne sais pas si cela se peut.
How can that be ?	Comment cela se peut-il ? *or* Comment cela peut-il être ?

---

before=previous to, avant ;   before=in front of, devant
before (Adverb)=previously, auparavant ;
before (followed by an Infinitive), avant de

Do this before that.	Faites ceci avant cela.
Don't put yourself before them.	Ne vous mettez pas devant eux.
We had never seen it before.	Nous ne l'avions jamais vu auparavant.
They will begin before[2] we arrive.[2]	Ils commenceront avant notre arrivée.
I drew the blinds down before[2] I went out.[2]	J'ai baissé les stores avant de sortir.
He will finish his work before I go out.	Il finira son travail avant que je sorte.[3]
They will do it before we start.	Ils le feront avant que nous partions.[3] [vant?
What was your trade previously ?	Quel était votre métier aupara-

2 best rendered as ' before our arrival,' ' before going out ' ; a similar change of construction should always be made, if possible, when translating into French, as avant que must be followed by the Subjunctive, a mood best avoided ; 3 the Subjunctive cannot be avoided here.

What is in question ?	De quoi s'agit-il ?
Is your watch gaining ?	Votre montre avance-t-elle ?
We shall get it copied as soon as possible.	Nous le ferons copier le plus tôt possible.
We have frightened them.	Nous leur avons fait peur.
When shall you call on him ?	Quand passerez-vous chez lui ?
I shall call for him at noon.	Je passerai le prendre à midi.
Arriving so late didn't trouble him much.	Cela lui importait peu d'arriver si tard.

to find fault with, **trouver à redire à**

He always finds fault with everything.	Il trouve toujours **à redire** à tout.
What do you find fault with in it ?	Qu'est-ce que vous y trouvez à redire ?
We found nothing to object to in it.	Nous n'y avons rien trouvé à redire.
There is nothing to find fault with in that.	Il n'y a rien à redire à cela.

---

the first of November, le premier novembre
the second, third, fourth, etc.* of June, le deux, trois, quatre juin

They will come on May 1st.	Ils viendront le premier mai.
She started on Tuesday, March the second.	Elle est partie mardi, le deux mars.
I was born on the first of August.	Je suis né le premier août.
She died on September 15th.	Elle est morte le **quinze** septembre.
It will take place on Sunday, October 21st.	Cela aura lieu dimanche, le vingt et un octobre.

*Cardinal Numbers are used when referring to the day of the month, the first (le premier) alone excepted.

I wanted very much to speak to you on this subject, but I could not find time.	J'avais envie de vous parler à ce sujet, mais le temps m'a manqué.[2]
What do you mean ?	Que voulez-vous dire ?
We are not at all anxious to do business with him.	Nous ne tenons pas du tout à faire des affaires avec lui.
We shall take our children with us.	Nous emmènerons nos enfants avec nous.
Would you advise them to strike ?	Leur conseilleriez-vous de faire grève ?
My husband slept for three hours and a half.	Mon mari a dormi pendant trois heures et demie.
We mistrusted his intentions.	Nous nous doutions de ses intentions.

[2] failed.

to get up, rise=raise one's self, se lever

I always get up early.	Je me lève toujours de[2] bonne heure.[2] [là.
She had risen late that day.	Elle s'était levée tard ce jour-
At what time used you to get up?	A quelle heure vous leviez-vous ?
Tell him to get up at once.	Dites-lui de se lever tout de suite.
We shall rise early in the morning.	Nous nous lèverons de bon matin.

to lie down, go to bed, se coucher

We go to bed about ten o'clock in the evening.	Nous nous couchons vers les dix heures du soir.
He will go to bed as soon as possible.	Il se couchera aussitôt que possible.
Do not lie down on that sofa.	Ne vous couchez pas sur ce canapé.
As soon as I am in bed, I shall fall asleep.	Dès que je serai couché, je m'endormirai.
When did they (fem.) go to bed ?	Quand se sont-elles couchées ?

It is to be hoped so.	Il faut l'espérer.[3]
Show them in.	Faites-les entrer.
Ask him to walk up.	Faites-le monter.[4]
He was born on April 22nd.	Il est né le vingt-deux avril.
How much money have you left ?	Combien d'argent vous reste-t-il ?
They ought not to wait.	Ils ne devraient pas attendre.
He ought to have waited for them longer.	Il aurait dû les attendre plus longtemps.
What does poverty matter to me ?	Que m'importe la gêne ?
I am used to it.	J'y suis habitué.
We only meet them once a week.	Nous ne les rencontrons qu'une fois par semaine.
I can do without that.	Je puis me passer de cela.

2=in good time ;   3 it is necessary to hope it ;   4 make him mount.

on *or* from all sides, from *or* in all directions, **de tous côtés**

The enemy fled in all directions.	Les ennemis s'enfuirent de tous côtés.
From all sides complaints were heard.	De tous côtés on entendait des plaintes.
An island is a piece⁰ of⁰ land surrounded by water on every side.	Une île est une terre entourée d'eau de tous côtés.

take care not to fall, **prenez garde de tomber***

Take care not to lose them.	Prenez garde de les perdre.
I shall take care not to hurt him.	Je prendrai garde de lui faire mal. [fatiguer.
He is very careful not to tire [himself.	Il prend bien garde de se
Let us be careful not to make ourselves dirty.	Prenons garde de nous tacher.
Mind the paint.	Prenez garde à la peinture.

*Or, **Ayez soin** (have care) **de ne pas tomber, de ne pas les perdre, J'aurai soin de ne pas lui faire mal,** etc. In such sentences, the **ne pas** should be omitted if **prendre garde** is used, as they are equivalent to 'guard yourself from falling,' etc.

Is he in a position to fulfil his engagements ?	Est-il à même de remplir ses engagements ?
We ought to have had it done six months ago.	Nous aurions dû le faire faire il y a six mois.
How far is it from here to the hotel ?	Combien y a-t-il d'ici à l'hôtel ?
Look straight before you.	Regardez droit devant vous.
I have just found it again.	Je viens de le retrouver.
Let us carry it away with us ; we shall need it.	Emportons-le ; nous en aurons besoin.
Some people go to sleep after their meals.	Quelques personnes s'endorment après leurs repas.
The price will come to three hundred francs a ton.	Le prix se montera à trois cents francs la tonne.
How many times a month do you see him ?	Combien de fois par mois le voyez-vous ?

nothing, not anything, ne...rien ; never, not ever, ne...jamais
not any more, no longer, ne...plus ; nobody, ne...personne

I heard nothing.	Je[2] n'ai rien entendu.[2]
He will never have finished it in time.	Il[2] ne l'aura jamais fini[2] à temps.
She has no more money.	Elle n'a plus d'argent.
We did not see anybody.	Nous n'avons vu personne.[3]
We have no doubt of it.	Nous n'en avons aucun doute.
I was neither hungry nor thirsty.	Je n'avais ni faim ni soif.
They would hardly have time.	Ils n'auraient guère de temps.

2 literally, I not have anything heard, he not will-have ever finished ;
3 personne, being practically a Noun, FOLLOWS the Past Participle in
Compound Tenses ; rien, jamais, etc. precede it.

Nothing is easier.	Rien n'est plus facile.
Nobody knows it better than he does.[0]	Personne ne le sait mieux que lui.
I should never have thought of that.	Jamais[2] je n'aurais[2] pensé à cela.
He will never accept those conditions.	Jamais[2] il n'acceptera[2] ces conditions.
Not a[0] single[0] one came.	Pas un n'est venu.
Nobody is more amiable than his cousin (fem.).	Personne n'est plus aimable que sa cousine.

2 more emphatic than je n'aurais jamais, il n'acceptera jamais.

What has he to say ?—Nothing.	Qu'a-t-il à dire ?—Rien.
Whom do you see on Sundays ? —Nobody.	Qui voyez-vous le dimanche ? —Personne.[2]
Do you ever lend him any money ?—Never.	Lui prêtez - vous parfois[3] de l'argent ?—Jamais.[2]
Have they no inclination to travel ?—None whatever.	N'ont-ils aucune envie de voyager ?—Aucune.
Do you think they will accept our terms ?—Never.	Pensez-vous qu'ils acceptent[4] nos conditions ?—Jamais.
Who (is it that) did that ?—No one.	Qui est-ce qui a fait cela ?— Personne.

2 ne is omitted if no Verb is used ; 3 at times, occasionally. ; 4 Subjunctive, after an interrogative form.

to go for a walk, se promener ; to go for a row, se promener en bateau
to take a drive, se promener en voiture

I go for a walk every evening.	Je me promène tous les soirs.
She goes for a drive every morning.	Elle se promène tous les matins en voiture.
Do you often ride out on horseback ?	Vous promenez-vous souvent à cheval ?
They went for a trip on the river.	Ils se sont promenés en bateau.
We shall go for a drive this afternoon.	Nous nous promènerons en voiture cette après-midi.
You had better go on horseback.	Promenez-vous plutôt[2] à cheval.
Did the ladies go on the river? 2 rather.	Les dames se sont-elles promenées en bateau ?

to get used to, become accustomed to, s'habituer à

He was getting used to the climate.	Il s'habituait au climat.
I am used to his way of speaking.	Je suis habitué à sa façon de [parler.
We are beginning to get accustomed to the noise.	Nous commençons à nous habituer au bruit.
I shall never get used to this custom.	Je ne m'habituerai jamais à cette coutume.
He will quickly get used to it.	Il s'y habituera vite.
Has she become used to it ?	S'y est-elle habituée ?

How long have you known how to swim ?	Depuis quand savez-vous nager[2] ?
You ought to have shown her in,—asked her to walk in.	Vous auriez dû la faire entrer.[3]
After a hard day's work, one goes to sleep easily.	Après une forte[4] journée[4] de travail, on s'endort facilement.
What has become of her ?	Qu'est-elle devenue ?
What has become of them ?	Que sont-ils devenus ?
That does not matter.	Cela ne fait rien.
There is a mistake somewhere.	Il y a une erreur quelque part.

2 since when do you know (how to) swim ?   3 you should-have ought-
to make her enter ;   4 strong daytime.

to come, venir   to have just ..., venir de ...
to happen to, chance to, venir à ...

We came here yesterday evening. [services.	Nous sommes venus ici hier soir. [vices.
I have[0] come to offer you my	Je viens vous offrir mes ser-
They have[0] come to ask you for some information.	Ils viennent vous demander un renseignement.
Where do you come from ?	D'où venez-vous ?
I come from home.	Je viens de chez moi.
If he happened to forget it, it would be a great misfortune.	S'il venait à l'oublier, ce serait un grand malheur.
He has just hurt himself.	Il vient de se blesser.
War has just been declared.	La guerre vient d'être déclarée.

---

to get tired, se fatiguer

We used to tire ourselves, in order to sleep better.	Nous nous fatiguions, pour mieux dormir.
I should soon get tired of his tales. [work.	Je me fatiguerais vite de ses histoires. [travail.
They had tired themselves at that	Ils s'étaient fatigués à ce
I never get tired of walking.	Je ne me fatigue jamais de la marche.
This game will soon tire you.	Ce jeu vous fatiguera vite.
How had you got so tired ?	Comment vous étiez-vous tant fatigué ?

I am afraid he is wrong.	Je crains qu'il ait[2] tort.
He has gone to the dentist's.	Il est allé chez le dentiste.
I have brought it from the	Je l'apporte de chez le bou-
I hope not. [butcher's.	J'espère que non. [cher.
We hope so.	Nous espérons que oui.
How long has he been here ?	Depuis quand est-il ici ?
He ought to have read it.	Il aurait dû le lire.
Try to make yourself competent to answer him.	Tâchez d'être à même de lui répondre.
After a short rest, I set out again. 2 or n'ait.	Après un court repos, je me remis en marche.

to keep to, abide by, act on, s'en tenir à
to stop short, stay at a certain point, s'en tenir là

He went by his instructions.	Il s'en[2] est tenu[2] à ses ordres.
We acted on what you had told us.	Nous nous en sommes tenus à ce que vous nous aviez dit.
I shall adhere to my first idea.	Je m'en tiendrai à ma première idée.
The matter will not rest there.	L'affaire ne s'en tiendra pas là.
If you had abided by the terms of the contract, you wouldn't have had any unpleasantness.	Si vous vous en étiez tenu aux conditions du contrat, vous n'auriez pas eu de désagréments.
Leave well alone,—let the matter remain as it is.	Tenez-vous-en là.

2 has held himself from it.

---

to make haste, hurry one's self, se dépêcher

Do not hurry so much.	Ne vous dépêchez pas tant.
We must make haste.	Il faut que nous nous dépêchions.
He says he is in a hurry.	Il se dit pressé.
They never hurry themselves.	Ils ne se dépêchent jamais.
Make haste and finish that work.	Dépêchez-vous de finir ce travail.
She had promised us she would make haste.	Elle nous avait promis de se dépêcher.

Will you take all your things away with you ?	Emporterez-vous tous vos effets ?
I have not slept well for some time.	Je ne dors pas bien depuis quelque temps.
I paid ten francs a pair for them.	Je les ai payés dix francs la paire.
No man has deserved it better than he.	Aucun homme ne l'a mieux mérité que lui.
Get up ; your breakfast is waiting for you.	Levez-vous ; votre déjeuner vous attend.
As one makes one's bed, one must lie on it.	Comme on fait son lit, on se couche.

He had his eyes open.   Il avait les* yeux ouverts.

Open your mouth, please.	Ouvrez la bouche, s'il vous plaît. [tête.
He completely lost his head.	
What have you got[0] in your hand ?	Il a complètement perdu le Qu'avez-vous à la main ?
She will put her hand on it.	Elle mettra la main dessus.
Move it with your foot.	Bougez-le du pied.
My chest hurts me.	La poitrine me fait mal.
He had just put his foot in the stirrup.	Il venait de mettre le pied à l'étrier.

*In all such sentences, where no confusion of meaning can arise, the Definite Article is substituted in French for the Possessive Adjective.

He saved my life.	Il m'a sauvé la vie.
Some one trod on his foot.	Quelqu'un lui a marché sur le pied.
An idea came into my mind.	Une idée m'est venue à l'esprit.
The surgeon will cut his leg off.	Le chirurgien lui coupera la jambe.
Take care, or you will burn your hand.	Prenez garde, ou vous[2] vous brûlerez à la main.[2]

2 you will burn yourself in the hand.

They are rubbing their eyes.	Ils se frottent les yeux.
He was washing his hands.	Il se lavait les mains.[2]
I will wipe my hands first.	Je m'essuierai les mains d'abord. [cheveux.
I am going to get my hair cut.	Je vais me faire couper les
She has broken her leg.	Elle s'est cassé la jambe.
I have burnt my tongue.	Je me suis brûlé la langue.
This little girl has scratched her(self in-the) face.	Cette fillette s'est égratignée au visage.

2 he to-himself (=of himself) was-washing the hands.

They do not like to go to bed without supper.	Ils n'aiment pas se coucher sans souper.
I shall use a screw-driver.	Je me servirai d'un tournevis.

to occupy one's self with, attend to, see to, **s'occuper de**

What is he occupied in ?	De quoi s'occupe-t-il ?
See to the luggage.	Occupez-vous des bagages.
Tell them to attend to it.	Dites-leur de s'en occuper.
Don't spend your time on that.	Ne vous occupez pas de cela.
The workman saw to it immediately.	L'ouvrier s'en est occupé immédiatement.
We shall deal with it in due course.	Nous nous en occuperons en temps^2 utile.^{2}
Don't you want us to deal with this matter ?	Ne voulez-vous pas que nous nous occupions^3 de cette affaire ?

nearly to do a thing, **faillir faire une chose**

We almost missed the train.	Nous avons failli manquer le train.
She slipped, and nearly fell.	Elle a glissé et a failli tomber.
We were on the point of starting for America.	Nous avons failli partir en Amérique.
His scheme almost suceeded.	Son artifice a failli réussir.

I will hurry, in order to gt there at the same time as you.	Je me dépêcherai, pour arriver en même temps que vous.
We shall have to pay twenty francs a head.	Il faudra payer vingt francs par tête.
If war were (=happened) to be declared, what would you do ?	Si la guerre venait à être déclarée, que feriez-vous ?
Why do you not make use of our horses ?	Pourquoi ne vous servez-vous pas de nos chevaux ?
Has she no more money ?—Not a halfpenny (more).	N'a-t-elle plus d'argent ?— Plus un sou.
You have only one thing to do now.	Vous n'avez qu'une chose à faire maintenant.
How did you get accustomed to it so easily ?	Comment vous y êtes-vous habitué si facilement ?
You ought to be careful what you say.	Vous devriez faire attention a ce que vous dites.

to happen, elapse. occur, se passer

This occurred last year.	Ceci se passait l'année dernière.
Some extraordinary things are happening just now.	Il[2] se passe[2] maintenant des choses extraordinaires.
Do you know what is going on ?	Savez-vous ce qui se passe ?
A great many more years will pass before this work is finished.	Il[3] se passera encore[3] de longues[1] années avant que cet ouvrage soit[4] fini.
I don't believe the week will go by without war breaking out.	Je ne crois pas que la semaine se passe sans que la guerre éclate.[4]

1 nearly the same as in English ;   2 =there are happening ;   3=there will still elapse ;   4 Subjunctive, after avant que, sans que.

to mind, pay attention to, faire attention à

Pay attention to what I tell you.	Faites attention à ce que je vous dis.
He didn't take any notice of that.	Il n'a pas fait attention à cela.
Mind what you are doing, sir ; you are pushing me.	Faites attention, Monsieur ; vous me poussez.
Look out ; here comes a carriage.	Faites attention ; voici une voiture.

We shall not be able to finish before ten o'clock.	Nous ne pourrons pas finir avant dix heures.
Where were you before[2] you came[2] to our house ?	Où étiez-vous avant de venir chez nous ?
Don't stay in front of me.	Ne restez pas devant moi.
I have never read this novel before.	Je n'ai jamais lu ce roman auparavant.
I fell asleep before he had finished his work.	Je me suis endormi avant qu'il ait fini son travail.
She has sprained her foot.	Elle s'est foulé le pied.
He whispered it in my ear.	Il me le souffla à l'oreille.
Did he call at your place ?	Est-il passé chez vous ?

2=before coming.

that is no use, **cela ne sert à rien**[2]

It will not be much use to you.	Cela ne vous servira pas à grand'chose.[3]
What is this tool used for ?	A quoi cet outil sert-il ?
What you say will be of no avail.	Ce que vous dites ne servira à rien.
This machine is used for printing the materials.	Cette machine sert à imprimer les étoffes.

2 that does not serve to anything ; 3 great thing.

to serve as, **servir de**

This room was used (=served) as a lumber-room.	Cette chambre servait de cabinet de débarras.
This flat serves him as a temporary resting place, when he comes to Paris.	Cet appartement lui sert de pied-à-terre,[2] quand il vient à Paris. [taire.
My friend acted as my secretary.	Mon ami m'a servi de secré-
Let this accident be a lesson to you !	Que cet accident vous serve de leçon !
His uncle was a father to him.	Son oncle lui a servi de père.
We shall make our journey our excuse.	Nous nous servirons de notre voyage comme excuse.

2 literally, foot to ground.

What did he make use of ?	De quoi s'est-il servi ?
We shall use your carriage this afternoon.	Nous nous servirons de votre voiture cette après-midi.
I made a mistake in the number.	Je me suis trompé de numéro.
Get these boxes weighed.	Faites peser ces boîtes.
We have got rid of the workmen.	Nous nous sommes débarrassés des ouvriers.
Enquire at the office.	Informez-vous au bureau.
He has got rid of it easily	Il s'en est facilement débarrassé.
If they had not hurried themselves, they would have arrived too late.	S'ils ne s'étaient pas dépêchés, ils seraient arrivés trop tard.

to seize on, take possession of, s'emparer de

He always takes possession of the best places.	Il s'empare toujours des meilleures places.
The enemy seized on the town.	Les ennemis se sont emparés de la ville. [d'eux.
A great dread came over them.	Une grande terreur s'empara
Hardly had he arrived when they seized hold of him.	A peine fut-il arrivé qu'on s'empara de lui.

to be at the disposal of, être à

If you will wait a minute, I shall be at your disposal.	Si vous voulez attendre une minute, je serai à vous.
I can't attend to you at the moment; I am very busy.	Je ne puis être à vous pour l'instant; je suis très occupé.
We shall be at their service in half an hour.	Nous serons à eux dans une demi-heure.

to pay cash, payer comptant

If you pay cash down, I will allow you a discount of five per cent.	Si vous payez comptant, je vous ferai un escompte de cinq pour cent.
They only sell for cash.	Ils ne vendent qu'au comptant.
Did he pay cash?	A-t-il payé comptant?

He looks an affable man.	Il a l'air d'un homme affable.
He was ready. So were they.	Il était prêt. Eux aussi.
I cannot understand this.	Je ne peux pas comprendre ceci.
Neither can his companion.	(Ni) son compagnon non plus.
Neither can we.	(Ni) nous non plus.
They were looking at each other.	Ils se regardaient l'un l'autre.
We ought to have kept to his method.	Nous aurions dû nous en être tenu à sa méthode.
If we make haste, we shall finish before eight o'clock.	Si nous nous dépêchons, nous finirons avant huit heures.
He will occupy himself in making me succeed.	Il s'occupera à me faire réussir.

to gain by, **gagner à**	to lose by, **perdre à**
You will not gain anything by acting thus.	Vous ne gagnerez rien à agir ainsi.
He improves on acquaintance.	Il gagne à[2] être connu.[2]
I do not think they will gain by it.	Je ne pense pas qu'ils y gagnent.
You have lost by not being there.	Vous avez perdu à ne pas y être.
You have lost nothing by not seeing it.	Vous n'avez rien perdu à ne pas le voir.
Be nice to him ; you will not lose by it.	Soyez aimable avec lui ; vous n'y perdrez pas.

to take it into one's head to, presume to, **s'aviser de**

If you presume to go out, you will be punished.	Si vous vous avisez de sortir, vous serez puni.
They would not think of going in without a ticket.	Ils ne s'aviseraient pas d'entrer sans billet.
He took it into his head to come and see me.	Il s'est avisé de venir me voir.
Let him dare to present himself here, and I will turn him out.	Qu'il s'avise de se présenter ici et je le[3] mettrai à la porte.[3]

2 =by being known ; 3 shall put him to the door.

They ask two francs and a half for each person.	Ils demandent deux francs cinquante par personne.
I formerly got up at eight in the morning ; now I have to rise at six o'clock.	Autrefois je me levais à huit heures du matin ; maintenant je dois me lever à six heures.
When will they do this work ? —Never.	Quand feront-ils cet ouvrage ? —Jamais.
I must go away in ten minutes.	Il faut que je m'en aille dans dix minutes.
If he happens to die, it will be a great loss to his party.	S'il vient à mourir, ce sera une grande perte pour son parti.
You have broken his arm.	Vous lui avez cassé le bras.
He owes you a grudge.	Il vous en veut.

to be sorry for, vexed at, être fâché de, désolé de, contrarié de

I am very sorry (for it), but I can't do it.	J'en suis bien fâché, mais je ne puis le faire.
I am sorry for what happened to you.	Je suis désolé de ce qui vous est arrivé.
We are grieved at it on their account.	Nous en sommes désolés pour eux.
It is useless to worry yourself about that.	Il est inutile de vous en désoler. [vous.
She will be very sorry for you.	Elle en sera très fâchée pour
He seemed very vexed at it.	Il en a paru très contrarié.
You will be sorry for having said that.	Vous serez fâché d'avoir dit cela.
He was sorry to hear the news.	Il a été désolé d'apprendre[2] la nouvelle. [moi.
He said he was sorry for me.	Il a dit en être désolé pour
I don't think they are very sorry for it.	Je ne crois pas qu'ils en soient[3] bien fâchés.

2 learn ;　3 Subjunctive, after a Negative Form.

---

to have a thing made for one's self, se faire faire une chose

I am having a pair of boots made (for myself).	Je me fais faire une paire de bottines.
He has had a suit made.	Il s'est fait faire un complet.
There is the bicycle he has had made.	Voilà la bicyclette qu'il s'est fait faire.
My brother has had one made too.	Mon frère s'en est fait faire une aussi.
We have had a country house built.	Nous nous sommes fait faire une maison de campagne.

Is she ill ?—Yes, she is.	Est-elle malade ?—Oui, elle
We are hungry.	Nous avons faim. [l'est.
They are not thirsty.	Ils n'ont pas soif.
I should not be ashamed of that.	Je n'aurais pas honte de cela.
Do you know what is the matter ?	Savez-vous ce qu'il y a ?

to get over, pull through, get through, se tirer de*

How shall we get out of this dilemma?	Comment nous tirerons-nous de cette impasse?
How are you getting on with your lessons?	Comment vous tirez-vous de vos leçons?
I manage to do them pretty well now.	Je m'en tire assez bien à présent.
Leave him to get out of the matter as best he can.	Laissez-le se tirer d'affaire comme il pourra.²

* to draw or extricate one's self from ; 2 will be able to.

to remain, be left, rester

What remains for you to do?	Que vous reste-t-il à faire?
How many are there left?	Combien en reste-t-il?
They remained there until the morning.	Ils sont restés là jusqu'au matin.
Let us stay where we are.	Restons où nous sommes.
There will be nothing of it left.	Il n'en restera rien.

to smell, feel, smell of, sentir

Does the wood smell of oil?	Le bois sent-il l'huile?
The whole house smells of gas.	Toute la maison sent le gaz.
This bottle smells of vinegar.	Cette bouteille sent le vinaigre.
The meat smells bad.	La viande sent mauvais.
Those flowers smell very nice.	Ces fleurs sentent très bon.
I can smell the sea air.	Je peux sentir l'air de la mer.
Do you feel the draught?	Sentez-vous le courant d'air?

Will you undertake this commission?	Voulez-vous vous charger de cette commission?
They will willingly take the responsibility of it.	Ils s'en chargeront volontiers.
Did you not have the ear-ache?	N'avez-vous pas eu mal à l'oreille?
Will you call on me to-morrow morning at ten?	Passerez-vous chez moi demain matin à dix heures?
Has anyone gone for the doctor?	Est-on allé chercher le médecin?

to trust to, rely on, se fier à

We (*or* you, they, etc.) must not trust to the first comer.	Il ne faut pas se fier au premier venu.
You may rely on her.	Vous pouvez vous fier à elle.
Don't trust flatterers.	Ne vous fiez pas aux flatteurs.
We shall trust to you.	Nous nous fierons à vous.
Rely on him.	Fiez-vous à lui.
I rely solely on you.	Je me fie entièrement à vous.

to put near, approcher ;   to go towards, come near, s'approcher de

Come near (to) the fire.	Approchez-vous du feu.
Don't let us go so near.	Ne nous approchons pas tant.
Put the inkstand nearer to me.	Approchez l'encrier de moi.
Why did she go near the window ?	Pourquoi s'est-elle approchée de la fenêtre ? [chien.
Don't go near that dog.	Ne vous approchez pas de ce
It is he that is coming near me.	C'est lui qui s'approche de moi.

to succeed in, réussir à

He has succeeded in finding the entrance.	Il a réussi à trouver l'entrée.
I did not succeed in doing it.	Je n'ai pas réussi à le faire.
Did you succeed in persuading him ?	Avez-vous réussi à le persuader ?

They had no desire to go out.	Ils n'avaient nulle envie de sortir. [courage.
That man has no courage.	Cet homme n'a point de
We shall have some trouble in accustoming ourselves to it.	Nous aurons de la peine à nous y habituer.
If you wrote to your uncle, he would make it his business to find you a situation.	Si vous écriviez à votre oncle il s'occuperait[1] de vous trouver un emploi.
I shall start on it after dinner.	Je m'y mettrai après le dîner
This vehicle will do for bringing back the goods.	Cette voiture servira à rapporter les marchandises.

to be a judge of, understand thoroughly, **se connaître à** *or* **en**

My friend is a good judge of horses.	Mon ami se[2] connaît en[2] chevaux.
Do you know all about them too?	Vous y connaissez-vous aussi?
I am an expert as regards motor-cars.	Je me connais très bien en automobiles.
In a few months, I shall know all about bicycles.	Dans quelques mois, je me connaîtrai parfaitement en bicyclettes.
You will soon be familiar with drugs.	Vous vous connaîtrez bientôt en médecines.
He must be a judge of the matter now.	Il doit s'y connaître maintenant.

to occupy by, on, *or* with, **occuper à**

I am very busy just now doing my correspondence.	Je suis très occupé en ce moment à faire ma correspondance.
What will you be occupied with to-morrow evening?	A quoi serez-vous occupé demain soir?
Keep them occupied with copying the addresses.	Occupez-les à copier les adresses.
He is engaged in writing a letter to them.	Il est occupé à leur écrire une lettre.
We are employing all our time in the drawing up of an important memorandum.	Nous occupons tout notre temps à la rédaction d'un important mémoire.

It is his good faith which is in question.	C'est de sa bonne foi qu'il s'agit.
When will he set to work?	Quand se mettra-t-il au travail?
I want very much to see it.	J'ai bien envie de le voir.
Have you ever seen that?—No, nowhere.	Avez-vous déjà vu cela?—Non, nulle part.
What you say will not matter much to him; he will not listen to you.	Peu lui importera ce que vous direz; il ne vous écoutera pas.

there is no occasion *or* need, **il n'y a pas de quoi**

I beg your pardon.	Je vous[2] demande pardon.
Don't mention it.	Il n'y a pas de quoi.[3]
I thank you for your offer.	Je vous remercie de votre offre.
There is no occasion to.	Il n'y a pas de quoi.
You were very kind to trouble yourself.	Vous avez été bien **aimable** de vous déranger.
There was really[2] no need to do so.	Vraiment il n'y avait pas de quoi.

2 to you=of you ;   3 more literally, there is no what (=ground, occasion, need, necessity) ; this is the phrase usually employed when thanks or apologies are deprecated as uncalled for.

---

to charge (a price)=to ask, take, cause to pay

How much do you charge for a full week ?	Combien demandez[2]-vous (*or* prenez[3]-vous) pour une semaine complète ?
He charged me too much.	Il m'a fait trop payer,[4] *or* Il m[5]'a trop pris.
We were charged five francs a head.	On nous[5] a pris cinq francs par tête.
They will charge us two francs an hour.	Ils nous demanderont deux francs par heure.

2 ask ;   3 take ;   4 he made me pay too much ;   5 literally, to me, to us ; 'to take something from somebody' is **prendre quelque chose à quelqu'un,**—see next page.

They had just arrived.	Ils venaient d'arriver.
Have you boiled the milk ?	Avez-vous fait bouillir **le lait**?
Which way has she gone ?	Par où est-elle allée ?
I value this watch very much.	Je tiens beaucoup à **cette** montre.
How do you do ? How are you ?	Comment vous **portez-vous** ?
It rests solely with you to get this work done.	Il ne tient qu'à vous de **faire** faire ce travail.
It depends only on me to tell them.	Il ne tient qu'à moi de **le** leur dire.
I will send for it (him *or* her).	Je l'enverrai **chercher.**

to take from, prendre à	to borrow from,* emprunter à
I know that he took it from some member of his family.	Je sais qu'il l'a pris à quelqu'un de sa famille.
Don't you know whom they took it from?	Ne savez-vous pas à qui ils l'ont pris?
I have borrowed twenty francs from a friend.	J'ai emprunté vingt francs à un ami.
You would do better not to borrow from anybody.	Vous feriez mieux de n'emprunter à personne.
X—, the banker, has been robbed of a hundred thousand francs.	On a volé cent mille francs à X—, le banquier.
Take the knife away from your brother.	Otez le couteau à votre frère.
The dressmaker has had to take a button off your dress.	La couturière a dû ôter un bouton à votre robe.
He concealed from her the real reason of his departure.	Il lui a caché la véritable raison de son départ.

Let him give it back to the person he took it from.	Qu'il le rende à qui il l'a pris.
Did she tell you whom she had bought it from?	Vous a-t-elle dit à qui elle l'avait acheté?
We hid our intentions from them.	Nous leur avons caché nos intentions.
He bought it from a friend.	Il l'a acheté à un ami.
She took this pencil from her brother.	Elle a pris ce crayon à son frère.
Whom had she stolen them from?	A qui les avait-elle volés?
Whom do you expect me to borrow from, if not from a friend?	A qui voulez-vous que j'emprunte, sinon à un ami?
I shall not conceal from you that I don't like that.	Je ne vous cacherai pas que je n'aime pas cela.

* There are several other Verbs, after which FROM must be rendered by à; the most important of them are introduced on this page.

I have hurt my hand.	Je me suis fait mal à la main.
Is he not very thirsty?	N'a-t-il pas grand'soif?
Who set this watch going?	Qui a fait aller cette montre?

to cut one's finger, **se couper au** doigt

She has hurt her finger.	Elle s'est blessé le doigt.[2]
She has hurt her finger.	Elle s'est blessée au doigt.[3]
She had cut her finger off.	Elle s'était coupé le doigt.[4]
I burnt my finger in poking the fire.	Je[5] me suis brûlé au doigt[5] en attisant le feu.
Has she cut her(self in-the) thumb ?	S'est-elle coupée au pouce ?
She has cut her thumb off.	Elle s'est coupé le pouce.
Has she scratched her arm ?	S'est-elle égratigné le bras[6] ?
Have you *(fem.)* cut your hand ?	Vous êtes-vous coupée à la main ?
One of the workmen has had his arm cut off by this machine.	Un des ouvriers s'est fait couper le bras par cette machine.

This workman had a very narrow escape of being killed in the fire at the works.	Cet ouvrier a failli périr[1] dans l'incendie de l'usine.
The study of languages tends to broaden the mind.	L'étude des langues sert à élargir la pensée.
I don't see what good that would do you.	Je ne vois pas à quoi cela vous servirait.
It is a question of knowing what must be done next.	Il s'agit de savoir ce qu'il faudra faire ensuite.
I have not been able to find it anywhere.	Je n'ai pu le trouver nulle part.
With time, one gets used to everything.	Avec le temps, on s'habitue à tout.

2 more literally, 'she has hurt to-herself (=of herself) the finger ';
when the Object Pronoun means TO myself, TO herself, TO ourselves, etc., the
Past Participle does not vary in Gender and Number ; 3 more literally, 'she
has hurt HERSELF in the finger ' ; the Participle is therefore made Feminine Singular, to agree with **se** ; Past Participles always agree with a preceding Direct Object, never with an Indirect Object ; 4 this construction is
often used in the meaning of 'she had cut her finger,' but **elle s'était
coupée au doigt** is preferable ;   5 I burnt myself in the finger ;   **6 this**
construction is correct, it being impossible to scratch one's **arm OFF.**

to fall into agreement=come to an agreement, **tomber d'accord**

My calculations agree exactly.	Mes calculs tombent parfaitement d'accord.
That agrees with what I had predicted.	Cela tombe d'accord avec ce que j'avais prédit.
We cannot come to an understanding as regards the price.	Nous ne pouvons tomber d'accord sur le prix.
Have you managed to agree at last	Etes-vous enfin tombés d'accord ?

to treat as=call, speak of as, **traiter de**

Didn't they call him a thief ?	Ne l'ont-ils pas traité de voleur ?
They would speak of you as rascals.	Ils vous traiteraient de coquins.
He called me a swindler.	Il m'a traité d'escroc.
We used to tell them they were lazy fellows.	Nous les traitions de fainéants.

Get this bottle filled for me.	Faites remplir cette bouteille pour moi.
Do not send for her (or him).	Ne l'envoyez pas chercher.
I shall have it done at once.	Je le ferai faire tout de suite.
They were born in Germany.	Ils sont nés en Allemagne.
Make use of it more.	Servez-vous-en davantage.
They have fallen asleep.	Ils se sont endormis.
I can easily swim across a river three hundred metres broad.	Je puis facilement traverser à la nage une rivière de trois cents mètres de largeur.
Are they good judges of materials ?	Se connaissent-ils en étoffes ?
No, they don't know anything about them.	Non, ils n'y connaissent rien.
He made me a deduction of six per cent.	Il m'a fait une remise de six pour cent.
One never loses anything by being polite.	On ne perd jamais rien à être poli.

How to translate "SHALL."

I shall[2] light the fire at once.	Je vais allumer le feu tout de suite. [feu ?
Shall I[3] light the fire ?	Voulez-vous que j'allume le
Shall I[3] write to him ?	Voulez-vous que je lui écrive ?
We shall[3] not write to them.	Nous ne leur écrirons pas.
Shall we[3] tell him to wait downstairs ?	Voulez-vous que nous lui disions d'attendre en bas ?
He shall[4] pay me.	Il faudra qu'il me paie.[5]
You shall[4] apologize.	Il faudra que vous vous excu-
We shall[2] apologize.	Nous nous excuserons. [siez.
Shall he send them a receipt ?	Doit-il[6]leur envoyer[6] un reçu ?

I haven't any more postage-stamps ; I am going to send for some.	Je n'ai plus de timbres-poste ; je vais en envoyer chercher.
They came to the station for us.	On est venu nous chercher à la gare.
See about the tickets ; I'll attend to the luggage.	Occupez-vous des billets ; je m'occuperai des bagages.
We have just met your brother.	Nous venons de rencontrer votre frère.
Were you at home yesterday ?	Etiez-vous chez vous hier ?
No, I was not.	Non, je n'y étais pas.
He bought this watch two years ago.	Il a acheté cette montre il y a deux ans.
They were here about three hours ago.	Ils étaient ici il y a environ trois heures.

2 When SHALL simply refers to the future, the Future Tense (or aller) must be employed ; 3 when SHALL I ? SHALL WE ? mean : do you wish me (or us) to ? vouloir que, followed by the Subjunctive, is used ; 4 when SHALL denotes compulsion, it is usually best to employ falloir ; 5 literally, it will be necessary that he pays me=he will have to pay me ; il doit me payer (he is to pay me) conveys the same idea, but less emphatically ; 6 this construction is equivalent to ' is he to send them,' etc. : voulez-vous qu'il leur envoie, etc., is equally correct. Similarly, dois-je allumer ? dois-je lui écrire ? could be used in the second and third sentences above.

I shall make him do it, je le lui ferai faire*

I made him wait.	Je l'ai fait attendre.
I made him wait for my answer.	Je lui ai fait attendre - ma réponse.
We made her (or him) pay.	Nous l'avons fait payer.
We made her (or him) pay the bill.	Nous lui avons fait payer la facture.
He is having it copied in a book.	Il le fait copier dans un livre.
He is getting him to copy the letters.	Il lui fait copier les lettres.
Make him work at the correspondence.	Faites-le travailler à la correspondance.
Make him finish this work.	Faites-lui finir ce travail.
You ought to show them upstairs.	Vous devriez les² faire monter.²
You ought to make them take the luggage upstairs.	Vous devriez leur faire monter les bagages.

* When an Infinitive following faire has a Direct Object (Accusative),
the Object of faire is made Indirect (Dative).   2 them make mount.

to succeed in=manage to, parvenir à

You will certainly succeed in making him understand it.	Vous parviendrez certainement à le lui faire comprendre.
We cannot manage (to do) it.	Nous ne pouvons y parvenir.
We arrived at nothing great.	Nous ne sommes² pas parvenus à grand'chose.
I shall succeed in finding it again.	Je parviendrai à le retrouver.
He succeeded in mending it.	Il est² parvenu à le reparer.

2 the Compound Tenses of parvenir are formed with être.

The walls are about five feet thick.	Les murs ont environ cinq pieds d'épaisseur.
How far is it from here to A— ?	Combien y a-t-il d'ici à A— ?
They had died the previous day.	Ils étaient morts la veille.
It was cold last month.	Il faisait froid le mois dernier.
She was dressed as a peasant-girl.	Elle était habillée en paysanne.
The patient was warm.	Le malade avait chaud.
She will not be sleepy.	Elle n'aura pas sommeil.

to cash, draw, receive money, toucher

When do you draw your pension?	Quand touchez-vous votre pension?
I draw it twice a year.	Je la touche deux fois par an.
I take half in cash, and leave the remainder on deposit.	J'en touche la moitié en argent, et laisse le reste en dépôt.
I have a number of coupons to cash.	J'ai nombre de coupons à toucher.
He is paid his salary on the last day of the month.	Il touche ses appointements le dernier jour du mois.

to walk up, carry up, monter	to go down, carry down, descendre
Walk upstairs, if you please.	Montez, s'il vous plaît.
Go down to the first floor.	Descendez au premier étage.
They came up by the main staircase.	Ils sont montés par le grand escalier.
I noticed you at the moment you were getting out of the train.	Je vous ai aperçu au moment où vous descendiez[1] du train.
We carried all the chairs up to the third floor.	Nous avons monté toutes les chaises au troisième étage.
We shall take the luggage downstairs.	Nous descendrons les bagages.
If you are not tall enough to reach the top shelf, get on a chair.	Si vous n'êtes pas assez grand pour atteindre le rayon supérieur, montez sur une chaise.

What will you gain by it?	Qu'est-ce que vous y gagnerez?
He will lose more by it than he gains (=will gain).	Il y perdra plus qu'il n'y gagnera.
There was a great deal more to do.	Il restait beaucoup à faire.
Nothing remains for me but to go away.	Il ne me reste plus qu'à m'en aller.
I hope I shall arrive in time.	J'espère arriver à temps.
He believed he was right.	Il croyait avoir raison.
My watch is losing.	Ma montre retarde.
He will not be long in doing it.	Il ne tardera pas à le faire.
He has gone to fetch them.	Il est allé les chercher.

move=stir, **bouger**

move (a piece)=play, **jouer**

move about, **remuer**

move=remove, **enlever, ôter**

to be moved=affected, **s'émouvoir**

move=change one's residence, **déménager**

Don't move now. [that.	Ne bougez pas maintenant.
Don't move (fidget) about like	Ne remuez pas comme cela.
I have moved the shade from this lamp.	J'ai enlevé l'abat-jour de cette lampe.
Move the chairs out of the way.	Otez les chaises du chemin.
He is a very unemotional man, whom it is difficult to move.	C'est un homme très froid,[2] qui s'émeut difficilement.
I am neither moved by his threats nor his entreaties.	Je ne m'émeus ni de ses menaces, ni de ses prières.
He will move (=change his address) next month.	Il déménagera le mois prochain.
It's your turn to move (at chess, at draughts).	C'est à vous à jouer (aux échecs, aux dames).
Mr. Duval moved (=proposed) a vote of thanks to the directors.	M. Duval a proposé de voter des remercîments aux directeurs.
He arrived as the train was moving off.	Il est arrivé comme le train s'ébranlait.
He moved me to tears.	Il m'a ému jusqu'aux larmes.
The earth moves (itself) round the sun.	La terre se meut autour du soleil.

He looks ill.	Il[3] a l'air d'être malade.[3]
You looked as if you were displeased.	Vous aviez l'air d'être mécontent.
I have hurt my arm. [eyes.	Je[4] me suis fait mal au bras.[4]
I was following them with my	Je les suivais des yeux.
What you do is quite immaterial to me.	Ce que vous faites m'est tout à fait indifférent.
If you go out shooting, take care not to injure yourself.	Si vous allez à la chasse, prenez garde de vous blesser.
He behaves like an honest man.	Il se conduit en honnête homme.

2 cold ;   3 he has the appearance of be(ing) ill ;   4=I to myself have caused injury in the arm.

6

How to translate " THE MORE..., THE MORE."

The more I go to Scotland, the more I want to go there again.	Plus je vais en Ecosse, plus je veux y retourner.
The more you warm yourself, the more you will feel the cold.	Plus vous vous chaufferez,[2] plus vous sentirez le froid.
The more he works, the more money he earns.	Plus il travaille, plus il gagne de l'argent.
The faster we walk, the less time we shall lose.	Plus nous marcherons[2] vite, moins nous perdrons de temps.

2 Future Tense, because future time is referred to.

He has changed his boots.	Il a changé de[2] bottines.
He has exchanged his boots.	Il a changé ses[3] bottines.
I shall not change my opinion,	Je ne changerai pas d'opinion.
Did she buy it secondhand ?	Est-ce qu'elle l'a acheté d'occasion ?
He only sells secondhand articles.	Il ne vend que des articles d'occasion.
We do not sell on credit.	Nous ne vendons pas à crédit.
He doesn't give credit to anybody.	Il ne fait crédit à personne.
I sold it to him on credit.	Je le lui ai vendu à crédit.

2 =put another pair on ;   3 =obtained another pair instead.

They want ten francs' worth.	Ils en veulent pour dix francs.
What is this used for ?	A quoi ceci sert-il ?
They have taken shelter.	Ils se sont mis à l'abri.
I am giving careful attention to your affair.	Je m'occupe soigneusement de votre affaire.
I can't get on without him.	Je ne puis me passer de lui.
You will have to dispense with it.	Il faudra que vous vous en passiez.
They went for a walk.	Ils sont allés se promener.
We shall get rid of them (or it) soon.	Nous nous en débarrasserons prochainement.
He would like to dispose of his motor-car.	Il voudrait se débarrasser de son automobile.

Have you heard from them ? **Avez-vous eu de leurs nouvelles ?**

I expect to hear from my brother-in-law to-morrow.	J'attends demain des nouvelles[2] de mon beau-frère.
When did you last hear from him ?	Quand avez-vous eu de ses nouvelles en dernier lieu[3] ?
We shall not hear from him (*or* her) again for a fortnight.	Nous n'aurons plus de ses nouvelles avant une quinzaine.

2 news ; 3 place.

---

to be upright, up, standing, **être debout**

That lady is standing ; offer her your chair.	Cette dame est debout ; offrez-lui votre chaise.
Everybody was up at six o'clock.	Tout[2] le monde[2] était debout à six heures.
The young lady was standing near the mantelpiece.	La demoiselle était debout près de la cheminée.
I have been up since four in the morning.	Je suis[3] debout depuis quatre heures du matin.
Nearly everybody was standing.	Presque tout le monde était debout. [merci !
I am still alive and well, thank God !	Je suis encore debout,[4] Dieu

2 literally, all the world ; ' the whole world ' is rendered as **le monde entier** ; 3 Present Tense, because the speaker is still up, at the moment of speaking ; 4 upright=on my feet, not laid up in bed.

I couldn't find it anywhere.	Je n'ai pu le trouver nulle part.
We do not in the least recollect what he said.	Nous ne nous souvenons pas du tout de ce qu'il a dit.
Make your friend do it.	Faites-le faire à votre ami.
They have changed their address.	Ils ont changé d'adresse.
There will be some difficulty in cleaning it.	Il y aura quelque difficulté à le nettoyer.
Would there be enough time to finish it ?	Y aurait-il assez de temps pour le finir ?
Was there no room for you on that seat ?	N'y avait-il pas de place pour vous sur ce banc ?
It is not worth while.	Cela n'en vaut pas la peine.

to shoot (literally, to pull, to draw), **tirer**

They have the reputation of being excellent shots.	Ils ont la réputation de[2] bien tirer.[2]
Practice is required to make a good marksman.	Il faut de la pratique pour faire un bon tireur.
He fires without troubling to take aim.	Il tire sans prendre la peine de viser.
The soldiers were firing on the enemy at a distance of six hundred mètres.	Les soldats tiraient sur l'ennemi à six cents mètres.

2 of shoot(ing) well

---

to dream of, meditate on, think over, **penser à, songer à, rêver à**

What are you dreaming of ?	A quoi rêvez-vous ?
I am thinking of the things I saw yesterday evening.	Je pense aux choses que j'ai vues hier soir.
Do not think too much about these events.	Ne pensez pas trop à ces événements.
Why do you think of that ?	Pourquoi songez-vous à cela ?
Don't think any more about it, then.	N'y songez donc plus.
We were thinking of sending you something.	Nous songions à vous envoyer quelque chose.
Think seriously of what you have to do.	Pensez sérieusement à ce que vous avez à faire.
Haven't you thought about it ?	N'y avez-vous pas pensé ?

My feet are cold.	J'ai froid aux pieds.
To-day is the first of July.	C'est aujourd'hui le premier juillet.
Get our luggage registered.	Faites enregistrer nos bagages.
She died three months ago.	Elle est morte il y a trois mois.
That is not much use.	Cela ne sert pas à grand'chose.
He bought two francs' worth of fruit.	Il a acheté pour deux francs de fruits.
I cannot do without it.	Je ne puis pas m'en passer.
They paid no attention to it.	Ils n'y firent aucune attention.
We must go away.	Il faut que nous partions.

somewhere, **quelque part**	nowhere, **nulle part**
I have left your book somewhere, but I don't know where.	J'ai laissé votre livre quelque part, mais je ne sais où.
He cannot be found anywhere.	On ne peut le trouver nulle part.
Shall you go anywhere this evening ?	Irez-vous quelque part ce soir ?
I don't go anywhere on Sundays.	Je ne vais nulle part le dimanche.

---

to wonder=ask one's self, **se demander**

I wonder who broke this.	Je me demande qui a brisé ceci.
We were wondering whether he would get back in time.	Nous nous demandions s'il reviendrait à temps.
I wonder whether they have succeeded this time.	Je me demande s'ils ont réussi cette fois-ci.
I wondered how they would do it.	Je me demandais comment ils le feraient.
I wonder such things can happen.	Je m'étonne que de telles choses puissent[2] arriver.[3]
We wonder it is allowed.	Nous nous étonnons que ce soit[2] permis.
Don't you wonder that he kept it ?	Ne vous étonnez-vous pas qu'il l'ait[2] gardé ?

2 **s'étonner que** (to wonder=marvel, be astonished) is followed by the Subjunctive ; 3 or **se passer**.

Have you ever been there before ?	Y avez-vous été auparavant ?
He has taken them downstairs to brush (them).	Il les a descendus pour les brosser.
Don't say anything about it.	N'en dites rien.
You will have to turn to the left after passing the farm.	Vous devrez prendre à gauche après avoir passé la ferme.
There is no time to lose.	Il n'y a pas de temp à perdre.
She has come from her milliner's.	Elle vient de chez sa modiste.
When will he call on us ?	Quand passera-t-il chez nous ?

to be there, to be ready, to understand, to be at home, **y être**

Are you ready ? You always keep us waiting. [start.	Y êtes-vous ? Vous nous faites toujours attendre.
Now then ! I am ready ; let us	Allons ! j'y suis ; partons.
I don't understand at all.	Je n'y suis pas du tout.
Ah, I see ! I didn't understand at first.	Ah, j'y suis ! je n'avais pas compris d'abord.
Is your mistress at home ?	Votre maîtresse y est-elle ?

do it when you come back, **faites-le quand vous reviendrez***

When he has begun, I shall help him.	Quand il aura commencé, je l'aiderai. [drez.
Pay me when you like.	Payez-moi quand vous vou-
As soon as you have finished this, you will be able to rest a little while.	Aussitôt que vous aurez fini ceci, vous pourrez vous reposer un peu.
He will probably not be at home when we get there.	Il ne sera probablement pas chez lui quand nous y arriverons.
We must do it as soon as we can.	Nous devons le faire, dès que nous le pourrons. [bien.
When he works, he works well.	Quand il travaille, il travaille

* The Verb following **quand** or **lorsque** (when), **dès que** (as soon as), and **aussitôt que** (immediately), must be put in the Future Tense, if future time is referred to. There is no difference in meaning between **quand** and **lorsque**, except that **lorsque** cannot be used interrogatively. It is best for foreigners always to employ **quand**.

We always treat him like a brother. [here.	Nous le traitons toujours en frère.
He talks as if he were master	Il parle en maître ici.
Have you at last succeeded in getting the money ?	Etes-vous enfin parvenu à toucher l'argent ?
The speaker could not make himself heard.	L'orateur n'a pu se faire entendre.
It was only by shouting very loudly that I was able to make him understand what I wanted.	Ce n'est qu'en criant très fort que j'ai pu lui faire comprendre ce que je désirais.
We have worked enough for this time.	Nous avons assez travaillé pour cette fois.

to ask some one for something, **demander** quelque chose à quelqu'un

Did you ask him for his address?	Lui avez-vous demandé son adresse?
I shall ask the guide the way.	Je demanderai le chemin au guide.
Why didn't you ask them (it)?	Pourquoi ne le leur avez-vous pas demandé?
We are going to ask him the reason of his refusal.	Nous allons lui demander la raison de son refus.
Ask him (it) as soon as you see him.	Demandez-le-lui aussitôt que vous le verrez.
I ought to have asked you for some small change.	J'aurais dû vous demander de la petite monnaie.
How often did they ask me? [money.	Combien² de fois² me l'ont-ils demandé? [rant.
Let us ask the manager for the	Demandons l'argent au gé-

2 how many times?

I am right, am I not?	J'ai raison, n'est-ce pas?
They were ready, weren't they?	Ils étaient prêts, n'est-ce pas?
We shall get there in time, shall we not?	Nous y arriverons à temps, n'est-ce pas?
You could understand what he meant, couldn't you?	Vous pouviez comprendre ce qu'il voulait dire, n'est-ce pas?
He ought not to start yet, ought he?	Il ne devrait pas partir encore, n'est-ce pas?
They never work more than eight hours a day, do they?	Ils ne travaillent jamais plus de huit heures par jour, n'est-ce pas?

Come near the fire.	Approchez-vous du feu.
Don't let us go so near.	Ne nous approchons pas tant.
Put the table nearer to me.	Approchez la table de moi.
Why isn't this table washed?	Pourquoi cette table n'est-elle pas lavée?
Hasn't she washed herself yet?	Ne s'est-elle pas encore lavée?
What did that mean?	Qu'est-ce que cela voulait dire?

to be on bad terms with..., être mal avec..., n'être pas bien avec...

He is on bad terms with his brother.	Il est mal[2] avec son frère.
We are not on good terms.	Nous ne sommes pas bien[3] ensemble.[3]
They are on exceedingly bad terms.	Ils sont tout[4] à fait[4] mal ensemble.
Are you not on very bad terms with your employer ?	N'êtes-vous pas très mal avec votre patron ?

2 bad ;   3 well together :   4 quite.

How to translate "TIME."*

That has happened to him several times.	Cela lui est arrivé plusieurs fois.
He has taken a long time to do this work.	Il a mis[2] beaucoup de temps à faire ce travail.
How many times have you (already) been to Paris ?	Combien de fois avez-vous déjà été à Paris ?
The time passes quickly.	Le temps passe vite.
What time will he come ?	A quelle heure viendra-t-il ?
He managed to attain his end three times in succession.	Il est parvenu trois fois de suite à atteindre son but.
What sort of weather is it ?	Quel temps fait-il ?
It is fine (weather).	Il fait beau.
What time is it ?	Quelle heure est-il ?
It is ten minutes to five.	Il est cinq heures moins dix.

*' Time' is usually temps; but heure must be used in referring to the time of day, and fois when ' occasion ' is meant.   If ' time' means : age, period in the world's history, portion of the year, époque should be employed.
2 put.

Will you manage to discover anything ?	Parviendrez-vous à découvrir quelque chose ?
You will soon have finished, if you make haste.	Vous aurez bientôt fini, si vous vous dépêchez.
Did he hurt himself in falling ?	S'est-il fait mal en tombant ?
It is very windy.	Il fait beaucoup de vent.
Where do you intend to spend your holidays ?	Où avez-vous l'intention de passer vos vacances ?

a tea-cup, une tasse à thé | a cup of tea, une tasse de thé

Give us the champagne glasses. | Donnez-nous les coupes à[2] champagne. [pagne.

He drank a glass of champagne. | Il a bu une coupe de cham-

Did you find anything in the letter-box ? | Avez-vous trouvé quelque chose dans la boîte aux lettres ? [papier.

Use this paper-knife. | Servez-vous de ce couteau à[2]

Where did you put the carving-knife ? | Où avez-vous mis le couteau à[2] découper ?

The matchbox is hanging up in the kitchen. | La boîte aux allumettes est accrochée[3] dans la cuisine.

2=used for, intended for ; 3 hung on a hook.

to put an end to, finish, mettre fin à

We must put an end to this state of things. | Il faut mettre fin à cet état de choses.

The treaty of Frankfort ended the war of 1870. | Le traité de Francfort mit fin à la guerre de 1870.

I wish you would (=I pray you to) stop that noise. | Je vous prie de mettre fin à ce bruit.

What did he do to put an end to their importunate applications ? | Qu'a-t-il fait pour mettre fin à leurs demandes importunes?

Night stopped the combat. | La nuit mit fin au combat.

Did you understand what his letter meant ? | Avez-vous compris ce que sa lettre voulait dire ?

I have hurried very much these last few days. | Je me suis beaucoup dépêché ces jours derniers.

How many times have you been to Switzerland ? | Combien de fois avez-vous été en Suisse ?

How much did you pay for this umbrella ? | Combien avez-vous payé ce parapluie ?

He retraced his steps,—turned back. [park ? | Il retourna sur ses pas.

Can you tell me the way to the | Pouvez-vous m'indiquer le chemin du parc ?

to set about a thing, **s'y prendre**

How do you begin doing that ?	Comment s'y[2] prend-on[2] pour faire cela ?
I don't know what steps to take to get rid of it	Je ne sais comment m'y prendre pour m'en débarrasser.
You didn't set about it in the right way.	Vous ne vous y êtes pas bien pris.
He will set to work in a better way another time.	Il s'y prendra mieux une autre fois.
I don't think they are going the right way to work.	Je ne crois pas qu'ils s'y prennent[3] bien.

2 does one take one's self there ?   3 Subjunctive, after a Negative Form.

each other, one another,
l'un (or l'une) l'autre, les uns (or les unes) les autres

My two brothers always help each other.	Mes deux frères s'aident* toujours l'un l'autre.
We all used to help each other.	Nous nous* aidions tous[2] les uns les autres.[2]
They *(fem.)* love one another.	Elles s'aiment l'une[3] l'autre.[3]
We looked at each other for a long time without speaking.	Nous nous sommes regardés l'un[4] l'autre[4] pendant longtemps sans parler.
Did they *(fem.)* speak to each other ?	Se sont-elles parlé l'une à l'autre ?

2 or **toutes les unes les autres ;**   3 or **les unes les autres,** if more than two persons are referred to ;   4 or **les uns (or les unes) les autres,** if more than two persons are referred to.

Come in.—Walk upstairs.	Entrez.—Montez.
Take a seat,—Sit down.	Asseyez-vous.
How long have they been in Germany ?	Depuis combien de temps sont-ils en Allemagne ?

*As Object of a Verb used reflectively, **nous, vous** and **se** sometimes mean EACH OTHER or TO EACH OTHER, rather than : (to) ourselves, (to) yourselves, (to) themselves. The addition of **l'un l'autre, l'une à l'autre, les unes les autres, les uns aux autres,** etc., is not necessary, unless required for clearness.

EXAMPLES OF THE VARIOUS TRANSLATIONS OF "GET."

The Verb ' TO GET,' which many people avoid on account of its supposed inelegance, has several entirely distinct meanings, such as POSSESS, OBTAIN, BECOME, EARN, ARRIVE, ATTAIN, RECEIVE, REACH, etc. The following sentences show some of the ways of rendering ' GET ' in French.

He got very rich at this trade.	Il est devenu[2] très riche à ce métier.
They seem to have had a lot of difficulties to get over.	Ils semblent avoir eu beaucoup de difficultés à vaincre.[3]
Where did you get this book ?	Où vous êtes-vous procuré[1] ce livre ?
Have you got what you were asking for ?	Avez-vous obtenu[4] ce que vous demandiez ?
Try to get me a ticket for this piece.	Tâchez de me[5] faire avoir[5] un billet pour cette pièce.
Can you get at that book ?	Pouvez-vous atteindre ce livre?
I can't get to it without a ladder.	Je ne peux pas l'atteindre sans échelle.
How high up can you get ?	A quelle hauteur pouvez-vous atteindre ? [pied.
We got to the town on foot.	Nous avons gagné[6] la ville à
We got there late in the evening.	Nous y sommes arrivés tard dans la soirée.
What time did we get this letter ?	A quelle heure avons-nous reçu[7] cette lettre ?
What day did they get married?	Quel jour se sont-ils mariés ?
Is your mother getting a little better ?	Votre mère se[8] porte-t-elle[8] un peu mieux ?
How were you able to get this trunk up here ?	Comment avez-vous pu monter cette malle ici ?
Get down from there.	Descendez de là.
Get on this chair.	Montez sur cette chaise.
When did they get back to London ?	Quand sont-ils revenus à Londres ?

1 nearly the same as in English ; 2 become ; 3 conquer ; 4 obtained ; 5 make me have ; 6 gained ; 7 received ; 8 does she carry herself ?

EXAMPLES OF THE IDIOMATIC USES OF "FAIRE."

We have no occasion for our umbrellas ; it will not rain.	Nous n'avons que faire de nos parapluies ; il ne pleuvra pas.
Don't you think he is pretending to be ill ?	Ne croyez-vous pas qu'il fasse[2] le malade[2] ?
It will not be fine this evening.	Il ne fera pas beau ce soir.
Get (*or* have) my clothes brushed.	Faites brosser mes habits.
We must first of all have these documents copied.	Il faut d'abord faire copier ces documents.
I have had a house built in the country.	Je me suis fait bâtir une maison à la campagne.
I shall have one built for myself at the seaside.	Je m'en ferai bâtir une au bord de la mer.

2 does (=feigns) the invalid.

to receive, to welcome, faire accueil à

They gave him a bad reception.	Ils lui ont fait mauvais accueil.
If he comes, receive him well.	S'il vient, faites-lui bon accueil.
What kind of a reception did they give them ?	Quel accueil leur ont-ils fait ?
I don't want to see them any more ; they always receive me coldly.	Je ne désire plus les voir ; ils me font toujours mauvais accueil.
It is useless for you to go there ; they will not welcome you.	Inutile que vous y alliez ; ils ne vous feront pas bon accueil.

I don't know whether that can be the case.	Je ne sais pas si cela se peut.
I have only two tickets left.	Il ne me reste que deux billets.
Do not eat too much sugar, or else you will have the toothache.	Ne mangez pas trop de sucre, autrement vous aurez mal aux dents.
I shall get some help from some one.	Je me ferai aider par quelqu'un.
Where did you get this bicycle made ?	Où vous êtes-vous fait faire cette bicyclette ?

to send word, faire dire

to let know, faire savoir

Have you sent word to him that you would not go ?

Lui[2] avez-vous fait dire[2] que vous n'iriez pas ?

I should have sent word to them, if I had had anyone.

Je le leur aurais fait dire, si j'avais eu quelqu'un.

Did you let him know that you would not allow it ?

Lui avez-vous fait savoir que vous ne le permettriez pas?

No, I have not been able to let him know (it).

Non, je n'ai pas pu le lui faire savoir.

He informed me that he had not received my letter.

Il[3] m'a fait savoir[3] qu'il n'avait pas reçu ma lettre.

I sent him your message this morning.

Je[3] lui ai fait tenir[3] votre message ce matin.

2=have you caused to be said to him ? 3=he caused me to know, I caused him to hold ; il m'a informé, je lui ai envoyé, is a simpler, and equally correct construction.

(all) alone, by myself, by yourself, etc., tout seul

The door opened by itself.

La porte s'est ouverte toute seule.

Did he send off the goods without any assistance ?

A-t-il expédié les marchandises tout seul ?

You will have to take some trouble in the matter ; the work won't do itself.

Il faudra vous donner de la peine ; le travail ne se fera pas tout seul.

It didn't do itself, I suppose ?

Cela ne s'est pas fait tout seul, je suppose ?

Why do you make her write ?

Pourquoi la faites-vous écrire?

Why do you make her write this letter ?

Pourquoi lui faites-vous écrire cette lettre ?

On Sundays, they spend their time in reading.

Le dimanche, ils passent leur temps à lire.

We must pay in advance, mustn't we ?

Il faut payer d'avance, n'est-ce pas ?

Does she succeed in passing herself off as a fine lady ?

Parvient-elle à se faire passer pour grande dame ?

I am anxious to make myself understood.

Je tiens à me faire comprendre.

to ... very nearly, **manquer de** ... (before a Verb)

In going up the staircase, I almost fell.	En montant l'escalier, j'ai manqué de tomber.
They nearly had a fight.	Ils ont manqué de se battre.
He has several times nearly gone bankrupt.	Il a plusieurs fois manqué de faire[2] faillite.[2]
He was very near not succeeding.	Il a bien manqué de ne pas réussir.

2 make failure.

to fail in, lack, be missing, **manquer à**... (before a Noun or a Pronoun)

I shall not fail in my duty.	Je ne manquerai pas à mes devoirs.
I am sure you will not be lacking in it.	Je suis sûr que vous n'y manquerez pas.
She has very often been wanting in it.	Elle y a bien souvent manqué. [ments.
He broke all his engagements.	Il a manqué à tous ses engage-
They have once more failed in their promises.	Ils ont encore une fois manqué à leurs promesses.
There are several metres short in the pieces of cloth you sent me.	Il manque plusieurs mètres aux pièces de drap que vous m'avez envoyées.
Nothing is lacking in this collection.	Il ne manque rien à cette collection.

You ought to attend to this to-night.	Vous devriez vous occuper de ceci ce soir. [main.
We shall attend to it to-morrow.	Nous nous en occuperons de-
Aren't they willing to undertake it ?	Ne veulent-ils pas s'en charger ?
He can't do without him.	Il ne peut se passer de lui.
We went away at five o'clock in the evening.	Nous nous en sommes allés à cinq heures du soir.
Come and see us from time to time.	Venez nous voir de temps en temps.
I am speaking to you as a friend.	Je vous parle en ami.

to feel cold in (some part of the body), **avoir froid à**

Are your hands cold ?	Avez-vous froid aux mains ?
Are his feet warm ?	A-t-il chaud aux pieds ?
We could not write ; our hands were too cold.	Nous ne pouvions pas écrire ; nous avions trop froid aux mains.
Avoid getting cold feet.	Evitez d'avoir froid aux pieds.
My legs feel cold, because of this draught.	J'ai froid aux jambes, à cause de ce courant d'air.
If you put your gloves on, your fingers will be warm.	Si vous mettez vos gants, vous aurez chaud aux doigts.

to take from (a place), **prendre dans, prendre sur, prendre sous**

I took the money from the cash-box—from the mantelpiece—from (out of) my salary.	J'ai pris l'argent dans la caisse—sur la cheminée—sur mes appointements.
I shall get the manuscript from the library.	Je prendrai le manuscrit dans la bibliothèque.
Which box did you take that from ? [from ?	Dans quelle boîte avez-vous pris cela ?
Which table did he take this	Sur quelle table a-t-il pris ceci?
I shall take the footstool from under the chair.	Je prendrai le tabouret sous la chaise.

Don't be afraid of disturbing me.	N'ayez pas peur de me déranger.
One thinks a great deal of the things one likes.	On tient beaucoup aux choses qu'on aime.
Which way did you get in ?	Par où êtes-vous entré ?
How were you able to get out of that room ?	Comment avez-vous pu sortir de cette pièce ?
What do you gain by complaining ?	Que gagnez-vous à vous plaindre ?
He had been working for several months in that firm.	Il travaillait depuis plusieurs mois dans cette maison.
Where do you meet (each other) ?	Où vous rencontrez-vous (l'un l'autre) ?
You are frightening him.	Vous lui faites peur.

to succeed in a thing, accomplish it, **en venir à bout**

Will you manage to do it ?	En viendrez-vous à bout[2] ?
I have been able to manage it.	J'ai pu en venir à bout.
He will never accomplish it.	Il n'en viendra jamais à bout.
We should easily succeed in doing it.	Nous en viendrions facilement à bout.
I hope to manage (to do) it.	J'espère en venir à bout.
Hasn't he been successful ?	N'en est-il pas venu à bout ?

2 of-it will you come to end ?

---

to be a member of, form part of, **faire partie de**

I am a member of this club.	Je fais partie de ce club.
Did you join the excursion to Normandy ?	Avez-vous[2] fait partie[2] de l'excursion en Normandie ?
Do you belong to our society ?	Faites-vous partie de notre société ?
That does not form part of the programme.	Cela ne fait pas partie du programme.
This picture is one of Mr. F—'s collection.	Ce tableau fait partie de la collection de M. F—.
Do you belong to the liberal or the conservative party ?	Faites-vous partie des libéraux ou des conservateurs ?

2 have you made part=did you take part ?

They have sent for the police.	On a envoyé chercher la police.
They called on us this morning.	Ils sont venus chez nous ce matin. [mi.
He was sound asleep.	Il était profondément endor-
How long have you been listening ? [new suit.	Depuis quand écoutez-vous ?
They have measured him for a	On lui a pris mesure d'un nouveau complet.
She goes for a drive every morning.	Elle se promène tous les matins en voiture.
I cannot remember it.	Je ne puis m'en souvenir.
Get hold of his hand ; he is going to strike you.	Emparez-vous de sa main ; il va vous frapper.
I always get up very late.	Je me lève toujours très tard.

to resist a thing, **résister à une chose**

He hasn't been able to resist the temptation.	Il n'a pas pu résister à la tentation.
They will not resist it.	Ils n'y résisteront pas.
The town was not in a condition to stand a siege.	La ville n'était pas en état de résister à un siège.
He resisted our threats and entreaties.	Il a résisté à nos menaces et à nos prières.
He cannot stand cold (weather).	Il ne peut pas résister au froid.

while, **tout en** (followed by a Present Participle)

He smoked (all the) while (he was) working.	Il fumait tout en travaillant.
We talked as we went along.	Nous causions tout en mar-[chant.
I answered him while I was writing.	Je lui répondis tout en écrivant.
As you go along, examine the shop windows.	Examinez, tout en vous promenant, les devantures des magasins.
He occupied himself by reading the posters while he was waiting for the train.	Il s'est occupé à lire les affiches tout en attendant le train.

Bring me some, please.	Apportez-m'en, s'il vous plaît.
Do not give him any more of it.	Ne lui en donnez plus.
The ladies have not sat down yet.	Les dames ne se sont pas encore assises.
Weren't they (*fem.*) seated ?	N'étaient-elles pas assises ?
You ought to have taken more precautions.	Vous auriez dû prendre plus de précautions.
He has had much too much.	Il en a eu beaucoup trop.
I have not thanked them for it yet.	Je ne les en ai pas encore remerciés.
Will you be able to get all these letters finished this evening ?	Pourrez-vous finir toutes ces lettres ce soir ?
Try to get away (=escape) for a few minutes.	Tâchez de vous échapper quelques minutes.

EXAMPLES OF THE USE OF VARIOUS NEGATIONS.

I have no desire for it.	Je n'en ai nulle envie.
You had no need of it.	Vous n'en aviez nul besoin.
They had no fear of falling.	Ils n'avaient nulle crainte de tomber.
We shall have no right to his protection.	Nous n'aurons nul droit à sa protection.
Have no anxiety about it.	N'en ayez nul souci.

Not one of you was invited.	Aucun de vous n'était invité.
None of these unfortunate[0] people used to complain.	Aucun de ces malheureux ne se plaignait.
Not one of them understands it.	Aucun d'eux ne le comprend.
Of all those who had attempted it, not one had succeeded.	De tous ceux qui l'avaient tenté, aucun n'avait réussi.
No sport pleases me so much.	Aucun sport ne me plaît tant.
No lady would venture on it.	Aucune dame ne s'y aventurerait.

We are in no way responsible for it.	Nous n'en sommes nullement responsables.
I do not reproach[2] you for it[2] in the faintest degree.	Je ne vous[2] le reproche[2] nullement.
He hasn't the slightest desire to come with us.	Il n'a nullement envie de venir avec nous.
Don't worry yourself in the least about the noise.	Ne vous inquiétez nullement du bruit.

2 =reproach it to you.

It was impossible to make them say anything.	Il a été impossible de leur faire dire quelque chose.
He smokes a great deal too much, doesn't he ?	Il fume beaucoup trop, n'est-ce pas ?
Let him have my answer at once.	Faites-lui tenir ma réponse tout de suite.
As soon as you have put it in motion, this machine goes by itself.	Dès que vous l'avez mise en mouvement, cette machine marche toute seule.

to say to, tell (a person), **dire à**
to say to=have an opinion concerning, **dire de**

Did you tell (it to) your friend ?	L'avez-vous dit à votre ami ?
He would not tell me.	Il n'a pas voulu me le dire.
I shall tell (it to) him.	Je le lui dirai.
Who told them so ?	Qui le leur a dit ?
What does he say to[2] that ?	Qu'est-ce qu'il dit de cela ?
What do you say to[2] it ?	Qu'en dites-vous ?
I don't believe what they say about[2] him.	Je ne crois pas ce qu'on dit de lui.
Don't say anything about[2] it.	N'en dites rien.
I shall not say anything about[2] it to anybody.	Je n'en dirai rien à personne.

2=of.

EXAMPLES OF THE USE OF "TELLEMENT."

I have been running so much that I am out of breath.	J'ai tellement[2] couru que je suis hors d'haleine.
There is not such a large amount of difference.	Il n'y a pas tellement de différence.
We have so many engagements that we cannot promise (you it).	Nous avons tellement d'occupations que nous ne pouvons pas vous le promettre.
You have seen such a number of people that you cannot remember him.	Vous avez vu tellement de monde que vous ne pouvez vous souvenir de lui.

2 so, to such an extent.

They would not use our name without telling us first.	Ils ne se serviraient pas de notre nom sans nous prévenir.
They don't look as if they were enjoying themselves.	Ils n'ont pas l'air de s'amuser.
Have you hurt your hand ?	Vous êtes-vous fait mal à la
They are not ashamed.	Ils n'ont pas honte. [main ?
We got better at once with the change of air.	Nous nous sommes tout de suite mieux portés en changeant d'air.
I have heard from them.	J'ai reçu de leurs nouvelles.

EXAMPLES OF THE USE OF "PLUS" AND "DAVANTAGE."

MORE is translated by **plus** whenever it precedes THAN ; in the sense of ' a larger number,' MORE must be rendered by **plus** ; NO MORE, in the sense of NO LONGER, must be rendered by **ne ... plus** ; **davantage** can only mean TO A GREATER EXTENT, and can only occur at the end of a sentence ; **davantage** can only modify a Verb ; **plus** can modify either a Verb or an Adjective.

He smokes more than you.	Il fume plus que vous.
He smokes more than six cigars a day.	Il fume plus de[2] six cigares par jour.
I smoke a little, and he smokes more.	Je fume un peu, et il fume davantage.
He smokes three cigars a day, and he ought not to smoke more.[3]	Il fume trois cigares par jour, et il ne devrait pas fumer davantage.
He ought not to smoke more.[4]	Il ne devrait pas en fumer plus.
He does not smoke any longer.[5]	Il ne fume plus.

2 THAN is rendered by **de** instead of **que** if a Numeral follows ; 3= to a greater extent ; 4=more than three cigars ; 5=he has left off smoking.

They inconvenience me a little, but you inconvenience me more.	Ils m'incommodent un peu, mais vous m'incommodez davantage.
He is industrious, and his brother is more so.	Il est laborieux, et son frère l'est davantage.*
This photograph is pretty, but the other is still more so.	Cette photographie est jolie, mais l'autre l'est encore davantage.

*When a comparison is expressed by two distinct statements, and **le** is used in the second statement to avoid the repetition of the Adjective in the first, **davantage** must be employed, not **plus**.

They never write to one another.	Ils ne s'écrivent jamais l'un à l'autre.
Take a sheet of paper from under the book.	Prenez une feuille de papier sous le livre.
Obtain some information about him.	Procurez-vous quelques renseignements sur lui.

IDIOMATIC USE OF THE FRENCH CONDITIONAL.

They say that the queen has given her consent.	La reine aurait[2] donné son consentement.
Did he perhaps come on purpose?	Serait-il venu exprès?
Some one seems to have seen me at the concert yesterday.	On m'aurait vu au concert hier.
He is said to have been employed at X—'s.	Il aurait été employé chez X—.
There has apparently been a serious accident.	Il y aurait eu un grave accident.
Do you happen to know his address? [France soon?	Connaîtriez-vous son adresse?
Is it true that you are going to	Iriez-vous en France prochainement?
I've lost my umbrella; have you (not) by chance seen it?	J'ai perdu mon parapluie; ne l'auriez-vous pas vu?
It seems that they got there in time.	Ils y seraient arrivés à temps.

2 would have=is alleged to have; the Conditional is frequently used in French instead of the Present Indicative, to suggest some degree of DOUBT and UNCERTAINTY, especially when the speaker repeats some statement he has heard or read, without vouching for its truth; on dit que la reine a donné, etc., is a simpler, and equally correct construction.

---

to thank for, remercier de

We thank you for your kindness.	Nous vous remercions de votre bonté.
I thanked him for his offer.	Je l'ai remercié de son offre.
You will have to thank them for having lent it to you.	Vous devrez les remercier de vous l'avoir prêté.
Thank you for the flowers you sent me.	Merci des fleurs que vous m'avez envoyées.
Thanks for your attention.	Merci de votre attention.

We shall be able to send them to you without delay.	Nous serons à même de vous les envoyer sans délai.
I shall not go out to-day; it is too muddy.	Je ne sortirai pas aujourd'hui; il fait trop de boue.
I have good reasons for owing them a grudge,	J'ai de bonnes raisons de leur en vouloir.

by=to the extent of, de   **by [speaking of dimensions], sur**

Charles is the taller.	Charles est le plus grand.
By how much ? Five inches.	De combien ? De cinq pouces.
The tower was higher by twelve feet.	La tour était plus haute de douze pieds.
This piece of linen is ten metres shorter than the other.	Cette pièce de toile est plus courte de dix mètres que l'autre.
She is (by) much the oldest of the three.	Elle est de beaucoup la plus âgée des trois.
Your trunk is the heaviest, by a long way.	Votre malle est la plus lourde de beaucoup.
This room is twenty feet (long) by twelve (wide).	Cette chambre a vingt pieds de long² sur douze pieds de large.²
This plot of land is two hundred metres by sixty.	Ce terrain a deux cents mètres de long² sur soixante mètres de large.²
2 *or* **longueur, largeur** ; see p. 13.	

to debit with, débiter de   **to credit with, créditer de**

Have you debited his account with that sum ?	Avez-vous débité son compte de cette somme ?
I am going to debit him with it.	Je vais l'en débiter.
I have forwarded the goods to them, and charged them to their account.	Je leur ai expédié les marchandises et j'en ai débité leur compte.
Have you credited him with it ?	L'en avez-vous crédité ?
Kindly credit us with it.	Veuillez nous en créditer.
I send you two hundred francs, with which please credit me.	Je vous envoie deux cents francs, dont je vous prie de me créditer.
Credit their account with it.	Créditez-en leur compte.

It is no use for her to hurry.	Elle a beau se dépêcher.
They always interfere with my affairs.	Ils se mêlent toujours de mes affaires.
Did you see to what I told you about ?	Vous êtes-vous occupé de ce que je vous ai dit ?

to perceive, notice (=actually see a person *or* a thing), **apercevoir**
to notice (a fact) =observe that it is the case, **s'apercevoir de**

I noticed a man going stealthily into the house.	J'ai aperçu un homme qui entrait furtivement dans la maison.
Do you observe that black spot in the sky? it is an airship.	Apercevez-vous ce point noir dans le ciel? c'est un ballon[1] dirigeable.[1]
Our horse was stolen during the night, and we did not notice anything.	On nous a volé notre cheval pendant la nuit et nous ne nous sommes aperçus de rien.
He did not notice his mistake at first.	Il ne s'est pas aperçu de son erreur au premier abord.
He took twenty francs out of the cash-box, and is afraid that his employer will notice it.	Il a pris vingt francs dans la caisse, et il craint que son patron (ne) s'en aperçoive.

to expect *or* wait for a person *or* a thing, **attendre**
to expect something to happen, **s'attendre à**

They were expecting us, but they did not expect to see us so soon.	Ils nous attendaient, mais ils ne s'attendaient pas à nous voir si tôt.
We were waiting for it.	Nous l'attendions.
We were expecting it (to happen).	Nous nous y attendions.
I am expecting him to ask me.	Je m'attends à ce[2] qu'il me le demande.
We were expecting his letter, but we did not expect to receive a telegram.	Nous attendions sa lettre, mais nous ne nous attendions pas à recevoir un télégramme.
He was expecting it, I believe.	Il s'y attendait, je crois.

2 when **s'attendre à** is followed by the Subjunctive, **à ce que** is used instead of **que**.

Which book did you copy it from?	Dans quel livre l'avez-vous copié?
I shall go and see him on Sunday.	J'irai le voir dimanche.
It is no use inviting him; he will not come.	Vous aurez beau l'inviter; il ne viendra pas.

to be able to=know how to, savoir*

I can (=know how to) dive.	Je sais plonger.
I could[2] not dive; there was not sufficient water.	Je ne pouvais pas plonger; il n'y avait pas assez d'eau.
Can you dance?	Savez-vous danser?
She could not dance, because she had sprained her foot.	Elle ne pouvait pas danser, parce qu'elle s'était foulé le pied.
Can he ride a bicycle?	Sait-il monter à bicyclette?
He could[2] not swim, because the current was too strong.	Il ne pouvait pas nager, parce que le courant était trop fort.
He could[3] not swim against the stream.	Il ne pourrait pas nager contre le courant.

2=was able to; 3 COULD, referring to the present or the future, must be rendered as WOULD BE ABLE TO.

*When CAN, COULD, etc., refer to an accomplishment that has to be ACQUIRED, it is customary to employ savoir instead of pouvoir. But pouvoir is often used, especially by Belgians, in such sentences, and therefore cannot be considered actually incorrect.

to afford=be able to pay, have the means to, be rich enough to

They cannot afford so much.	Ils ne peuvent pas tant payer.
They haven't the means to pay so much.	Ils n'ont pas les moyens de tant payer.
We can't (afford to) allow him any discount.	Nous ne pouvons pas lui faire d'escompte. [cela.
I cannot afford that.	Je ne suis pas assez riche pour
He can't afford to go abroad this year.	Il n'a pas les moyens d'aller à l'étranger cette année.

I have to go out now.	J'ai à sortir maintenant.
He has to write several letters.	Il a à écrire plusieurs lettres.
We should not have time to finish it.	Nous n'aurions pas le temps de* le finir.
I have the pleasure to inform you that the goods reached me in good condition.	J'ai le plaisir de* vous informer que les marchandises me sont parvenues en bon état.
I have the honor to salute you.	J'ai l'honneur de vous saluer.

*TO HAVE TO=BE COMPELLED TO, is avoir à; but TO following 'to have' and a NOUN is rendered by de.

EXAMPLES OF THE USE OF "ON" (one=you, people, we, they)

You are wanted in the office.	On[2] a besoin de vous[2] au bureau. [près d'ici.
They say that there is a fire close by.	On dit qu'il y a un incendie
It is supposed that he escaped during the night.	On suppose qu'il s'est échappé pendant la nuit.
Where do they sell postage-stamps? [head?	Où vend-on des timbres-poste?
How much do they charge per	Combien prend-on[3] par tête?
People say that the news is not French spoken here. [true.	On dit que la nouvelle n'est pas
	Ici on parle français. [vraie.
There is a knock at the door.	On frappe à la porte.

2 one has need of you ; 3 takes one?

both=all the two, tous (les) deux, toutes (les) deux

You (*masc.*) both went there, didn't you?	Vous y êtes allés tous (les)* deux, n'est-ce pas?
Did they (*fem.*) both come yesterday morning?	Sont-elles venues toutes (les) deux hier matin?
They (*masc.*) are both tired.	Ils sont fatigués tous les deux.
We (*fem.*) were both going for a walk.	Nous allions nous promener toutes (les) deux.
They (*fem.*) were both very tall.	Toutes les deux étaient très grandes.

* Tous deux usually means 'both together'; tous les deux would simply imply that they both went, but not necessarily together. As this faint distinction is not always observed, it is better for foreigners always to insert the les.

out of=from among, sur

One out of four of the pupils was absent.	Un sur quatre des élèves était absent.
There are ten thousand protestants out of a population of twenty-five thousand.	Il y a dix mille protestants sur une population de vingt-cinq mille.
Of all the cartridges that I fired, only one out of two was good.	De toutes les cartouches que j'ai tirées, une sur deux seulement était bonne.

EXAMPLES OF THE OMISSION OF "PAS."*

He cannot see us.	Il ne peut nous voir.
I don't know where to go.	Je ne sais où aller.
They don't dare to own it.	Ils n'osent l'avouer.
I do not cease to repeat it to them.	Je ne cesse de le leur répéter.

*Pas is often omitted from the negative forms of pouvoir, savoir, oser, and cesser ; but as this omission is never compulsory, and is sometimes not even permissible, it is safer for foreigners always to insert the pas.

It is a long time since I met him.	Il y a longtemps que je n.² l'ai rencontré.
How long is it since we wrote to them ?	Combien de temps y a-t-il depuis que nous ne² leur avons écrit ?
It is about six months since he was here. 2 see page 9.	Il y a environ six mois qu'il n'a² été ici.

I am afraid he will lose it.	J'ai peur qu'il ne² le perde.
We fear that you will run great risks.	Nous craignons que vous ne² couriez de grands risques.
I shall do it, unless business prevents me (from it).	Je le ferai, à moins que mes affaires ne² m'en empêchent.
It is later than I thought.	Il est plus tard que je ne³ pensais.
The parcel is less heavy than I expected.	Le paquet est moins lourd que je ne³ m'y attendais.

2 ne is usually inserted before a Subjunctive following certain Verbs and Conjunctions,—see Rule 160 in Grammar ; but as this insertion of ne is now optional, it is simplest for foreigners to ignore the ne when translating from French, and not to use it when translating into French ; 3 the same applies to ne following the Comparative Form of an Adjective.

They came to our house ; let us go to theirs to-morrow.	Ils sont venus chez nous ; allons chez eux demain.
They have managed without it.	Ils s'en sont passés.
How much money have you left ?	Combien d'argent vous reste-t-il ?
You ought to have let him have it yesterday evening.	Vous auriez dû le lui faire tenir hier soir.

to wait for=await, attendre — to listen to, écouter

Where will they wait for* us ?	Où nous attendront-ils ?
Wait for him at the entrance.	Attendez-le à l'entrée.
We were listening to* the band.	Nous écoutions la musique.
You ought to listen to them.	Vous devriez les écouter.
How much did you pay for this ?	Combien avez-vous payé ceci ?
I am going to pay for these ar-	Je vais payer ces articles.
Ask for it again. [ticles.	Demandez-le de nouveau.
When did he ask for them ?	Quand les a-t-il demandés ?
What are they looking at ?	Que regardent-ils ?
Look at this.	Regardez ceci.
Will you ring for the servant, please ?	Voulez-vous sonner la bonne, s'il vous plaît ?
I have rung for her twice.	Je l'ai sonnée deux fois.

*Some Verbs are followed by a Preposition in English, but not in French, as the above examples show.

I saw him speak to the workmen.	Je l'ai vu parler aux ouvriers.
I saw him speaking to the crew.	Je l'ai vu qui parlait à l'équi-
We can hear them carrying it upstairs. [trance.	page. [monter.
He saw me waiting at the en-	Nous pouvons les entendre le Il m'a vu attendre à l'entrée.

We saw it (being) mended.	Nous l'avons vu réparer.
I saw it (after it was) mended.	Je l'ai vu réparé.
I saw somebody shutting the door.	J'ai vu quelqu'un qui fermait la porte.
I saw it closing (itself).	Je l'ai vu se fermer.
I saw it (when it was) closed.	Je l'ai vue fermée.

to cut off, cut down, cut loose, couper

His leg has been cut off.0	On lui a coupé la jambe.
Cut the pages of this book.	Coupez les pages de ce livre.
They are cutting down0 the trees.	Ils coupent les arbres.
He cut off0 their retreat.	Il leur coupa la retraite.
They cut loose0 the mooring-rope.	Ils coupèrent l'amarre.

0 not to be translated.

SOME USEFUL IDIOMATIC PHRASES.

I am quite certain of it.	J'en suis tout à fait certain.
He hasn't quite finished yet.	Il n'a pas encore tout à fait fini.
Does he earn as much as you? —No, not quite.	Est-ce qu'il gagne autant que vous?—Non, pas tout à fait.

He went away directly.	Il est parti sur-le-champ.[2]
He wants people to obey him immediately.	Il veut qu'on lui obéisse sur-le-champ.
We answered them at once.	Nous leur avons répondu sur-le-champ.

We shall come for that purpose.	Nous viendrons à cet effet.[1]
He will come with the intention of speaking to you about it.	Il viendra à l'effet de vous en parler.
It is not about this that I want to see him.	Ce n'est pas à cet effet que je désire le voir.

Up to the present moment, we know nothing definite.	En attendant,[3] nous ne savons rien de précis.[1]
So far I have received no answer from him.	En attendant, je n'ai pas de réponse de lui.
Read the newspaper until I am ready.	Lisez le journal en attendant que je sois prêt.

We took it, in the absence of anything better.	Nous l'avons pris, faute[4] de mieux.
He has not succeeded, through lack of industry and energy.	Il n'a pas réussi, faute de travail[5] et d'énergie.
If he doesn't know it, it will not be for want of being told.	S'il ne le sait pas, ce ne sera pas faute de le lui avoir dit.

They won the prize three times in succession.	Ils ont gagné le prix trois fois de[6] suite.[6]
I went there two days together.	J'y suis allé deux jours de suite.
She wrote several letters straight off.	Elle a écrit plusieurs lettres de suite.

2 on the field;   3 waiting;   4 fault, want;   5 work;   6 of continuation.

USEFUL IDIOMATIC PHRASES (*continued*)

Do it directly.	Faites-le tout[2] de suite.[2]
Tell him to come downstairs at once.	Dites-lui de descendre tout de suite. [suite.
They replied to us immediately.	Ils nous ont répondu tout de
I shall go out directly after lunch.	Je sortirai tout de suite après déjeuner.

He didn't come, because of the bad weather.	Il n'est pas venu, à cause du mauvais temps.
I dismissed my assistant on account of his unpunctuality.	J'ai congédié mon employé, à cause de son inexactitude.
I did it for his sake.	Je l'ai fait à cause de lui.

They say his parents are well off.	On dit que ses parents sont à leur aise.[3]
Is he rich ?—He is comfortably off.	Est-il riche ?—Il est à son aise.
I don't think they are independent.	Je ne crois pas qu'ils soient à leur aise.

He acted very badly towards me.	Il a très mal agi à[4] mon égard.[4]
What steps will you take about them ? [him ?	Quelles mesures prendrez-vous à leur égard ? [égard ?
How will you act with respect to	Comment agirez-vous à son
I shall do it out of regard for you.	Je le ferai par égard pour vous.

I shall send them to you as fast as they arrive.	Je vous les enverrai au[5] fur et à mesure de[5] leur arrivée.
He pays for them as he receives them.	Il les paye au fur et à mesure qu[6]'il les reçoit.
He sends them off as fast as he manufactures them.	Il les expédie au fur et à mesure qu'il les fabrique.

I have to speak to you with regard to this affair.	J'ai à vous parler à propos de cette affaire.
You come in the nick of time.	Vous arrivez à propos.
For what reason did he say that ?	A propos de quoi a-t-il dit cela ?
She wants to speak to you about her nephew.	Elle veut vous parler à propos de son neveu.

? all of follow ; 3 ease ; 4 to my respect ; 5=in proportion to ; 6 as.

EXAMPLES OF THE EMPLOYMENT OF "C'EST" AND "IL EST"

Who is smoking over there?	Qui fume là-bas?
It is my cousin.	C'est[2] mon cousin.
He is your uncle, isn't he?	C'est vôtre oncle, n'est-ce pa~?
Wasn't that true?	N'était-ce pas vrai?
It will be he; was it you?	Ce sera lui; était-ce vous?
Is this possible? it is I.	Est-ce possible? c'est moi.
Who are those men?	Qui sont ces hommes?
They are my comrades.	Ce[3] sont mes camarades.
They are not Belgians.	Ce ne sont pas des Belges.
It amuses me greatly.	Cela[4] m'amuse beaucoup.
It goes without saying.	Cela va sans dire.
Who wrote this?	Qui est ce qui a écrit ceci?
It was (=is) your son, wasn't it?	C'est votre fils, n'est-ce pas?
Are they your nieces, or your daughters? [cousins?	Sont-ce vos nièces, ou vos filles? [cousines?
Are those young ladies his	Ces demoiselles sont-elles ses

2 IT, THIS, and THAT, used with part of TO BE, are usually translated
ce; 3 THESE, THOSE, HE, SHE, and THEY, are also usually translated ce,
if used with any tense of TO BE, singular or plural, followed by a Noun or
a Pronoun; 4 with any other Verb, IT is rendered by cela.

Where is the parcel?	Où est le paquet?
It is upstairs, I believe.	Il[2] est en haut, je crois.
I have read their letter; it is rather long.	J'ai lu leur lettre; elle est assez longue.
Where are our trunks?	Où sont nos malles?
They are at the railway-station.	Elles sont à la gare.
This bottle is full, but that one is empty.	Cette bouteille-ci est pleine, mais celle-là[2] est vide.
Here are several coins; these are French, and those are Swiss.	Voici plusieurs pièces d'argent; celles-ci sont françaises, et celles-là sont suisses.

2 il, elle, ils, elles, are used for IT, HE, SHE, THEY, and celui-ci,
celle-ci, ceux-ci, ceux-là, etc., for THIS, THAT, THESE, THOSE, when a
Noun *just previously mentioned* is referred to.

"C'EST" AND "IL EST" (continued).

It is easy.	C'est facile.
It is easy to see them.	Il[2] est facile de les voir.
It was interesting.	C'était intéressant.
It was interesting to hear them speak.	Il[2] était intéressant de les entendre parler.
It is not one o'clock yet.	Il n'est pas encore une heure.
It is necessary to begin.	Il[3] faut commencer.
It was raining in torrents.	Il[3] pleuvait à verse.
What time is it?	Quelle heure est-il[3]?
It is true, isn't it?	C'est vrai, n'est-ce pas?
It is true that I had promised it to him.	Il est vrai que je le lui avais promis.
Is it possible that they have lost it?	Est-il possible qu'ils l'aient perdu?
Walk up, please.	Montez, s'il[4] vous plaît.[4]

2 IT, used with part of TO BE, and followed by an Adjective, should be rendered by il, if de or que follows; 3 il is also used in impersonal expressions,—that is to say, when the IT is not used instead of a Noun; 4 literally, if it pleases you.

He is not tired.	Il[2] n'est pas fatigué.
Isn't she upstairs?	N'est-elle[2] pas en haut?
He is the station-master, isn't he?	C'est[3] le chef de gare, n'est-ce pas?
She is your sister-in-law, isn't she?	C'est[3] votre belle-sœur, n'est-ce pas?
He was in Paris,—in France,—in the country,—in town.	Il était à Paris,—en France, —à la campagne,—en ville.
They (fem.) are absent to-day, —ill,—travelling,—away on leave,—over there.	Elles sont absentes aujourd'hui,—malades,—en voyage,—en congé,—là-bas.
She is the queen of England.	C'est la reine d'Angleterre.
Is he the manager of the firm?	Est-ce le gérant de la maison?

2 HE, SHE, or THEY, used with any part of TO BE, is rendered by il, elle, ils, elles, if a temporary condition or position is referred to; 3 ce is usually employed when something permanent, such as character, rank, profession, or relationship to others, is referred to.

FURTHER EXAMPLES OF THE IDIOMATIC USES OF "FAIRE."

This news must have afforded you much pleasure.	Cette nouvelle a dû vous faire bien[2] plaisir.
You will give me pleasure by remaining here.	Vous me ferez plaisir en restant ici.
Don't you think she is only making believe to be ill?	Ne croyez-vous pas qu'elle fasse semblant[3] d'être ma-
He acts as if he were ill.	Il fait le malade. [lade?
Let us pretend not to hear the noise.	Faisons semblant[3] de ne pas entendre le bruit.
Have you acquainted him with your decision?	Lui avez-vous fait part de votre décision?
Don't let anyone know of it.	N'en faites part à personne.
Why pretend to be rich, if you have nothing?	Pourquoi faire le riche, si vous n'avez rien?
You must pay attention.	Vous devez faire attention.
He is going to be a sailor.	Il va se faire matelot.
Do you know the price he charges?	Savez-vous le prix qu'il fait[4]?
They never allow any discount.	Ils ne font jamais d'escompte.

2=indeed ; 3 seeming=pretence ; 4 or fait payer.

Can you recommend me a general servant?	Pouvez-vous me recommander une bonne[2] à tout faire[2]?
Not just now ; you had better apply to Mrs. Dumas.	Pas en ce moment ; vous feriez mieux de vous adresser à Madame Dumas.
I thought your servant was leaving you ; that is why I asked you.	Je croyais que votre bonne vous quittait ; c'est[3] ce qu' fait que[3] je vous demandais cela.
I will see Mrs. X——, although I do not know her.	Je verrai Madame X——, quoique je ne la connaisse pas.
Oh! that does not matter ; she will receive you with pleasure if you mention my name.	Oh! cela ne fait rien ; elle vous recevra avec plaisir s vous venez[4] de ma part.[4]

2 servant to do everything=maid of all work ; 3 simpler, c'est pourquoi ; 4 come on my part=come from me.

KEY

TO

FRENCH
GRAMMAR

SIMPLIFIED

PHILADELPHIA

DAVID McKAY, Publisher

604-8 S. Washington Square

KEY to HUGO'S FRENCH GRAMMAR

EXERCISE I.—1. un frère; 2. une sœur; 3. un soldat; 4. une tante; 5. un jour; 6. une porte; 7. un hôtel; 8. une église; 9. un ami.

EXERCISE II.—1. le papier; 2. la porte; 3. l'oncle; 4. l'église; 5. la table; 6. le sac; 7. l'adresse; 8. le jour; 9. l'heure; 10. l'hôtel; 11. le soldat; 12. l'ami.

EXERCISE III.—1. les papiers; 2. les oncles; 3. les tables; 4. les sacs; 5. les hôtels; 6. les adresses; 7 les soldats; 8. les heures.

EXERCISE IV.—1. Il a acheté une maison. 2. Nous avons trouvé deux sacs. 3. Elles ont reçu une lettre. 4. Le frère et la sœur ont acheté un hôtel. 5. J'ai reçu deux paquets. 6. Vous avez trouvé les adresses. 7. Elle a une chaise.

EXERCISE V.—1. de notre porte; 2. à vos hôtels; 3. les portes de l'église; 4. à leur table; 5. de votre maison à notre jardin; 6. à leur église; 7. de nos chaises; 8. de leurs amis.

EXERCISE I.—1. un couteau, les couteaux; 2. un bras, deux bras; 3. le journal, les journaux; 4. la voix, les voix; 5. le feu, les feux; 6. un fils, trois fils.

EXERCISE II.—1. Ai-je vu vos neveux? 2. Ont-ils envoyé une lettre? 3. Avez-vous écrit l'adresse? 4. Avons-nous reçu les journaux? 5. A-t-il vu les chevaux? 6. Ont-elles écrit à leurs amis? 7. Ils ont deux fils. 8. Avez-vous vu vos amis? 9. Ont-ils acheté votre maison? 10. A-t-elle reçu le paquet?

✳ EXERCISE III.—1. ma nièce; 2. son père; 3. mon chapeau; 4. sa mère; 5. mes neveux; 6. ses nièces; 7. ma chambre; 8. sa plume; 9. sa plume; 10. son crayon; 11. son crayon; 12. ses chapeaux.

EXERCISE IV.—1. son écriture; 2. son école; 3. sa chambre; 4. son oncle; 5. sa rue; 6. son église; 7. son église.

Exercise V.—1. N'avez-vous pas mon livre ? 2. Il n'a pas vu son écriture. 3. Nous n'avons pas trouvé les gants. 4. N'ont-ils pas écrit à vos amis ? 5. Je n'ai pas lu sa lettre.

KEY to 3rd Lesson on pages 12 and 14.

Exercise I.—1. quelle école ? 2. quel mois ? 3. quelles chambres ? 4. quel homme ! 5. quels chapeaux ? 6. quelle heure ? 7. quels paquets ?

Exercise II.—1. cette voiture ; 2. ce fusil ; 3. ces couteaux ; 4. ces fourchettes ; 5. cet encrier ; 6. cette écriture ; 7. cette heure ; 8. ces jours ; 9. cet hôtel ; 10. ces jardins ; 11. cette encre.

Exercise III.—1. le mari de ma nièce ; 2. le cheval de l'officier ; 3. les fusils de ces soldats ; 4. le parapluie de ma sœur ; 5. la voiture de quelle dame ? 6. les chevaux de ces officiers ; 7. l'adresse de votre ami.

8. Avez-vous trouvé le parapluie de cette dame ? 9. Son mari a écrit à l'ami de son neveu. 10. Leurs nièces n'ont pas lu la lettre de cette dame. 11. Les fenêtres de notre voisin.

Exercise IV.—1. Qui est là ? 2. Où sont nos couteaux ? 3. Je suis très fatigué. 4. Il est très riche. 5. Elle est à l'église. 6. Nous sommes à son hôtel. 7. Vous êtes en retard. 8. L'encrier est sur la table. 9. Qui sont ces hommes ? 10. Où sont nos journaux ? 11. Vos amis sont à la gare.

Exercise V.—1. Nos amis sont absents. 2. Ces hommes sont riches. 3. Sa maison est trop petite. 4. Nous sommes fatigués. 5. Cette eau est chaude. 6. Cette encre est mauvaise. 7. Vous êtes très poli. 8. Je suis malade. 9. Son chapeau est trop petit. 10. Mes gants sont trop grands.

KEY to 4th Lesson on pages 16 and 18.

Exercise I.—1. Elle n'est pas vaine. 2. Ces chevaux ne sont pas vieux. 3. N'êtes-vous pas satisfait ? 4. N'est-il pas trop jeune ? 5. Ne suis-je pas en retard ? 6. Nous (*f.*) ne sommes pas fatiguées. 7. Ces dames sont jolies. 8. Nos chambres ne sont pas petites. 9. Vos voisins sont très riches.

EXERCISE II.—1. Le facteur a-t-il apporté une lettre ? 2. Ces officiers ont-ils acheté vos chevaux ? 3. Ces fleurs ne sont-elles pas très jolies ? 4. Votre sœur est-elle à l'église ? 5. Ce monsieur a-t-il deux fils ou trois ? 6. Le docteur a-t-il vu votre ami ? 7. Les journaux ne sont-ils pas sur la table ? 8. Le garçon n'est-il pas ici ? 9. Sa maison est-elle grande ?

EXERCISE III.—1. J'ai reçu. 2. Mon ami a brisé le verre. 3. Avez-vous entendu le bruit ? 4. Elle a perdu son parapluie. 5. Le docteur a-t-il lu ma note ? 6. Il n'a pas ouvert le paquet. 7. N'ont-ils pas vu l'incendie ? 8. Nous n'avons pas ouvert la porte.

EXERCISE IV.—1. du jardin ; 2. au docteur ; 3. du couteau ; 4. au bras ; 5. de l'église ; 6. à l'hôtel ; 7. Avez-vous reçu le compte du docteur ? 8. Qui a trouvé les gants du monsieur ? 9. Le dernier jour du mois. 10. Le fusil du soldat est ici. 11. Avez-vous vu la voiture du docteur ?

KEY to 5th Lesson on pages 20 and 22.

EXERCISE I.—1. Avez-vous entendu sa voix ? Oui, elle est très forte. 2. J'ai lu sa lettre ; elle est très courte. 3. Nous avons acheté ce roman ; il est très intéressant. 4. Avez-vous acheté la maison ? Non, elle est vendue. 5. Où sont les fourchettes ? Elles ne sont pas bonnes.

EXERCISE II.—1. les pages des livres ; 2. les plumes des oiseaux ; 3. les bott(in)es* des garçons ; 4. les souliers des filles ; 5. Nous avons donné l'argent aux garçons. 6. Ils ont parlé aux femmes des ouvriers. 7. J'ai écrit aux frères de notre ami. 8. Nous avons envoyé le paquet aux fils de votre oncle. 9. Ils ont vu les soldats des fenêtres de notre maison.

EXERCISE III.—1. de la bière ; 2. du fromage ; 3. de l'encre ; 4. des verres ; 5. du beurre ; 6. du sel ; 7. de la salade ; 8. de l'eau ; 9. des fleurs. 10. Il a acheté des plumes et des crayons. 11. Avez-vous trouvé de l'argent sur la table ? 12. Ils ont eu de la soupe. 13. Avez-vous entendu du bruit ?

---

*Botte, a long boot reaching to or above the knee ; bottine, an ordinary boot ; soulier, a shoe.

Exercise IV.—1. Nous n'avons pas de soupe. 2. N'a-t-il pas d'allumettes ? 3. N'avez-vous pas d'argent ? 4. Je n'ai pas de temps. 5. Elle n'a pas de gants. 6. N'avons-nous pas de sucre ? 7. Ce monsieur n'a pas de sœurs. 8. N'ont-ils pas de bière ? 9. Ils n'ont pas reçu de lettres. 10. Les hommes ont eu du pain, du fromage et du vin. 11. Avez-vous des amis à Paris ?

KEY to 6th Lesson on pages 26 and 28.

Exercise I.—1. il parle ; 2. nous copions ; 3. vous passez ; 4. ils acceptent ; 5. je visite ; 6. il ferme ; 7. elles ferment ; 8. nous parlons ; 9. elle copie ; 10. ils passent ; 11. j'accepte ; 12. elle visite.

Exercise II.—1. Il donne du pain et du beurre aux hommes. 2. Les hommes parlent aux facteurs. 3. Son fils copie une lettre. 4. Nous parlons aux hommes. 5. Vous acceptez son argent. 6. Ils visitent la maison. 7. Elle ferme la porte. 8. Les hommes passent devant la maison. 9. Nous donnons du pain et du fromage aux ouvriers. 10. Ils ferment les fenêtres. 11. Il visite cette école. 12. Ils copient les comptes.

Exercise III.—1. Il fume sa pipe. 2. Nous coupons le papier. 3. Elle cherche l'adresse. 4. Ils allument le feu. 5. Je porte le paquet. 6. Vous cherchez vos amis. 7. Il porte des bott(in)es. 8. Je parle à mon neveu. 9. Elle donne de l'argent aux ouvriers.

Exercise IV.—1. Fument-ils des cigares ou des cigarettes ? 2. Cherche-t-elle une lettre ? 3. Porte-t-il une canne ? 4. Allumez-vous votre pipe ? 5. Ces hommes portent-ils des chapeaux ? 6. Ferment-elles leurs fenêtres ? 7. Acceptent-ils ces cadeaux ? 8. Cherchez-vous votre oiseau ? 9. Votre ami parle-t-il à son voisin ?

KEY to 7th Lesson on pages 30 and 32.

Exercise I.—1. Il ne trouve pas le chemin. 2. Ils ne payent pas leurs dettes. 3. Ne demeurez-vous pas dans cette maison ? 4. Ne chante-t-elle pas souvent ? 5. Ne cherchent-ils pas leurs sacs ? 6. Pourquoi ne coupez-vous pas cette ficelle ? 7. Il ne demeure pas là. 8. Ne chanté-je pas bien ?

EXERCISE II.—1. Qui ferme la porte ? 2. Qui a mis les allumettes sur la table ? 3. Que copiez-vous ? 4. Qu'a-t-elle accepté ? 5. Qui cherchent-ils ? 6. Qui a ouvert la fenêtre ? 7. Qu'avez-vous dit ? 8. Que porte-t-il ? 9. Qui porte des gants ? 10. Qu'avons-nous payé ? 11. Qui a eu le temps ? 12. Que donne-t-il au facteur ? 13. À qui avez-vous écrit ?

EXERCISE III.—1. pour son fils ; 2. dans le feu ; 3. sur la chaise ; 4. sous la table ; 5. avec votre couteau ; 6. sans ce monsieur.

EXERCISE IV.—1. j'ai payé ; 2. nous avons visité ; 3. elle a donné ; 4. il n'a pas trouvé ; 5. ont-ils passé ? 6. n'avez-vous pas accepté ? 7. Il a copié une lettre. 8. Ils ont fermé la porte. 9. Nous n'avons pas parlé au docteur. 10. N'ai-je pas donné d'argent au garçon ?

EXERCISE V.—1. Il n'allume pas le feu. 2. N'ont-ils pas allumé le gaz ? 3. Nous ne portons pas de parapluies. 4. N'ont-ils pas porté de fusils ? 5. Ne payez-vous pas vos dettes ? 6. J'ai payé votre compte.

KEY to 8th Lesson on pages 34 and 36.

EXERCISE I.—1. J'ai votre clef (*or* clé) et vous avez la mienne. 2. A-t-elle pris mon billet ou le sien ? 3. Nous avons leurs tableaux, et ils ont les nôtres. 4. Il n'a pas allumé sa lampe, mais la leur. 5. Avez-vous rencontré mes filles ou les siennes ? 6. J'ai perdu sa montre et la mienne. 7. Ils n'ont pas pris mes papiers, mais les siens. 8. N'a-t-il pas dépensé son argent et le vôtre ?

EXERCISE II.—1. Sur quoi avez-vous écrit l'adresse ? 2. Qu'avez-vous dit ? 3. Quel tableau ont-ils acheté ? 4. Qui a-t-il rencontré au concert ? 5. Dans quoi a-t-elle envoyé les choses ? 6. Pourquoi chantez-vous ? 7. Qu'a-t-il trouvé dans le livre ?

EXERCISE III.—1. une ville anglaise ; 2. des officiers allemands ; 3. des vaisseaux français ; 4. cette table ronde ; 5. ces hommes riches ; 6. ma main droite ; 7. son bras gauche ; 8. Ont-ils apporté ces fleurs jaunes ? 9. Avez-vous bu du vin rouge ?

EXERCISE IV.—1. une porte fermée ; 2. deux enfants perdus ; 3. La ficelle est coupée. 4. Ses dettes sont payées. 5. Les fenêtres sont-elles ouvertes ? 6. Les enfants ne sont pas encore trouvés. 7. A-t-il vendu ses chevaux ? 8. Ses chevaux ne sont pas encore vendus. 9. Ont-ils bu l'eau ?

KEY to 9th Lesson on pages 38 and 40.

EXERCISE I.—1. Ils le portent. 2. Nous leur donnons les fleurs. 3. Je la fume. 4. Elle nous cherche. 5. Vous les trouvez. 6. Il vous rencontre. 7. Les dames nous parlent. 8. Le docteur lui parle. 9. La fille lui chante.

EXERCISE II.—1. Nous l'invitons. 2. Je l'invite. 3. Elle nous oublie. 4. Ils m'oublient. 5. Nous l'acceptons. 6. Ils les acceptent. 7. Le garçon l'apporte. 8. Les dames leur chantent. 9. Ils la trouvent. 10. Votre sœur le copie. 11. Il l'aime. 12. Nous les aimons. 13. Il nous apporte du pain et du beurre.

EXERCISE III.—1. Vos amis vous cherchent. 2. Nous les rencontrons. 3. Notre tante lui parle. 4. Vous les oubliez. 5. Où est la lettre ? Il la copie. 6. Les garçons les portent-ils ? 7. Je leur donne l'argent.

EXERCISE IV.—1. Vous parle-t-il ? 2. Nous ne la louons pas. 3. Les remerciez-vous ? 4. Nous regarde-t-il ? 5. Le frappent-ils ? 6. Me regardez-vous ? 7. Nous vous remercions. 8. Votre ami nous cherche-t-il ? 9. Ils la brisent. 10. Pourquoi les cachez-vous ? 11. L'avez-vous ? 12. Nous les avons.

EXERCISE V.—1. Il ne le copie pas. 2. Ne nous remerciez-vous pas ? 3. Ne lui parlez-vous pas ? 4. Nous ne leur donnons pas les livres. 5. Pourquoi ne me regardez-vous pas ? 6. Il ne la cache pas. 7. Pourquoi ne nous apporte-t-elle pas la lettre ? 8. Mon ami ne les aime pas. 9. Son maître ne le loue-t-il pas ? 10. Pourquoi ne leur chantez-vous pas ? 11. Ne les rencontrez-vous pas tous les jours ? 12. Pourquoi ne fume-t-il pas ces cigares ? 13. Il ne les aime pas. 14. Pourquoi cette fenêtre n'est-elle pas fermée ? 15. Je la ferme.

KEY to 10th Lesson on pages 42 and 44.

EXERCISE I.—1. il perd ; 2. nous rendons ; 3. vous vendez ; 4. ils répondent ; 5. j'attends ; 6. elle vend ; 7. ils perdent ; 8. nous répondons ; 9. vous attendez ; 10. votre ami rend ; 11. l'officier répond ; 12. ces hommes perdent ; 13. L'homme fume un cigare. 14. Pourquoi ne payent-ils pas la montre ? 15. Ils nous répondent toujours par retour du courrier. 16. Avez-vous vu sa maison ? Oui, il la vend. 17. Ci-inclus je vous rends l'échantillon. 18. Il nous attend à cinq heures.

EXERCISE II.—1. vend-elle ? 2. perdez-vous ? 3. répondent-ils ? 4. je ne rends pas ; 5. elle n'attend pas ; 6. ne vendons-nous pas ? 7. ne rend-elle pas ? 8. pourquoi ne répondez-vous pas ?

EXERCISE III.—1. J'attends le train. 2. Ne vendent-ils pas de timbres-poste ? 3. Ne perd-il pas son argent ? 4. Je leur prête mon dictionnaire, et ils ne le rendent pas. 5. J'ai rencontré votre frère aujourd'hui ; ne l'attendez-vous pas ce soir ?

EXERCISE IV.—1. Je corresponds avec vous, et il a correspondu avec nous. 2. Il les entend, et elle a entendu le bruit. 3. Ils ne descendent pas, et ils n'ont pas descendu. 4. Le rend-il ? A-t-il rendu l'argent ? 5. Ne m'attendez-vous pas ? N'avez-vous pas attendu votre voisin ? 6. L'homme ne le vend-il pas ? 7. L'homme n'a-t-il pas vendu les chevaux ?

KEY to 11th Lesson on pages 46 and 48.

EXERCISE I.—1. Ils vous ont écrit. 2. Lui avez-vous parlé ? 3. Nous ne leur avons pas répondu. 4. Ne nous ont-ils pas envoyé ? 5. Je lui ai apporté les lettres. 6. Nous l'avons vu aujourd'hui. 7. Elle ne m'a pas donné l'adresse. 8. Ne vous a-t-il pas rendu les timbres (*or* timbres-poste) ? 9. Ils ne l'ont pas trouvé.

EXERCISE II.—1. Elle ne remplit pas la lampe. 2. Ces garçons n'obéissent-ils pas ? 3. Nous ne choisissons pas ces couleurs. 4. Ne punissez-vous pas votre chien ? 5. Pourquoi ne finissent-ils pas leurs devoirs ? 6. Pourquoi ne remplissez-vous pas l'encrier ? 7. Il finit votre habit aujourd'hui. 8. Mon chien n'obéit pas.

EXERCISE III.—1. Pourquoi n'avez-vous pas rempli la bouteille ?
2. Ils n'ont pas encore fini leur travail. 3. Nous n'avons pas puni
le voleur. 4. A-t-elle choisi ce chapeau ? 5. Ces garçons n'obéissent-ils pas à leur maître ? 6. Ne l'ont-ils pas trop puni ? 7. Nous
lui avons obéi avec plaisir. 8. Ne l'ont-ils pas choisi d'abord ?

EXERCISE IV.—1. Pourquoi l'homme vous a-t-il parlé ? 2. Où
le monsieur demeure-t-il ? 3. Comment la dame a-t-elle chanté ?
4. Qu'a envoyé votre voisin *or* qu'est-ce que votre voisin a envoyé ?
5. Où les soldats sont-ils ? 6. Pourquoi les garçons ne copient-ils
pas leurs leçons ? 7. Que vous a dit le facteur ? *or* qu'est-ce que
le facteur vous a dit ? 8. Que répond votre ami ? *or* qu'est-ce que
votre ami répond ?

———————

KEY to 12th Lesson on pages 52 and 54.

EXERCISE I.—1. une bonne chose ; 2. ces belles pommes ;
3. son petit chat ; 4. un joli oiseau ; 5. quel petit pied ! 6. un
vieux fou ; 7. ces grands fleuves ; 8. sa jolie bague ; 9. une
mauvaise opinion ; 10. ces méchants hommes ; 11. un gros
paquet ; 12. notre nouvelle maison.

EXERCISE II.—1. Voici de vieux vin. 2. Voici de belles bagues.
3. Voilà un joli oiseau. 4. Voilà de gros paquets. 5. Voici un bon
chat. 6. Voilà de petites maisons. 7. Voici de bonnes plumes.
8. Voilà de bon beurre. 9. Ils vendent de bonne bière et de bon vin.

EXERCISE III.—1. Avez-vous de bon beurre ? 2. Nous avons bu
de mauvais vin. 3. Ils ont acheté de belles bagues. 4. Nous avons
une mauvaise opinion de vous. 5. Elle porte un nouveau chapeau
chaque jour.

EXERCISE IV.—1. Nos voisins sont plus riches que nous.
2. Votre jardin est plus grand que le nôtre. 3. Cet arbre n'est-il
pas le plus haut du jardin ? 4. Ces filles sont les plus jeunes de
l'école. 5. Son pied est plus petit que le sien. 6. N'est-elle pas
plus jolie que sa sœur ? 7. La femme la plus pauvre de la ville
demeure là.

EXERCISE V.—1. Ma montre est aussi bonne que la sienne. 2. Il est moins actif que son frère. 3. Ce soldat est le meilleur du régiment. 4. Mes mains ne sont pas si petites que les vôtres. 5. Sa bague est la moins belle. 6. Son sac est le plus grand. 7. Voici l'arbre le plus haut du jardin. 8. N'est-il pas le meilleur homme du monde ? 9. Ces pommes ne sont-elles pas meilleures que les vôtres ? 10. Mes cigares sont aussi bons que les siens. 11. Il a reçu moins de dix francs aujourd'hui. 12. Je lui ai donné plus de huit timbres-poste.

KEY to 13th Lesson on pages 56 and 58.

EXERCISE I.—1. Il sera ici demain. 2. Nous serons là. 3. Je parlerai à son père. 4. Il vendra sa maison. 5. Aurez-vous le temps demain ? 6. Nous finirons nos leçons aujourd'hui. 7. Ils répondront à notre lettre par retour du courrier. 8. Ne punirez-vous pas votre chien ? 9. Je ne donnerai pas l'argent à l'homme. 10. Où demeureront-ils ? 11. Ne fermeront-ils pas la porte ? 12. Elle choisira cette couleur.

EXERCISE II.—1. Je lui parlerai demain. 2. Nous leur rendrons le paquet. 3. Il ne le finira pas avant ce soir. 4. Ne nous inviteront-ils pas au concert ? 5. Ils ne lui répondront pas. 6. Ne vous attendra-t-elle pas ? 7. Vous l'aurez. 8. Nous ne le trouverons pas à la maison. 9. Ne l'accepteront-ils pas ? 10. Elle vous apportera les choses.

EXERCISE III.—1. Ne parlez pas au garçon. 2. Répondez à sa lettre par retour. 3. Invitons nos voisins. 4. Remplissez les verres. 5. N'attendez pas le train. 6. Regardez ces tableaux ; ne sont-ils pas jolis ? 7. Ne punissez pas le petit garçon. 8. Ne vendez pas vos livres. 9. Fermez la fenêtre, s'il vous plaît. 10. Ne dépensez pas plus de cinq francs. 11. Coupez du pain, s'il vous plaît. 12. N'apportez pas votre parapluie.

EXERCISE IV.—1. Quelle sera sa position ? 2. Quelles seront leurs dépenses ? 3. Quel est son nom ? 4. Quelle est votre maison ? 5. Quels sont vos amis ? 6. Quelles sont leurs adresses ? 7. Quelle est sa sœur ? 8. Quelles sont vos idées ? 9. Lesquels de ces soldats ont gagné les prix ? 10. Laquelle de vos filles chante ? 11. Lequel des livres est là ?

KEY to 14th Lesson on pages 60 and 62.

EXERCISE I.—1. Nous oublierions son nom. 2. Il serait là à temps. 3. Je n'allumerais pas le gaz. 4. Ils ne perdraient pas le chemin. 5. Finiriez-vous votre travail avant le soir ? 6. Ils n'auraient pas le temps. 7. Elle serait seule. 8. Nous briserions la fenêtre. 9. Ils ne seraient pas à la maison. 10. Auriez-vous frappé à la porte ?

EXERCISE II.—1. La dame qui vous a parlé est ma nièce. 2. Le monsieur que vous avez vu hier est son oncle. 3. La maison qu'il vous a vendue est très bonne. 4. La lettre qui est sur la table est pour vôtre ami. 5. Les journaux qui sont ici sont français. 6. L'oiseau qui est dans cette cage ne chante pas. 7. Les plumes que nous avons sont très mauvaises.

EXERCISE III.—1. L'homme que vous avez vu est là. 2. Les garçons que vous rencontrez sont mes neveux. 3. Les chevaux qu'ils vendent sont très vieux. 4. Les tableaux que nous regardons sont très jolis. 5. Les souliers qu'ils vendent sont bons. 6. Les choses que nous leur rendrons sont sur la table.

EXERCISE IV.—1. Quelle page avez-vous lue ? 2. J'ai trouvé les timbres-poste que vous avez perdus. 3. Le facteur a apporté trois lettres pour vous ; les avez-vous reçues ? 4. Quels animaux avez-vous vus ? 5. L'eau qu'il vous a apportée est-elle chaude ? 6. Sa sœur est très jolie ; ne l'avez-vous pas vue ?

KEY to 15th Lesson on pages 64 and 66.

EXERCISE I.—1. Je lui donnais une leçon. 2. Elle avait deux sœurs. 3. Ils étaient seuls. 4. Elle finissait la robe pour cette dame. 5. Ils écoutaient la musique. 6. Nous attendions le train. 7. Elle nous parlait. 8. Vous fumiez un cigare. 9. Ils avaient les échantillons. 10. Nous étions à la maison. 11. Je remplissais la lampe.

EXERCISE II.—1. Ils jouaient tous les jours. 2. Elle déchirait les papiers. 3. Nous étudiions ensemble le français. 4. Ils
marchaient au marché avec leurs paniers. 5. Ne jouaient-ils pas aux
cartes hier soir ? 6. Elle gagnait toujours et je perdais tout mon
argent. 7. Il finissait mon habit. 8. Ils ne réussissaient pas dans
ces choses. 9. Ils n'étaient pas ici. 10. Nous avions une petite maison. 11. N'était-elle pas très jolie ? 12. Ils n'avaient pas le temps.

EXERCISE III.—1. Le livre dans lequel il étudiait est une
grammaire française. 2. Le train par lequel elle arrive est toujours en retard. 3. La dame avec laquelle (*or* avec qui) nous
dansions hier n'est pas ici. 4. Les filles pour lesquelles (*or* pour
qui) vous avez acheté les bottines. 5. L'enveloppe sur laquelle il a
écrit l'adresse. 6. L'homme par lequel (*or* par qui) il a envoyé
l'argent.

EXERCISE IV.—1. Avez-vous loué les chambres dont nous parlions ? 2. Où est la liste dont (*or* de laquelle) il copiait les noms ?
3. Voilà l'homme à qui (*or* auquel) je l'ai donné. 4. L'incendie
dont nous avons entendu parler était très sérieux. 5. Nous parlions
de notre jardin et non (pas) du vôtre. 6. Nous l'avons prêté à nos
amis et non (pas) aux leurs. 7. Auquel de ces hommes l'avez-vous
envoyé ? 8. Desquelles de ces filles parliez-vous ? 9. L'avez-vous
donné à notre garçon ou au sien ? 10. L'ont-ils appris de mon
(*or* ma) domestique ou du sien (*or* de la sienne) ?

KEY to 16th Lesson on pages 70 to 73.

EXERCISE I.—1. En parlant à son ami ; 2. en rendant le
paquet ; 3. en finissant la robe ; 4. sans répondre à la lettre ;
5. après avoir écrit ; 6. j'ai le plaisir de vous informer ; 7. pour
avoir perdu l'argent ; 8. en cherchant la rue ; 9. sans copier la
lettre ; 10. en allumant le gaz ; 11. ayant perdu le chemin ; 12. en
vous obéissant ; 13. pour avoir vendu ; 14. en entendant le bruit ;
15. sans étudier ses leçons.

EXERCISE II.—1. Donnez ceci à votre frère. 2. Cela coûte
plus de six schellings. 3. Pourquoi n'avez-vous pas choisi cela ?

4. C'est la meilleure couleur. 5. N'était-ce pas stupide ? 6. C'est trop cher. 7. Ce sera joli. 8. Ne lui montrez pas ceci. 9. C'est trop bon. 10. Ceci fume trop. 11. Ne sera-ce pas difficile ? 12. Ce n'était pas facile.

EXERCISE III.—1. Il parla ; 2. je ne copiai pas ; 3. fermas-tu ? 4. nous acceptâmes ; 5. oubliâtes-vous ? 6. ils coupèrent ; 7. nous trouvâmes ; 8. ils ne donnèrent pas ; 9. ne rencontrâtes-vous pas ? 10. nous fermâmes la porte ; 11. ils ne payèrent pas le compte ; 12. il me regarda.

EXERCISE IV.—1. Nous finîmes ; 2. il ne vendit pas ; 3. j'obéis ; 4. nous perdîmes ; 5. ils répondirent ; 6. choisîtes-vous ? 7. elle rendit ; 8. je remplis ; 9. vous descendîtes ; 10. ils ne réussirent pas.

EXERCISE V.—1. Je fus ; 2. il eut ; 3. nous fûmes ; 4. ils eurent ; 5. elles furent ; 6. nous eûmes ; 7. fûtes-vous ? 8. n'eus-tu pas ? 9. je n'eus pas ; 10. il ne fut pas ; 11. ils ne furent pas ; 12. n'eurent-ils pas ?

EXERCISE VI.—1. C'est mon chapeau. 2. Est-ce votre chaise ? 3. Ce sont mes gants. 4. Ce ne sont pas ses chevaux. 5. N'est-ce pas votre billet ? 6. Etait-ce notre musique ? 7. Sera-ce votre place ? 8. C'était notre régiment. 9. N'est-ce pas sa boutique ? 10. Ne sont-ce pas leurs bagues ? 11. Quelles chansons étaient-ce ?

EXERCISE VII.—1. C'était son mari. 2. Sont-ce vos gants ? 3. Ce ne sera pas sa place. 4. C'est bon. 5. Ce sont des Allemands. 6. Est-ce un Espagnol ? 7. Était-ce joli ? 8. Ce ne sont pas des Français.

EXERCISE VIII.—1. Donnez-lui le livre. 2. Montrez-nous le chemin. 3. Prêtez-leur l'argent. 4. Rendez-nous les lettres. 5. Parlez-moi ce soir. 6. Ne l'acceptez pas. 7. Parlons-leur. 8. Ne lui donnez pas la bague. 9. Ne les vendez pas. 10. Répondez-moi. 11. Ne leur répondez pas. 12. Ne nous oubliez pas.

KEY to 17th Lesson on pages 74, 75 and 76.

EXERCISE I.—1. Voyez-vous cet homme ? 2. Je vous verrai demain. 3. Je l'ai vu la semaine dernière. 4. Les avez-vous vus ? 5. Ils virent le vapeur. 6. Ils ne nous voient pas. 7. En voyant cela. 8. Après l'avoir vu. 9. Nous les voyions tous les jours. 10. Je les verrais, s'ils étaient là.

EXERCISE II.—1. Avez-vous acheté ces livres-ci ou ceux-là ? 2. Quel est le prix de ces montres ? 3. Celles-ci coûtent cent francs, et celles-là deux cents francs. 4. Je n'ai pas trouvé votre clef, mais celle-ci. 5. Cette bouteille-ci est pleine et celle-là est vide. 6. Voici plusieurs pièces d'argent ; celles-ci sont anglaises et celles-là sont françaises. 7. Voulez-vous ces gants-ci ou ceux-là ?

EXERCISE III.—1. Est-ce votre chambre ou celle de votre sœur ? 2. Il a apporté mon fusil et celui de Henri. 3. Nous avons cherché vos parapluies, mais non ceux de ces messieurs. 4. Notre jardin est plus grand que celui de notre voisin. 5. Ces tableaux sont plus beaux que ceux que nous avons vus hier. 6. Est-ce votre voiture ou celle de votre cousine ?

EXERCISE IV.—1. Avez-vous lu cette histoire ? 2. Pas encore, je lis celle-ci. 3. Lirez-vous celle que je lisais ? 4. Lisez ce livre-ci ou celui de Henri. 5. Lisons ses lettres et celles de son oncle. 6. Dans quel livre lisiez-vous ? 7. Dans celui qui est sur la table. 8. Liriez-vous ma réponse ou celle de mon ami ? 9. Je lirai celle qui est ici. 10. Ces plumes sont meilleures que celles qu'il a apportées.

EXERCISE V.—1. Nous élirons un maire. 2. Il a été (*or* fut) réélu notre député. 3. Je relisais la lettre. 4. Nous ne relirons pas l'histoire. 5. Qui a été élu ? 6. En le relisant. 7. Sans être élu.

KEY to 18th Lesson on pages 78, 79 and 80.

EXERCISE I.—1. Vous a-t-il montré ce que nous avons trouvé ? 2. Elle nous a donné ce qu'elle a acheté. 3. Ce que vous avez dit n'est pas juste. 4. Ce qui est sur la table est à vous. 5. Tout ce qu'il a dit n'est pas vrai. 6. Je sais ce qu'il a fait. 7. Ce n'est pas ce que j'ai vu. 8. Je ne sais pas ce qui est dans cette boîte.

EXERCISE II.—1. J'écris ce que vous dictez.   2. Pourquoi ne leur avez-vous pas écrit ? 3. J'écrirai plusieurs lettres après le dîner. 4. Il écrivit son nom sur un morceau de papier. 5. N'écrivait-elle pas dans sa chambre ?

EXERCISE III.—1. Avez-vous quelque chose pour lui ? 2. Je l'ai reçu de vous. 3. Nous ne continuerons pas sans eux. 4. Qui chantait ? Elle. 5. Qui passe devant la maison ? Lui. 6. Qui a montré la ville à vos amis ? Moi. 7. Parle-t-il d'elle ? 8. Avez-vous reçu l'argent d'eux ? 9. Elle n'est pas si âgée que lui. 10. Nous sommes plus riches qu'eux. 11. Mon ami et moi. 12. Lui et elles.

EXERCISE IV.—1. Qui est là ?   C'est moi. 2. N'était-ce pas vous ? Non, c'était elle. 3. Ce sera lui. 4. Ce ne sont pas elles. 5. Ce n'est pas moi. 6. C'est votre frère. 7. Non, ce n'était pas lui. 8. N'est-ce pas eux ? 9. C'est Henri. 10. Était-ce Guillaume ? 11. Est-ce Marie ?

EXERCISE V.—1. Cet argent est à moi. 2. Ces crayons ne sont pas à vous ; ils sont à Henri. 3. Ces poneys ne sont-ils pas à nous ? 4. Non, ils sont à eux. 5. Ce porte-monnaie est à Guillaume. 6. Ces poires sont-elles à Marie ? 7. Cette assiette est-elle à moi ? 8. Non, elle est à cette dame.

EXERCISE VI.— 1. Il disait cela. 2. Ils le diront. 3. Je ne le dirais pas. 4. Que lui avez-vous dit ? 5. Dites-lui ce que j'ai dit. 6. Vous ne dites pas ce qu'ils vous ont répondu. 7. Je vous dirai quelque chose demain. 8. Dites-moi votre nom, s'il vous plaît. 9. Il ne dit que oui. 10. Que disiez-vous tout à l'heure ?

KEY to 19th Lesson on pages 82, 83 and 84.

EXERCISE I.—1 Il ne comprend pas votre question. 2. Pourquoi n'avez-vous pas appris vos leçons ? 3. Prenez un siège. 4. Je ne l'entreprendrai pas. 5. Est-ce que cela vous surprend *or* Cela vous surprend-il ? 6. Il prit son chapeau. 7. Me comprenez-vous ? 8. Il ne prend pas de thé. 9. Nous les surprendrons demain matin.

10. Qu'est-ce que vous apprenez *or* Qu'apprenez-vous ? le français ou l'allemand ?   **11.** A quelle heure prenez-vous votre bain ? **12.** Prenez cet argent.

EXERCISE II.—**1.** Elle écrit poliment.   **2.** Ils parlent sagement.   **3.** Nous marchons lentement.   **4.** Nous les voyons rarement.   **5.** Elle répondit fièrement.   **6.** Je travaillerai activement. **7.** Ecrivez-le soigneusement.   **8.** Heureusement, il était là.   **9.** Il nous passa rapidement.

EXERCISE III.—**1.** A-t-il copié autant de pages que moi ? **2.** Combien de sucre avez-vous mis dans mon café ?   **3.** Mangez-vous plus de viande que lui ?   **4.** Je n'ai pas assez de papier pour cela.   **5.** Elle a mis trop de sel dans la soupe.   **6.** Nous avons moins d'argent qu'eux.   **7.** Avez-vous beaucoup d'amis dans cette ville ?   **8.** Donnez-moi un peu de pain.   **9.** Cela m'a donné beaucoup de peine.   **10.** Combien d'enfants ont-ils ?

EXERCISE IV.—**1.** Nous envoyons un paquet à Paris.   **2.** Quand renverrez-vous mon parapluie ?   **3.** Avez-vous envoyé les billets à l'hôtel ?   **4.** Je le renverrais tout de suite.   **5.** Envoyez-nous votre compte aussitôt que possible.   **6.** Ne renvoyez pas les choses.   **7.** L'enverra-t-il par la poste ?

EXERCISE V.—**1.** Cette demoiselle apprend bien ses leçons. **2.** Nous prenons toujours du café après le dîner.   **3.** Les garçons l'ont souvent vu.   **4.** Nous avons reçu une lettre de lui hier. **5.** Je refuserai poliment l'invitation.   **6.** Elle chante souvent ces chansons.   **7.** Mes amis ont déjà dîné.   **8.** Le facteur a-t-il été ici ce matin ?   **9.** Ils l'ont envoyé par retour (du courrier).

EXERCISE VI.—**1.** Avez-vous le journal ? Non, notre voisin ne me l'a pas rendu.   **2.** Je ne les lui montrerai pas.   **3.** Nous ne la leur donnerons pas.   **4.** Envoyez-le-lui.   **5.** Nous les ont-ils vendus ?   **6.** Prêtez-moi votre couteau.   **7.** Je l'ai prêté à votre ami, mais il ne me l'a pas rendu.   **8.** Pourquoi les lui avez-vous vendus ?   **9.** Apportez-les-moi.

KEY to 20th Lesson on pages 86, 87 and 88.

EXERCISE I.—1. Voici les allumettes ; donnez-les-lui. 2. C'est mon adresse ; ne la leur montrez pas. 3. Voilà un couteau ; ne le lui prêtez pas. 4. Est-ce son porte-monnaie ? donnez-le-lui. 5. Je lui ai prêté de l'argent, mais il ne me l'a pas rendu.

EXERCISE II.—1. Que faites-vous ? 2. Je fais ce que vous m'avez dit. 3. Vous faites toujours la même chose. 4. Qu'a-t-il fait ce matin ? 5. Faisons autre chose (or quelque chose d'autre). 6. Que faisait-il ? 7. Avez-vous fait cela ? 8. Je ne le ferai pas. 9. Feriez-vous cela ? 10. Ces enfants font trop de bruit. 11. Faites-le tout de suite. 12. Nous faisions nos leçons. 13. Combien de fautes avez-vous faites ?

EXERCISE III.—1. Je reçois une lettre presque chaque jour *or* presque tous les jours. 2. Chacun de ces garçons a reçu un prix. 3. Vous recevrez une invitation du maire. 4. Recevez-les poliment. 5. N'a-t-il pas reçu l'argent que nous lui avons envoyé la semaine dernière ? 6. Combien de livres avez-vous reçues pour cette somme ? 7. Le roi reçut la députation. 8. Ils ne recevront pas le paquet avant après-demain.

EXERCISE IV.—1. Combien vous dois-je ? 2. Il me doit vingt francs. 3. Vous devez fermer la porte. 4. Dois-je payer son compte ? 5. Il doit le faire. 6. Vous devriez dire la vérité. 7. Ils ne lui doivent pas d'argent. 8. Vous ne devez pas lui écrire. 9. Ne devons-nous pas faire notre travail ? 10. Ils ne doivent pas le voir.

EXERCISE V.—1. Voici des poires ; en voulez-vous ? 2. Voilà l'argent, j'en ai dépensé un schelling. 3. Il a apporté ses croquis ; il m'en a montré deux. 4. Combien de bagues porte-t-elle ? 5. Elle en porte trois. 6. Quelle en est la couleur ? 7. Quel en était le prix ? 8. Qu'en a-t-elle dit ? 9. Voici le poivre ; j'en ai pris.

EXERCISE VI.—1. Y avez-vous mis de l'encre ? 2. Oui, j'y en ai mis. 3. Avez-vous été à Paris ? 4. Oui, j'y ai été. 5. Avez-vous mangé des pommes ? 6. Non, il n'y en a pas. 7. Avez-vous mis de l'huile dans la salade ? 8. J'y en ajouterai.

KEY to 21st Lesson on pages 90, 91 and 92.

EXERCISE I.—1. Je ne bois pas de bière. 2. Ils ne boivent pas de vin. 3. Elle buvait son café. 4. Ne buvez pas ceci ; ce n'est pas très bon. 5. Je n'en boirai pas. 6. En avez-vous bu ? 7. Nous boirions du thé et du café.

EXERCISE II.—1. Tous ces timbres-poste sont à moi. 2. Toute la maison est pleine de fumée. 3. Où sont vos amis ? Sont-ils tous ici ? 4. Avez-vous invité les dames ? 5. Oui, j'ai écrit à toutes. 6. Avez-vous tout trouvé ? 7. Toute sa famille demeure à Paris. 8. Ils ont perdu tout leur argent. 9. C'est tout ce que j'ai à vous demander. 10. Toutes ces règles sont utiles. 11. Avez-vous lu toute l'histoire ? 12. Est-ce tout ?

EXERCISE III.—1. Il ne veut pas chanter. 2. Voulez-vous le chercher ? 3. Elle n'a pas voulu l'apprendre. 4. Veuillez me dire—. 5. Je voudrais vous aider. 6. N'a-t-il pas voulu le faire? 7. Voulez-vous nous raconter une histoire ? 8. Ils ne veulent pas nous voir. 9. Il voudra vous payer. 10. Ne veulent-ils pas nous aider ?

EXERCISE IV.—1. Il ne boit rien. 2. Elle n'apprend jamais ses leçons. 3. Ils n'en avaient plus. 4. Nous n'étions que trois. 5. Il n'est ni vieux ni jeune. 6. Je ne boirai plus. 7. Elle ne m'a jamais vu. 8. Il ne mange ni viande ni poisson.

EXERCISE V.—1. Je ne puis pas vous parler aujourd'hui. 2. Il pouvait le faire aussi bien que vous. 3. Je pourrai y être avant six heures. 4. Pourriez-vous y aller cet après-midi ? 5. Ils ne peuvent pas boire ce thé, parce qu'il est trop fort. 6. Nous ne pouvions pas comprendre sa question. 7. N'avez-vous pas pu finir la lettre ? 8. Je ne pourrai pas renvoyer les choses la semaine prochaine. 9. Ne peuvent-ils pas venir ?

EXERCISE VI.—1. Nous les rencontrons tous les jeudis. 2. Ils voient un exemplaire tous les six mois. 3. Tout le monde le disait. 4. Quelques-uns de ses amis étaient ici. 5. Nous avons rencontré quelques-unes des demoiselles. 6. J'ai dépensé quelques schellings. 7. Quelqu'un a brisé les fenêtres. 8. Nous avons mangé quelques pommes et quelques poires. 9. N'a-t-il pas parlé à quelques-uns de ces hommes ?

KEY to the 22nd Lesson on pages 94, 95 and 96.

EXERCISE I.—1. Je le sais. 2. Nous savions toujours notre leçon. 3. Vous le saurez demain. 4. Ne savez-vous pas où il demeure ? 5. Si je savais qu'il avait fait cela, je lui donnerais un soufflet. 6. Ne sait-il pas le numéro du cocher ? 7. Il le savait, mais il l'a oublié.

EXERCISE II.—1. Attentive. 2. Russe. 3. Complète. 4. Première. 5. Verte. 6. Heureuse. 7. Basse. 8. Cruelle. 9. Autrichienne. 10. Sotte.

EXERCISE III.—1. A qui ceci appartient-il ? 2. Cette page contient toute l'information. 3. Le matelot tenait le câble. 4. Ces choses appartenaient à notre voisin. 5. Tenez ceci, s'il vous plaît. 6. Ces boîtes ne contiennent rien.

EXERCISE IV.—1. Il reviendra demain. 2. Venez ici. 3. Ils venaient tous les jours. 4. Il vient de Paris. 5. D'où viennent-ils ? 6. Je ne viendrai pas seul. 7. Nous viendrions avec vous, si nous avions le temps. 8. Il vint à la fin du mois dernier. 9. Cela ne me convient pas.

EXERCISE V.—1. Ils sont allés à un bal. 2. Elle n'est pas entrée. 3. Les filles sont-elles parties ? 4. Personne n'était venu. 5. Les chasseurs seront revenus. 6. Elle serait restée avec sa tante. 7. N'est-elle pas tombée en bas de l'escalier ? 8. Nos amis sont restés toute la semaine.

EXERCISE VI.—1. Ils lisaient des journaux français. 2. Les tableaux qu'il a achetés sont très beaux. 3. Quelles belles fleurs bleues ! 4. Mes cousins n'étaient pas présents. 5. Quelles grandes mains il a ! 6. Je voudrais voir des gants noirs. En avez-vous en magasin ? 7. Ces règles sont très difficiles à comprendre.

KEY to the 23rd Lesson on pages 98, 99 and 100.

EXERCISE I.—1. Où allez-vous ? 2. Il allait au théâtre. 3. Nous irons à Paris demain. 4. Pourquoi ne va-t-il pas avec vous ? 5. Il n'ira pas seul. 6. Allons ensemble. 7. N'allez pas dans la rue. 8. Ces hommes vont-ils au marché ? 9. Ils ne vont pas chanter. 10. Nous allons commencer. 11. Je ne vais pas l'acheter. 12. Elle n'allait pas le faire.

EXERCISE II.—1. Chauffez-vous dans cette chambre. 2. Il se flatte trop. 3. Pourquoi ne vous habillez-vous pas ? 4. Ne s'amusent-ils pas ? 5, Ne s'habille-t-il pas le soir ? 6. Amusez-vous bien au théâtre. 7. Ne se chauffaient-ils pas ? 8. Nous ne nous flattions pas. 9. Ne vous chauffez pas trop. 10. Les dames ne s'habillaient-elles pas ?

EXERCISE III.—1. Elle ne veut pas nous accompagner. 2. Vous ne devriez pas dire cela. 3. Nous nous laverons. 4. Les enfants ne voulaient pas s'amuser. 5. Ne doivent-ils pas l'informer ? 6. Ne devrions-nous pas l'accompagner chez elle ? 7. Ils ne viendraient pas sans nous en informer. 8. Ils n'ont pas voulu venir avec nous. 9. Je ne veux pas lui parler. 10. Dois-je y aller sans vous ? 11. Elle ne doit pas garder cela. 12. Je veux l'écrire moi-même. 13. Ils ne le trouveront pas chez lui. 14. Il n'a pas voulu s'excuser.

EXERCISE IV.—1. Les chevaux courent. 2. Ne courez pas si vite. 3. Il courait tout le temps. 4. Courons après eux. 5. Pourquoi courez-vous ? 6. Les garçons courront ce soir. 7. Pourquoi courez-vous toujours ? 8. Je ne courrais pas si j'étais à votre place.

EXERCISE V.—1. Nous ne nous sommes pas amusés. 2. Ils se seraient habillés. 3. Les garçons ne s'étaient pas lavés. 4. Ne s'est-elle pas flattée ? 5. Ils se sont établis. 6. Il ne s'était pas dépêché. 7. Pourquoi ne s'est-elle pas habillée ? 8. Les filles ne se seront pas habillées à temps.

KEY to 24th Lesson on pages 102, 103 and 104.

EXERCISE I.—1. Pourquoi riez-vous ? 2. Il ne nous suit pas. 3. Il ne suffisait pas. 4. Ne riez pas si haut. 5. Je ne vous suis pas. 6. Cela ne suffira pas. 7. Il rira s'il voit cela. 8. Vous a-t-il suivi ?

EXERCISE II.—1. Ils se disputent tous les jours. 2. Vous vous reposez trop souvent. 3. Pourquoi vous êtes-vous écrié ? 4. Il ne se porte pas bien. 5. Elle ne s'est pas disputée avec sa sœur. 6. Vous êtes-vous reposés ? 7. Je ne me porte pas bien. 8. Nous nous portons très bien. 9. Comment se porte votre cousin aujourd'hui ? 10. Les soldats se battaient. 11. Ils ne voulaient pas se battre. 12. Nous devons nous excuser.

Exercise III.—1. J'ai oublié de lui écrire. 2. Nous avons attendu à la gare pour les rencontrer. 3. J'ai regretté d'avoir parlé. 4. Il l'a dit pour vous calmer. 5. Elle essaye de m'aider. 6. Ils étudient pour passer un examen. 7. Nous travaillons pour gagner de l'argent. 8. Il se souvient d'avoir écrit ceci.

Exercise IV.—1. Il apprend à écrire. 2. N'allez-vous pas commencer ? 3. Ils nous ont invités à venir avec eux. 4. Permettez-moi de (*or* Laissez-moi) passer. 5. Nous avons à obéir. 6. Ne pouvaient-ils pas vous aider ? 7. Les soldats ne pouvaient pas traverser le fleuve. 8. N'ont-ils pas à faire ceci ? 9. Les dames voudront danser. 10. Aimez-vous à patiner ? 11. N'avez-vous rien à faire ? 12. Ils doivent l'essayer.

Exercise V.—1. Sentez-vous le courant d'air ? 2. Elle ne se sent pas bien. 3. Pourquoi êtes-vous sortis sans moi ? 4. Ils partiront avant six heures. 5. Votre cousine est-elle sortie ? 6. À quelle heure reviendra-t-elle ? 7. Vous le sentirez demain. 8. Sortons ensemble. 9. Ils servent dans le même régiment. 10. Il ne dort pas bien. 11. Ne mentez pas. 12. Le dîner était servi en haut.

Exercise VI.—1. Il va chez lui. 2. Elle sortait de chez le boucher. 3. Il ecrit une lettre en Allemagne. 4. Ne sont-ils pas à Paris ? 5. Nous les avons rencontrés chez notre tante. 6. N'est-il pas chez lui ? 7. Elle n'était pas chez elle ; elle était chez ses voisins. 8. Nous les avons rencontrés comme ils sortaient de chez eux.

KEY to 25th Lesson on pages 106, 107, and 108.

Exercise I.—1. Il commence, nous ne commençons pas ; 2. jugez-vous ? ils jugeaient ; 3. nous achetons, il n'achète pas ; 4. a-t-il mené ? mènerez-vous ? 5. il répétait, ne répète-t-il pas ? 6. il ne vous payera pas, ne le payez pas ; 7. Il cachette sa lettre. 8. Ils renouvelleront leur commande.

Exercise II.—1. Ouvrez-vous la boutique à huit heures ? 2. Il souffre beaucoup. 3. Elle m'offrait une chaise. 4. Qu'avez-vous découvert ? 5. Ouvrez la porte. 6. Ne couvrez pas les choses. 7. Vous a-t-il offert quelque chose ? 8. J'ouvrirai les portes et les fenêtres.

Exercise III.—1. Il y a des (*or* quelques) personnes qui disent cela. 2. N'y a-t-il pas de chaises pour nous ? 3. Il n'y aura rien à faire. 4. Y a-t-il un bureau de poste dans cette rue ? 5. Il n'y avait pas de tableaux sur le mur. 6. Y a-t-il des souris dans votre cuisine ? 7. N'y avait-il pas de cigares dans mon étui ?

Exercise IV.—1. Sur quoi écrivez-vous ? 2. Les enfants avec qui ils jouaient. 3. Il part avant cinq heures. 4. Le journal dans lequel il lit. 5. Nous étions ici avant vous. 6. La table était devant nous. 7. Le monsieur à qui ii parle. 8. Dans quel paquet l'avez-vous mis ? 9. Il est venu (*or* il vint) lui-même. 10. Ils l'ont donné aux dames elles-mêmes.

Exercise V.—1. Ne les admettez-vous pas ? 2. Il ne l'a pas promis. 3. Nous ne le permettrons pas. 4. Pourquoi les ont-ils omis ? 5. Il ne l'admettra pas. 6. Ils me le promirent. 7. N'omettez pas de le leur dire. 8. Ne le permettrait-il pas ?

Exercise VI.—1. À qui était ce chapeau ? 2. Qu'est-ce que vous peignez ? 3. De qui est-il l'ami ? 4. Qu'est-ce qui sent si fort ? 5. Pourquoi est-ce qu'il se plaint ? *or* Pourquoi se plaint-il ? 6. Qu'est-ce qui vous amuse ? 7. À qui sont ces gants ? 8. Ils ne craignent rien. 9. Tout le monde le craignait. 10. Pourquoi vous êtes-vous plaint ? 11. Qui peindra le tableau ? 12. Pourquoi n'éteint-il pas la lampe ?

Exercise VII.—1. On frappe. 2. On vous demande. 3. On parle de vous. 4. On aime à être chez soi. 5. On chantait dans la rue. 6. On ne fume pas ici. 7. On dit qu'elle va mourir. 8. Si l'on demande votre adresse.

Exercise VIII.—1. Ces livres sont meilleurs que ceux-là. 2. Elle écrit mieux que vous. 3. Il a acheté une livre et demie de beurre. 4. Son parapluie est le meilleur. 5. Il travaille plus mal qu'hier. 6. Elle mange moins chaque jour. 7. Ce garçon travaille le mieux de tous.

KEY to 26th Lesson on pages 110 to 114.

Exercise I.—1. Que je ferme, que tu fermes, qu'il ferme, que nous fermions, que vous fermiez, qu'ils ferment ; que j'attende, que tu attendes, qu'il attende, que nous attendions, que vous attendiez, qu'ils attendent ; que je remplisse, que tu remplisses, qu'il remplisse, que nous remplissions, que vous remplissiez, qu'ils remplissent. 2. parte,* partes, parte ; partions, partiez, partent ; écrive, écrives, écrive ; écrivions, écriviez, écrivent ; lise, lises, lise ; lisions, lisiez, lisent. 3. sache, saches, sache ; sachions, sachiez, sachent ; voie, voies, voie ; voyions, voyiez, voient ; dise, dises, dise ; disions, disiez, disent. 4. que je passe ; 5. qu'il ne parle pas ; 6. que nous perdions ; 7. que vous ne rendiez pas ; 8. qu'ils réussissent ; 9. qu'elle obéisse ; 10. qu'il écrive ; 11. qu'ils ne sachent pas ; 12. que vous vendiez.

EXERCISE II.—1. que j'aille, que tu ailles, qu'il aille ; que nous allions, que vous alliez, qu'ils aillent ; que je fasse, que tu fasses, qu'il fasse ; que nous fassions, que vous fassiez, qu'ils fassent ; boive,* boives, boive ; buvions, buviez, boivent ; 2. puisse, puisses, puisse ; puissions, puissiez, puissent ; prenne, prennes, prenne ; prenions, preniez, prennent ; vienne, viennes, vienne ; venions, veniez, viennent ; 3. aie, aies, ait ; ayons, ayez, aient ; sois, sois, soit ; soyons, soyez, soient ; veuille, veuilles, veuille ; voulions, vouliez, veuillent ; 4. que je vienne ; 5. qu'il ne puisse pas ; 6. que nous voulions ; 7. que vous ne teniez pas ; 8. qu'ils n'aillent pas ; 9. que nous revenions ; 10. que vous ne receviez pas ; 11. qu'ils le fassent.

EXERCISE III.—1. que j'eusse, que tu eusses, qu'il eût; que nous eussions, que vous eussiez, qu'ils eussent ; que je fusse, que tu fusses, qu'il fût ; que nous fussions, que vous fussiez, qu'ils fussent ; que je fermasse, que tu fermasses, qu'il fermât ; que nous fermassions, que vous fermassiez, qu'ils fermassent ; 2. attendisse,* attendisses, attendît ; attendissions, attendissiez, attendissent ; remplisse, remplisses, remplît ; remplissions, remplissiez, remplissent ; lusse, lusses, lût ; lussions, lussiez, lussent ; 3. pusse, pusses, pût ; pussions, pussiez, pussent ; tinsse, tinsses, tînt ; tinssions, tinssiez, tinssent ; prisse, prisses, prît; prissions, prissiez, prissent ; 4. que je répondisse ; 5. qu'elle ne réussît pas ; 6. qu'ils n'eussent pas ;

* For brevity, que and the PRONOUN are omitted from this point.

7. qu'elle vînt ; **8.** que nous parlassions ; **9.** que vous fussiez ; **10.** qu'il écrivît.

EXERCISE IV.—**1.** C'est la seule chose qu'il vende. **2.** Le meilleur livre que j'aie jamais lu. **3.** Le plus beau tableau qu'il ait peint. **4.** Donnez-le au premier homme qui vienne. **5.** Attendez jusqu'à ce que je sois prêt. **6.** Quoiqu'il soit riche, il n'est pas heureux. **7.** Nous leur parlerons, avant qu'ils l'aient fini. **8.** Il est venu, afin que nous puissions en parler.

EXERCISE V.—**1.** Pensez-vous qu'il soit à la maison ? **2.** Je ne crois pas qu'elle veuille danser. **3.** N'espérez-vous pas que nous passions l'examen ? **4.** Je ne pensais pas qu'il vînt. **5.** Faut-il que nous partions ? **6.** N'est-il pas probable qu'il le voie ? **7.** Ne savez-vous pas qu'il y sera ? **8.** Il n'a pas dit qu'il pouvait le faire. **9.** Est-il possible que l'argent soit à lui (*or* le sien) ? **10.** Je ne pense pas qu'il reçoive un prix.

EXERCISE VI.– **1.** Nous regrettons qu'il ne nous ait pas trouvés. **2.** Elle craint qu'il ne vienne. **3.** Faut-il que nous attendions ? **4.** Je doutais qu'ils vinssent. **5.** J'ai peur qu'il ne vous attende. **6.** Nous craignions que vous ne le reçussiez pas. **7.** Nous voudrions qu'ils ne l'eussent pas commencé. **8.** Je voudrais qu'elle ne fût pas ici.

EXERCISE VII.—**1.** Faut-il que vous le fassiez ? **2.** Il faudra que vous lui écriviez. **3.** Il ne faudrait pas qu'il le finît. **4.** Il faut que nous le sachions. **5.** Il ne faut pas que nous copiions l'adresse. **6.** Il ne fallait pas qu'ils parlassent.

EXERCISE VIII.—**1.** Veut-il qu'elle le lise ? **2.** Ils veulent que je lui parle. **3.** Voudra-t-il que vous leur écriviez ? **4.** Elle veut que vous acceptiez ceci. **5.** Ils ne voudront pas que nous le gardions. **6.** Ne veut-elle pas que nous y restions ? **7.** Nous ne voulons pas qu'ils nous entendent. **8.** Vouliez-vous que je le fisse pour vous ? **9.** Voulez-vous que je le fasse pour lui ? **10.** Ne voulez-vous pas que nous y allions ? **11.** Ne voulez-vous pas que je le lui envoie ? **12.** Voulez-vous que nous le cherchions ? **13.** Voulez-vous que je ferme la fenêtre ?

FOREIGN DICTIONARIES, TRAVELLERS' MANUALS, EDUCATIONAL AND COMMERCIAL TEXT-BOOKS, Etc.

卍 卍

Hill's Vest-Pocket Dictionaries
Cheapest and Most Reliable

Each Volume, Cloth Binding, 50 Cents

No expense has been spared in compiling these books. As a result, the most complete Dictionaries of handy size have been produced. Not only are they the most convenient for the student, but also the most practical for the use of the progressive business man. They are the most reliable Dictionaries of this style on the market, and each one contains a complete guide to pronunciation, with rules for same. Condensation and usefulness are the chief features of these books. Unusual and self-explanatory terms are left out to make room for more needful words.

Dano-Norwegian Eng., Eng. Dano-Norwegian Dict.

French-English and English-French Dictionary

German-English and English-German Dictionary

Italian-English and English-Italian Dictionary

Latin-English and English-Latin Dictionary

Portuguese-English and English-Portuguese Dictionary

Russian-English Dictionary

English-Russian Dictionary

Spanish-English and English-Spanish Dictionary

Swedish-English and English-Swedish Dictionary

Webster Dictionary A Pronouncing Dictionary of the English Language

Wessely's Handy Dictionaries

FRENCH-ENGLISH AND ENGLISH-FRENCH. By J. E. Wessely. Re-written, Improved, and Greatly Enlarged by L. Tolhausen and G. Payn, in collaboration with M. Eng. Heymann. 509 pages. 12mo, cloth........ $1.00

GERMAN-ENGLISH AND ENGLISH-GERMAN. By J. E. Wessely. Revised, Altered, and Greatly Enlarged by C. Stoffel and G. Payn, assisted by George Berlit. 594 pages. 12mo, cloth................................. 1.00

SPANISH-ENGLISH AND ENGLISH-SPANISH. By Wessely and Gironés. Thoroughly Revised and Entirely Rewritten by Louis Tolhausen and George Payn. 477 pages. 12mo, cloth..................................... 1.00

ITALIAN-ENGLISH AND ENGLISH-ITALIAN. By J. E. Wessely. Thoroughly Revised and Rewritten by G. Rigutini and G. Payn. 430 pages. 12mo, cloth 1.00

LATIN-ENGLISH AND ENGLISH-LATIN. With an Appendix of Latin Geographical, Historical, and Mythological Proper Names. 414 pages. 12mo, cloth... 1.00

SYNONYMS—A DICTIONARY OF ENGLISH. Alphabetically Classified by Thomas Fenby. Fourth Edition, Revised and Enlarged. Latin and French quotations with English translations; a list of French and English abbreviations; a brief outline of English Grammar. 12mo, cloth......... 1.00

GREEK-ENGLISH DICTIONARY. A Pocket Dictionary of the Greek and English Languages. By Prof. Karl Feyerabend, Ph.D., with an introduction of Greek sounds. 420 pages. 12mo, cloth................. 1.00

POLISH-ENGLISH AND ENGLISH-POLISH DICTIONARY WITH CONVERSATIONS AND IDIOMS. By Francis Bauer Czarnomski. 382 pages. 12mo, cloth... 1.00

RUSSIAN-ENGLISH AND ENGLISH-RUSSIAN DICTIONARY AND SELF-INSTRUCTOR WITH CONVERSATIONS AND IDIOMS. By S. J. Luboff. Cloth binding..................................... 1.00

FRENCH-ENGLISH AND ENGLISH-FRENCH COMMERCIAL DICTIONARY, by F. W. Smith. A complete work of reference for Students and Teachers of French, and for those engaged in foreign correspondence, containing all the Words and Terms used in Commerical Correspondence which are not contained in the Dictionaries in ordinary use, Compound Phrases, Idiomatic and Technical Expressions, etc. Large 12mo, cloth, 563 pages ....*net,* 2.00

SPANISH-ENGLISH AND ENGLISH-SPANISH COMMERCIAL DICTIONARY. By G. R. MacDonald. Society of Art's First Prizeman and Silver Medallist for Spanish, Portuguese, Italian, and Dano-Norwegian; Lecturer in Spanish at the Municipal School of Commerce, Manchester. Large 12mo, cloth, 652 pages ....*net,* 2.00

PETIT LAROUSSE. Illustre. Nouveau Dictionnaire Encyclopedique, public sous la direction, de Claude Augé.................................*net,* 2.50

PEQUENO LAROUSSE ILLUSTRADO. Nuevo Diccionario Enciclopédico. Publicado bajo la dirección de Claude Augé, adaptación Española de Miguel De Toro y Gisbert...*net,* 4.00

PORTUGUESE-ENGLISH AND ENGLISH-PORTUGUESE DICTIONARY. By R. De Mesquita. 580 pp. 16mo, cloth..............*net,* 2.00

RUSSIAN-ENGLISH AND ENGLISH-RUSSIAN PRONOUNCING DICTIONARY. By A. Wassilieff. 736 pages. 16mo, cloth............*net,* 2.00

Hugo's Simplified System

HUGO'S FRENCH SIMPLIFIED

The book comprises the following:

I. A SIMPLE BUT COMPLETE GRAMMAR, containing all the rules necessary for speaking and writing French correctly.

II. FRENCH PRONUNCIATION; a series of Easy Anecdotes, with the Translation and Pronunciation of every word, and complete rules on Pronunciation.

III. FRENCH IDIOMS: Practical Sentences, introducing all the Important Idioms and peculiarities of French construction.

IV. A KEY to the Conversational Exercises in the Grammar.

296 Pages. 12mo, Cloth, $1.50 net

FRENCH VERBS SIMPLIFIED

All the difficulties usually encountered in the study of French Verbs speedily disappear with the help of this handy little book. It gives clear rules by which one tense can be formed from another, and shows a natural and easy way of learning the full conjugation, instead of the arbitrary order usually adopted. It also groups the irregular Verbs in sections, and points out how the irregularities can best be mastered.

The book also deals fully with IMPERSONAL and REFLECTIVE VERBS, the PASSIVE VOICE, IDIOMATIC USES of Verbs, the Verbs which govern *a* or *de*, the agreement of the PAST PARTICIPLE, etc., etc. The whole forms a handy and comprehensive guide to every point connected with the study of the French Verb, invaluable to beginners as a text-book, and to advanced students as a book of reference.

12mo, Cloth, 75 Cents net

HUGO'S L'ANGLAIS SIMPLIFIE

GRAMMAIRE PRATIQUE.
VOCABULAIRES DIVERS.
CONVERSATION D'UTILITÉ PRATIQUE.

PHRASES UTILES À L'USAGE DES VOYAGEURS.
IDIOTISMES, LISTE D'ABRÉVIATIONS, etc.

256 Pages. 12mo, Cloth, $1.50 net

HUGO'S ITALIAN SIMPLIFIED

The book comprises the following:

I. A SIMPLE BUT COMPLETE GRAMMAR.

II. ITALIAN READING MADE EASY.

III. ITALIAN CONVERSATION SIMPLIFIED.

IV. A KEY to the Exercises in the Grammar.

273 Pages. 12mo, Cloth, $1.50 net

MARLBOROUGH'S SELF-TAUGHT SERIES
REVISED AND ENLARGED
12mo. Flexible Cloth. (Authorized Edition.)

These books contain systematized Vocabularies and useful Phrases and Conversations, with the ENGLISH PHONETIC PRONUNCIATION of every word, so arranged that they may be learned AT A GLANCE, and a simplified Grammar which will prepare the way for more advanced study.

French Self-Taught, by C. A. Thimm. Revised by T. de Marney. With Phonetic Pronunciations. Containing Vocabularies of the words in general use; Elementary Grammar; Idiomatic Phrases and Dialogues; Commercial Trading, Legal, Religious, Naval and Military Terms; Travel Talk; Photography; Cycling; Motoring; Amusements, etc.; Table of French Money with English and American equivalents; Weights and Measures, etc., 120 pages, 12mo, cloth............................*net,* $0.50

German Self-Taught, by C. A. Thimm. With Pronunciation. Containing Vocabularies, Elementary Grammar; Colloquial and Idiomatic Phrases; Travel Talk, Commercial and Trading, Legal, Religious, Naval and Military Terms and Phrases; Motoring; Cycling; Photography; Amusements, and many other Vocabularies and Conversations; Tables of German coinage and English and American values; Weights and Measures. 120 pages. 12mo, cloth..................*net,* .50

Italian Self-Taught, by C. A. Thimm. Revised by G. Dalla Vecchia. With English Phonetic Pronunciation. Containing Vocabularies; Elementary Grammar; Colloquial and Idiomatic Phrases; Travel Talk; Conversations, Commercial and Trading, Legal, Religious Terms; Amusements; Motoring; Cycling; Photography; Musical Terms; Money of Italian coinage and English and American values; Weights and Measures. Fourth Edition. 12mo, cloth, 120 pp...*net,* .50

Norwegian Self-Taught, by C. A. Thimm. Revised and Enlarged by P. Th. Hanssen. With Phonetic Pronunciation. Containing Vocabularies; Elementary Grammar; Conversations; Phrases and Sentences; Forms of Letters; Commercial, Legal and Religious Terms, Travel Talk; Motoring; Cycling; Photography; Fishing; Shooting; Amusements; Money of Norwegian coinage and English and American values; Weights and Measures. Fifth Edition. 12mo, cloth, 128 pp................................*net,* .50

Russian Self-Taught, by C. A. Thimm and J. Marshall, M.A. (In Russian and Roman Characters.) With English Phonetic Pronunciation Containing Vocabularies of words in general use; Elementary Grammar; Colloquial and Idiomatic Phrases; Travel Talk; Cycling, Photographic, Shooting, Fishing, Naval, Military, Commercial and Trading Terms and Conversations; Money of Russian coinage and English and American values; Weights and Measures. Fourth Edition. 12mo, cloth, 134 pp.....................*net,* .50

Spanish Self-Taught, by W. F. Harvey, M.A. (Thimm's System) with English Phonetic Pronunciation. Containing Vocabularies; Idiomatic Phrases and Dialogues; Elementary Grammar; Commercial, Trading, Legal, and Religious Terms; Travel Talk; Photography; Cycling, and Amusements; Money with English and American equivalents of Spanish coinage; Weights and Measures. Revised and Enlarged Edition. 12mo, cloth, 120 pp..*net,* .50

Swedish Self-Taught, by C. A. Thimm and W. F. Harvey, M.A. Revised by Carl Cederlöf, with English Phonetic Pronunciation. Containing Elementary Grammar; Colloquial and Idiomatic Phrases; Travel Talk; Cycling, Photographic, Shooting, Fishing, and other Vocabularies and Conversations; Money, Weights and Measures. Second Edition. 12mo, cloth, 100 pp...*net*, $0.50

Greek (Modern) Self-Taught, by Nicolaos Anastassiou. (In Greek and Roman Characters.) With Phonetic Pronunciation. Containing Vocabularies; Idiomatic Phrases and Dialogues; Elementary Grammar; Commercial, Trading, Archæological and Religious Terms; Travel Talk; Photography; Amusements; Tables of Money with English and American values and Weights and Measures. 12mo, cloth, 120 pp..................*net*, 1.00

Hungarian Self-Taught, by the Count de Soissons. With Phonetic Pronunciation. Containing The Alphabet; Preliminary Notes; Vocabularies; Elementary Grammar; Etymology; Modes of Address; Conversational Phrases and Sentences; Travel Talk; Commercial and Trading, Legal, Religious Terms and Phrases; Cycling; Photography; Amusements; Hungarian coinage and English and American values; Weights and Measures, Postal Rates, etc. 12mo, cloth, 112 pp.............................*net*, 1.00

Chinese Self-Taught. 12mo, cloth...................................*net*, 1.50

Japanese Self-Taught. 12mo, cloth..................................*net*, 1.50

ENGLISH for the French, Germans, Italians, Spaniards, etc.

L'Anglais sans Maître (English Self-Taught for the FRENCH), Méthode Thimm, by M. H. Hébert. Quatrième édition, Revue et agrandie. Avec la prononciation de tous les mots, pour apprendre L'Anglais soi-même. Vocabulaires, La Grammaire Anglaise, Phrases et Locutions de Conversation, Le Voyage, Le Commerce, Divertissements, Cyclisme, Automobilisme, Photographie, La Monnaie, Poids et Mesures, etc. 128 pages, 12mo, cloth...*net*, .50

Der Englische Dolmetscher (English Self-Taught for GERMANS), Methode Thimm, by W. von Knoblauch. Mit englischer Aussprache. Zweite Auflage. Durchgesehen von Heinrich Dorgeel. Wörterverzeichnisse, gebräuchliche Redensarten und Gespräche, Elementar-Grammatik, Lese- und Schreibübungen, kaufmännische, militärische, juridische, religiöse Redensarten und Gespräche, Ausdrücke und Gespräche für Rad-, Motorfahrer und Photographen, Gespräche über Theater und Vergnügungen. 120 pages, 12mo, cloth...*net*, .50

L'Inglese Imparato da sé (English Self-Taught for ITALIANS), by G. Dalla Vecchia. Con la pronuncia fonetica. Contenete: Vocabolari, Parole e Frasi di Conversazione, La Grammatica Inglese, Termini Commerciali e Religioso, Frasario per Viaggio, Velocipede, Automobile e Fotografia, Divertimenti, Monete, Pesi e Misure, ecc. 120 pages, 12mo, cloth...*net*, .50

El Inglés para Cada Cual (English Self-Taught for SPANIARDS), Método Marlborough, por William Chevob. Con pronunciacion fonetica. Para aprender el Ingles por si mismo. El Alfabeto con sa Pronunciacion, Vocabularios, La Gramática Inglesa, Ejercícios Locuciones conversacionales y Frases, El Viaje, Vocablos comerciales, La Bicicleta, El Automovil, Fotografía, Diversiones, Las Monedas, Moneda, Pesos y Medidas, Tarifa Postal. 128 pages, 12mo, cloth...*net*, .50

English Self-Taught for Yiddish. 128 pages, 12mo, cloth...........*net*, .50

A Complete Treatise on the Conjugation of French Verbs,
by J. Castaréde, French Professor, Graduate (Académie
de Paris). Comprising the Auxiliary Verbs; the Four Regular
Conjugations; the Peculiar and All the Irregular and Defective
Verbs; Fully Conjugated with the English in the Opposite
Columns and Numerous Notes and Remarks founded upon the
best Authorities. 148 pages. Limp cloth . . . . *net,* $0.80

French Conversational Course, by Cesar Dussault. 12mo.
cloth . . . . *net,* 1.00

Spanish Conversational Course, by Cesar Dussault. 12mo,
cloth . . . . *net,* 1.00

CONTENTS

1. A Complete French or Spanish course as used by the Dussault Schools
of Languages, Inc.

2. A clear and concise appendix of over 500 French or Spanish verbs, without
which one cannot hope to speak French or Spanish satisfactorily.

3. The subjunctive in a nutshell.

4. Over 2400 words and over 500 idioms in ordinary use.

5. French or South American money together with its American equivalents.

6. Social correspondence.

7. Interesting themes and up-to-date conversations on every-day topics,
such as: To find one's way; at the hotel; a journey; at the restaurant; at the
theatre; the weather; shopping, etc.

8. Chosen anecdotes, short stories, poems, etc.

9. The principal grammatical rules (just enough and not too much).

10. Masterful chapters on pronunciation and forceful drills on phonetics.

Spanish in a Week, by T. S. Romero, of the T. S. Romero
Spanish School. Embodying a new method, scientific,
exact, comprehensive, by an expert teacher of pure Castilian
Spanish. This book contains the elements of the language,
easily grasped and of sufficient vocabulary to enable anyone
to obtain a working knowledge of Spanish. Every word
phonetically pronounced. Appendix contains geographical
and commercial information in Spanish and English of all
Latin-America. 12mo, cloth 75

Spanish, Commercial and Professional, by T. S. Romero, of
the T. S. Romero Spanish School. Containing in a simple
way all the important definitions and technical terms in
Spanish and English for Commerce, Banking, Medicine,
Agriculture, Stock Raising, Irrigation, Mining, and Com-
mercial Correspondence. 12mo, cloth 1.00

A NEW PRONOUNCING DICTIONARY

OF THE

GERMAN AND ENGLISH LANGUAGES

CONTAINING

An Exhaustive Vocabulary of the Colloquial
and Literary English and German Languages,
as Well as a Great Many Scientific, Technical
and Commercial Terms and Phrases

AND

Preceded by a Study of the German Pronunciation

BY

F. C. HERBERT *and* L. HIRSCH

Professors of Modern Languages at the Lycée of Bordeaux

ENGLISH-GERMAN
GERMAN-ENGLISH

1749 PAGES, CLOTH BINDING, $2.50, NET

DAVID McKAY COMPANY
PHILADELPHIA